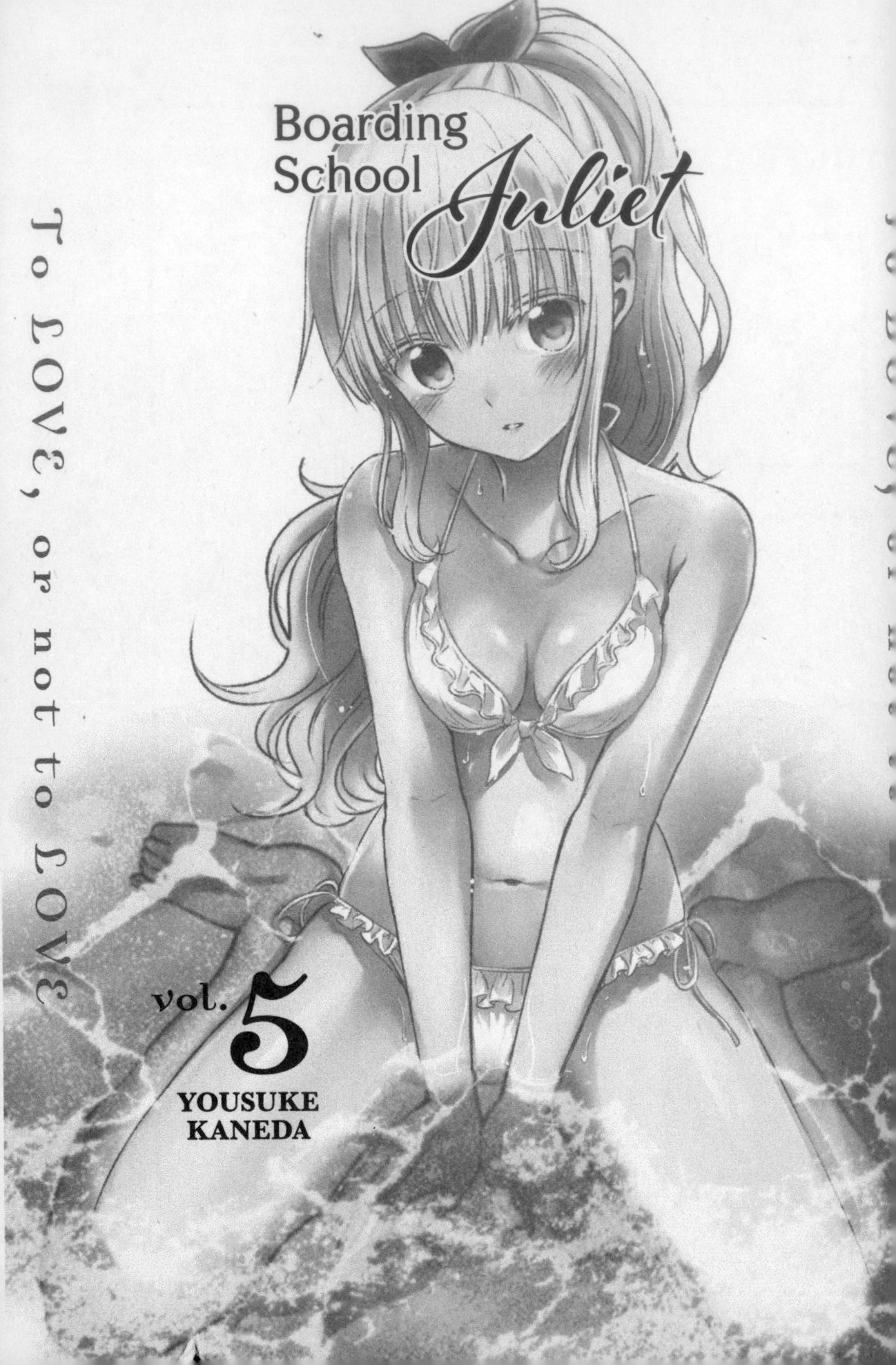
Boarding School Juliet
To LOVE, or not to LOVE
vol. 5
YOUSUKE KANEDA

THE PLAYERS

character

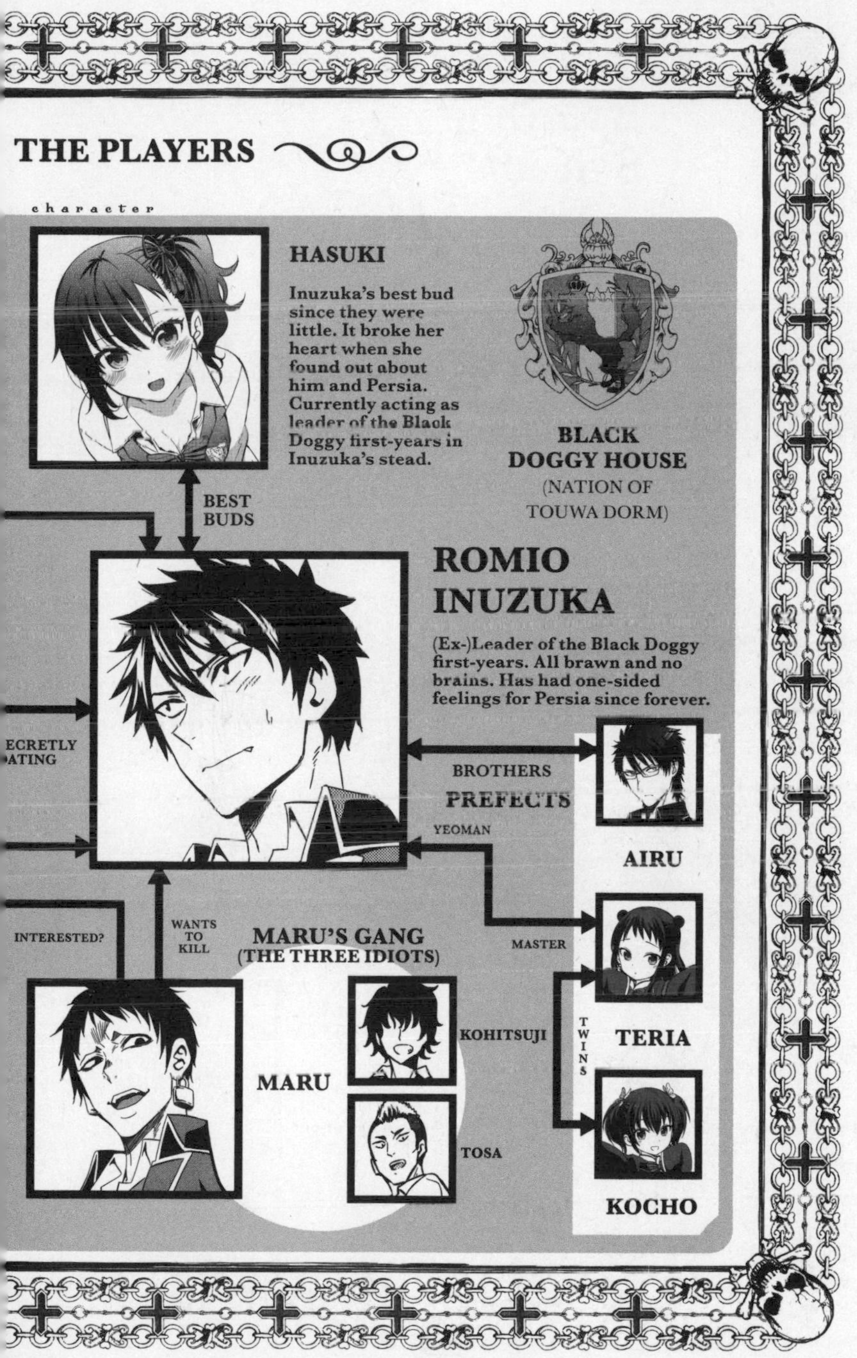

HASUKI
Inuzuka's best bud since they were little. It broke her heart when she found out about him and Persia. Currently acting as leader of the Black Doggy first-years in Inuzuka's stead.
BLACK DOGGY HOUSE
(NATION OF TOUWA DORM)
BEST BUDS
ROMIO INUZUKA
(Ex-)Leader of the Black Doggy first-years. All brawn and no brains. Has had one-sided feelings for Persia since forever.
ECRETLY
ATING
BROTHERS
PREFECTS
YEOMAN
AIRU
MASTER
INTERESTED?
WANTS TO KILL
MARU'S GANG
(THE THREE IDIOTS)
MARU
KOHITSUJI
TOSA
TWINS
TERIA
KOCHO

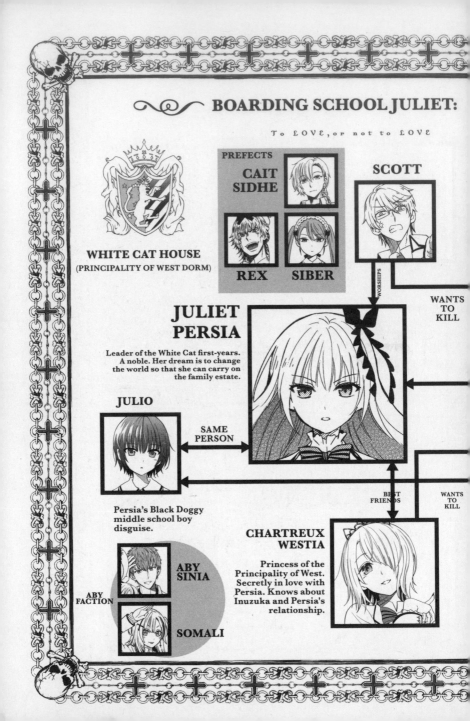

BOARDING SCHOOL JULIET:

To LOVE, or not to LOVE

PREFECTS

CAIT SIDHE

SCOTT

REX **SIBER**

WHITE CAT HOUSE
(PRINCIPALITY OF WEST DORM)

WORSHIPS

WANTS TO KILL

JULIET PERSIA

Leader of the White Cat first-years. A noble. Her dream is to change the world so that she can carry on the family estate.

JULIO

SAME PERSON

Persia's Black Doggy middle school boy disguise.

ABY SINIA

ABY FACTION

SOMALI

BEST FRIENDS

WANTS TO KILL

CHARTREUX WESTIA

Princess of the Principality of West. Secretly in love with Persia. Knows about Inuzuka and Persia's relationship.

contents

story

At boarding school Dahlia Academy, attended by students from two feuding countries, one first-year longs for a forbidden love. His name: Romio Inuzuka, leader of the Black Doggy House first-years. The apple of his eye: Juliet Persia, leader of the White Cat House first-years. It all begins when Inuzuka confesses his feelings to her. This is Inuzuka and Persia's star-crossed, secret love story...

Thanks to Persia's quick wit, Inuzuka managed to worm his way out of his big brother Airu's investigation of the pair's relationship. In order to change their school, Inuzuka vowed to become a prefect. Now, in mid-July, Inuzuka and Persia find themselves at the beach for a seaside summer camp...

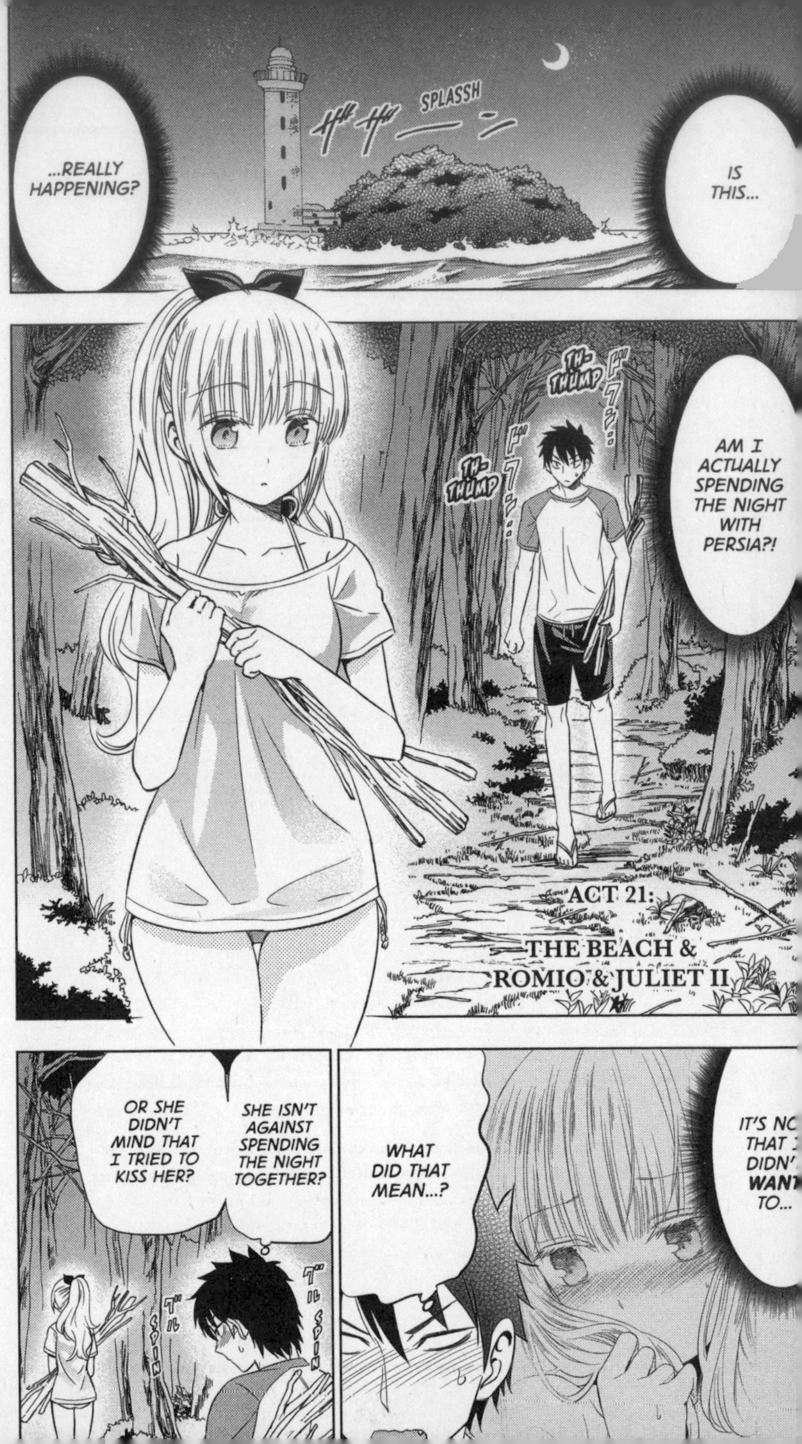
IS THIS...
SPLASSH
...REALLY HAPPENING?
TH-THUMP
TH-THUMP
AM I ACTUALLY SPENDING THE NIGHT WITH PERSIA?!
ACT 21:
THE BEACH & ROMIO & JULIET II
IT'S NO THAT I DIDN' WANT TO...
WHAT DID THAT MEAN...?
SHE ISN'T AGAINST SPENDING THE NIGHT TOGETHER?
OR SHE DIDN'T MIND THAT I TRIED TO KISS HER?
SPIN
SPIN

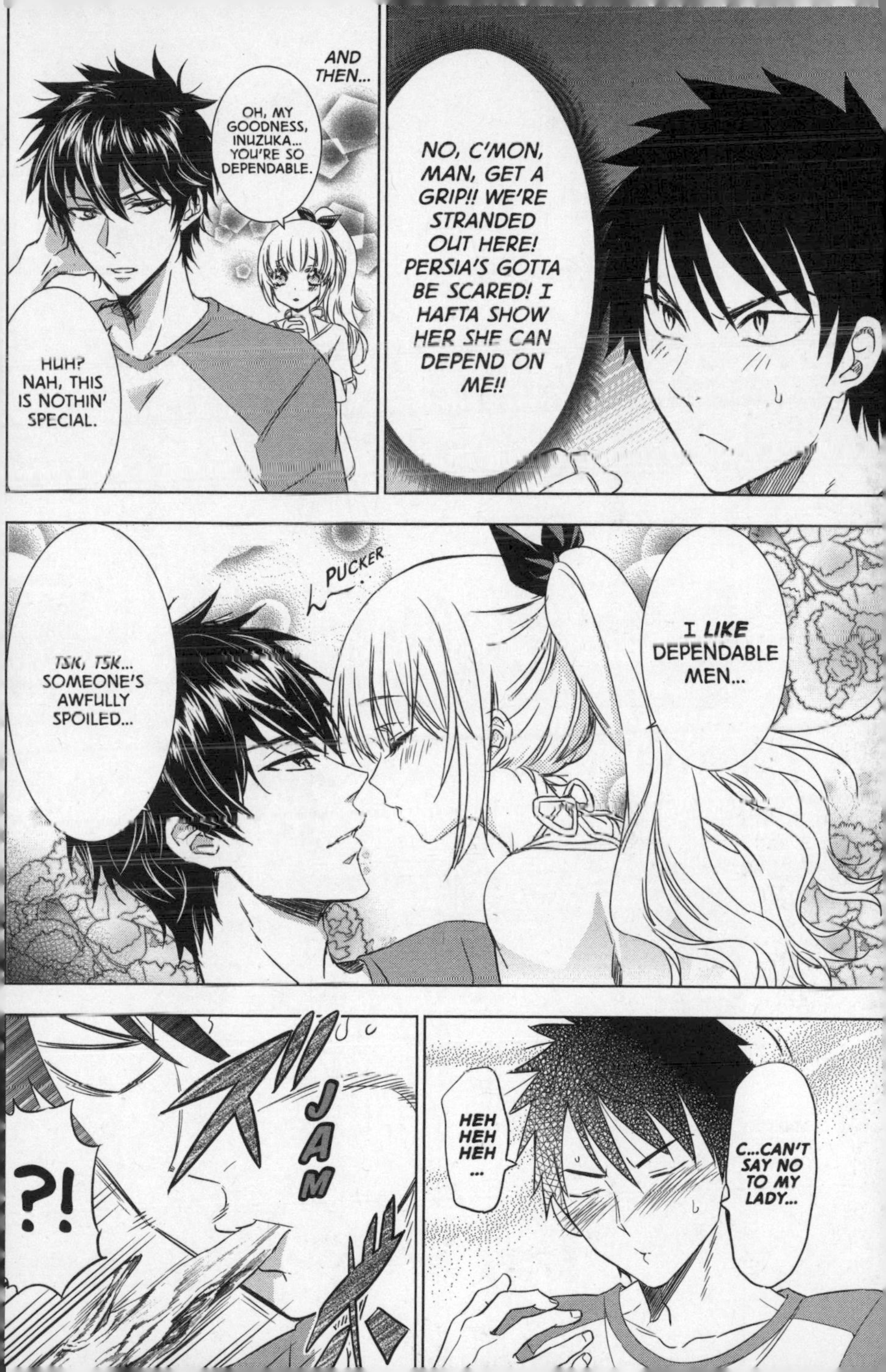
NO, C'MON, MAN, GET A GRIP!! WE'RE STRANDED OUT HERE! PERSIA'S GOTTA BE SCARED! I HAFTA SHOW HER SHE CAN DEPEND ON ME!!
AND THEN...
OH, MY GOODNESS, INUZUKA... YOU'RE SO DEPENDABLE.
HUH? NAH, THIS IS NOTHIN' SPECIAL.
I LIKE DEPENDABLE MEN...
PUCKER
TSK, TSK... SOMEONE'S AWFULLY SPOILED...
C...CAN'T SAY NO TO MY LADY...
HEH HEH HEH ...
JAM
?!

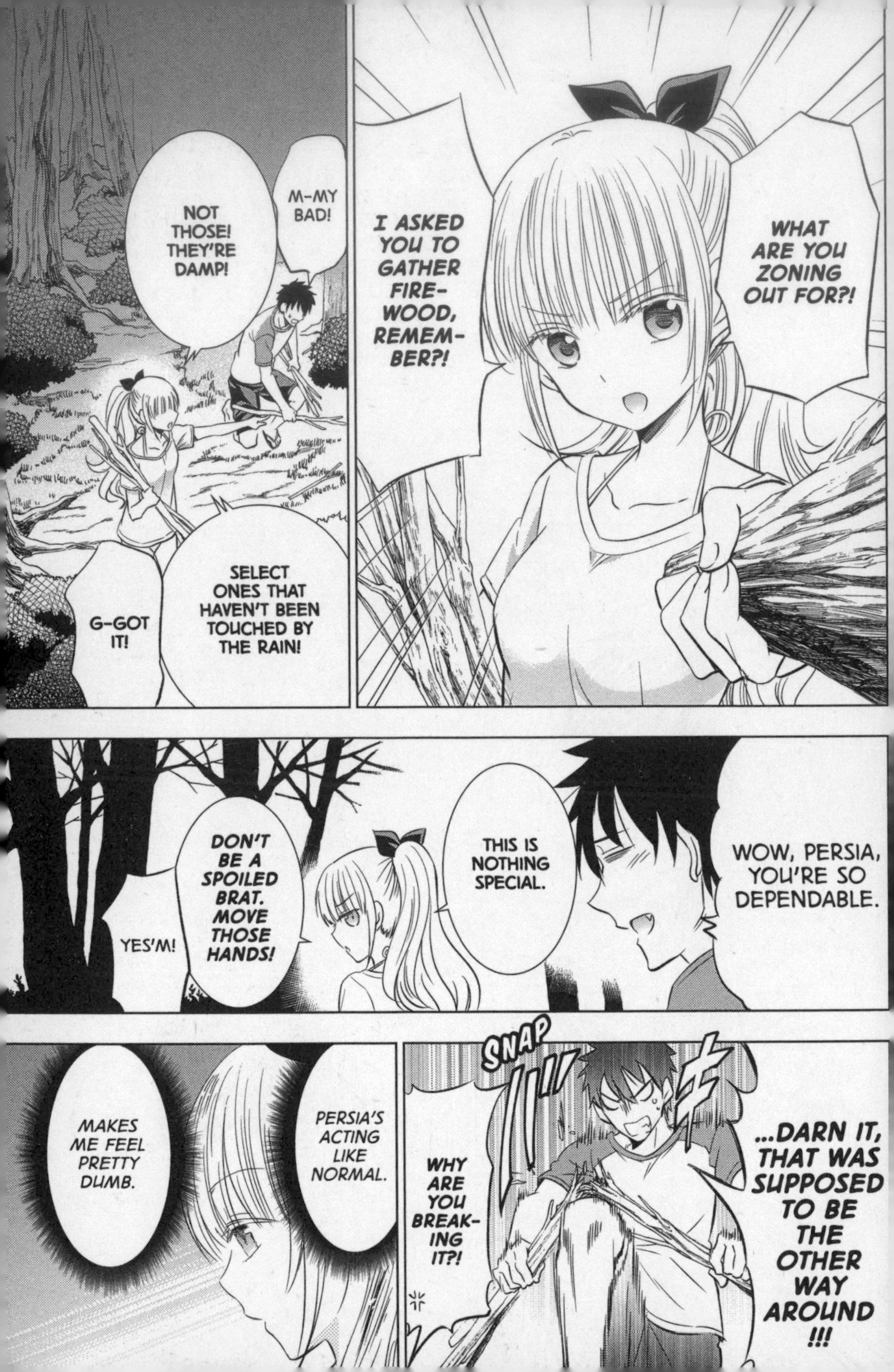
WHAT ARE YOU ZONING OUT FOR?!
I ASKED YOU TO GATHER FIRE-WOOD, REMEMBER?!
M-MY BAD!
NOT THOSE! THEY'RE DAMP!
SELECT ONES THAT HAVEN'T BEEN TOUCHED BY THE RAIN!
G-GOT IT!
WOW, PERSIA, YOU'RE SO DEPENDABLE.
THIS IS NOTHING SPECIAL.
DON'T BE A SPOILED BRAT. MOVE THOSE HANDS!
YES'M!
SNAP
...DARN IT, THAT WAS SUPPOSED TO BE THE OTHER WAY AROUND!!!
WHY ARE YOU BREAKING IT?!
PERSIA'S ACTING LIKE NORMAL.
MAKES ME FEEL PRETTY DUMB.

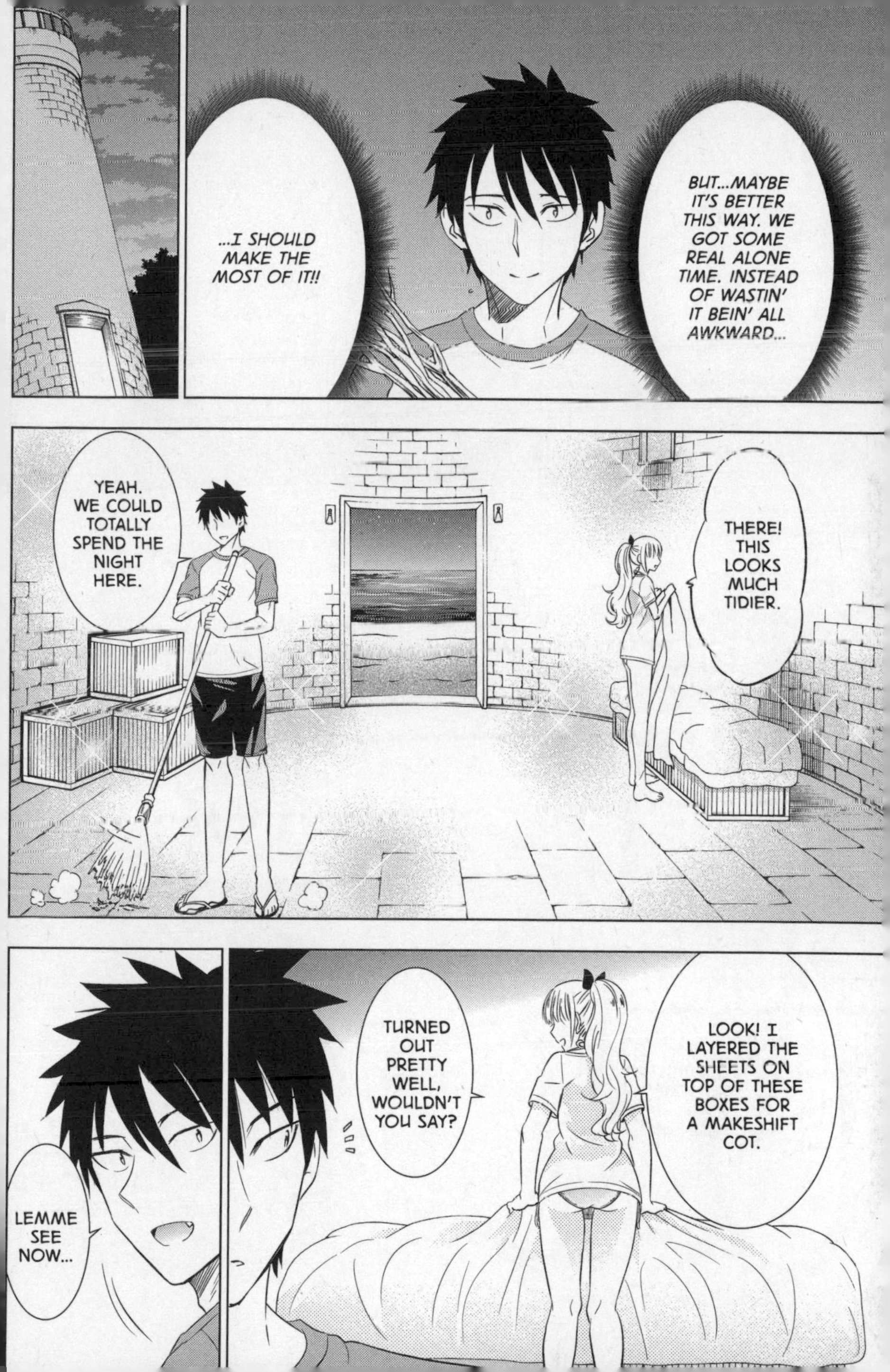
BUT...MAYBE IT'S BETTER THIS WAY. WE GOT SOME REAL ALONE TIME. INSTEAD OF WASTIN' IT BEIN' ALL AWKWARD...
...I SHOULD MAKE THE MOST OF IT!!
THERE! THIS LOOKS MUCH TIDIER.
YEAH. WE COULD TOTALLY SPEND THE NIGHT HERE.
LOOK! I LAYERED THE SHEETS ON TOP OF THESE BOXES FOR A MAKESHIFT COT.
TURNED OUT PRETTY WELL, WOULDN'T YOU SAY?
LEMME SEE NOW...

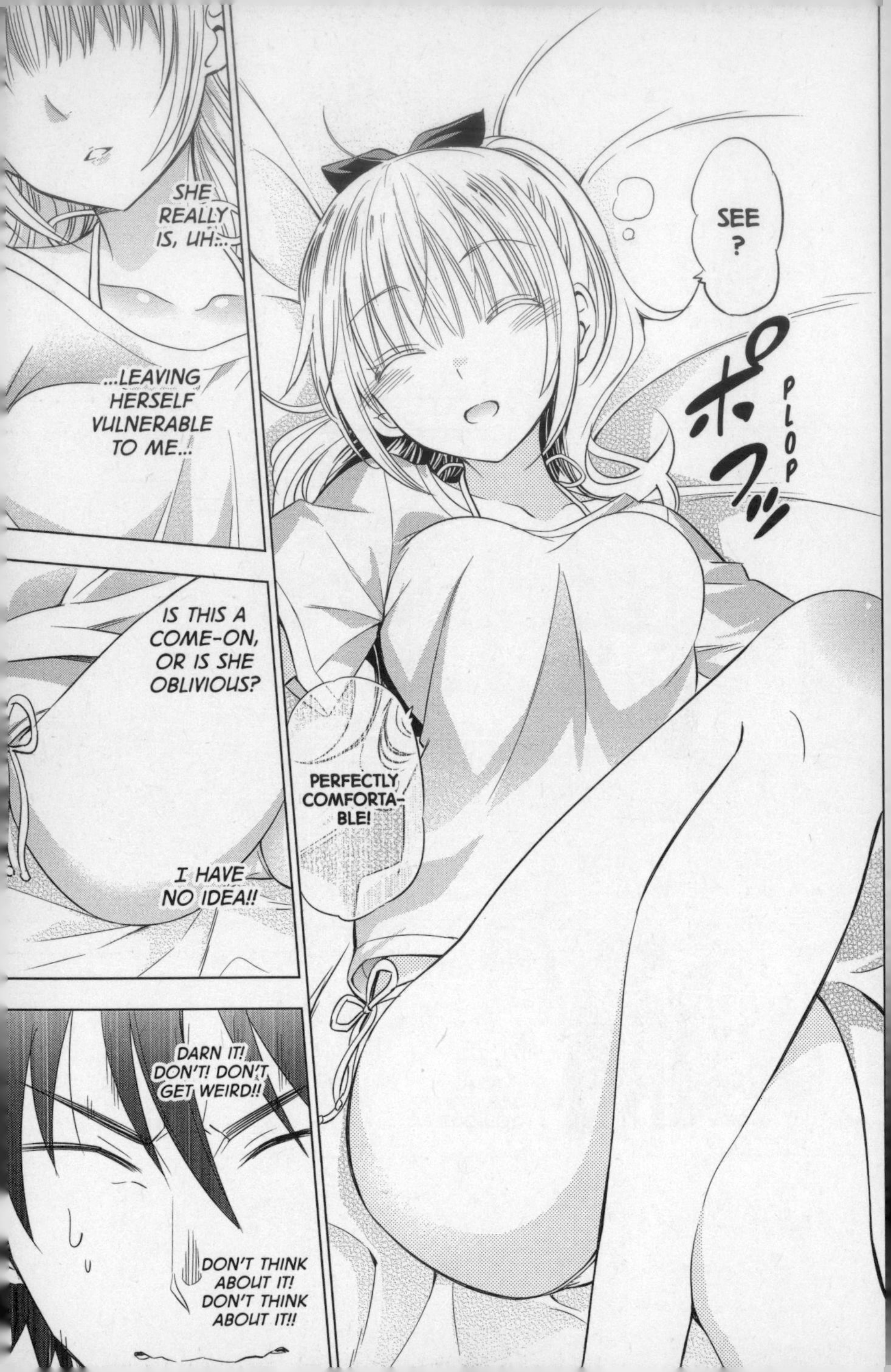
SEE?
ポフッ
PLOP
PERFECTLY COMFORTA-BLE!
SHE REALLY IS, UH...
...LEAVING HERSELF VULNERABLE TO ME...
IS THIS A COME-ON, OR IS SHE OBLIVIOUS?
I HAVE NO IDEA!!
DARN IT! DON'T! DON'T GET WEIRD!!
DON'T THINK ABOUT IT! DON'T THINK ABOUT IT!!

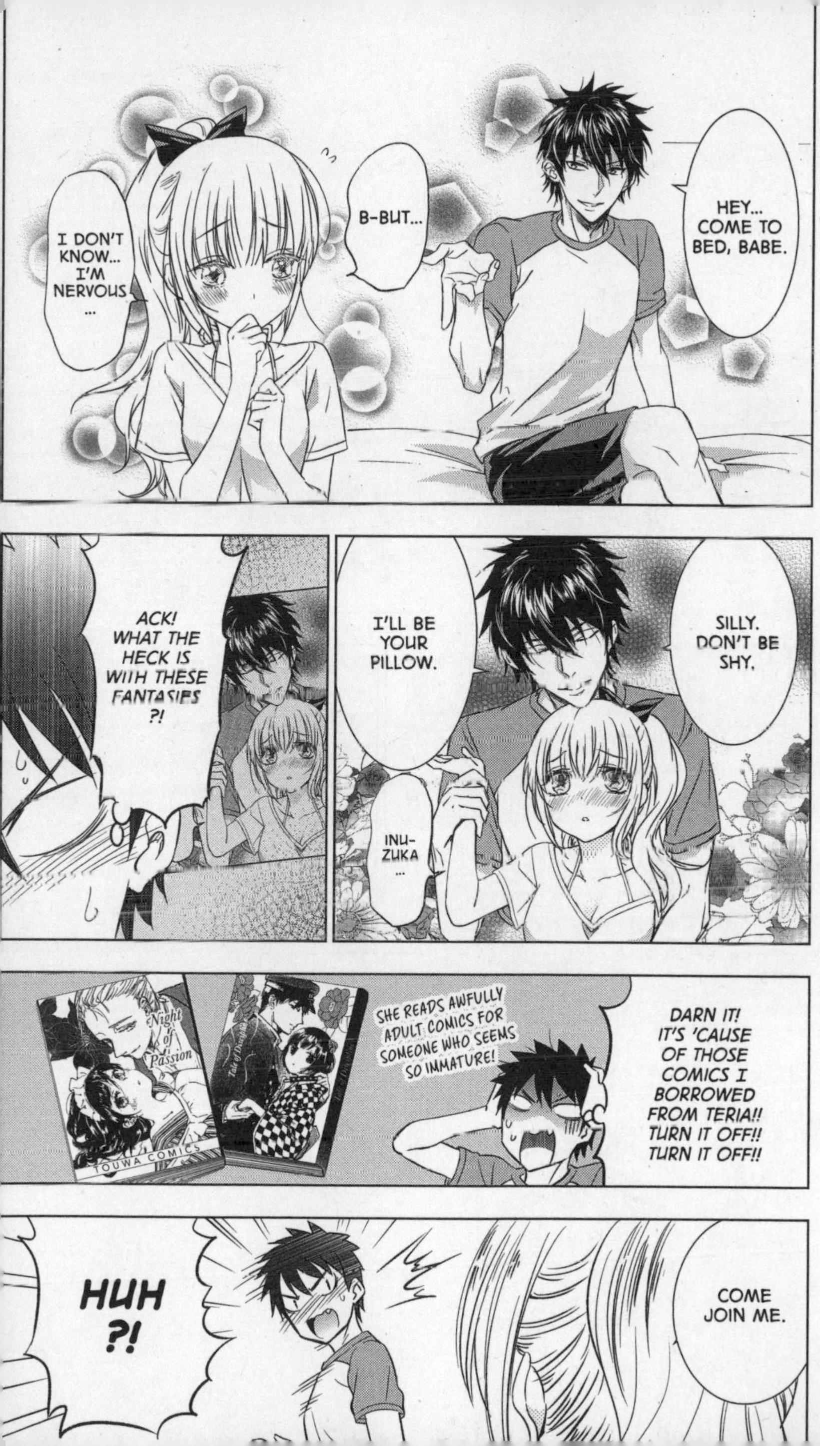
HEY... COME TO BED, BABE.
B-BUT...
I DON'T KNOW... I'M NERVOUS...
SILLY. DON'T BE SHY.
I'LL BE YOUR PILLOW.
INU-ZUKA...
ACK! WHAT THE HECK IS WITH THESE FANTASIES?!
DARN IT! IT'S 'CAUSE OF THOSE COMICS I BORROWED FROM TERIA!! TURN IT OFF!! TURN IT OFF!!
SHE READS AWFULLY ADULT COMICS FOR SOMEONE WHO SEEMS SO IMMATURE!
Night of Passion
TOUWA COMICS
COME JOIN ME.
HUH?!

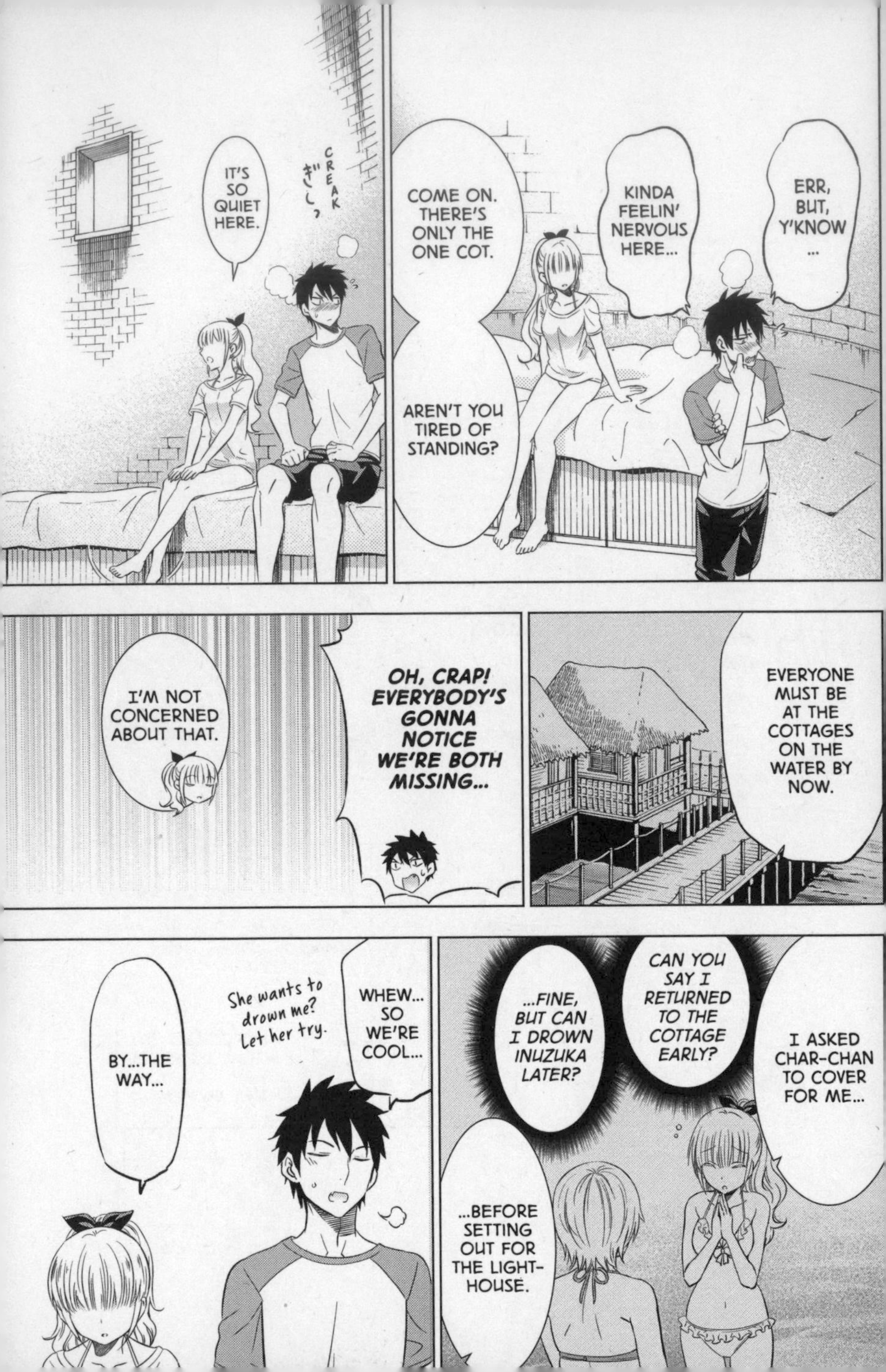
ERR, BUT, Y'KNOW ...
KINDA FEELIN' NERVOUS HERE...
COME ON. THERE'S ONLY THE ONE COT.
AREN'T YOU TIRED OF STANDING?
CREAK
ぎしっ
IT'S SO QUIET HERE.
EVERYONE MUST BE AT THE COTTAGES ON THE WATER BY NOW.
OH, CRAP! EVERYBODY'S GONNA NOTICE WE'RE BOTH MISSING...
I'M NOT CONCERNED ABOUT THAT.
I ASKED CHAR-CHAN TO COVER FOR ME...
CAN YOU SAY I RETURNED TO THE COTTAGE EARLY?
...BEFORE SETTING OUT FOR THE LIGHT-HOUSE.
...FINE, BUT CAN I DROWN INUZUKA LATER?
WHEW... SO WE'RE COOL...
She wants to drown me? Let her try.
BY...THE WAY...

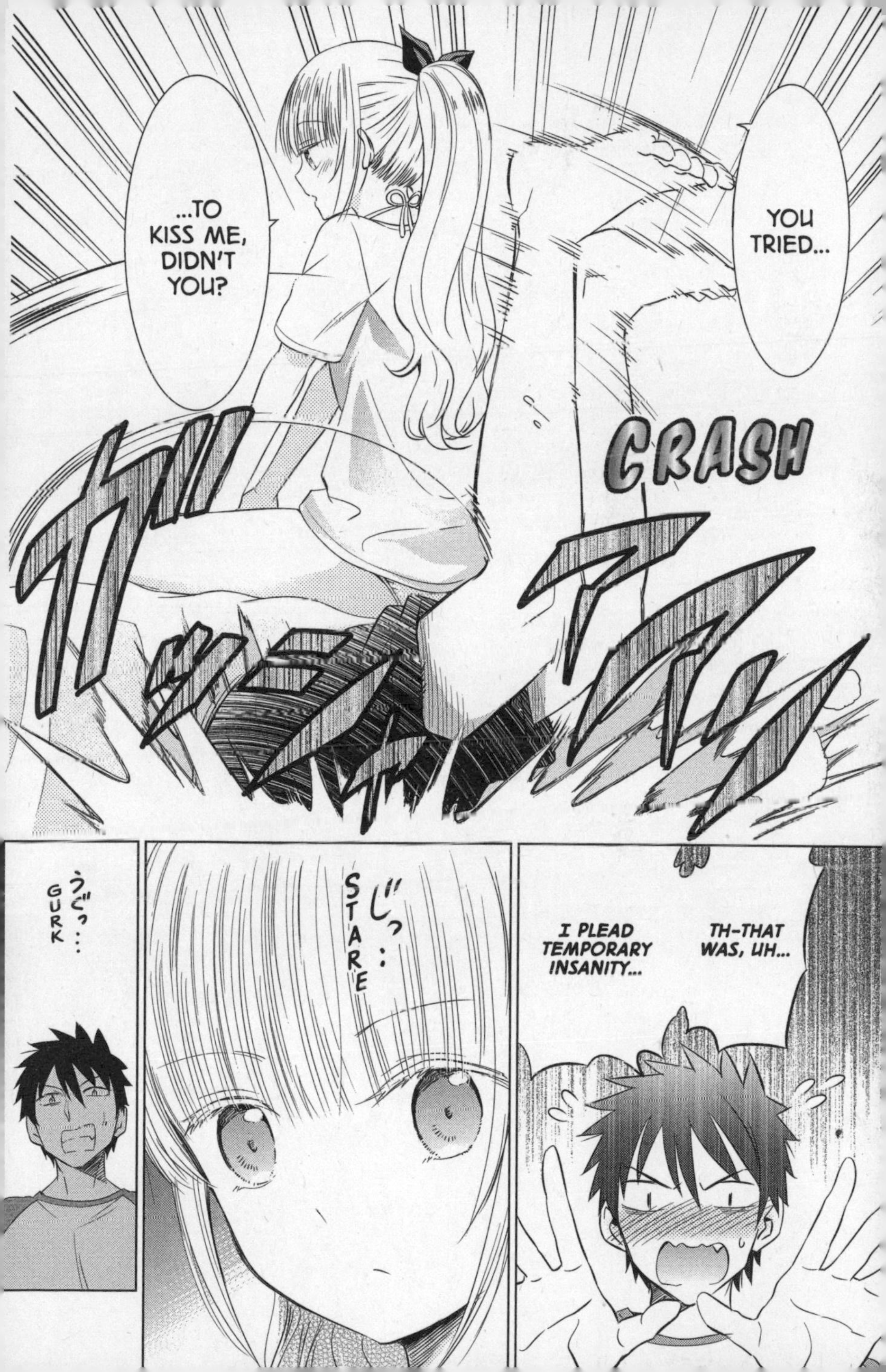
YOU TRIED...
...TO KISS ME, DIDN'T YOU?
CRASH
TH-THAT WAS, UH...
I PLEAD TEMPORARY INSANITY...
じっ…
STARE
うぐっ…
GURK

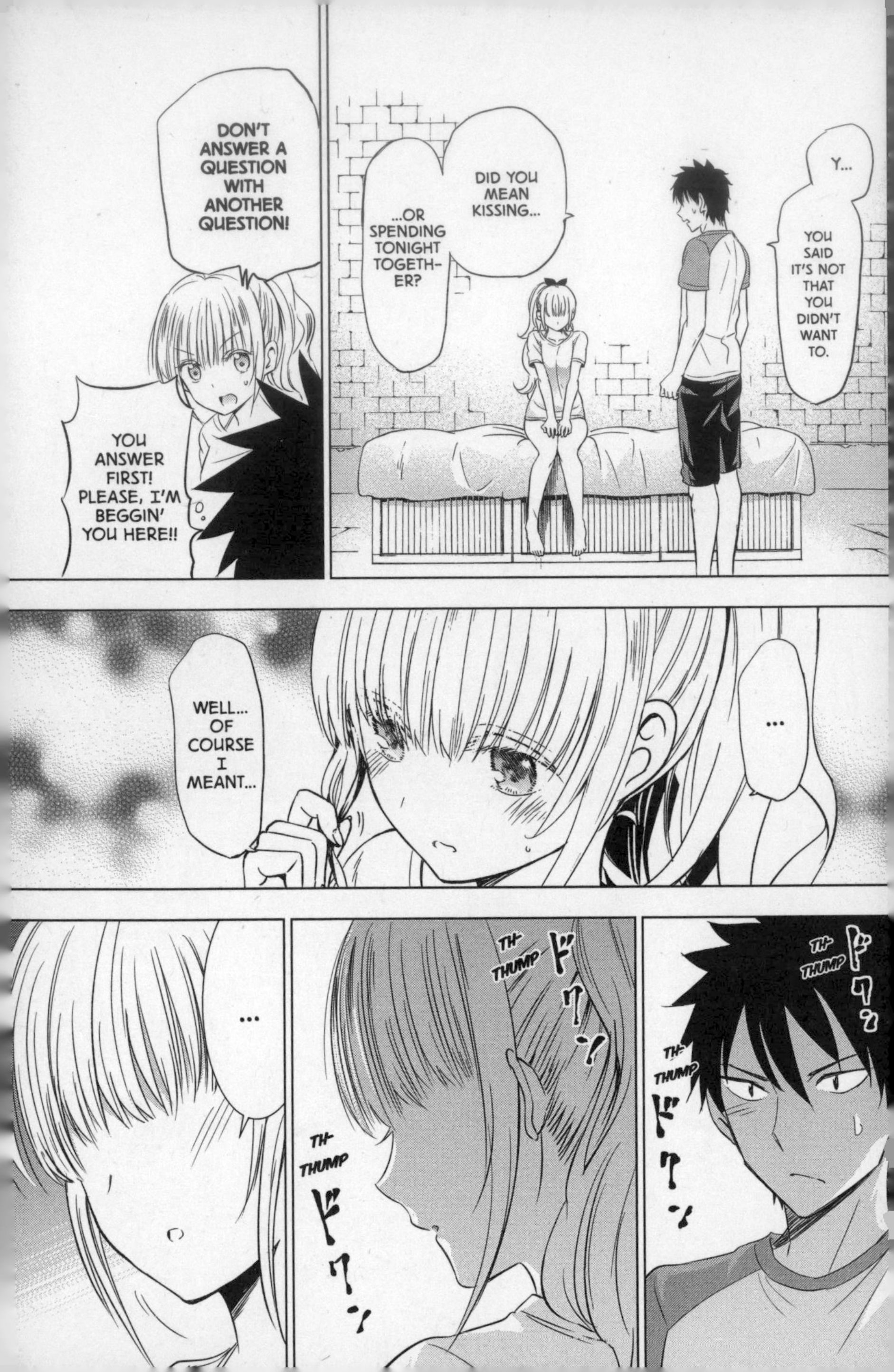
Y...
YOU SAID IT'S NOT THAT YOU DIDN'T WANT TO.
DID YOU MEAN KISSING...
...OR SPENDING TONIGHT TOGETH-ER?
DON'T ANSWER A QUESTION WITH ANOTHER QUESTION!
YOU ANSWER FIRST! PLEASE, I'M BEGGIN' YOU HERE!!
...
WELL... OF COURSE I MEANT...
TH-THUMP
TH-THUMP
TH-THUMP
TH-THUMP
...

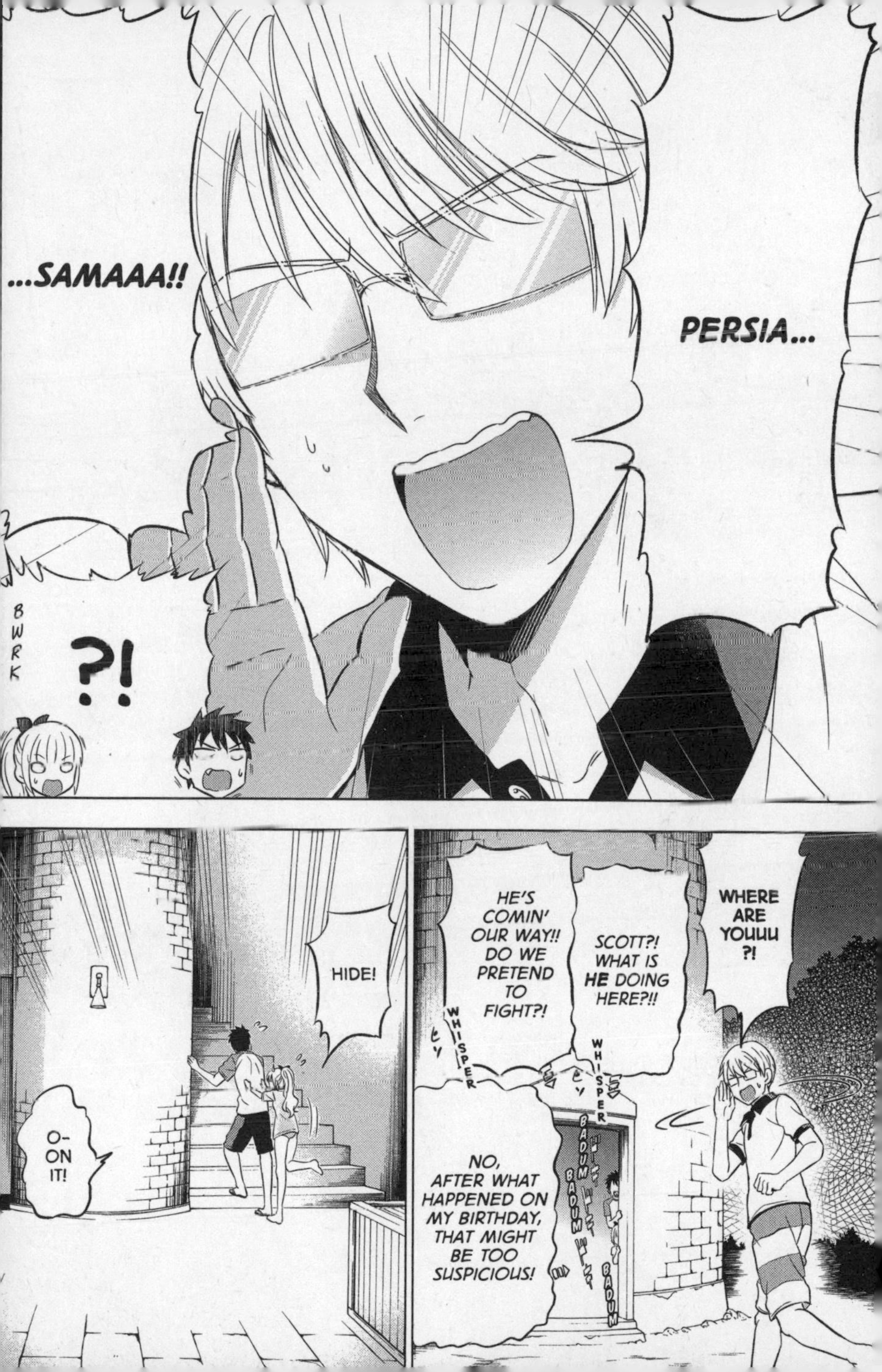
PERSIA...
...SAMAAA!!
BWRK
?!
WHERE ARE YOUUU?!
SCOTT?! WHAT IS HE DOING HERE?!!
WHISPER
HE'S COMIN' OUR WAY!! DO WE PRETEND TO FIGHT?!
WHISPER
NO, AFTER WHAT HAPPENED ON MY BIRTHDAY, THAT MIGHT BE TOO SUSPICIOUS!
BADUM BADUM BADUM BADUM
HIDE!
O- ON IT!

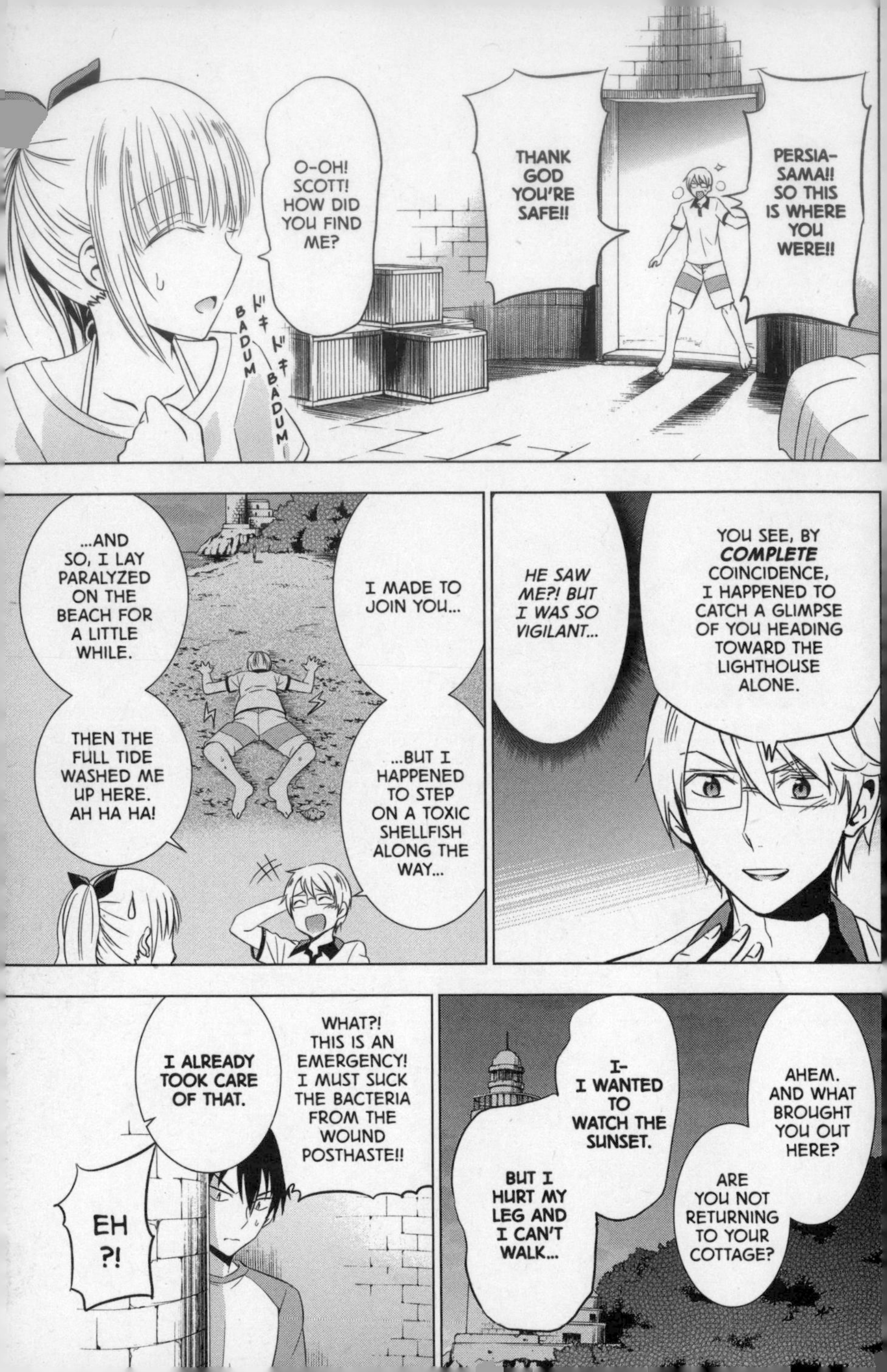
PERSIA-SAMA!! SO THIS IS WHERE YOU WERE!!
THANK GOD YOU'RE SAFE!!
O-OH! SCOTT! HOW DID YOU FIND ME?
BADUM BADUM
ドキドキ
YOU SEE, BY **COMPLETE** COINCIDENCE, I HAPPENED TO CATCH A GLIMPSE OF YOU HEADING TOWARD THE LIGHTHOUSE ALONE.
HE SAW ME?! BUT I WAS SO VIGILANT...
I MADE TO JOIN YOU...
...BUT I HAPPENED TO STEP ON A TOXIC SHELLFISH ALONG THE WAY...
...AND SO, I LAY PARALYZED ON THE BEACH FOR A LITTLE WHILE.
THEN THE FULL TIDE WASHED ME UP HERE. AH HA HA!
AHEM. AND WHAT BROUGHT YOU OUT HERE?
ARE YOU NOT RETURNING TO YOUR COTTAGE?
I- I WANTED TO WATCH THE SUNSET.
BUT I HURT MY LEG AND I CAN'T WALK...
WHAT?! THIS IS AN EMERGENCY! I MUST SUCK THE BACTERIA FROM THE WOUND POSTHASTE!!
I ALREADY TOOK CARE OF THAT.
EH?!

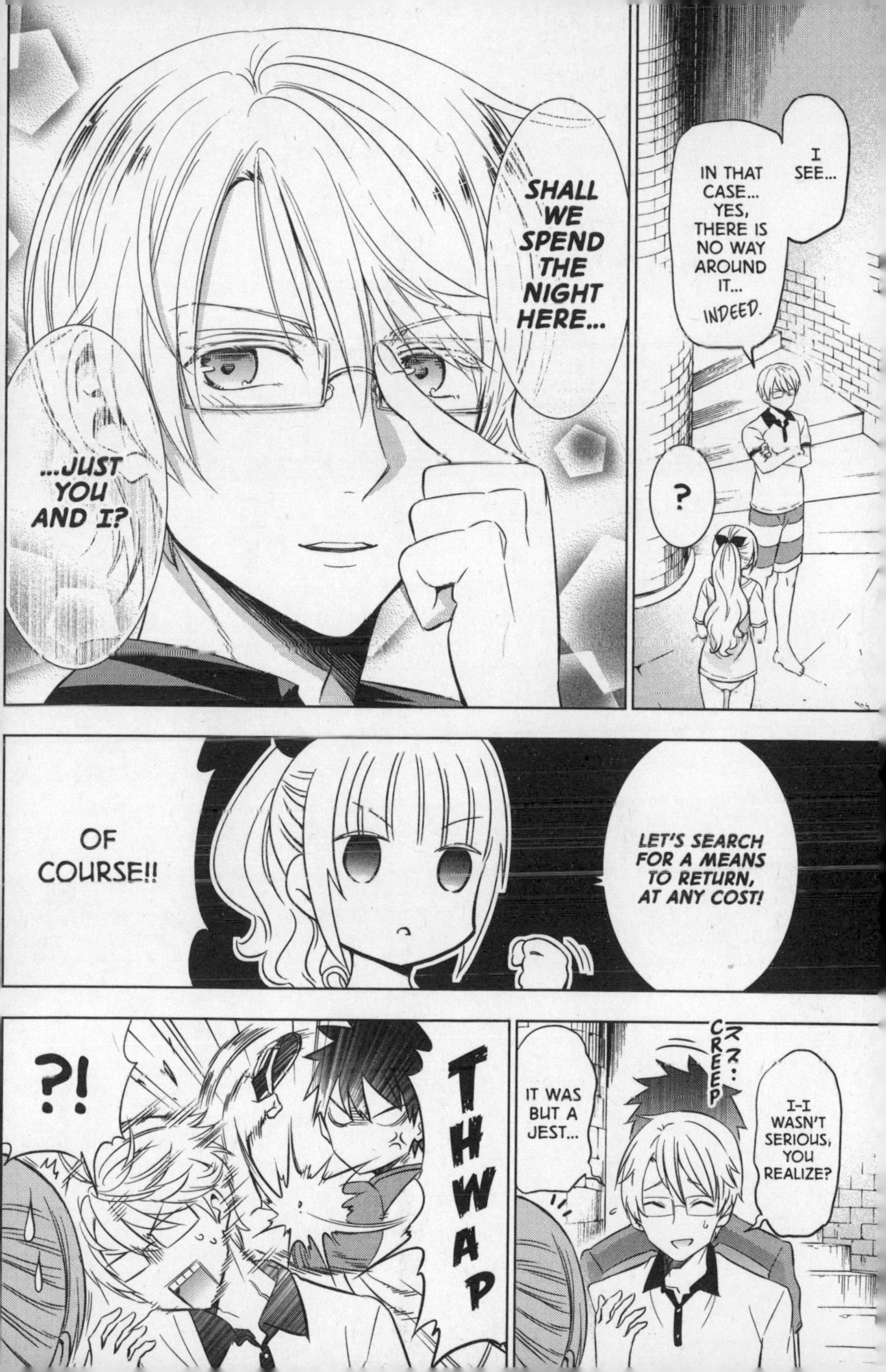

I SEE...
IN THAT CASE... YES, THERE IS NO WAY AROUND IT... INDEED.
?
SHALL WE SPEND THE NIGHT HERE...
...JUST YOU AND I?
LET'S SEARCH FOR A MEANS TO RETURN, AT ANY COST!
OF COURSE!!
スス… CREEP
I-I WASN'T SERIOUS, YOU REALIZE?
IT WAS BUT A JEST...
THWAP
?!

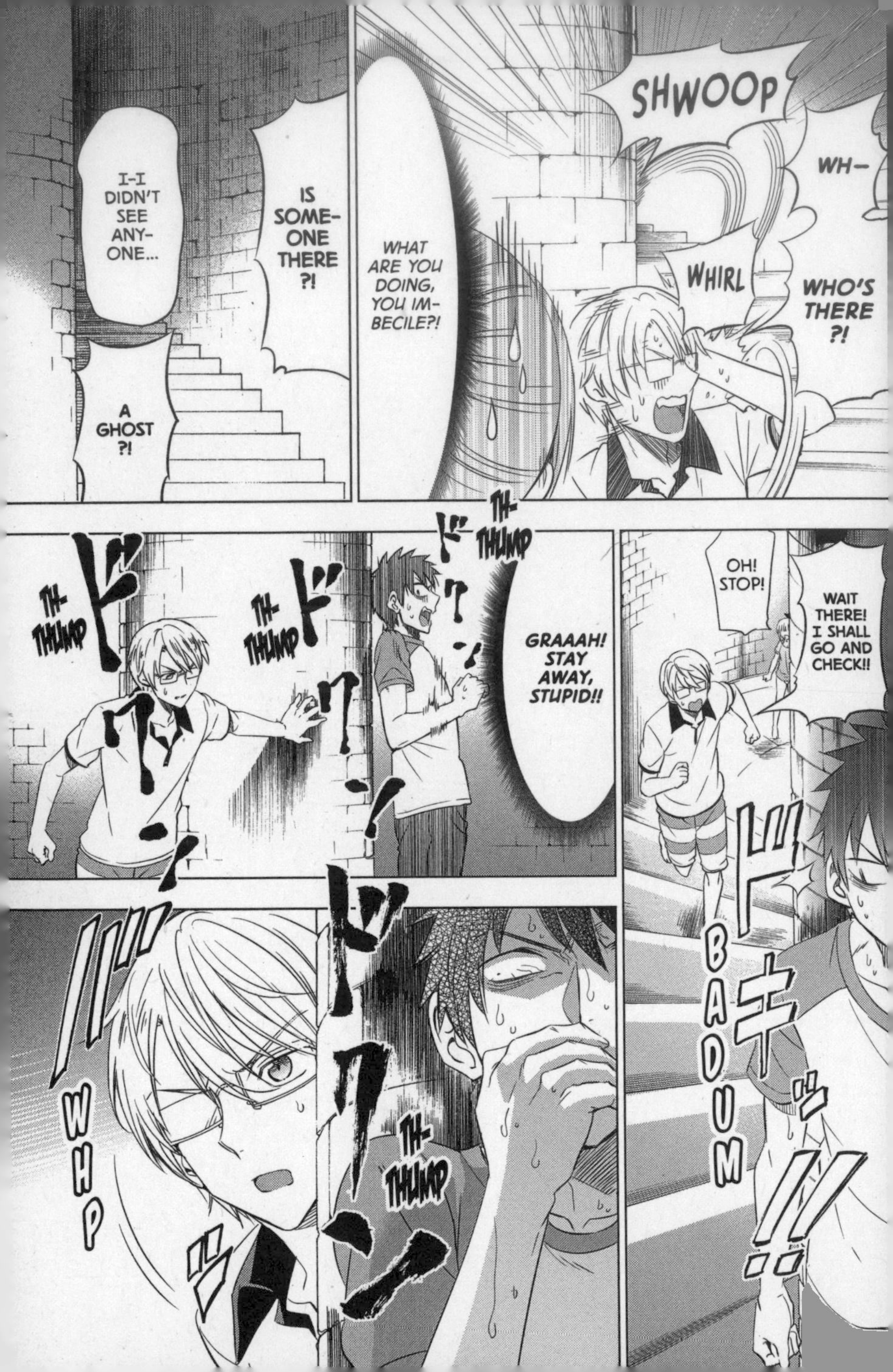
SHWOOP
WH—
WHIRL
WHO'S THERE ?!
WHAT ARE YOU DOING, YOU IMBECILE?!
IS SOMEONE THERE ?!
I-I DIDN'T SEE ANYONE...
A GHOST ?!
WAIT THERE! I SHALL GO AND CHECK!!
OH! STOP!
TH-THUMP
GRAAAH! STAY AWAY, STUPID!!
TH-THUMP
TH-THUMP
BADUM
TH-THUMP
WHP

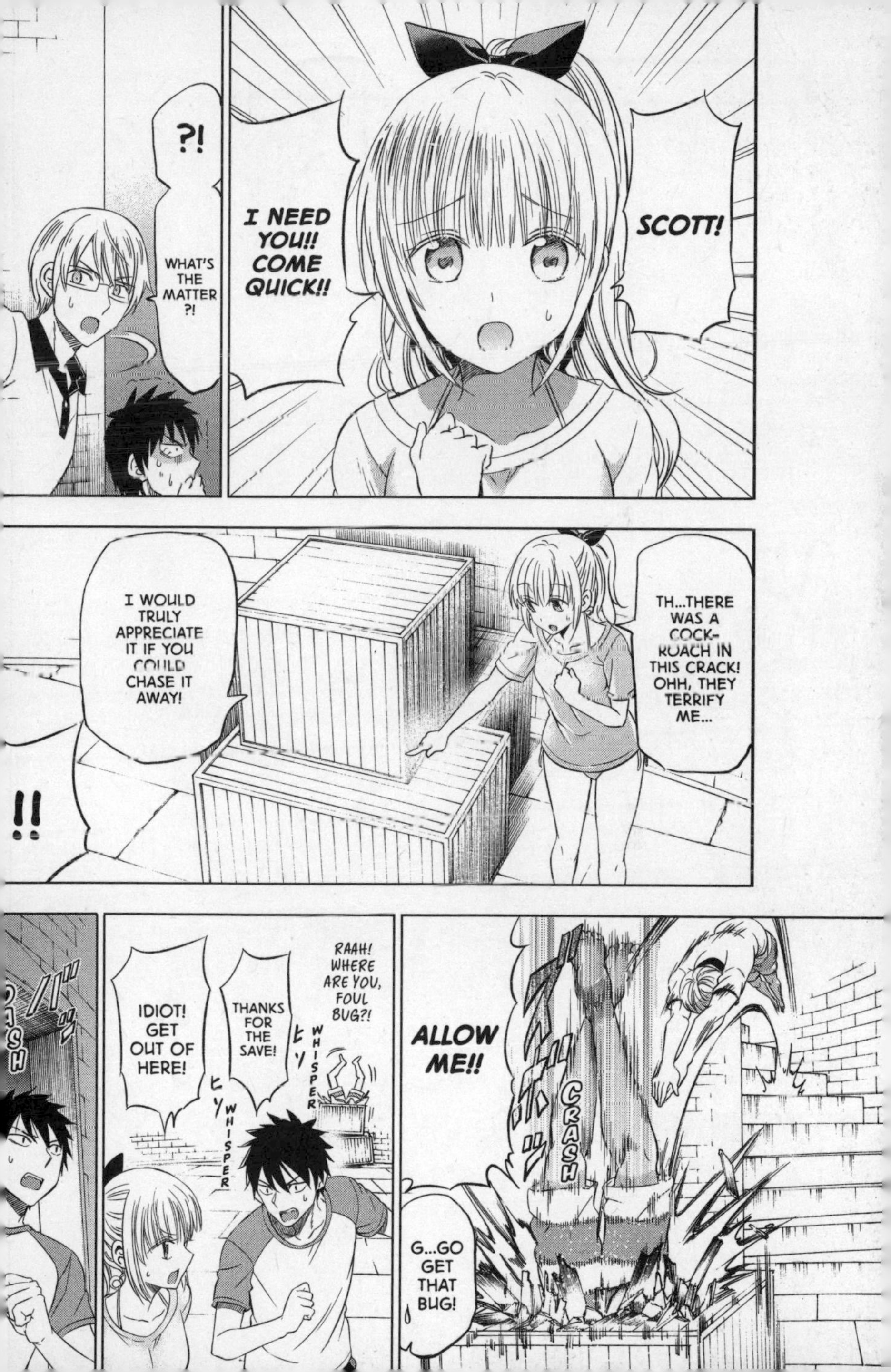
SCOTT!
I NEED YOU!! COME QUICK!!
?!
WHAT'S THE MATTER ?!
TH...THERE WAS A COCK-ROACH IN THIS CRACK! OHH, THEY TERRIFY ME...
I WOULD TRULY APPRECIATE IT IF YOU COULD CHASE IT AWAY!
!!
ALLOW ME!!
CRASH
G...GO GET THAT BUG!
RAAH! WHERE ARE YOU, FOUL BUG?!
THANKS FOR THE SAVE!
WHISPER
IDIOT! GET OUT OF HERE!
WHISPER
CRASH

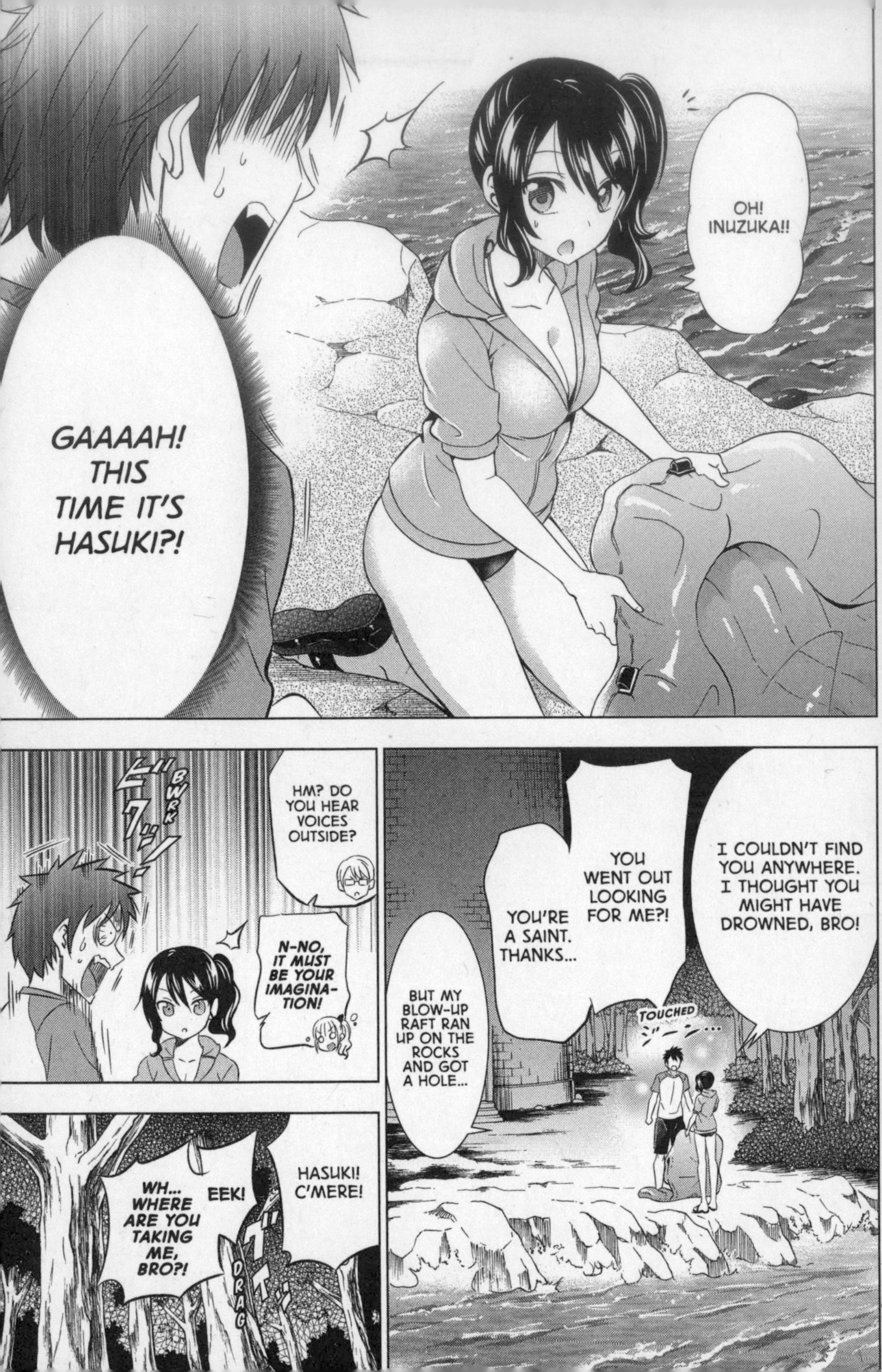

OH! INUZUKA!!
GAAAAH! THIS TIME IT'S HASUKI?!
I COULDN'T FIND YOU ANYWHERE. I THOUGHT YOU MIGHT HAVE DROWNED, BRO!
YOU WENT OUT LOOKING FOR ME?!
YOU'RE A SAINT. THANKS...
BUT MY BLOW-UP RAFT RAN UP ON THE ROCKS AND GOT A HOLE...
TOUCHED
HM? DO YOU HEAR VOICES OUTSIDE?
BWRK
N-NO, IT MUST BE YOUR IMAGINATION!
HASUKI! C'MERE!
EEK!
WH... WHERE ARE YOU TAKING ME, BRO?!
DRAG

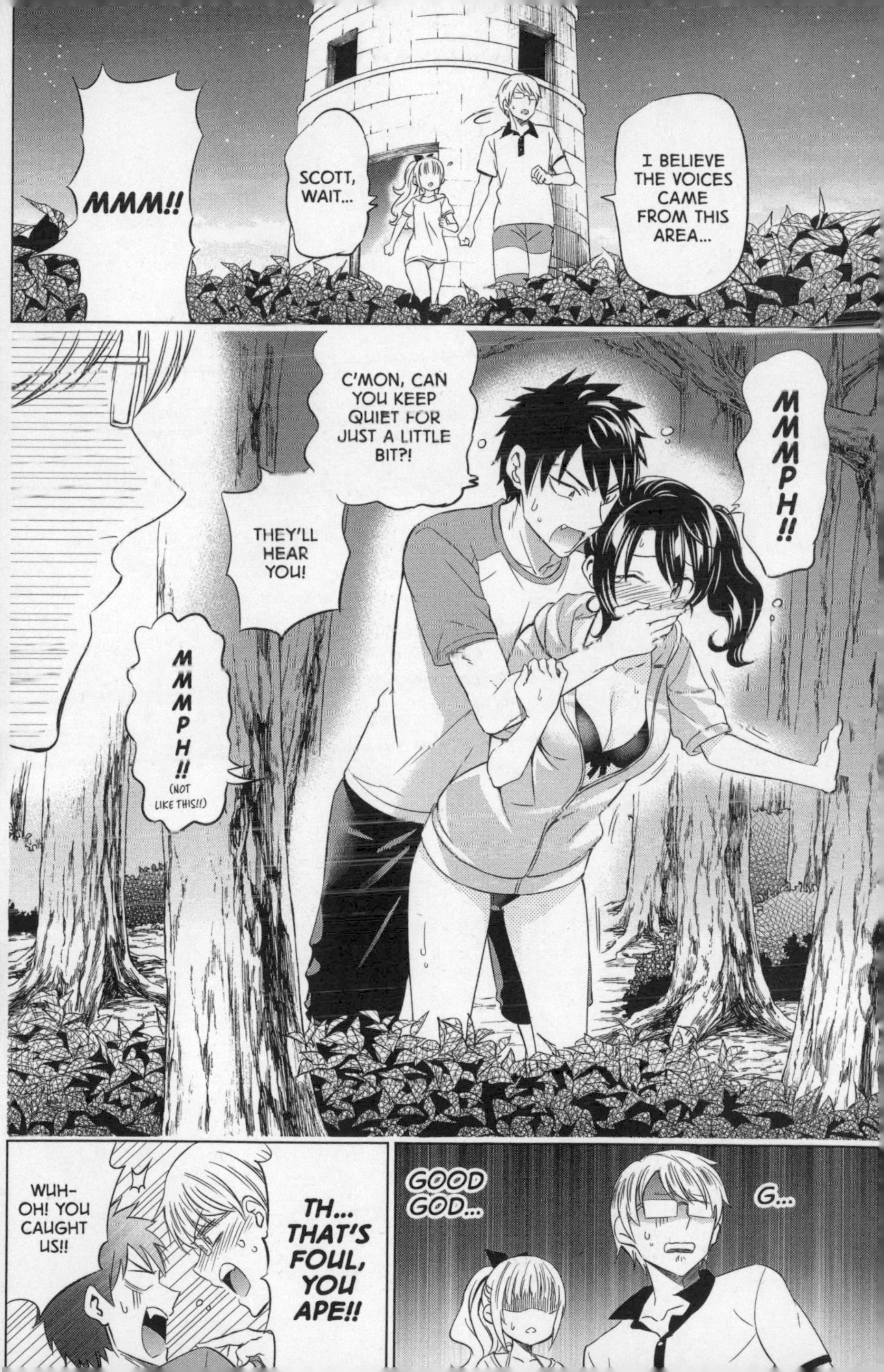
I BELIEVE THE VOICES CAME FROM THIS AREA...
SCOTT, WAIT...
MMM!!
MMMPH!!
C'MON, CAN YOU KEEP QUIET FOR JUST A LITTLE BIT?!
THEY'LL HEAR YOU!
MMMPH!!
(NOT LIKE THIS!!)
G...
GOOD GOD...
TH... THAT'S FOUL, YOU APE!!
WUH-OH! YOU CAUGHT US!!

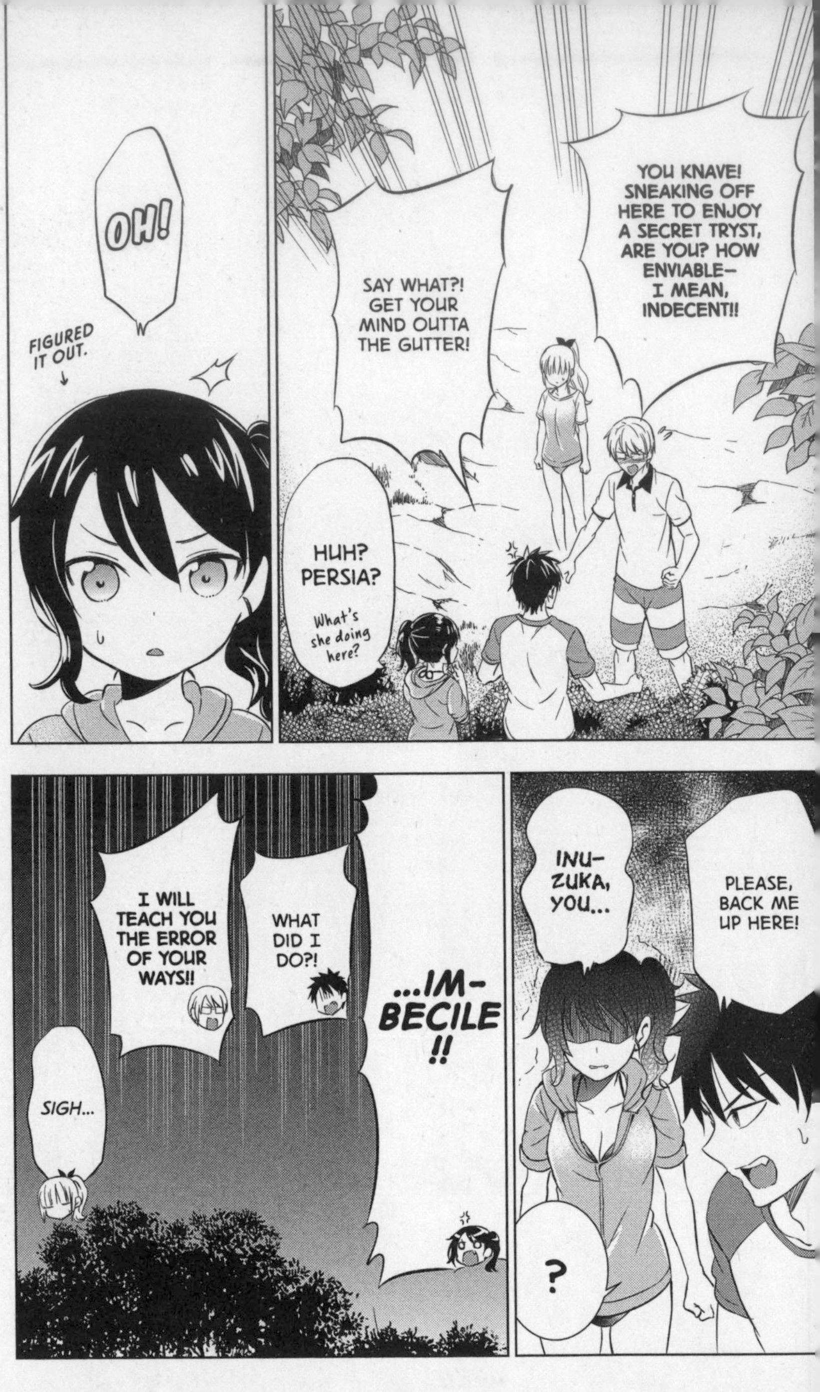
YOU KNAVE! SNEAKING OFF HERE TO ENJOY A SECRET TRYST, ARE YOU? HOW ENVIABLE– I MEAN, INDECENT!!
SAY WHAT?! GET YOUR MIND OUTTA THE GUTTER!
HUH? PERSIA?
What's she doing here?
OH!
FIGURED IT OUT.
PLEASE, BACK ME UP HERE!
INU-ZUKA, YOU...
?
...IM-BECILE!!
WHAT DID I DO?!
I WILL TEACH YOU THE ERROR OF YOUR WAYS!!
SIGH...

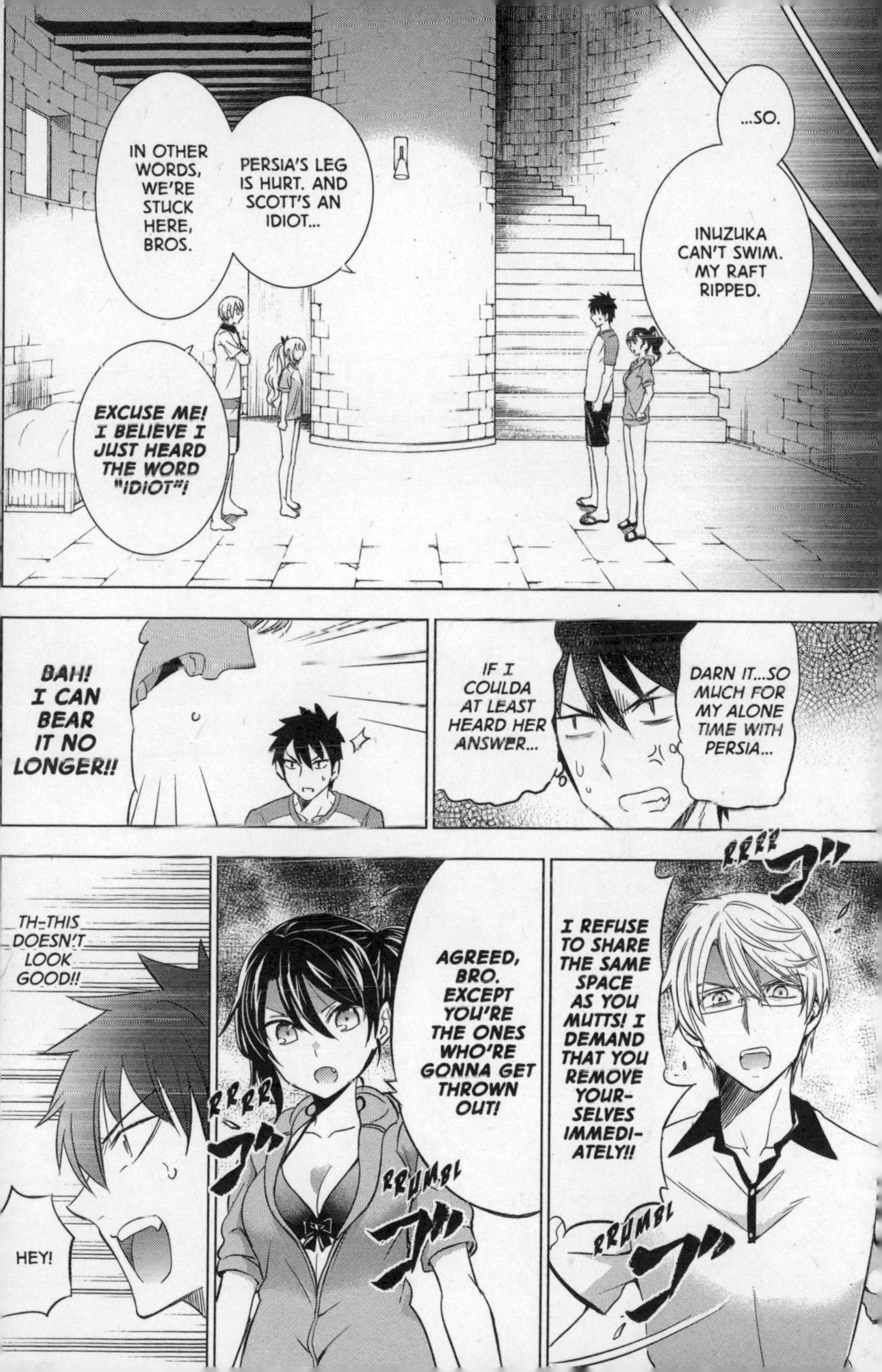
...SO.
INUZUKA CAN'T SWIM. MY RAFT RIPPED.
PERSIA'S LEG IS HURT. AND SCOTT'S AN IDIOT...
IN OTHER WORDS, WE'RE STUCK HERE, BROS.
EXCUSE ME! I BELIEVE I JUST HEARD THE WORD "IDIOT"!
DARN IT...SO MUCH FOR MY ALONE TIME WITH PERSIA...
IF I COULDA AT LEAST HEARD HER ANSWER...
BAH! I CAN BEAR IT NO LONGER!!
RRRR
I REFUSE TO SHARE THE SAME SPACE AS YOU MUTTS! I DEMAND THAT YOU REMOVE YOURSELVES IMMEDIATELY!!
RRUMBL
AGREED, BRO. EXCEPT YOU'RE THE ONES WHO'RE GONNA GET THROWN OUT!
RRRR
RRUMBL
TH-THIS DOESN'T LOOK GOOD!!
HEY!

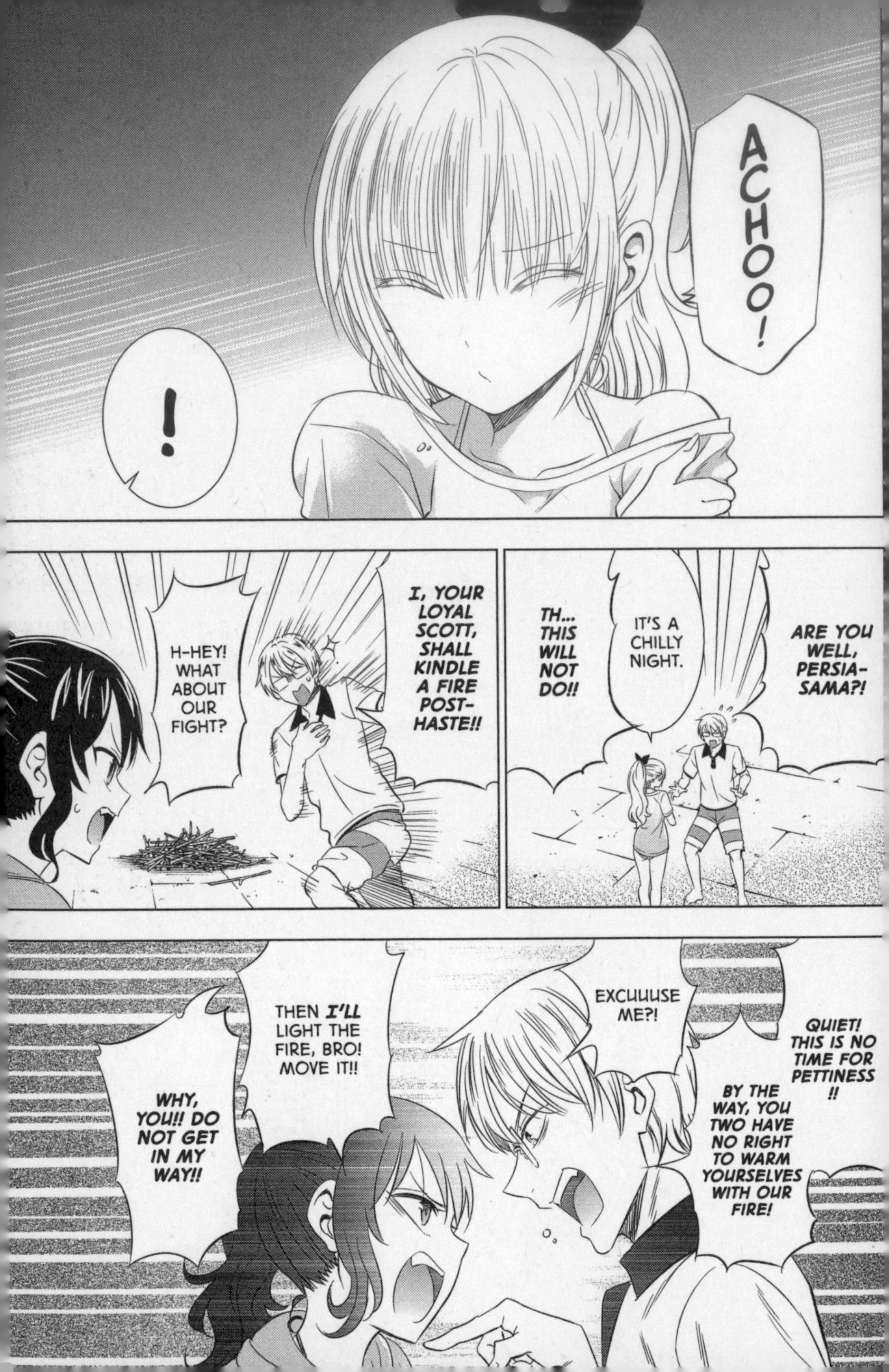
ACHOO!
!
ARE YOU WELL, PERSIA-SAMA?!
IT'S A CHILLY NIGHT.
TH... THIS WILL NOT DO!!
I, YOUR LOYAL SCOTT, SHALL KINDLE A FIRE POST-HASTE!!
H-HEY! WHAT ABOUT OUR FIGHT?
QUIET! THIS IS NO TIME FOR PETTINESS!!
BY THE WAY, YOU TWO HAVE NO RIGHT TO WARM YOURSELVES WITH OUR FIRE!
EXCUUUSE ME?!
THEN I'LL LIGHT THE FIRE, BRO! MOVE IT!!
WHY, YOU!! DO NOT GET IN MY WAY!!

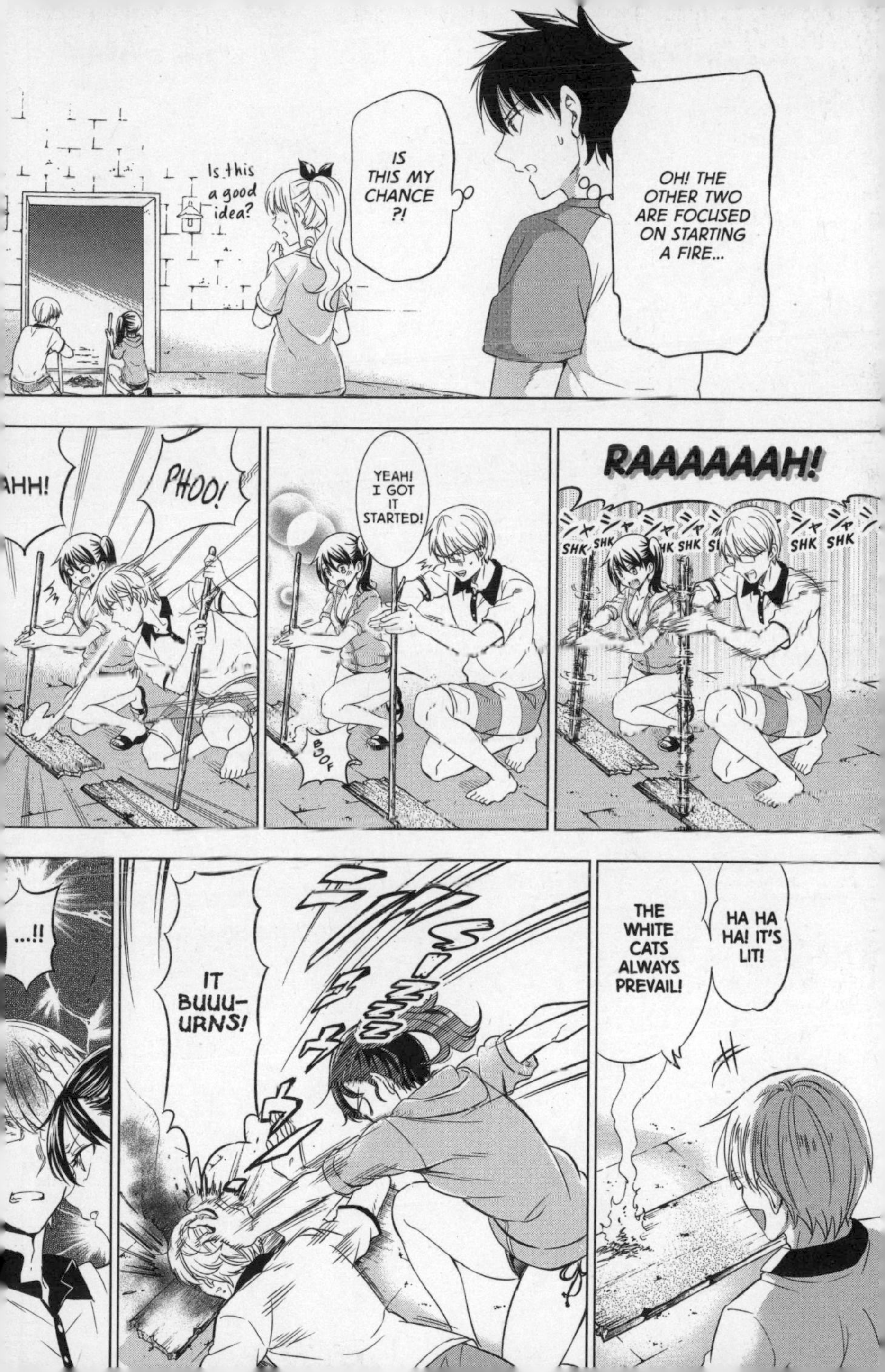
OH! THE OTHER TWO ARE FOCUSED ON STARTING A FIRE...
IS THIS MY CHANCE ?!
Is this a good idea?
RAAAAAAH!
SHK SHK SHK SHK SHK SHK
YEAH! I GOT IT STARTED!
BOOF
PHOO!
AHH!
HA HA HA! IT'S LIT!
THE WHITE CATS ALWAYS PREVAIL!
IT BUUU-URNS!
...!!

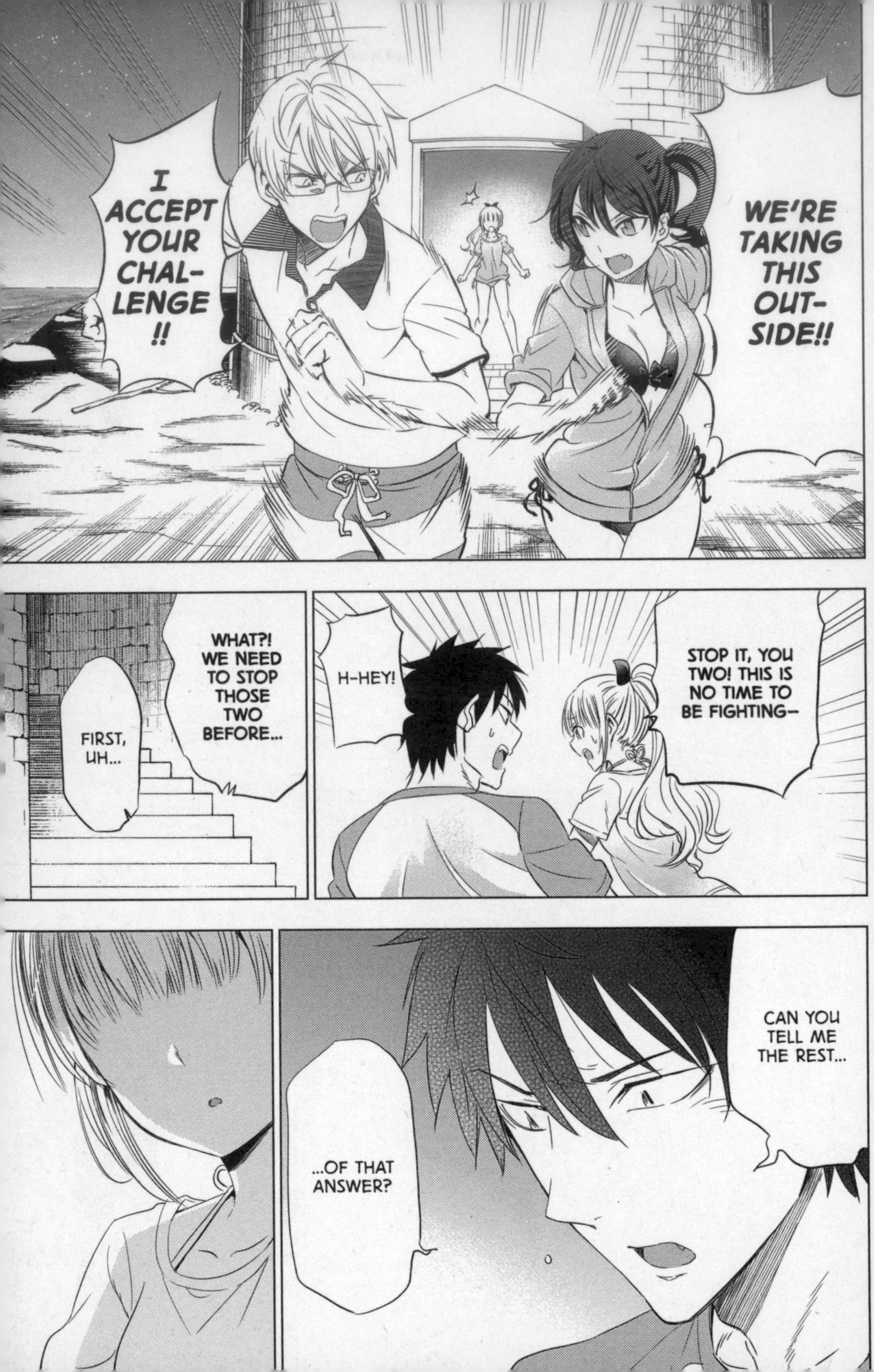
WE'RE TAKING THIS OUT-SIDE!!
I ACCEPT YOUR CHAL-LENGE!!
STOP IT, YOU TWO! THIS IS NO TIME TO BE FIGHTING–
H-HEY!
WHAT?! WE NEED TO STOP THOSE TWO BEFORE...
FIRST, UH...
CAN YOU TELL ME THE REST...
...OF THAT ANSWER?

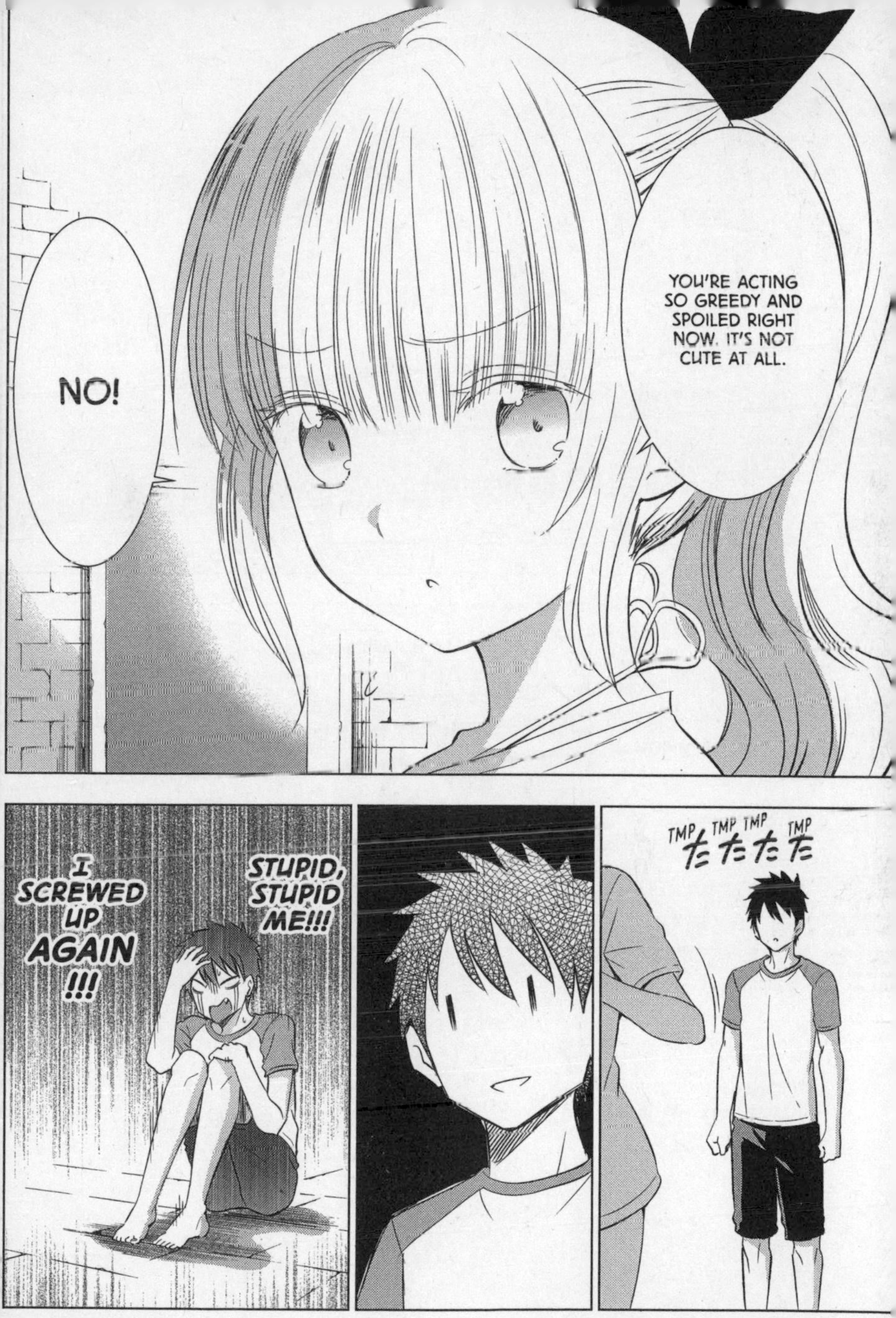
YOU'RE ACTING SO GREEDY AND SPOILED RIGHT NOW. IT'S NOT CUTE AT ALL.
NO!
TMP TMP TMP TMP
たたたた
STUPID, STUPID ME!!!
I SCREWED UP AGAIN!!!

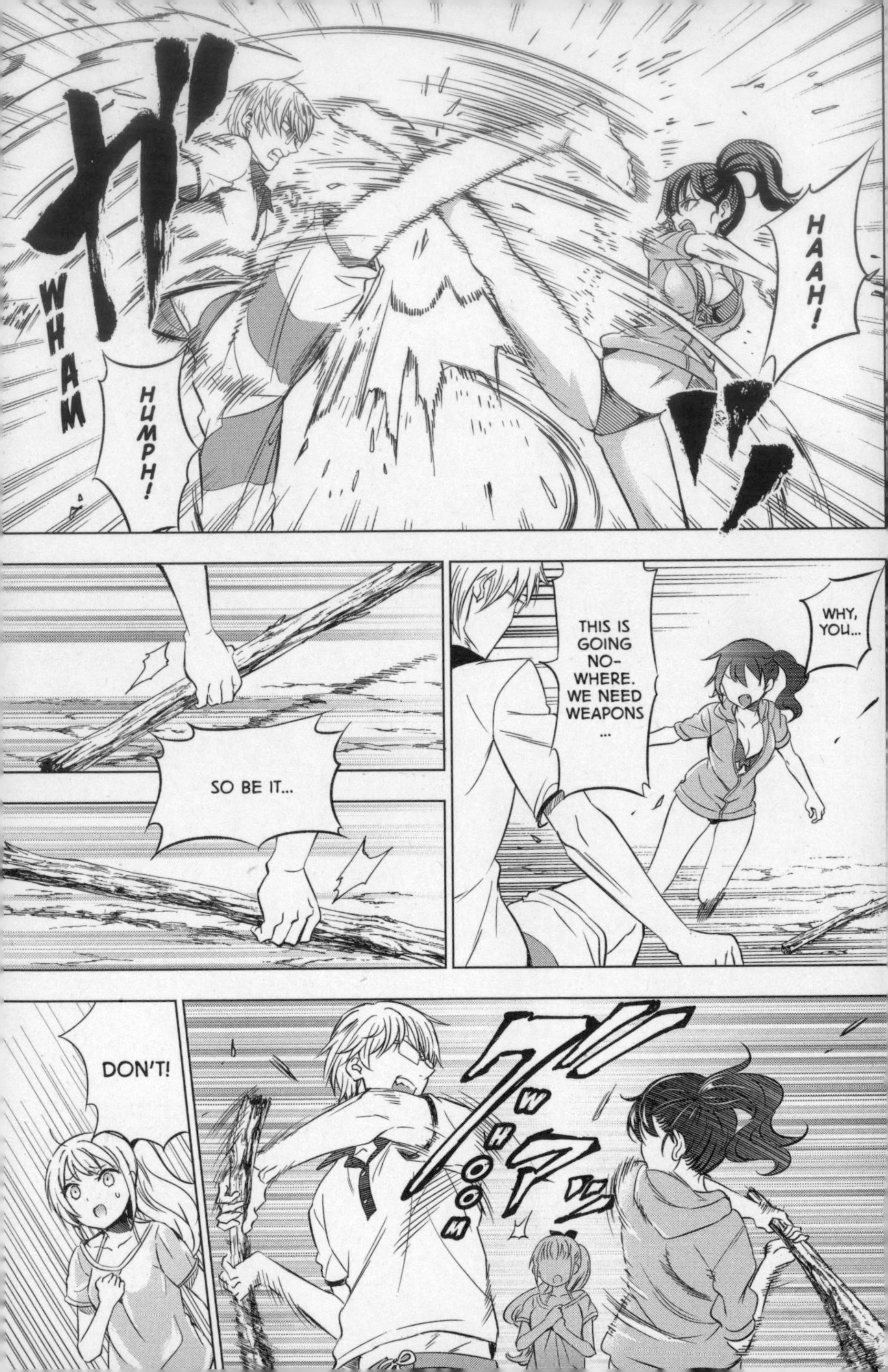
HAAH!
WHAM
HUMPH!
WHY, YOU...
THIS IS GOING NO-WHERE. WE NEED WEAPONS ...
SO BE IT...
WHOOOM
DON'T!

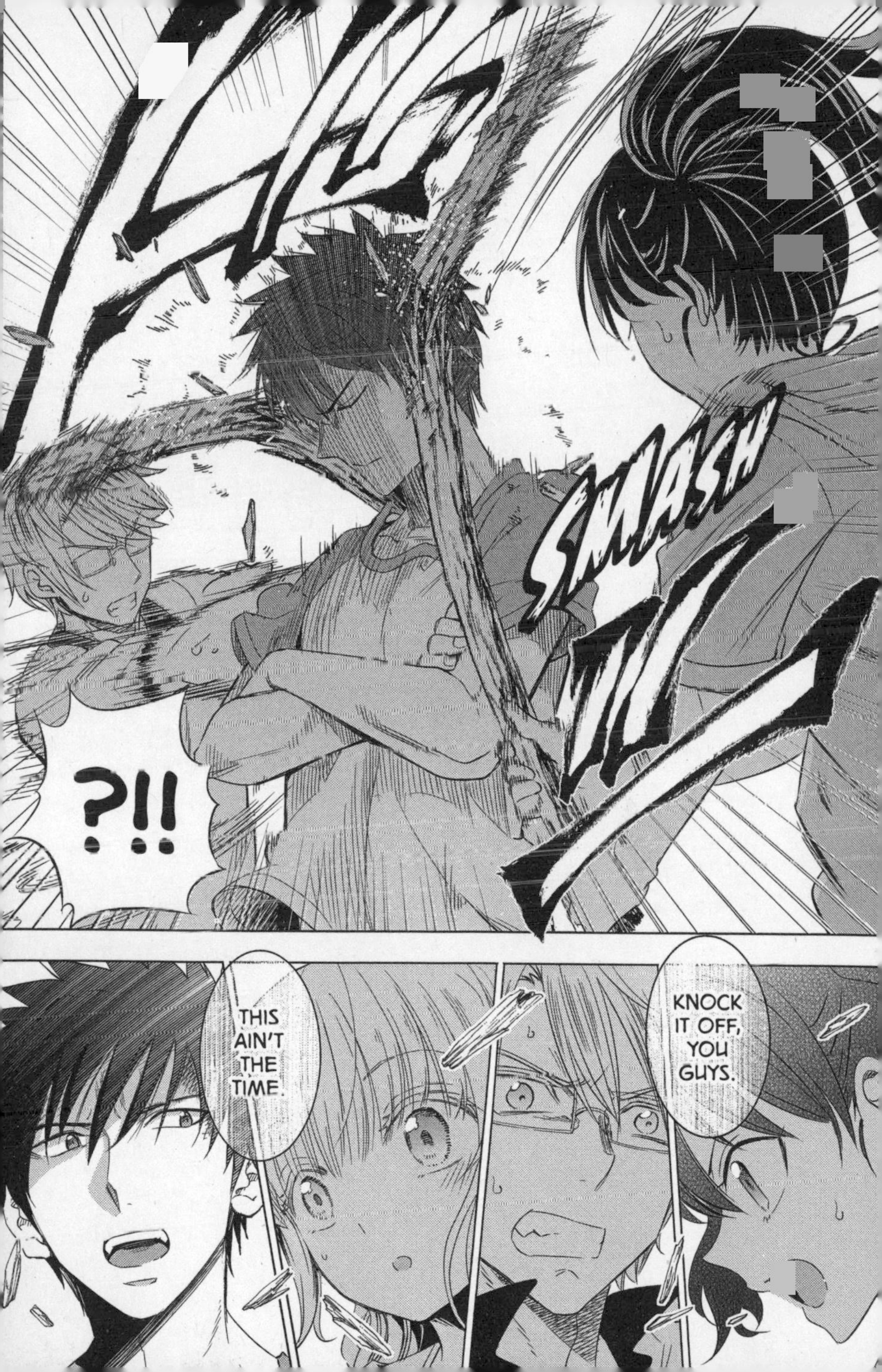
SMASH
?!!
KNOCK IT OFF, YOU GUYS.
THIS AIN'T THE TIME.

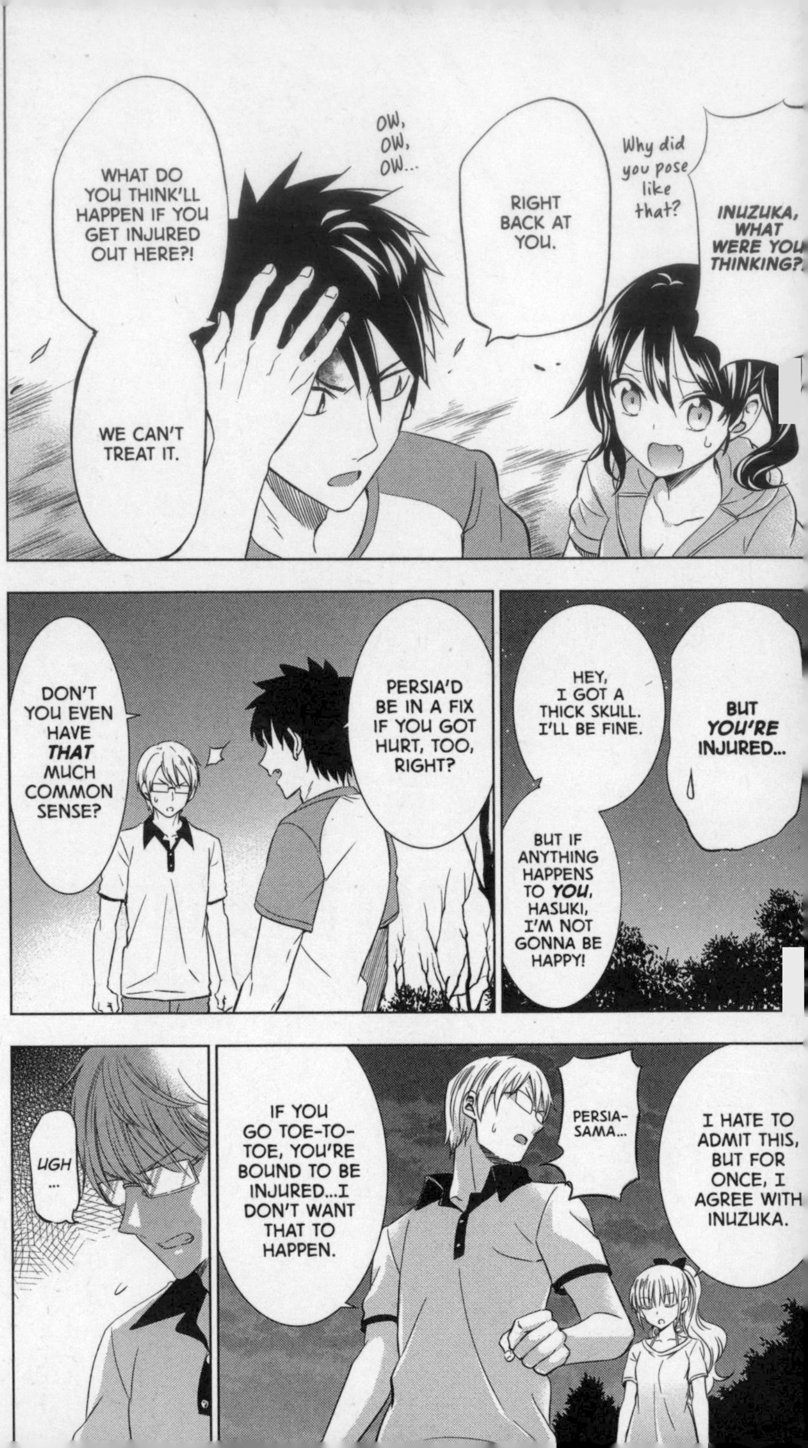
INUZUKA, WHAT WERE YOU THINKING?!
Why did you pose like that?
RIGHT BACK AT YOU.
OW, OW, OW...
WHAT DO YOU THINK'LL HAPPEN IF YOU GET INJURED OUT HERE?!
WE CAN'T TREAT IT.
BUT YOU'RE INJURED...
HEY, I GOT A THICK SKULL. I'LL BE FINE.
BUT IF ANYTHING HAPPENS TO YOU, HASUKI, I'M NOT GONNA BE HAPPY!
PERSIA'D BE IN A FIX IF YOU GOT HURT, TOO, RIGHT?
DON'T YOU EVEN HAVE THAT MUCH COMMON SENSE?
I HATE TO ADMIT THIS, BUT FOR ONCE, I AGREE WITH INUZUKA.
PERSIA-SAMA...
IF YOU GO TOE-TO-TOE, YOU'RE BOUND TO BE INJURED...I DON'T WANT THAT TO HAPPEN.
UGH ...

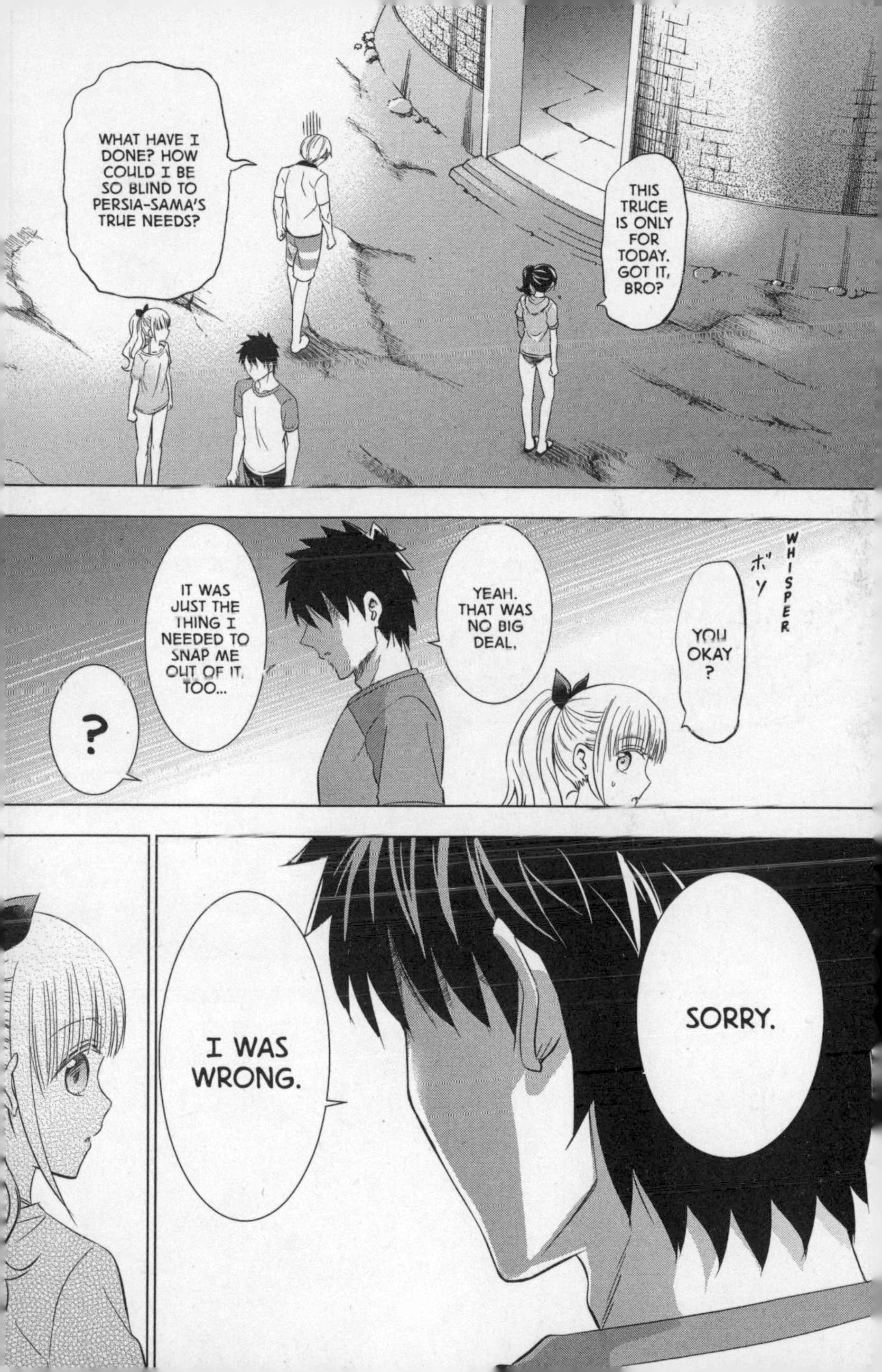
THIS TRUCE IS ONLY FOR TODAY. GOT IT, BRO?
WHAT HAVE I DONE? HOW COULD I BE SO BLIND TO PERSIA-SAMA'S TRUE NEEDS?
WHISPER
ボソ
YOU OKAY?
YEAH. THAT WAS NO BIG DEAL,
IT WAS JUST THE THING I NEEDED TO SNAP ME OUT OF IT, TOO...
?
SORRY.
I WAS WRONG.

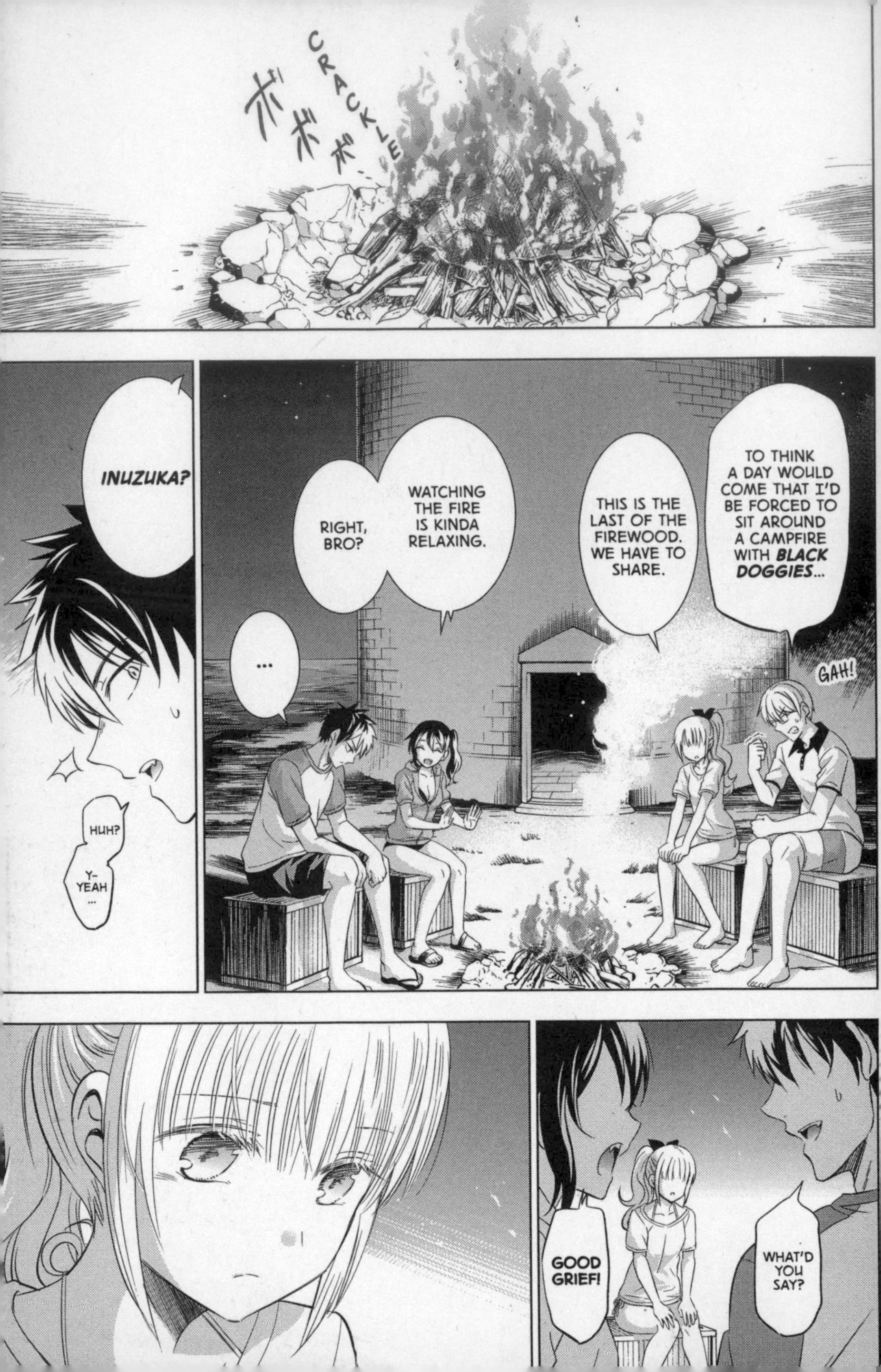
ボボボ
CRACKLE
TO THINK A DAY WOULD COME THAT I'D BE FORCED TO SIT AROUND A CAMPFIRE WITH **BLACK DOGGIES**...
GAH!
THIS IS THE LAST OF THE FIREWOOD. WE HAVE TO SHARE.
WATCHING THE FIRE IS KINDA RELAXING.
RIGHT, BRO?
...
INUZUKA?
HUH?
Y-YEAH ...
WHAT'D YOU SAY?
GOOD GRIEF!

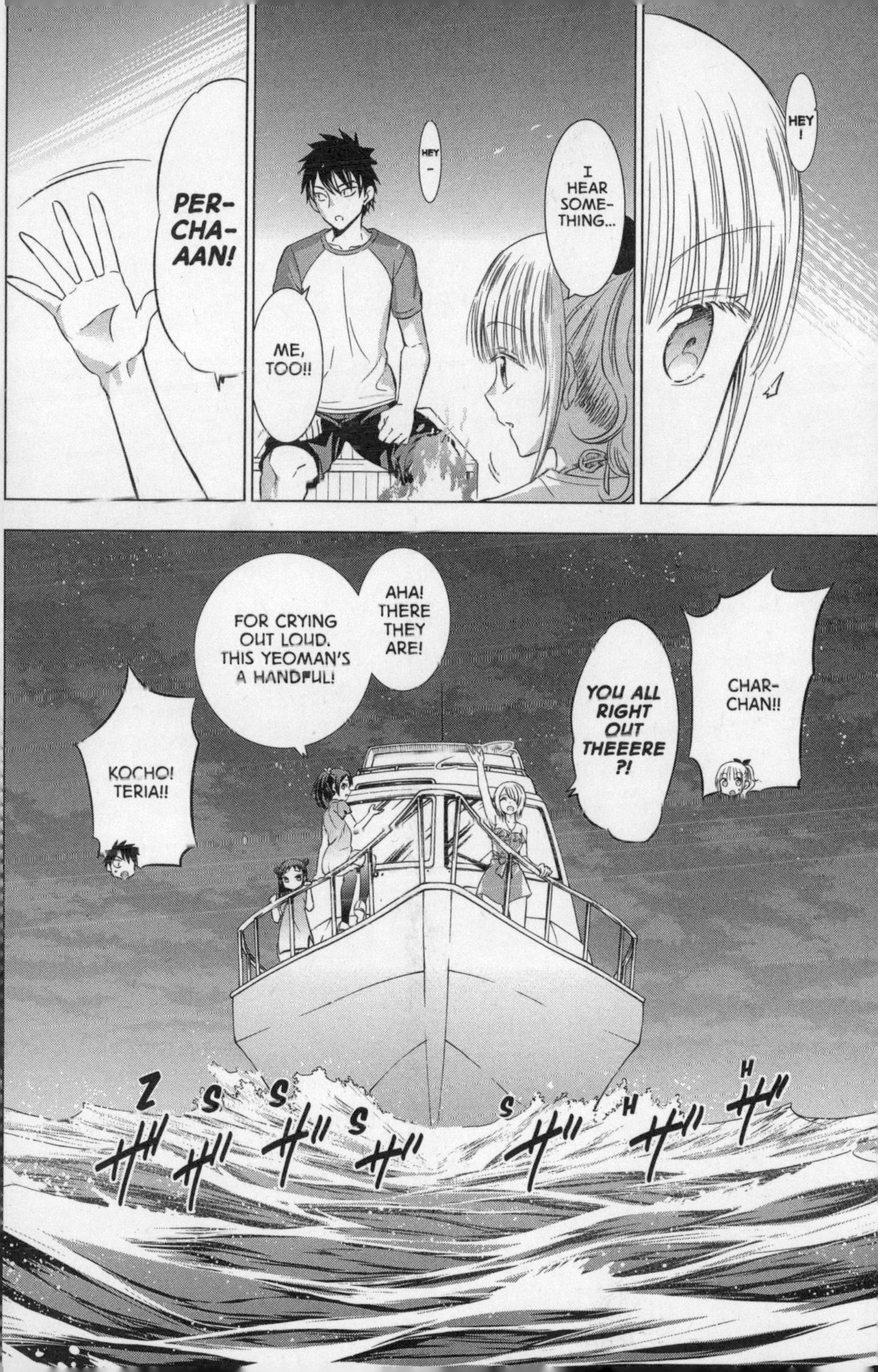
HEY !
I HEAR SOME-THING...
HEY –
ME, TOO!!
PER-CHA-AAN!
CHAR-CHAN!!
YOU ALL RIGHT OUT THEEERE ?!
AHA! THERE THEY ARE!
FOR CRYING OUT LOUD. THIS YEOMAN'S A HANDFUL!
KOCHO! TERIA!!
Z S S S S H H

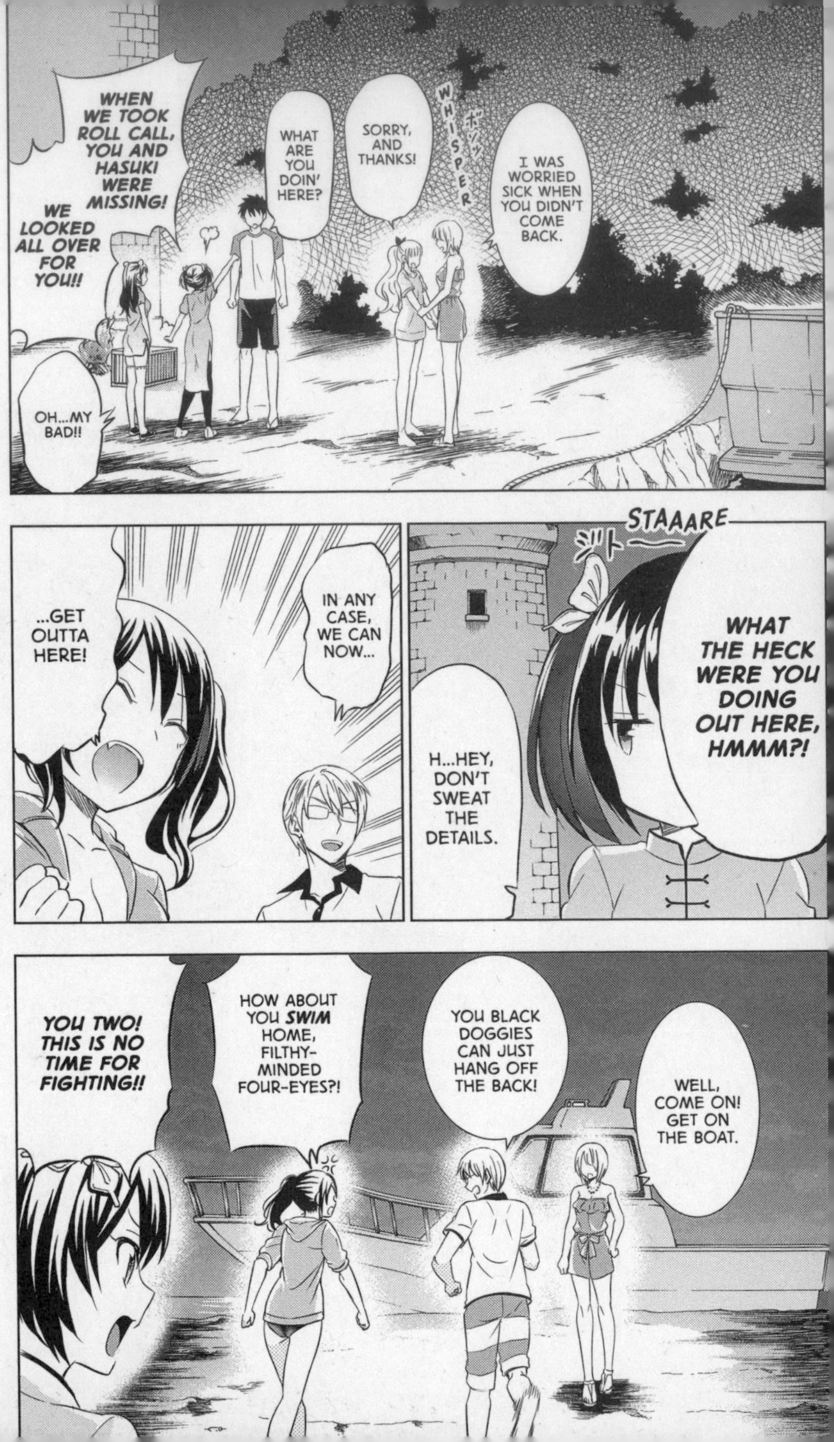
I WAS WORRIED SICK WHEN YOU DIDN'T COME BACK.
WHISPER
SORRY, AND THANKS!
WHAT ARE YOU DOIN' HERE?
WHEN WE TOOK ROLL CALL, YOU AND HASUKI WERE MISSING!
WE LOOKED ALL OVER FOR YOU!!
OH...MY BAD!!
STAAARE
WHAT THE HECK WERE YOU DOING OUT HERE, HMMM?!
H...HEY, DON'T SWEAT THE DETAILS.
IN ANY CASE, WE CAN NOW...
...GET OUTTA HERE!
WELL, COME ON! GET ON THE BOAT.
YOU BLACK DOGGIES CAN JUST HANG OFF THE BACK!
HOW ABOUT YOU **SWIM** HOME, FILTHY-MINDED FOUR-EYES?!
YOU TWO! THIS IS NO TIME FOR FIGHTING!!

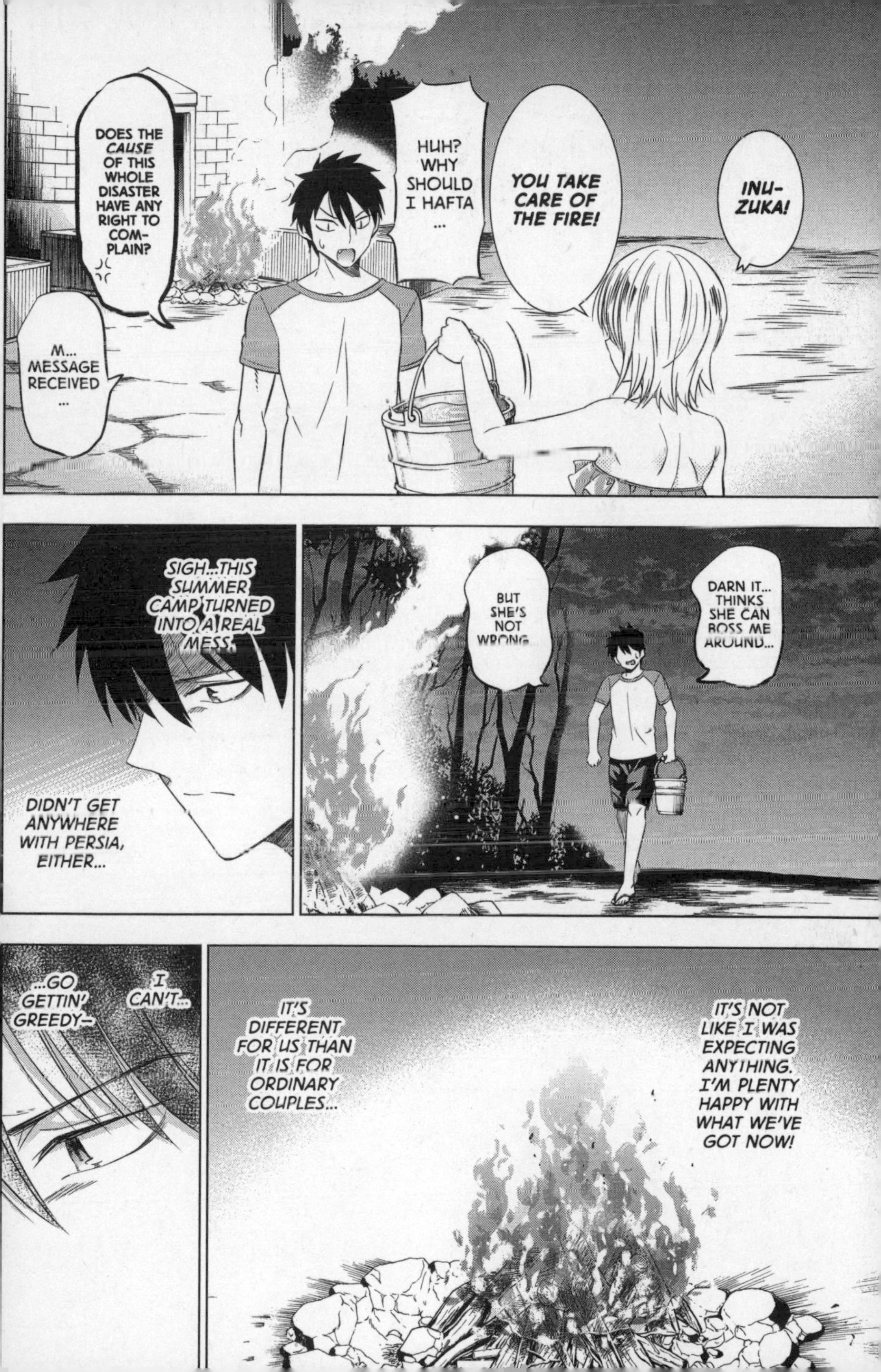
INU-ZUKA!
YOU TAKE CARE OF THE FIRE!
HUH? WHY SHOULD I HAFTA ...
DOES THE CAUSE OF THIS WHOLE DISASTER HAVE ANY RIGHT TO COMPLAIN?
M... MESSAGE RECEIVED ...
DARN IT... THINKS SHE CAN BOSS ME AROUND...
BUT SHE'S NOT WRONG...
SIGH...THIS SUMMER CAMP TURNED INTO A REAL MESS.
DIDN'T GET ANYWHERE WITH PERSIA, EITHER...
IT'S NOT LIKE I WAS EXPECTING ANYTHING. I'M PLENTY HAPPY WITH WHAT WE'VE GOT NOW!
IT'S DIFFERENT FOR US THAN IT IS FOR ORDINARY COUPLES...
I CAN'T...
...GO GETTIN' GREEDY-

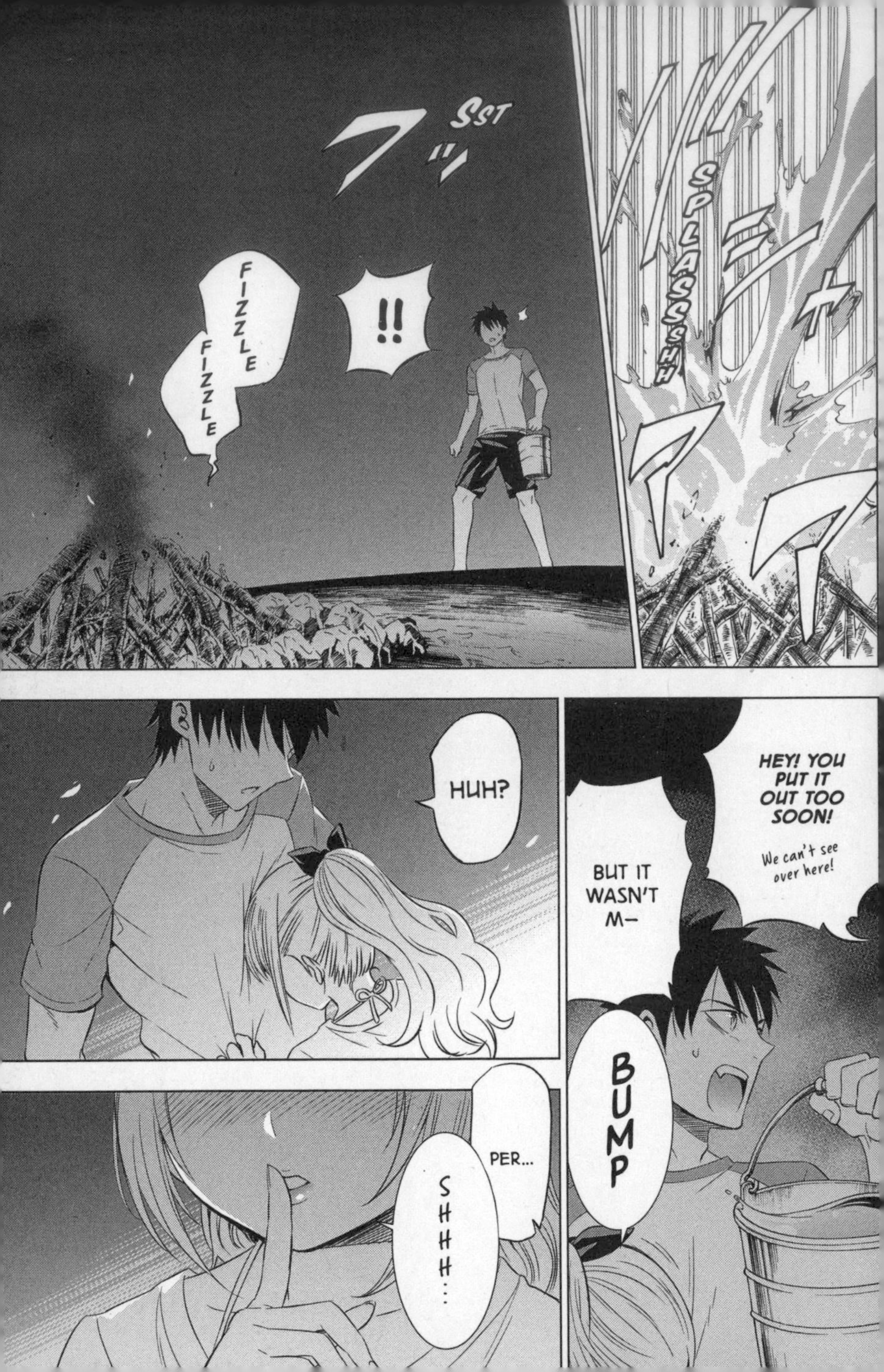
SPLASSSHH
SST
!!
FIZZLE FIZZLE
HEY! YOU PUT IT OUT TOO SOON!
We can't see over here!
BUT IT WASN'T M—
BUMP
HUH?
PER...
SHHH...

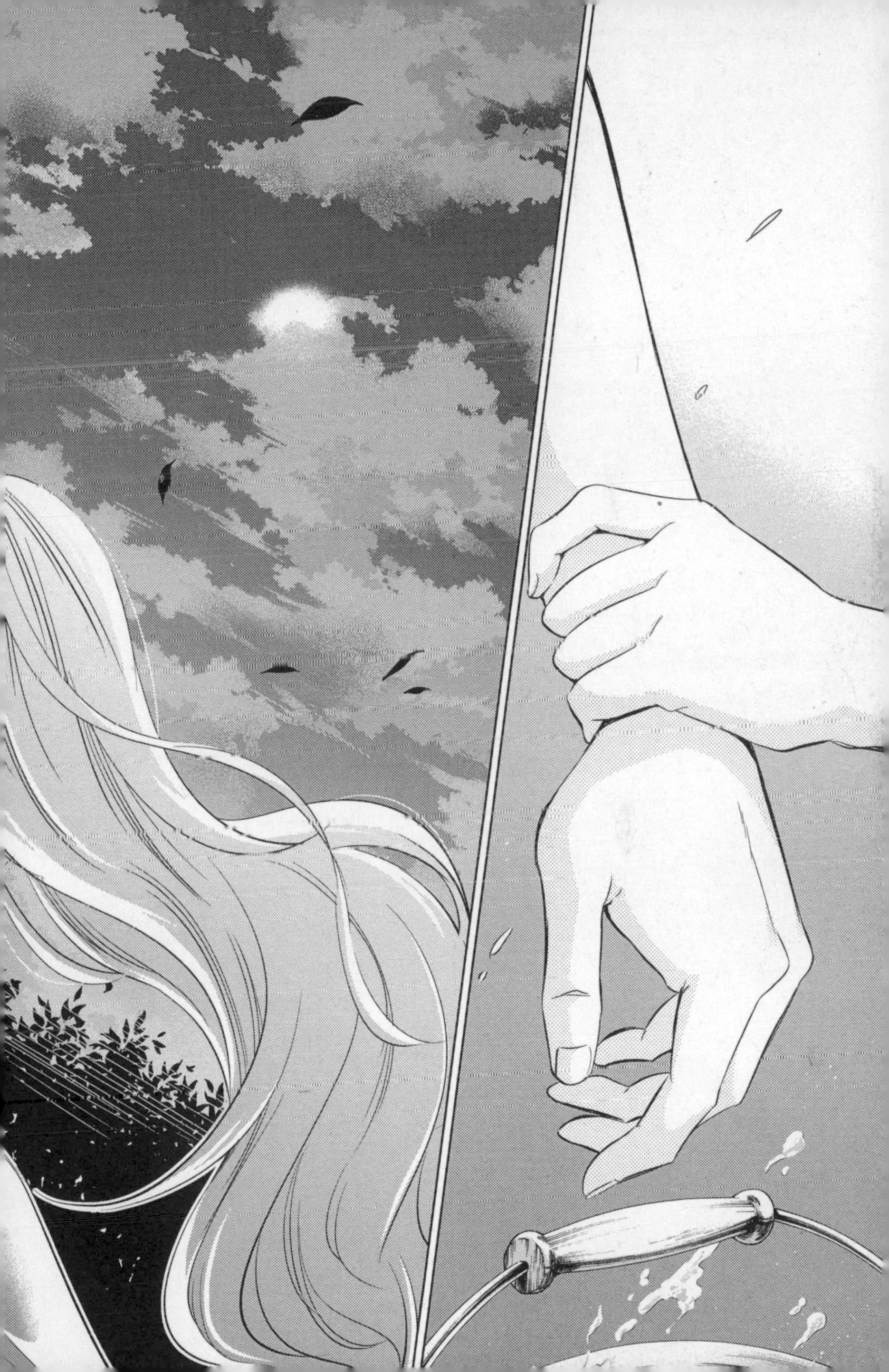

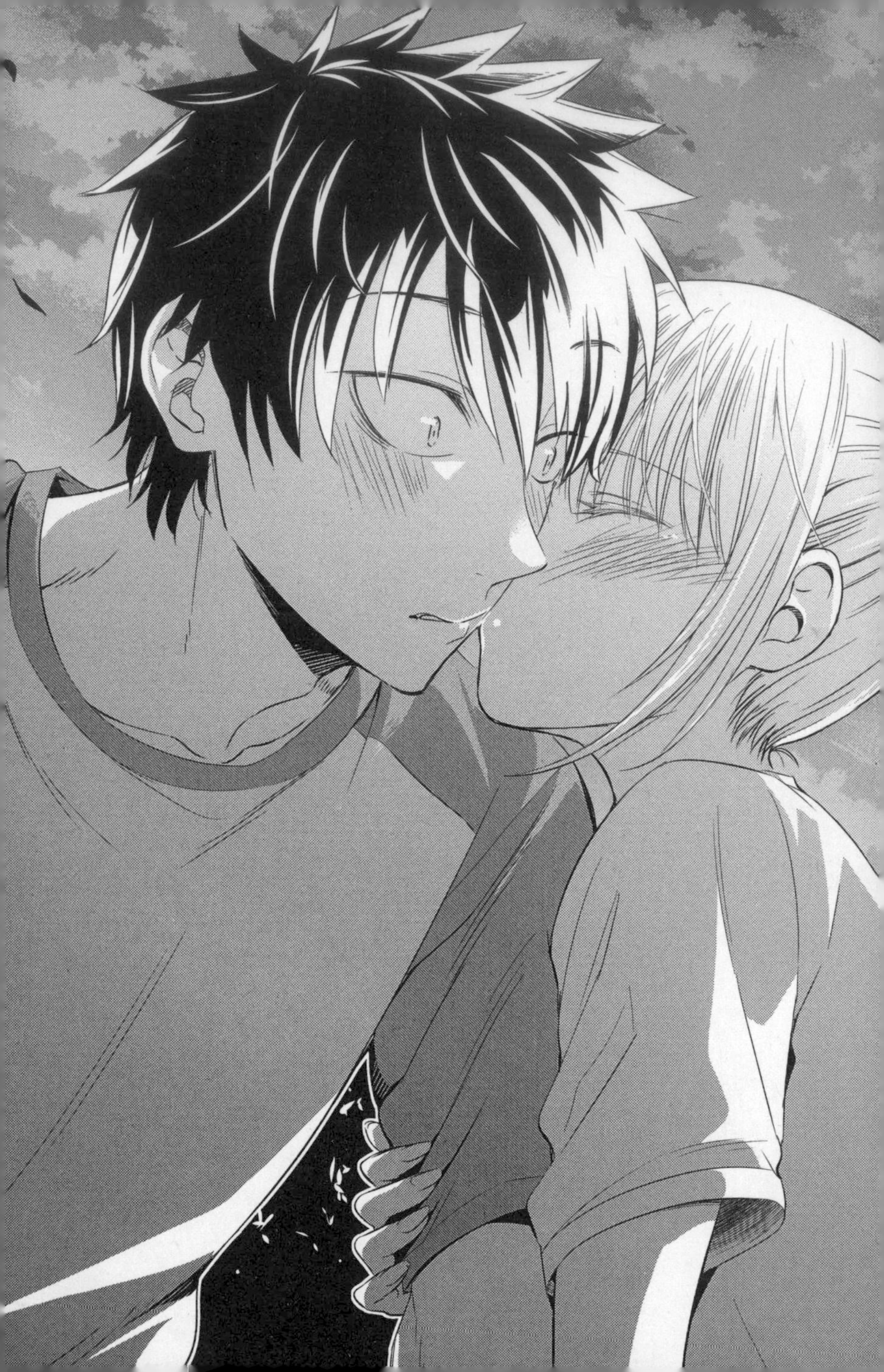

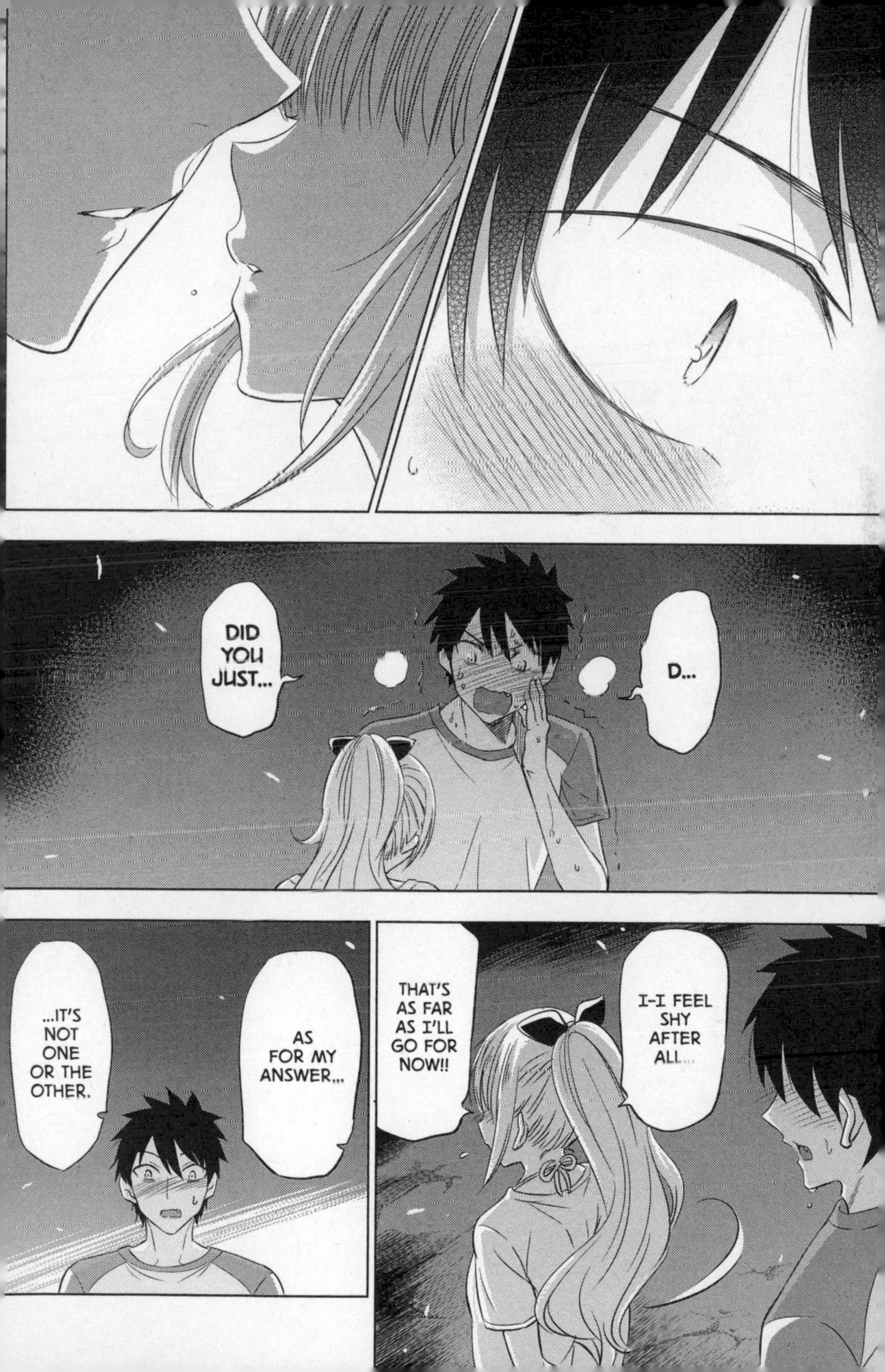
D...
DID YOU JUST...
I-I FEEL SHY AFTER ALL...
THAT'S AS FAR AS I'LL GO FOR NOW!!
AS FOR MY ANSWER...
...IT'S NOT ONE OR THE OTHER.

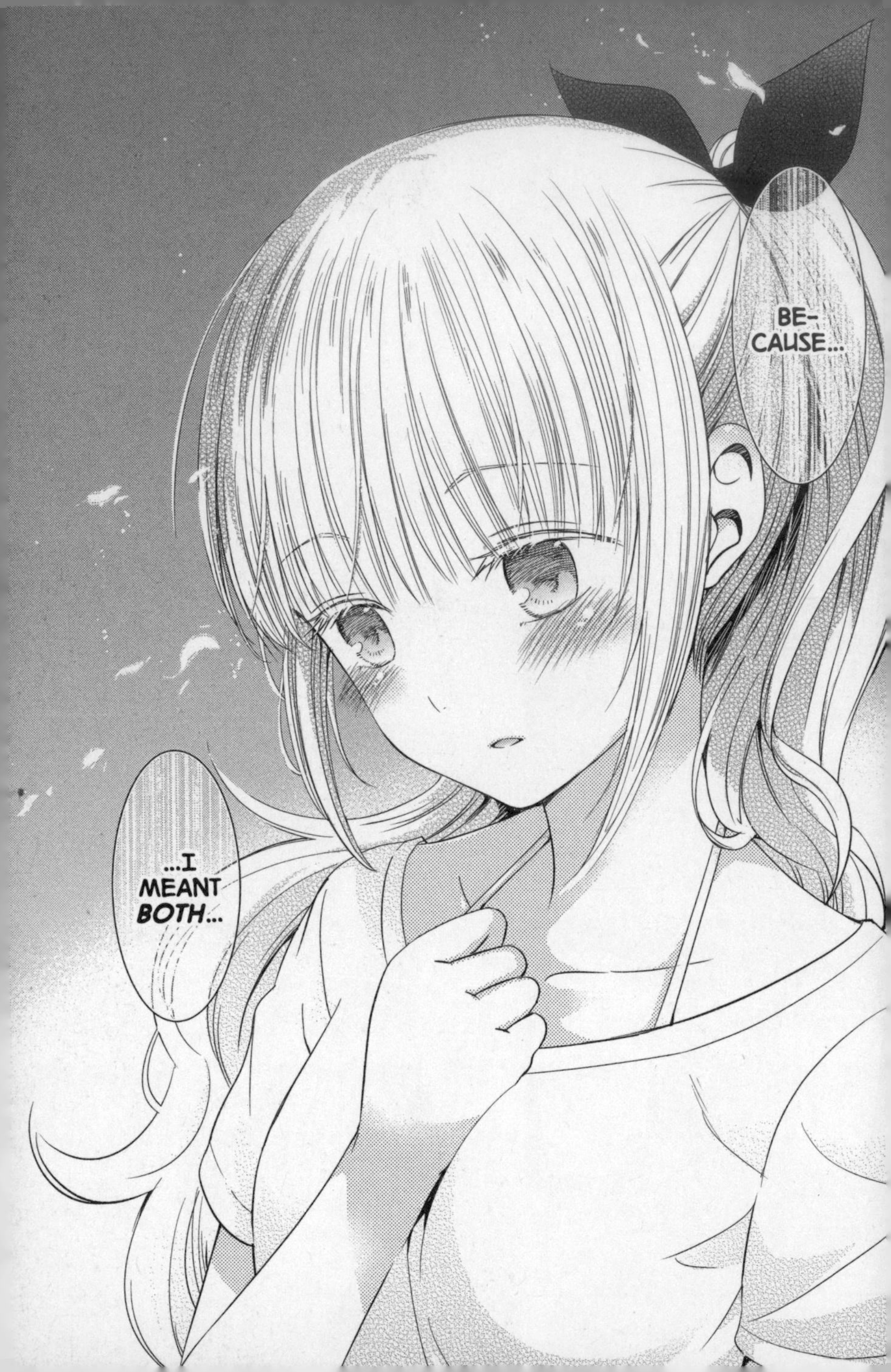
BE-CAUSE...
...I MEANT BOTH...

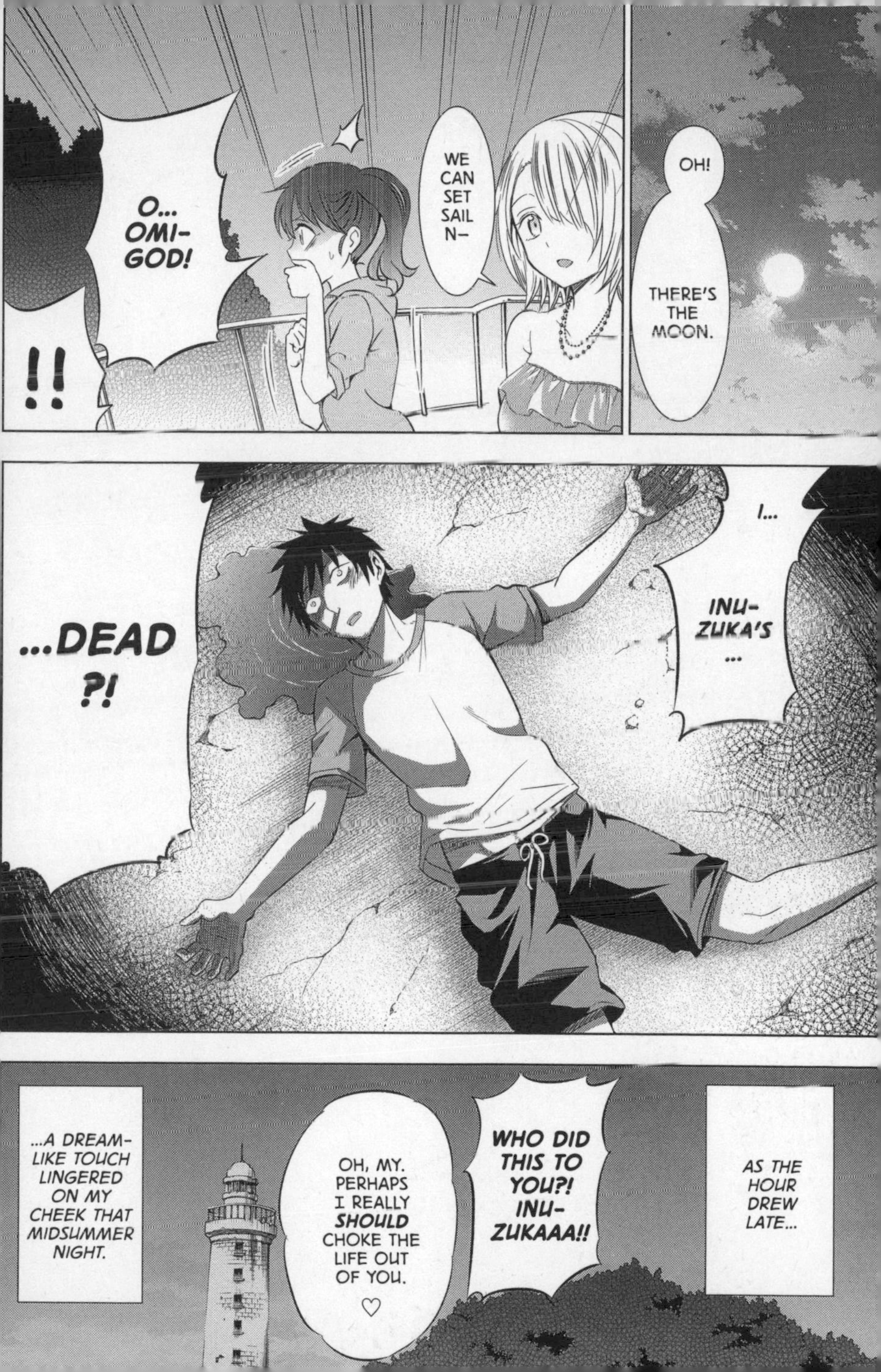
OH! THERE'S THE MOON.
WE CAN SET SAIL N—
O... OMI-GOD!
!!
I... INU-ZUKA'S ...
...DEAD ?!
AS THE HOUR DREW LATE...
WHO DID THIS TO YOU?! INU-ZUKAAA!!
OH, MY. PERHAPS I REALLY SHOULD CHOKE THE LIFE OUT OF YOU. ♡
...A DREAM-LIKE TOUCH LINGERED ON MY CHEEK THAT MIDSUMMER NIGHT.

ACT 22: CHARTREUX & JULIET

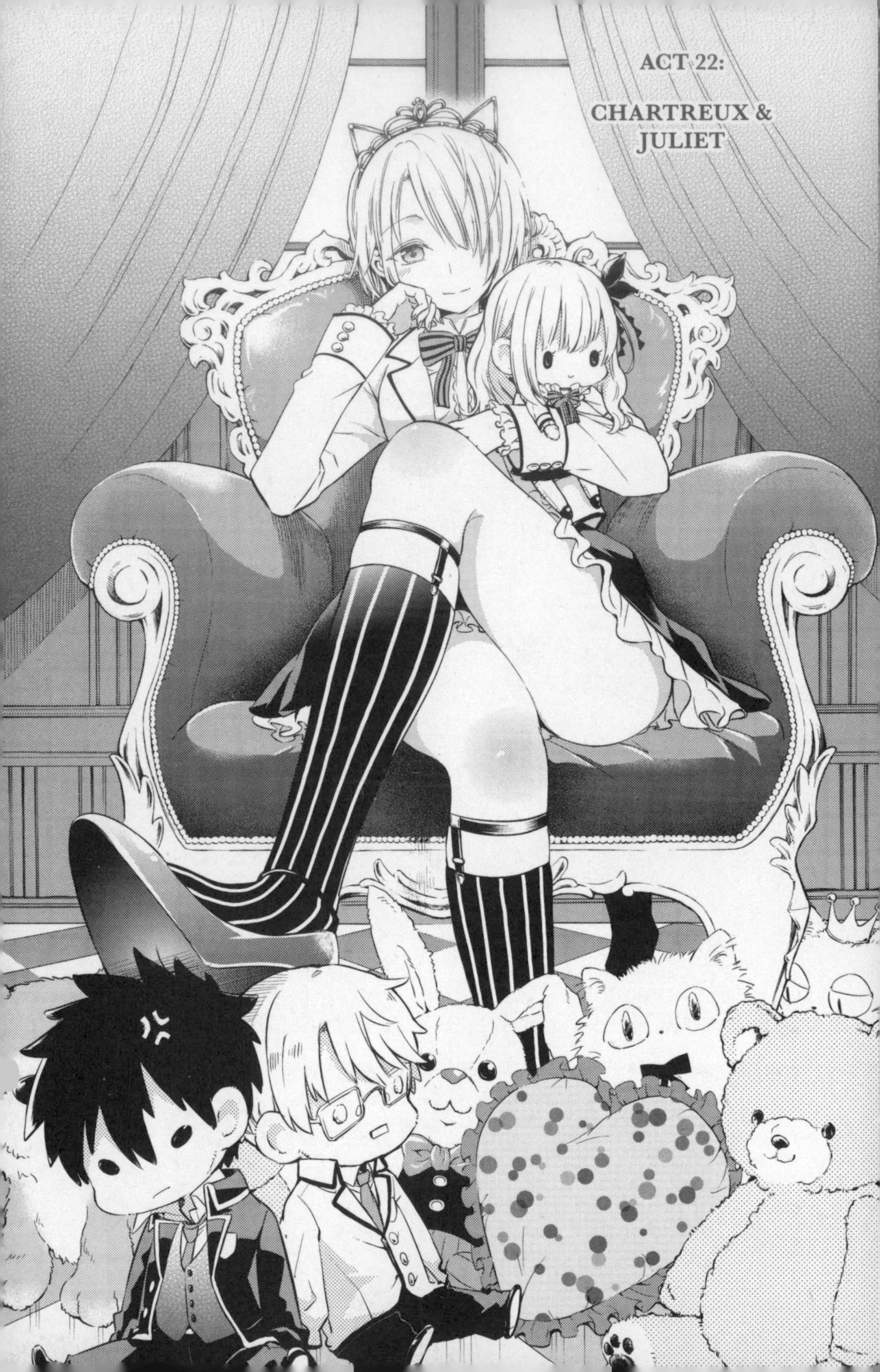

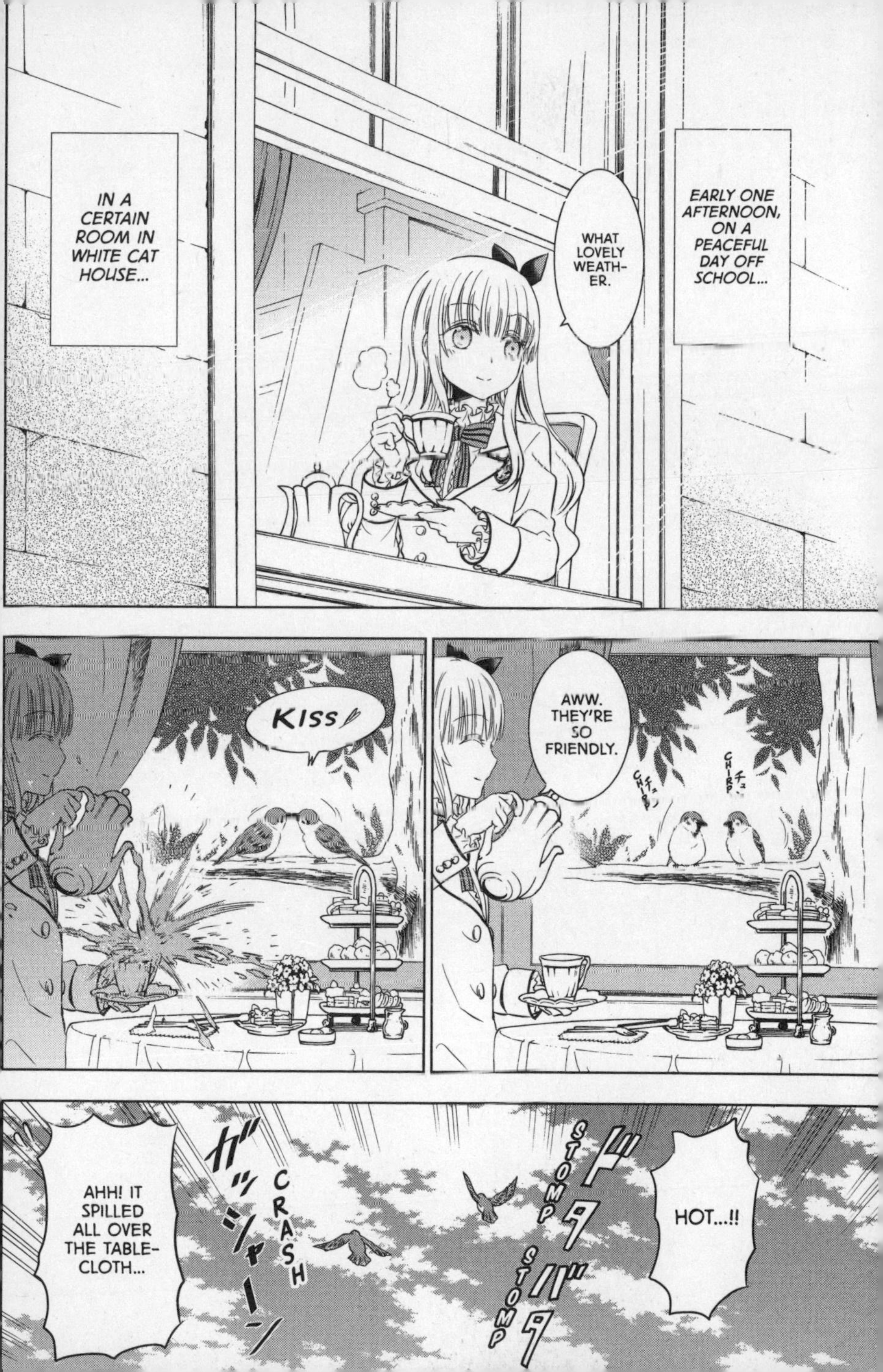
EARLY ONE AFTERNOON, ON A PEACEFUL DAY OFF SCHOOL...
WHAT LOVELY WEATH-ER.
IN A CERTAIN ROOM IN WHITE CAT HOUSE...
AWW. THEY'RE SO FRIENDLY.
CHIRP チュン
CHIRP チュン
KISS
HOT...!!
STOMP STOMP ドタバタ
CRASH ガッシャーン
AHH! IT SPILLED ALL OVER THE TABLE-CLOTH...

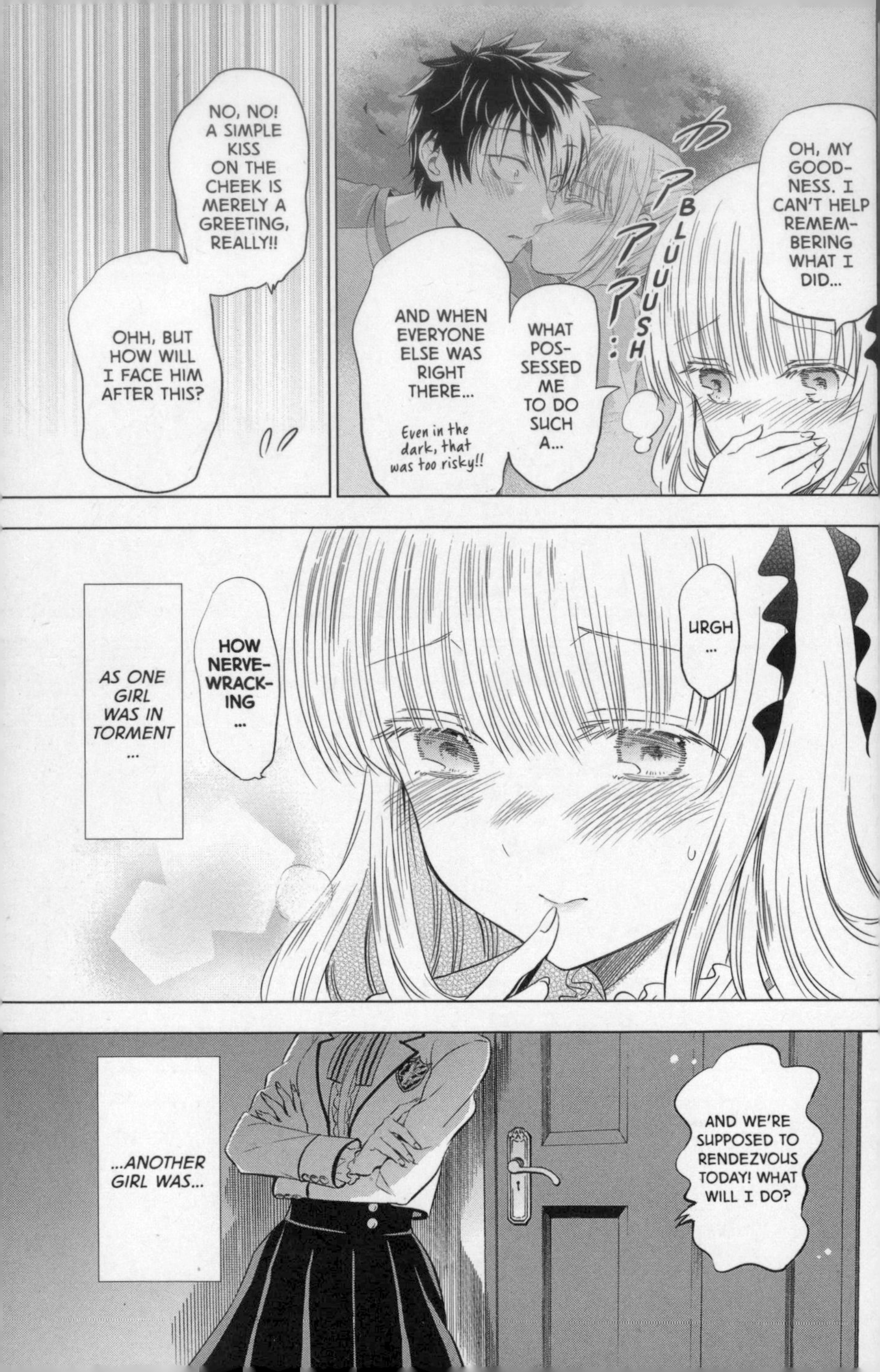
OH, MY GOOD-NESS. I CAN'T HELP REMEM-BERING WHAT I DID...
BLUUUSH
WHAT POS-SESSED ME TO DO SUCH A...
AND WHEN EVERYONE ELSE WAS RIGHT THERE...
Even in the dark, that was too risky!!
NO, NO! A SIMPLE KISS ON THE CHEEK IS MERELY A GREETING, REALLY!!
OHH, BUT HOW WILL I FACE HIM AFTER THIS?
URGH...
HOW NERVE-WRACK-ING...
AS ONE GIRL WAS IN TORMENT...
AND WE'RE SUPPOSED TO RENDEZVOUS TODAY! WHAT WILL I DO?
...ANOTHER GIRL WAS...

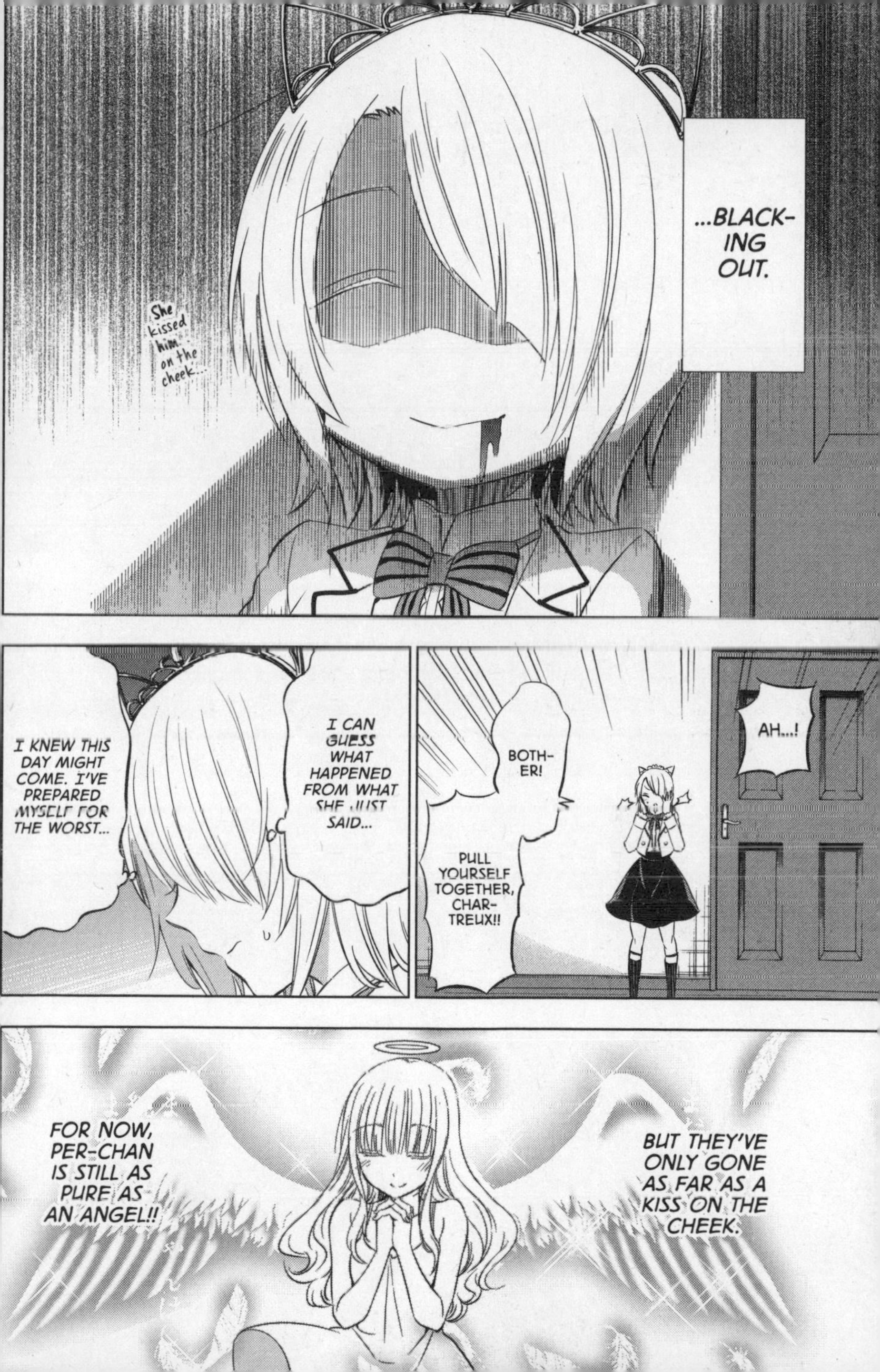
...BLACK-ING OUT.
She kissed him on the cheek...
AH...!
BOTHER!
PULL YOURSELF TOGETHER, CHAR-TREUX!!
I CAN GUESS WHAT HAPPENED FROM WHAT SHE JUST SAID...
I KNEW THIS DAY MIGHT COME. I'VE PREPARED MYSELF FOR THE WORST...
BUT THEY'VE ONLY GONE AS FAR AS A KISS ON THE CHEEK.
FOR NOW, PER-CHAN IS STILL AS PURE AS AN ANGEL!!

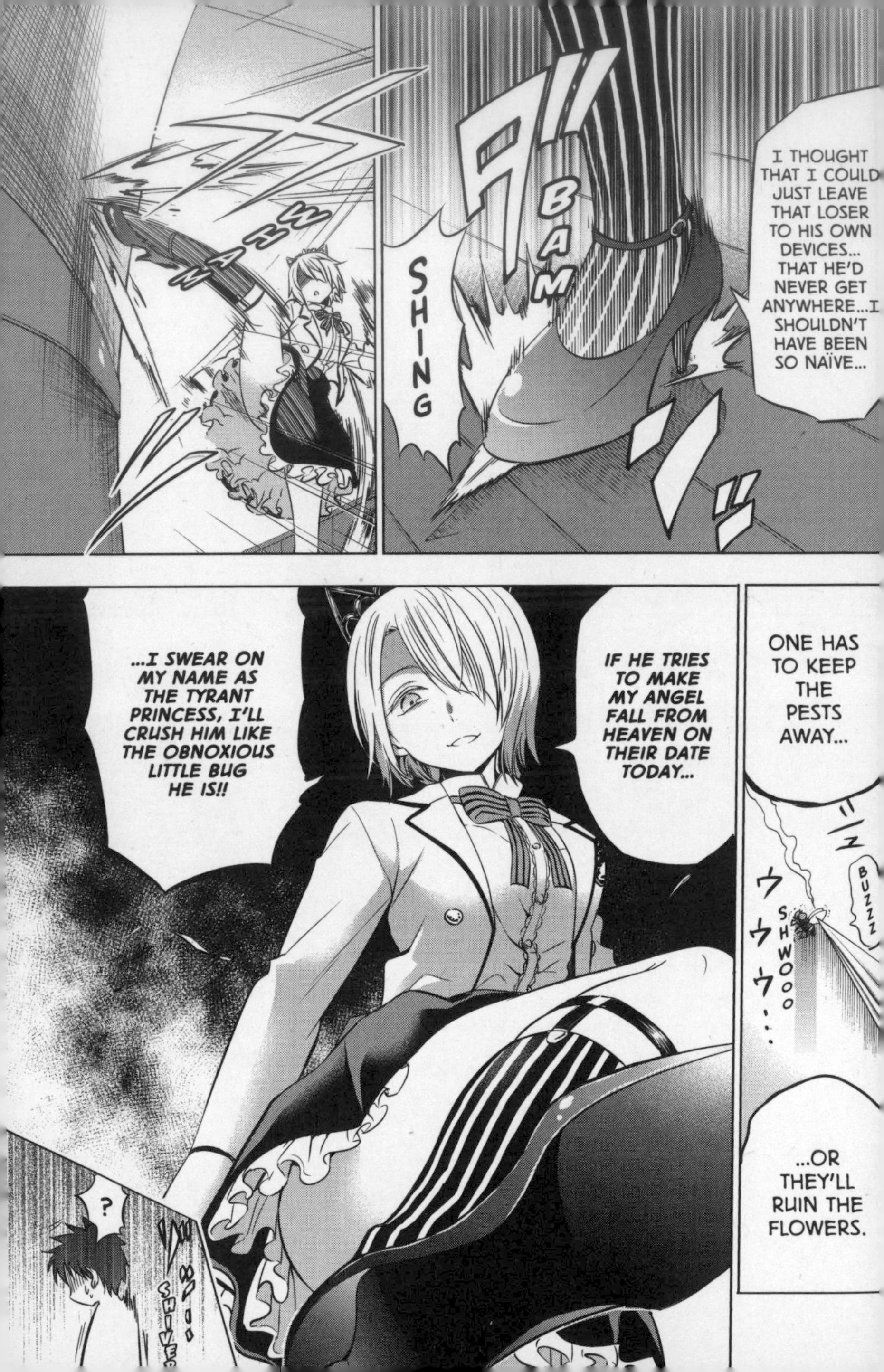
I THOUGHT THAT I COULD JUST LEAVE THAT LOSER TO HIS OWN DEVICES... THAT HE'D NEVER GET ANYWHERE...I SHOULDN'T HAVE BEEN SO NAÏVE...
BAM
SHING
WHAM
ONE HAS TO KEEP THE PESTS AWAY...
BUZZZ
SHWOOO
...OR THEY'LL RUIN THE FLOWERS.
IF HE TRIES TO MAKE MY ANGEL FALL FROM HEAVEN ON THEIR DATE TODAY...
...I SWEAR ON MY NAME AS THE TYRANT PRINCESS, I'LL CRUSH HIM LIKE THE OBNOXIOUS LITTLE BUG HE IS!!
?

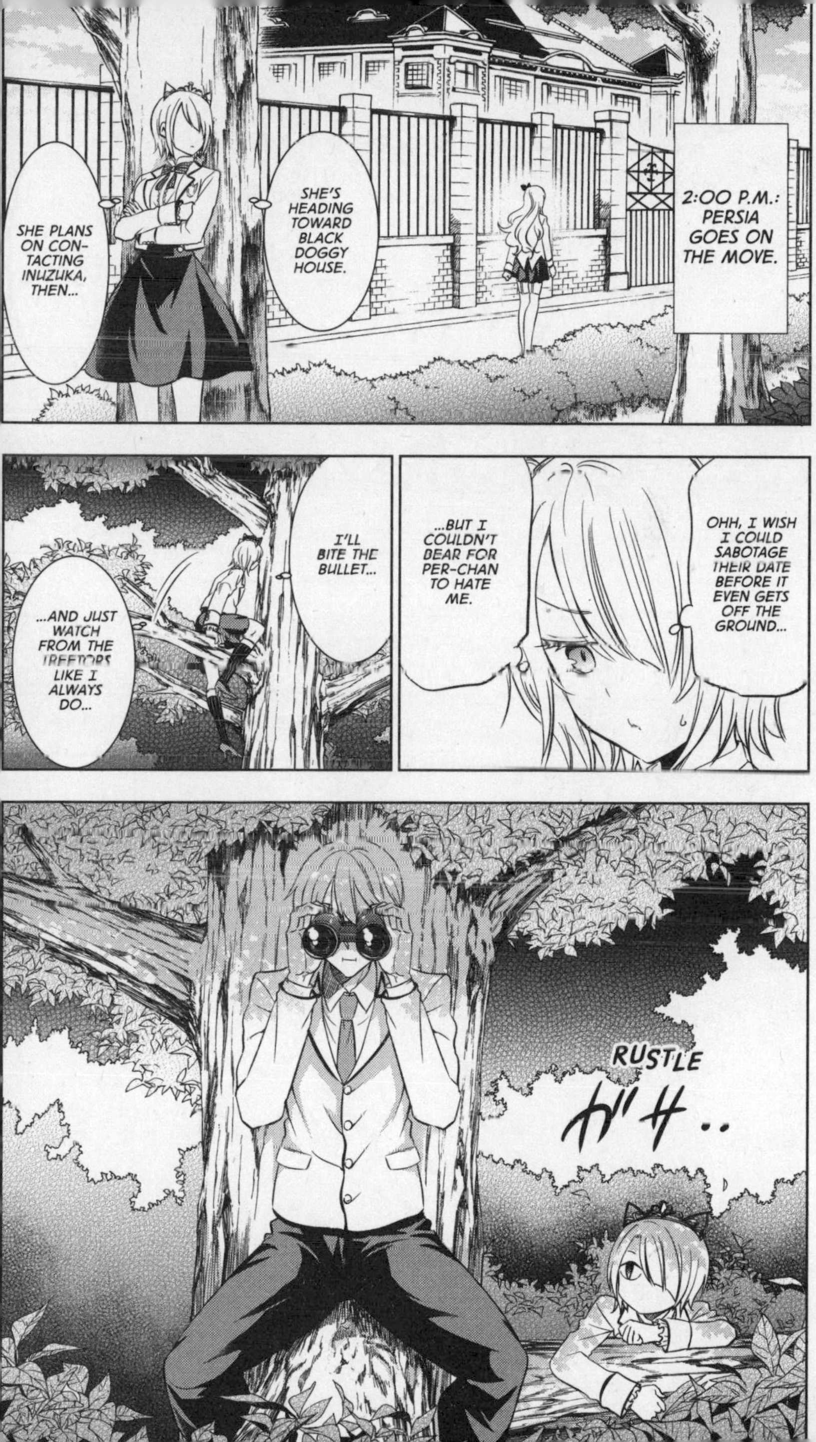
2:00 P.M.: PERSIA GOES ON THE MOVE.
SHE'S HEADING TOWARD BLACK DOGGY HOUSE.
SHE PLANS ON CONTACTING INUZUKA, THEN...
OHH, I WISH I COULD SABOTAGE THEIR DATE BEFORE IT EVEN GETS OFF THE GROUND...
...BUT I COULDN'T BEAR FOR PER-CHAN TO HATE ME.
I'LL BITE THE BULLET...
...AND JUST WATCH FROM THE TREETOPS LIKE I ALWAYS DO...
RUSTLE
ガサ‥

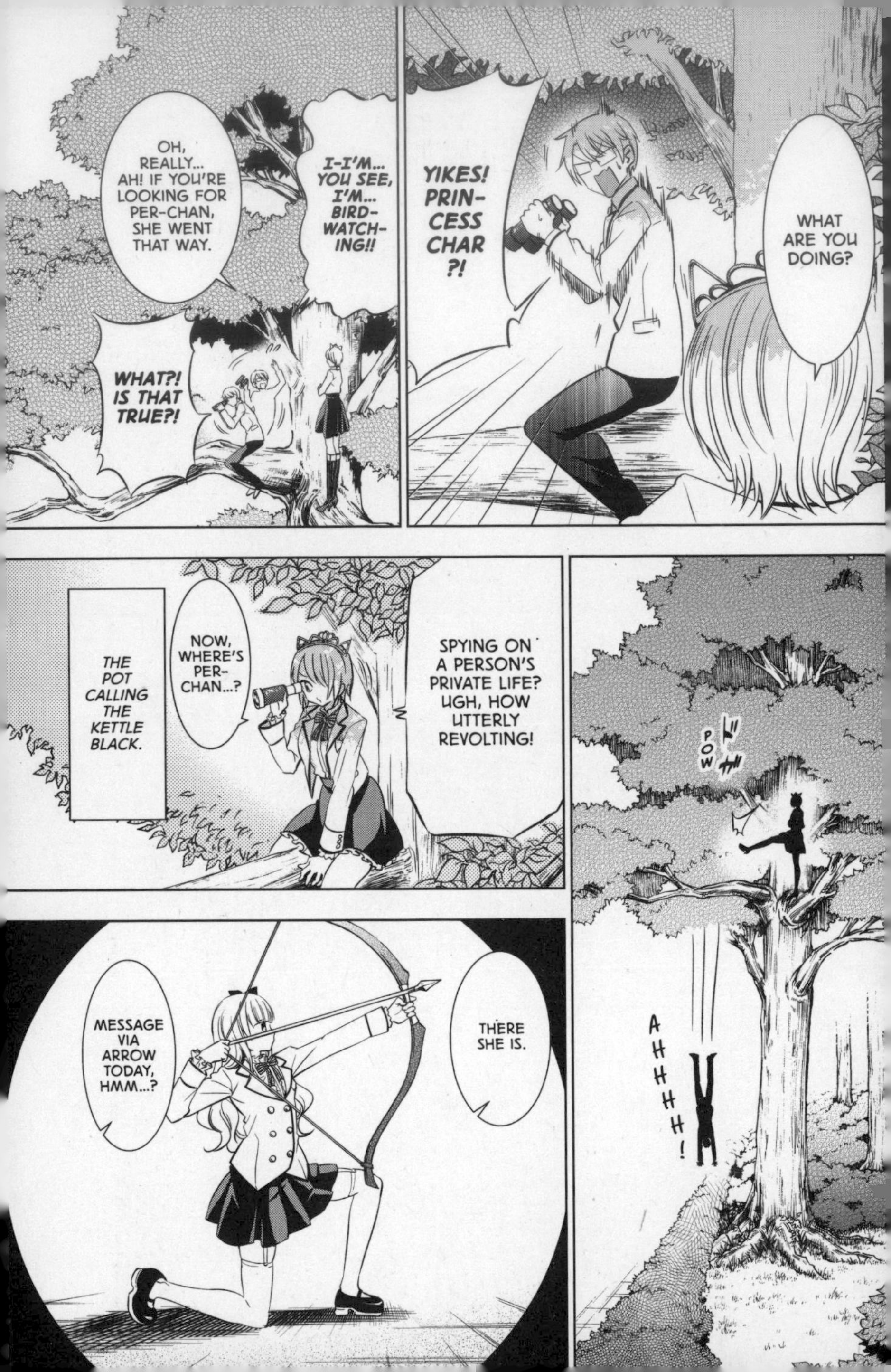
WHAT ARE YOU DOING?
YIKES! PRIN-CESS CHAR ?!
I-I'M... YOU SEE, I'M... BIRD-WATCH-ING!!
OH, REALLY... AH! IF YOU'RE LOOKING FOR PER-CHAN, SHE WENT THAT WAY.
WHAT?! IS THAT TRUE?!
POW
AHHHHH!
SPYING ON A PERSON'S PRIVATE LIFE? UGH, HOW UTTERLY REVOLTING!
NOW, WHERE'S PER-CHAN...?
THE POT CALLING THE KETTLE BLACK.
THERE SHE IS.
MESSAGE VIA ARROW TODAY, HMM...?

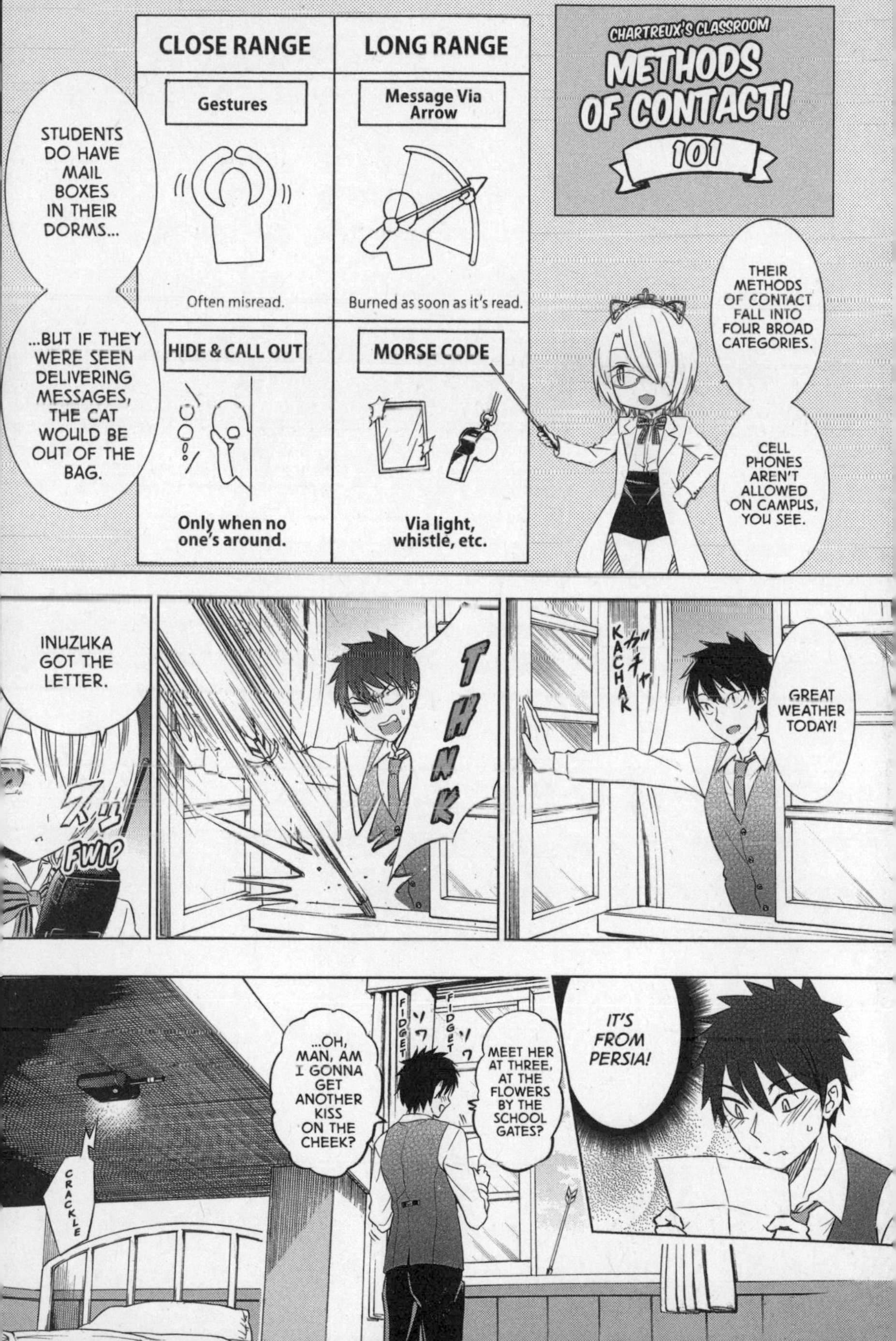
CHARTREUX'S CLASSROOM
METHODS OF CONTACT!
101
THEIR METHODS OF CONTACT FALL INTO FOUR BROAD CATEGORIES.
CELL PHONES AREN'T ALLOWED ON CAMPUS, YOU SEE.
CLOSE RANGE
LONG RANGE
Gestures
Often misread.
Message Via Arrow
Burned as soon as it's read.
HIDE & CALL OUT
Only when no one's around.
MORSE CODE
Via light, whistle, etc.
STUDENTS DO HAVE MAIL BOXES IN THEIR DORMS...
...BUT IF THEY WERE SEEN DELIVERING MESSAGES, THE CAT WOULD BE OUT OF THE BAG.
KACHAK
GREAT WEATHER TODAY!
THNK
INUZUKA GOT THE LETTER.
FWIP
IT'S FROM PERSIA!
MEET HER AT THREE, AT THE FLOWERS BY THE SCHOOL GATES?
FIDGET
FIDGET
...OH, MAN, AM I GONNA GET ANOTHER KISS ON THE CHEEK?
CRACKLE

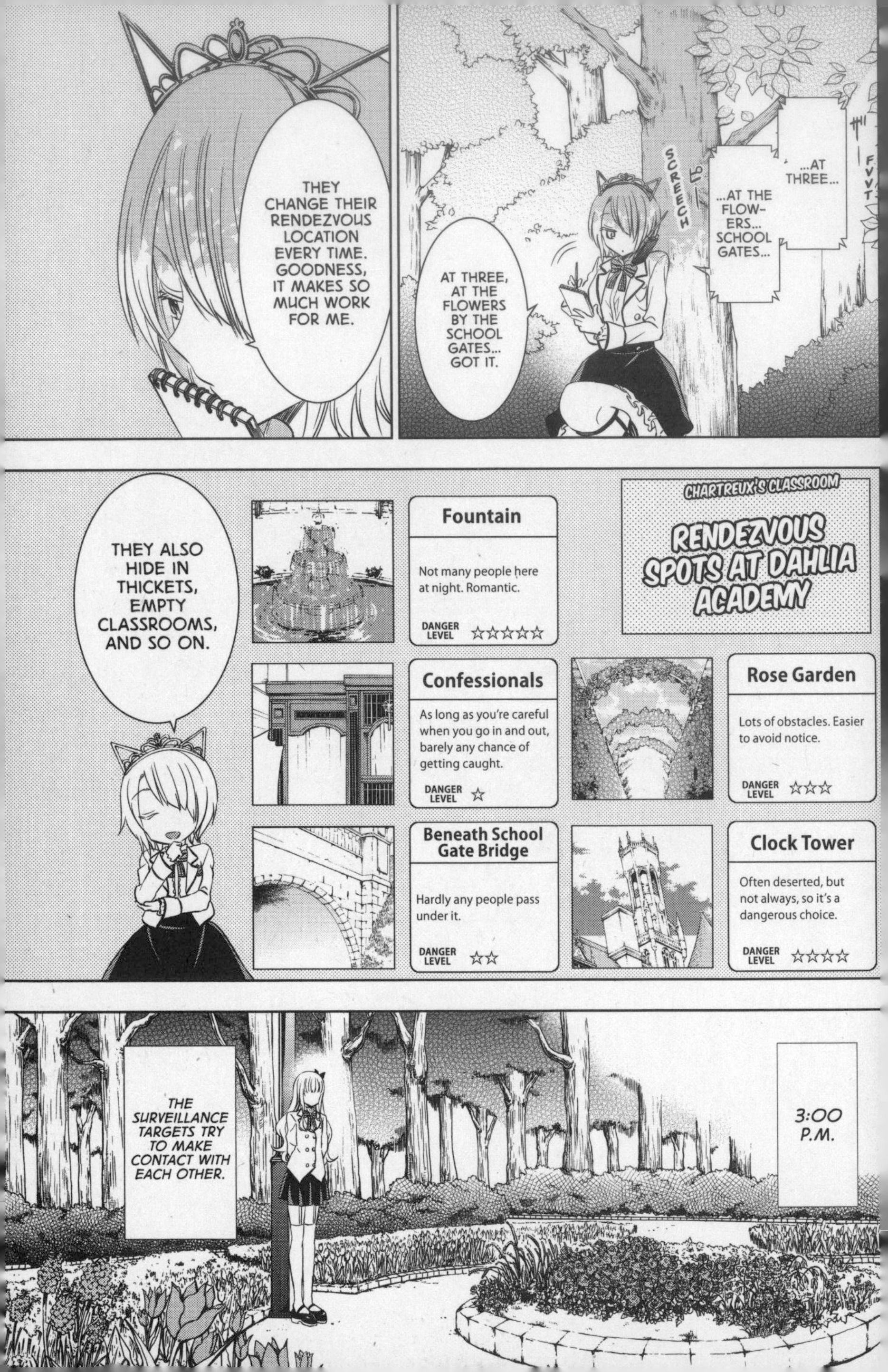

SCREECH
FVVT
...AT THREE...
...AT THE FLOW-ERS... SCHOOL GATES...
AT THREE, AT THE FLOWERS BY THE SCHOOL GATES... GOT IT.
THEY CHANGE THEIR RENDEZVOUS LOCATION EVERY TIME. GOODNESS, IT MAKES SO MUCH WORK FOR ME.
CHARTREUX'S CLASSROOM
RENDEZVOUS SPOTS AT DAHLIA ACADEMY
Fountain
Not many people here at night. Romantic.
DANGER LEVEL ☆☆☆☆☆
Rose Garden
Lots of obstacles. Easier to avoid notice.
DANGER LEVEL ☆☆☆
Confessionals
As long as you're careful when you go in and out, barely any chance of getting caught.
DANGER LEVEL ☆
Clock Tower
Often deserted, but not always, so it's a dangerous choice.
DANGER LEVEL ☆☆☆☆
Beneath School Gate Bridge
Hardly any people pass under it.
DANGER LEVEL ☆☆
THEY ALSO HIDE IN THICKETS, EMPTY CLASSROOMS, AND SO ON.
3:00 P.M.
THE SURVEILLANCE TARGETS TRY TO MAKE CONTACT WITH EACH OTHER.

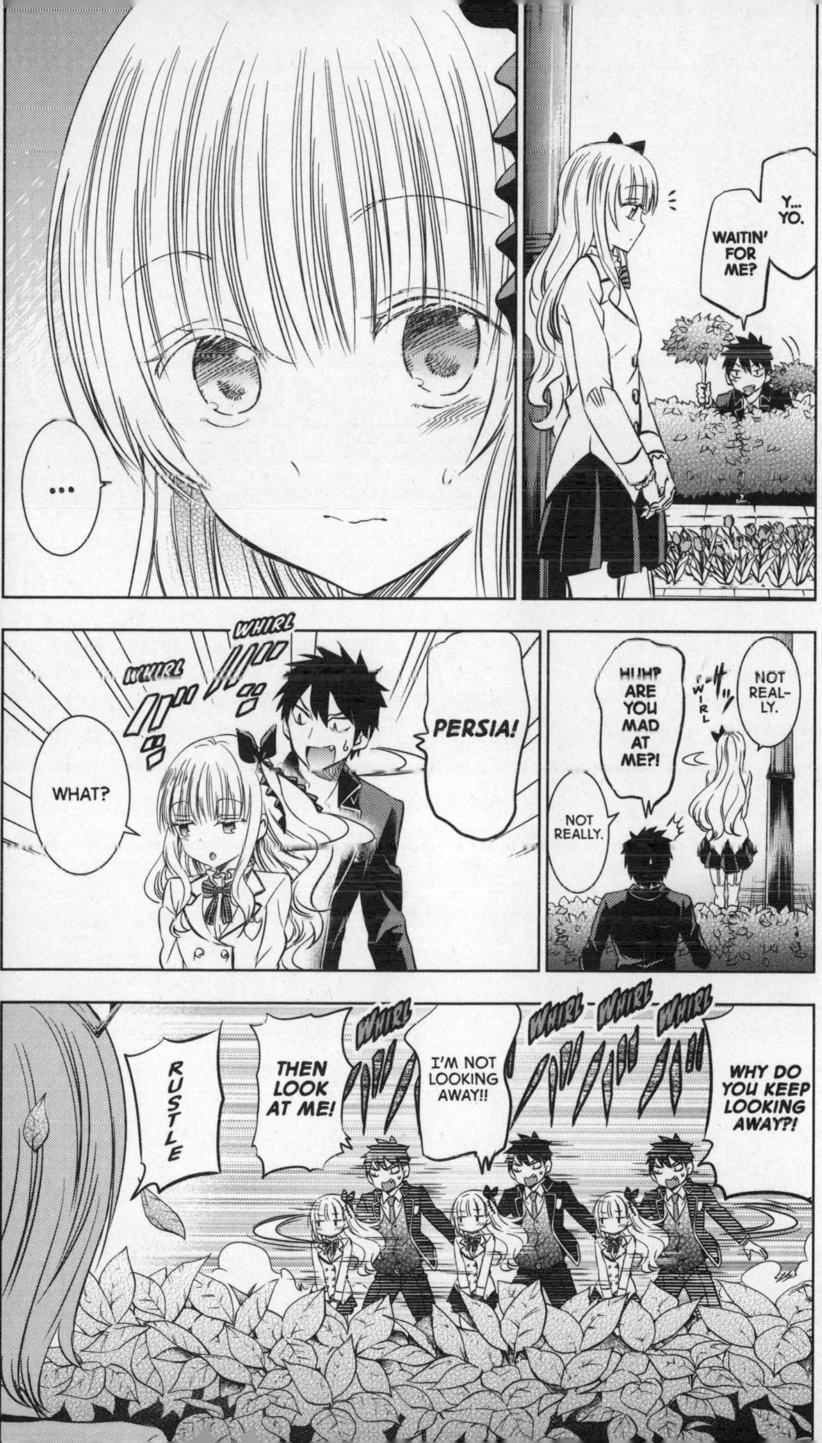
Y... YO.
WAITIN' FOR ME?
...
NOT REALLY.
HUMP ARE YOU MAD AT ME?!
NOT REALLY.
PERSIA!
WHIRL
WHIRL
WHAT?
WHY DO YOU KEEP LOOKING AWAY?!
WHIRL
WHIRL
WHIRL
I'M NOT LOOKING AWAY!!
WHIRL
THEN LOOK AT ME!
RUSTLE

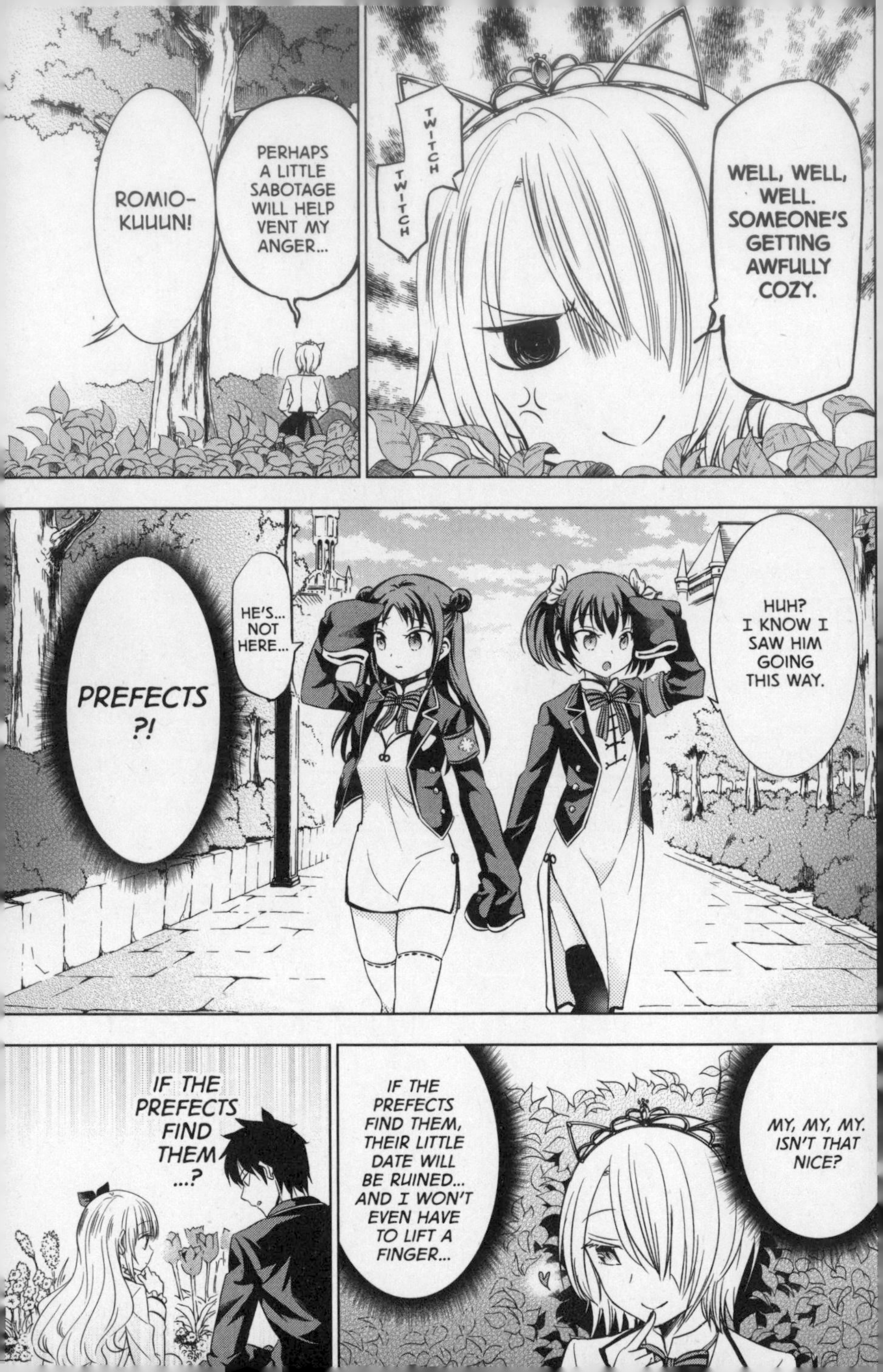

TWITCH TWITCH
WELL, WELL, WELL. SOMEONE'S GETTING AWFULLY COZY.
PERHAPS A LITTLE SABOTAGE WILL HELP VENT MY ANGER...
ROMIO-KUUUN!
HUH? I KNOW I SAW HIM GOING THIS WAY.
HE'S... NOT HERE...
PREFECTS ?!
MY, MY, MY. ISN'T THAT NICE?
IF THE PREFECTS FIND THEM, THEIR LITTLE DATE WILL BE RUINED... AND I WON'T EVEN HAVE TO LIFT A FINGER...
IF THE PREFECTS FIND THEM ...?

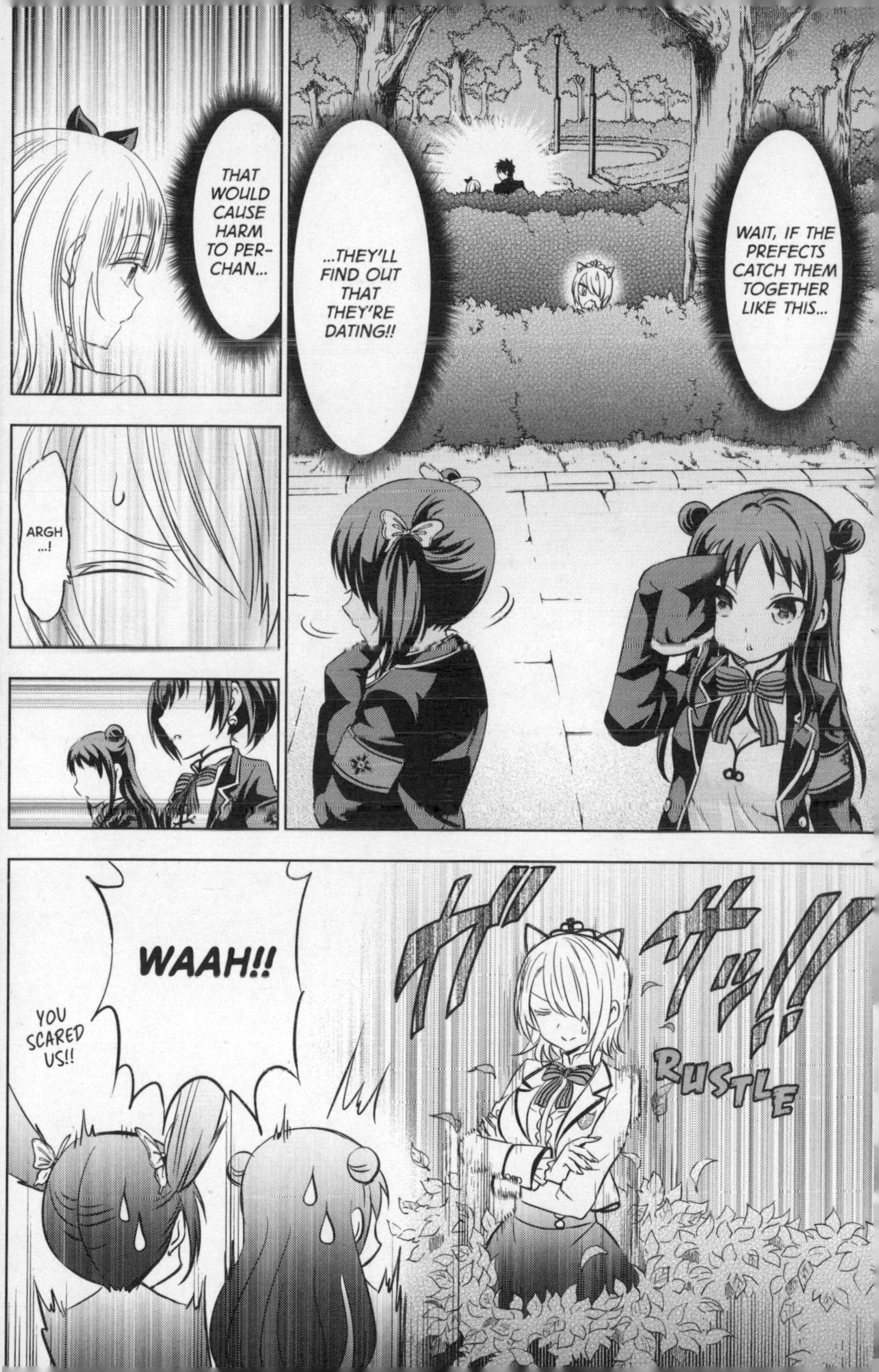
WAIT, IF THE PREFECTS CATCH THEM TOGETHER LIKE THIS...
...THEY'LL FIND OUT THAT THEY'RE DATING!!
THAT WOULD CAUSE HARM TO PER-CHAN...
ARGH ...!
RUSTLE
WAAH!!
YOU SCARED US!!

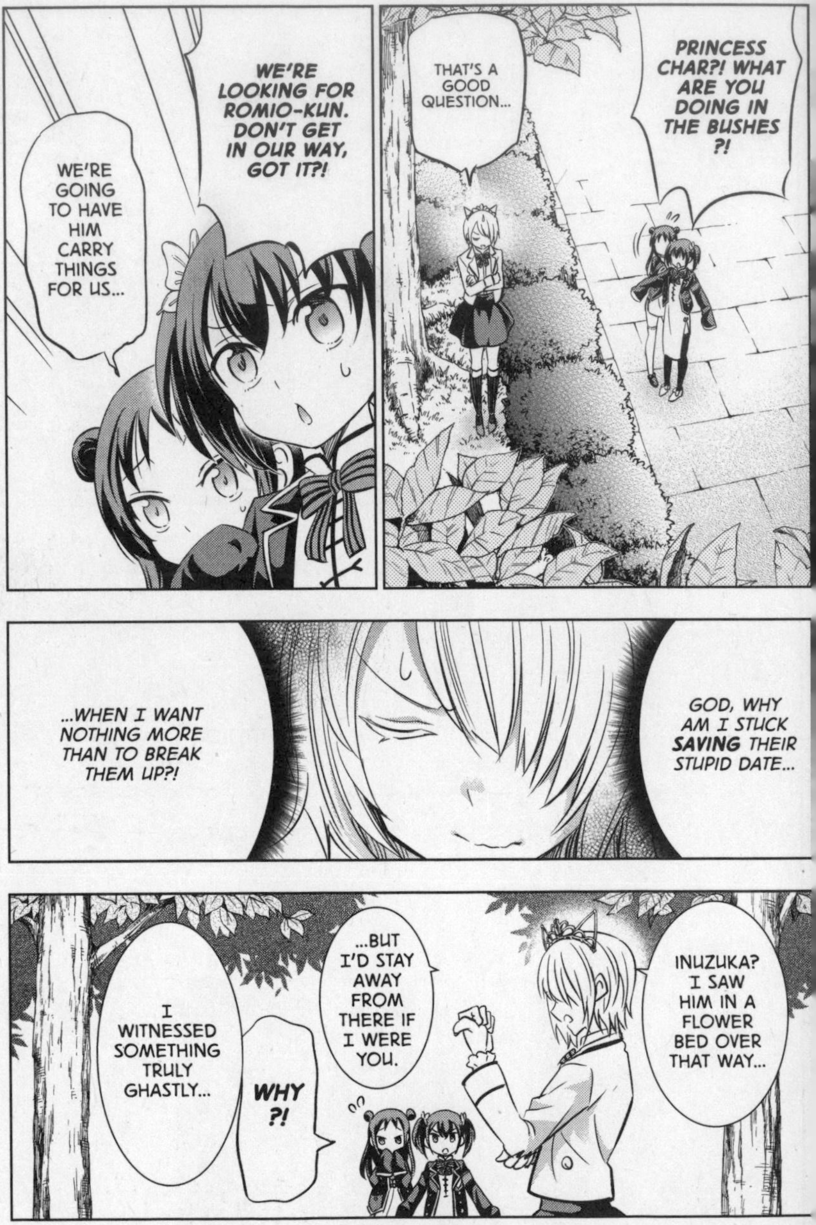
PRINCESS CHAR?! WHAT ARE YOU DOING IN THE BUSHES ?!
THAT'S A GOOD QUESTION...
WE'RE LOOKING FOR ROMIO-KUN. DON'T GET IN OUR WAY, GOT IT?!
WE'RE GOING TO HAVE HIM CARRY THINGS FOR US...
GOD, WHY AM I STUCK **SAVING** THEIR STUPID DATE...
...WHEN I WANT NOTHING MORE THAN TO BREAK THEM UP?!
INUZUKA? I SAW HIM IN A FLOWER BED OVER THAT WAY...
...BUT I'D STAY AWAY FROM THERE IF I WERE YOU.
WHY ?!
I WITNESSED SOMETHING TRULY GHASTLY...

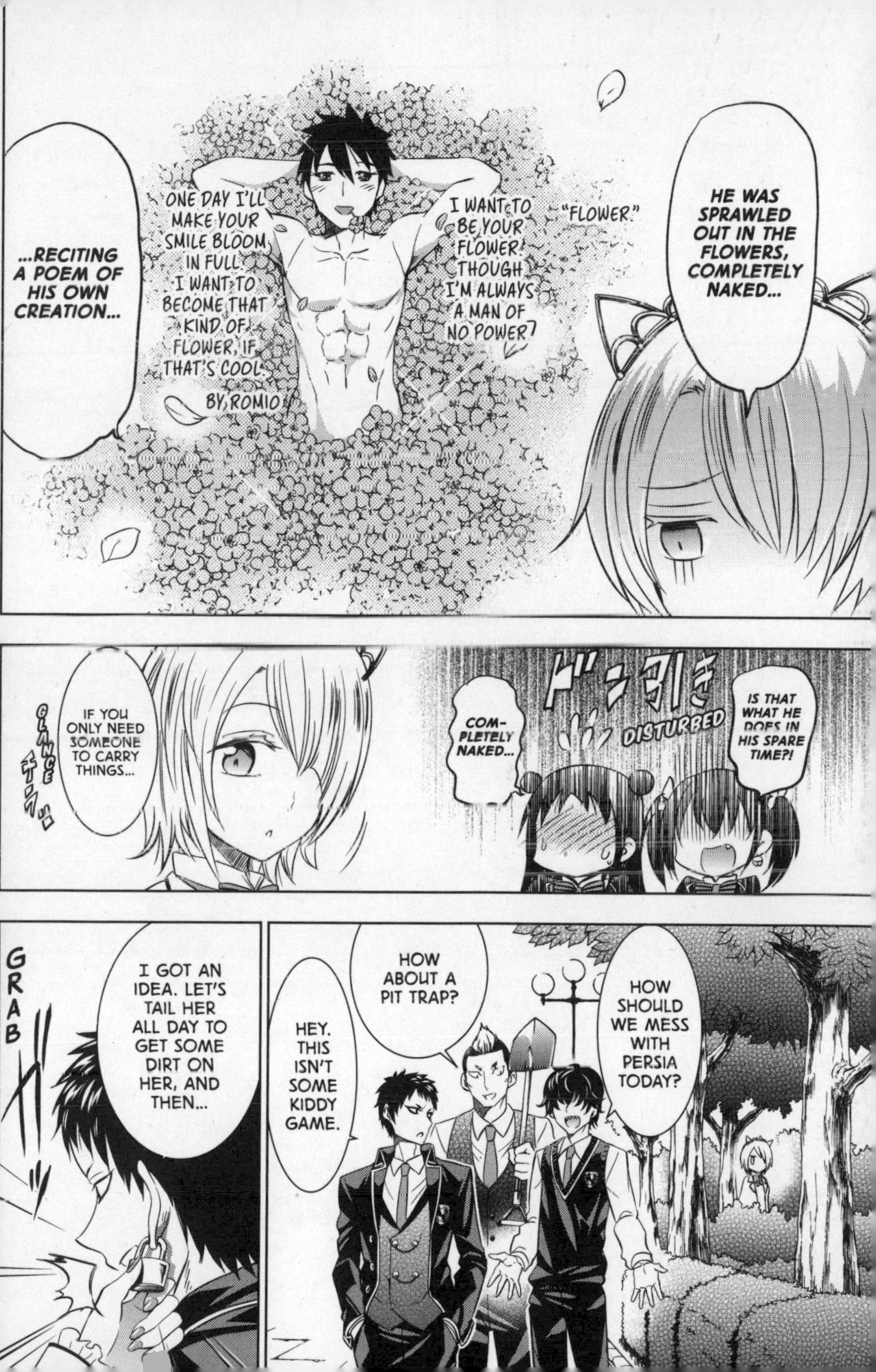
HE WAS SPRAWLED OUT IN THE FLOWERS, COMPLETELY NAKED...
"FLOWER."
I WANT TO BE YOUR FLOWER THOUGH I'M ALWAYS A MAN OF NO POWER?
ONE DAY I'LL MAKE YOUR SMILE BLOOM IN FULL. I WANT TO BECOME THAT KIND OF FLOWER, IF THAT'S COOL.
BY, ROMIO
...RECITING A POEM OF HIS OWN CREATION...
IS THAT WHAT HE DOES IN HIS SPARE TIME?!
ドン引き
DISTURBED
COM-PLETELY NAKED...
GLANCE
IF YOU ONLY NEED SOMEONE TO CARRY THINGS...
HOW SHOULD WE MESS WITH PERSIA TODAY?
HOW ABOUT A PIT TRAP?
HEY. THIS ISN'T SOME KIDDY GAME.
I GOT AN IDEA. LET'S TAIL HER ALL DAY TO GET SOME DIRT ON HER, AND THEN...
GRAB

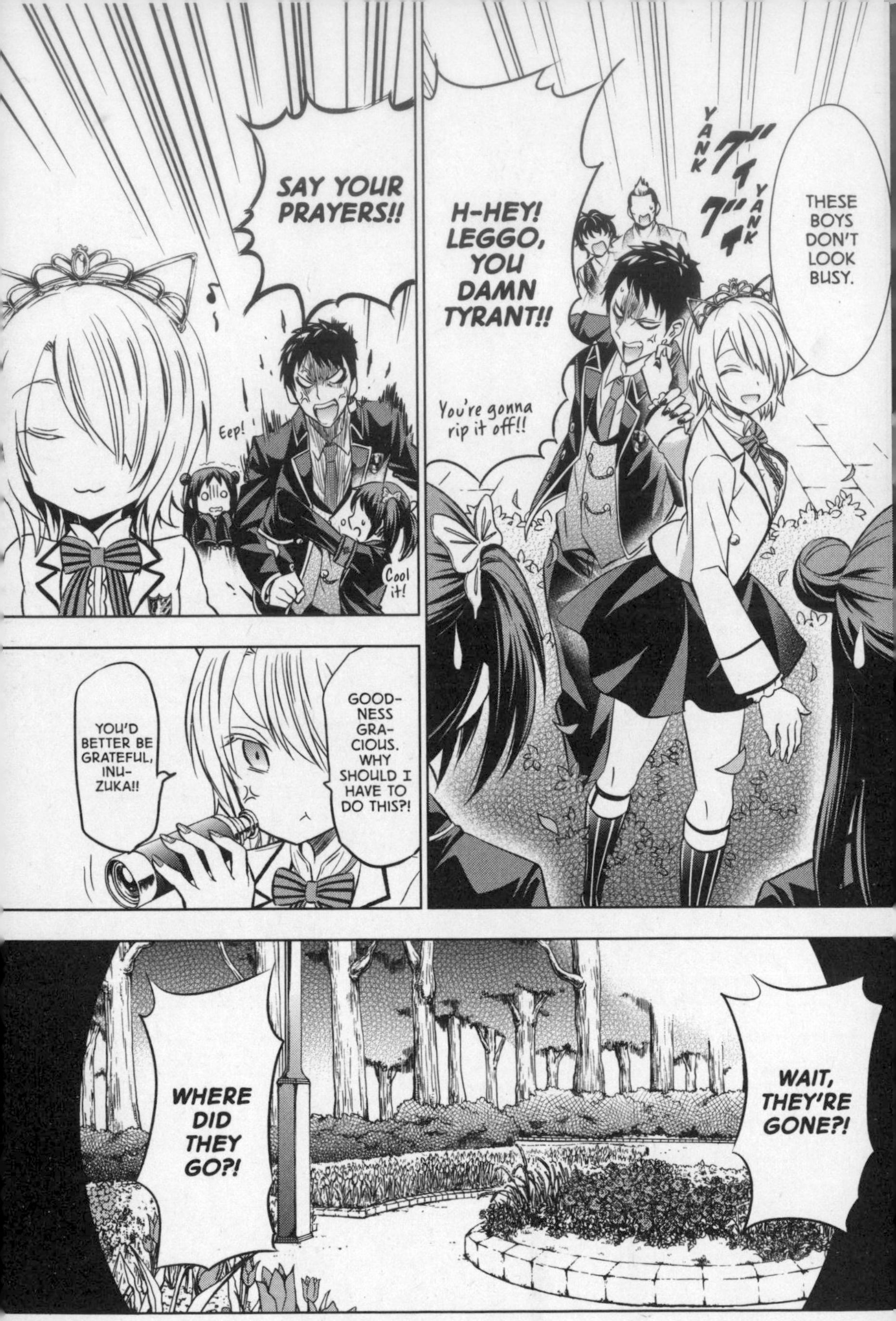
THESE BOYS DON'T LOOK BUSY.
YANK
YANK
H-HEY! LEGGO, YOU DAMN TYRANT!!
You're gonna rip it off!!
SAY YOUR PRAYERS!!
Eep!
Cool it!
GOODNESS GRACIOUS. WHY SHOULD I HAVE TO DO THIS?!
YOU'D BETTER BE GRATEFUL, INUZUKA!!
WAIT, THEY'RE GONE?!
WHERE DID THEY GO?!

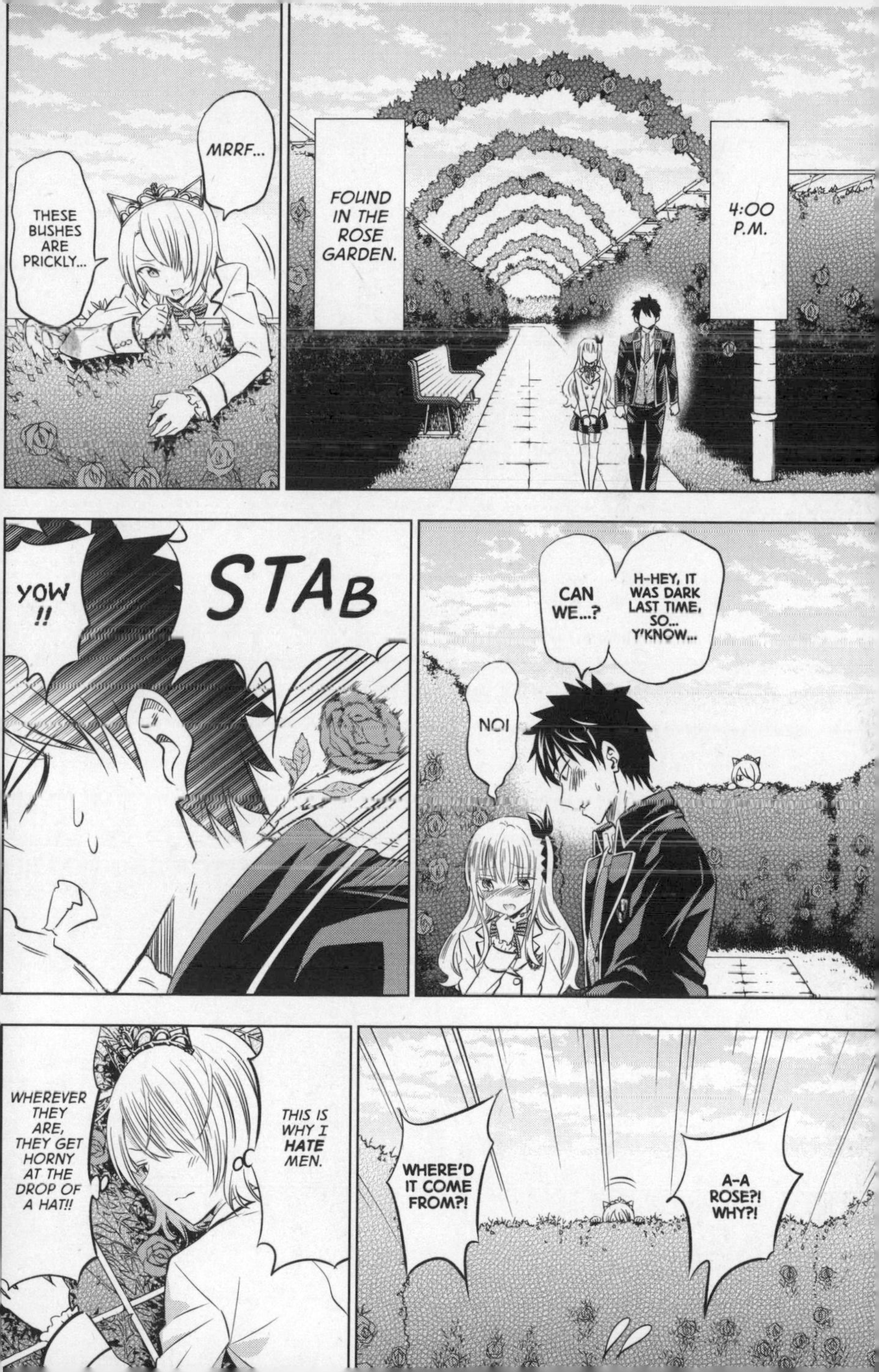
4:00 P.M.
FOUND IN THE ROSE GARDEN.
MRRF...
THESE BUSHES ARE PRICKLY...
H-HEY, IT WAS DARK LAST TIME, SO... Y'KNOW...
CAN WE...?
NO!
STAB
YOW!!
A-A ROSE?! WHY?!
WHERE'D IT COME FROM?!
THIS IS WHY I HATE MEN.
WHEREVER THEY ARE, THEY GET HORNY AT THE DROP OF A HAT!!

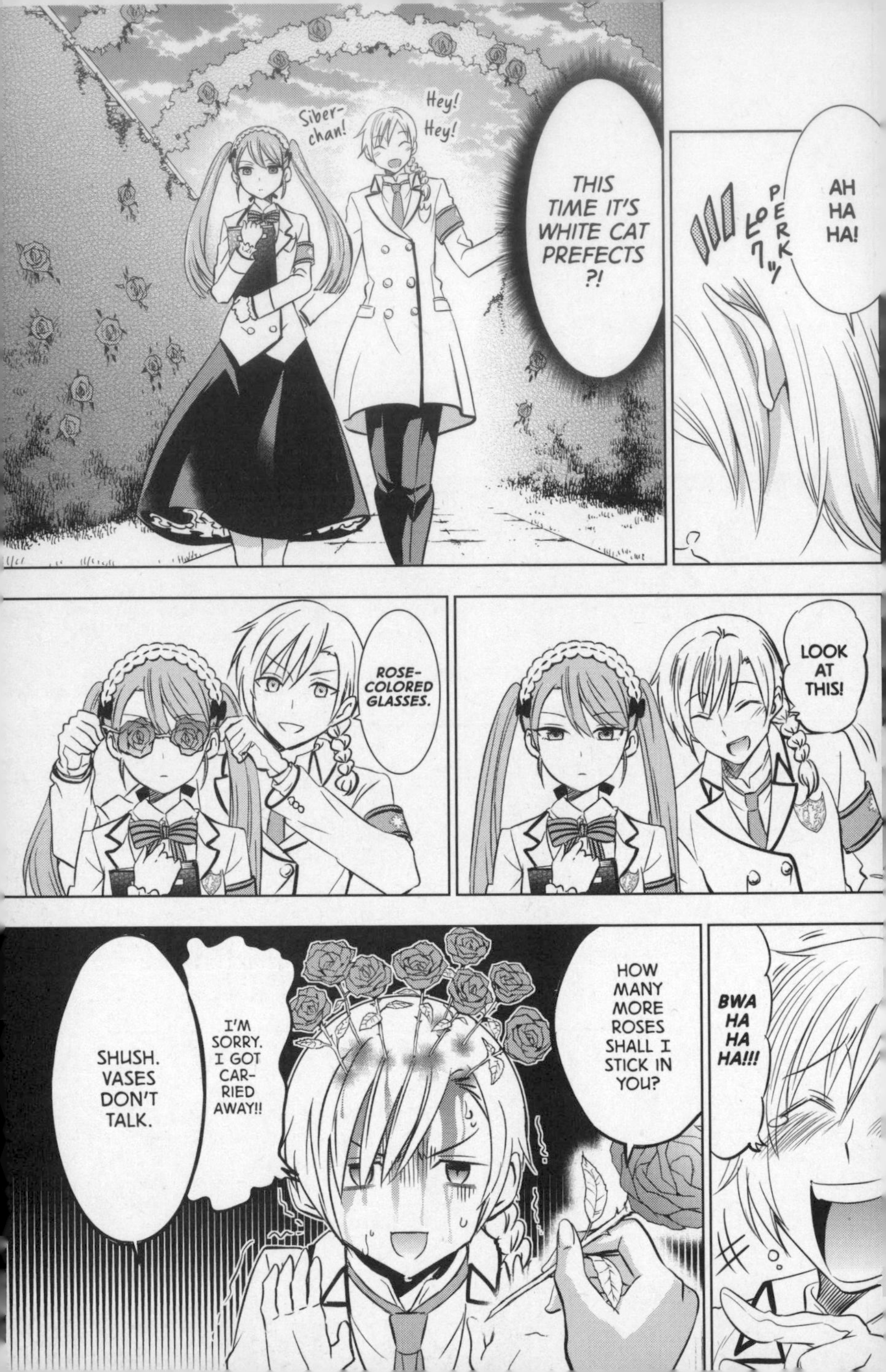
AH HA HA!
PERK
THIS TIME IT'S WHITE CAT PREFECTS ?!
Hey! Hey!
Siber-chan!
LOOK AT THIS!
ROSE-COLORED GLASSES.
BWA HA HA HA!!!
HOW MANY MORE ROSES SHALL I STICK IN YOU?
I'M SORRY. I GOT CAR-RIED AWAY!!
SHUSH. VASES DON'T TALK.

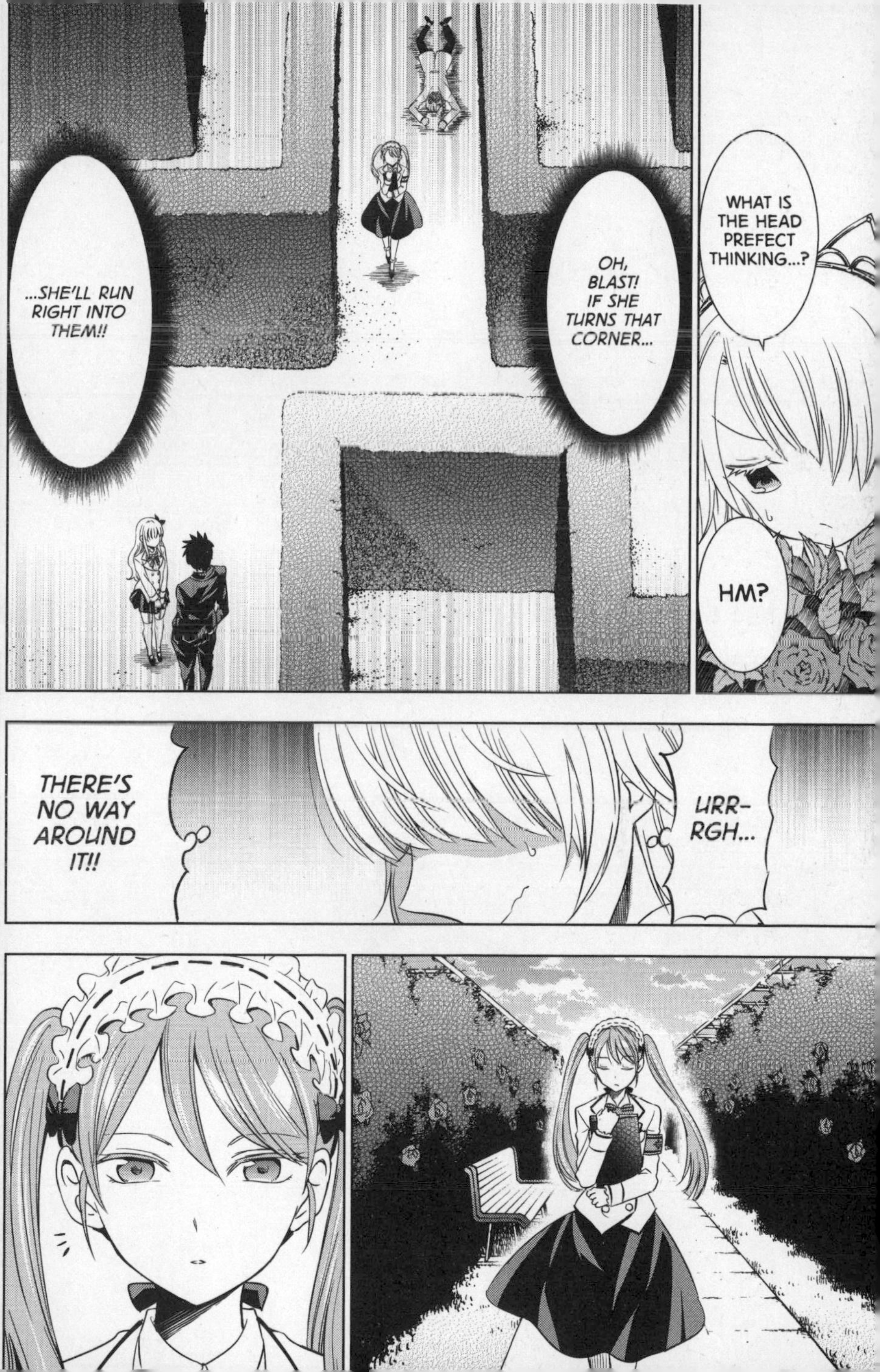
WHAT IS THE HEAD PREFECT THINKING...?
HM?
OH, BLAST! IF SHE TURNS THAT CORNER...
...SHE'LL RUN RIGHT INTO THEM!!
URR-RGH...
THERE'S NO WAY AROUND IT!!

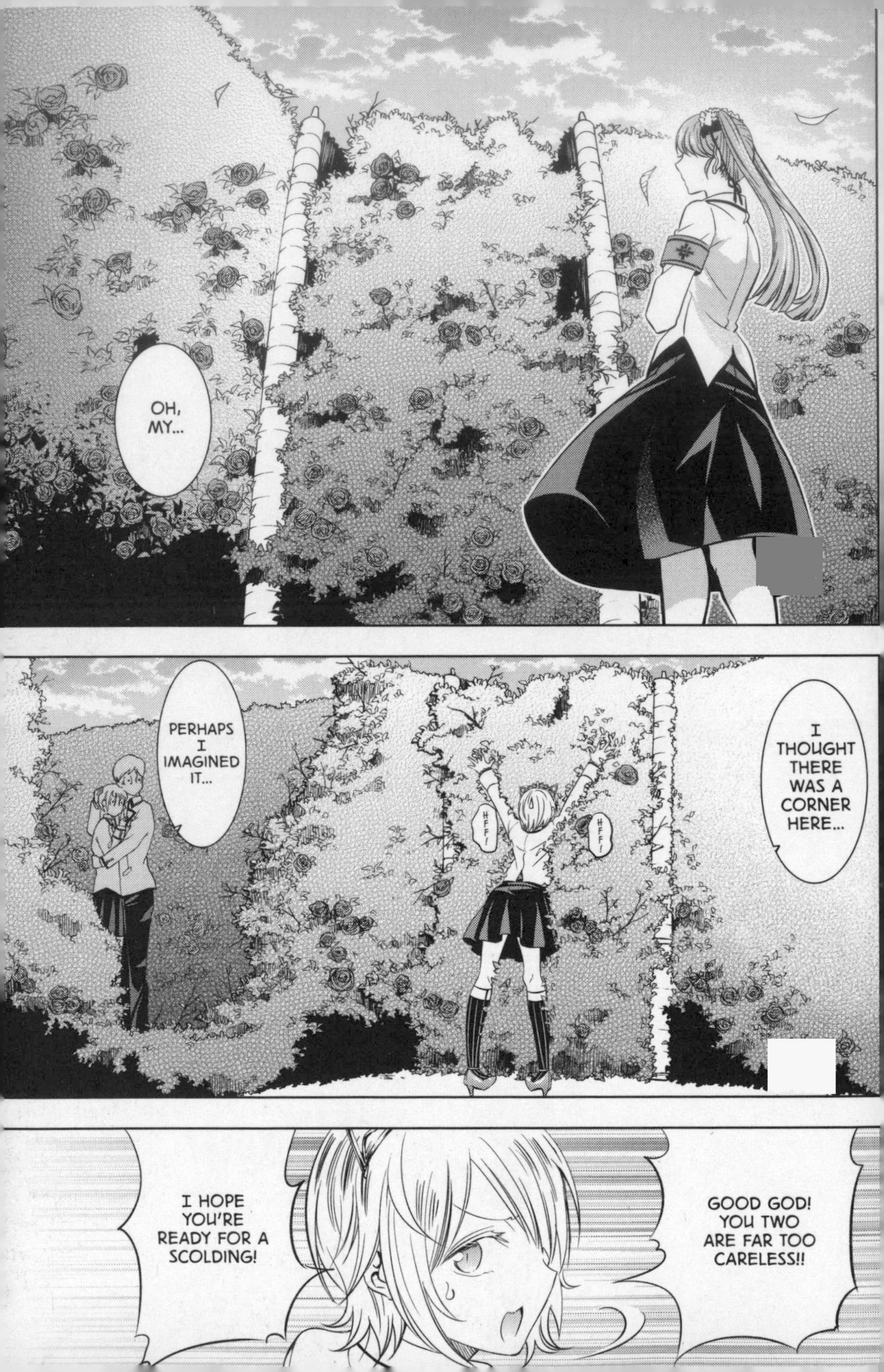
OH, MY...
I THOUGHT THERE WAS A CORNER HERE...
HFF!
HFF!
PERHAPS I IMAGINED IT...
GOOD GOD! YOU TWO ARE FAR TOO CARELESS!!
I HOPE YOU'RE READY FOR A SCOLDING!

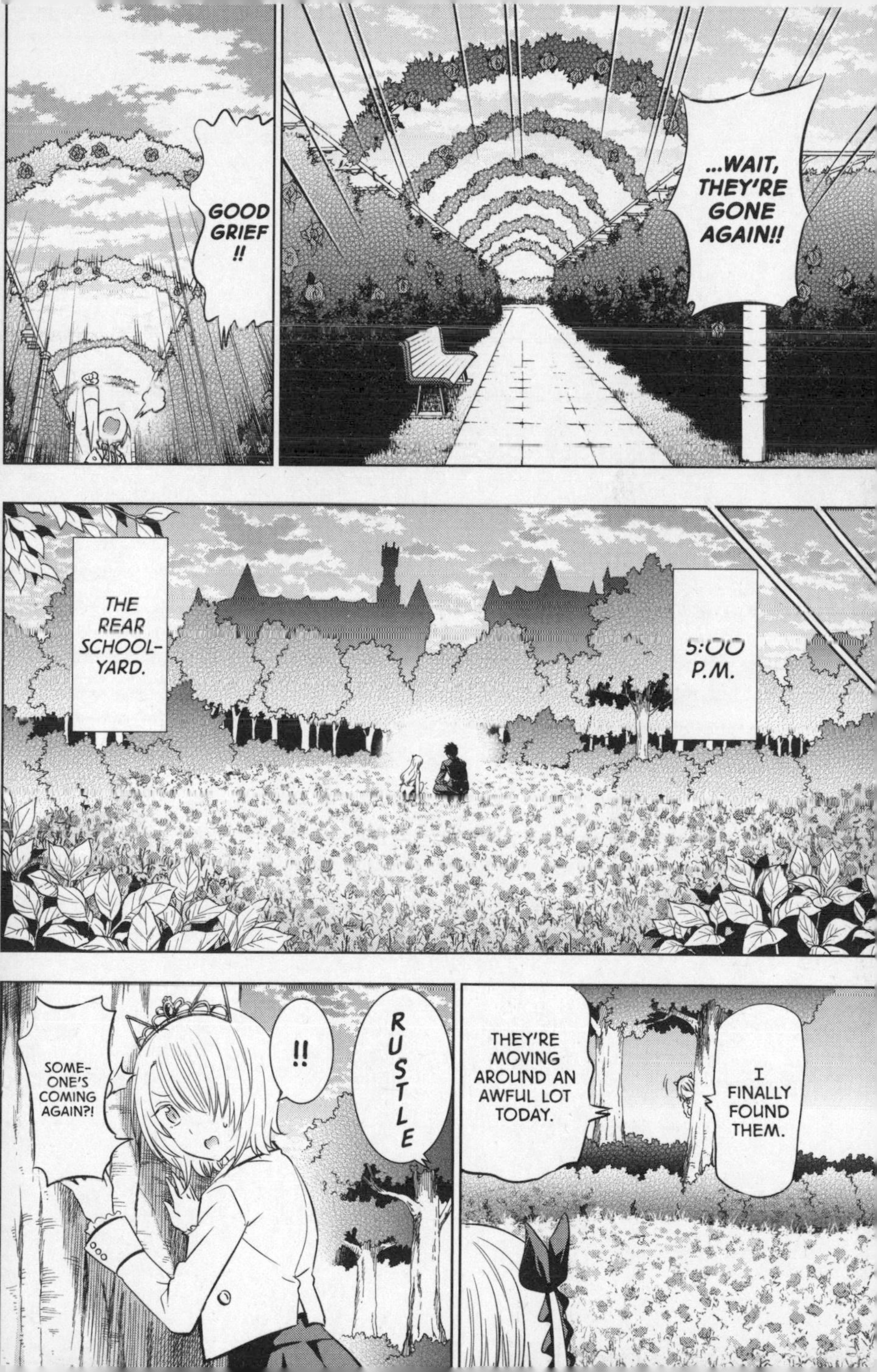
...WAIT, THEY'RE GONE AGAIN!!
GOOD GRIEF !!
5:00 P.M.
THE REAR SCHOOL-YARD.
I FINALLY FOUND THEM.
THEY'RE MOVING AROUND AN AWFUL LOT TODAY.
RUSTLE
!!
SOME-ONE'S COMING AGAIN?!

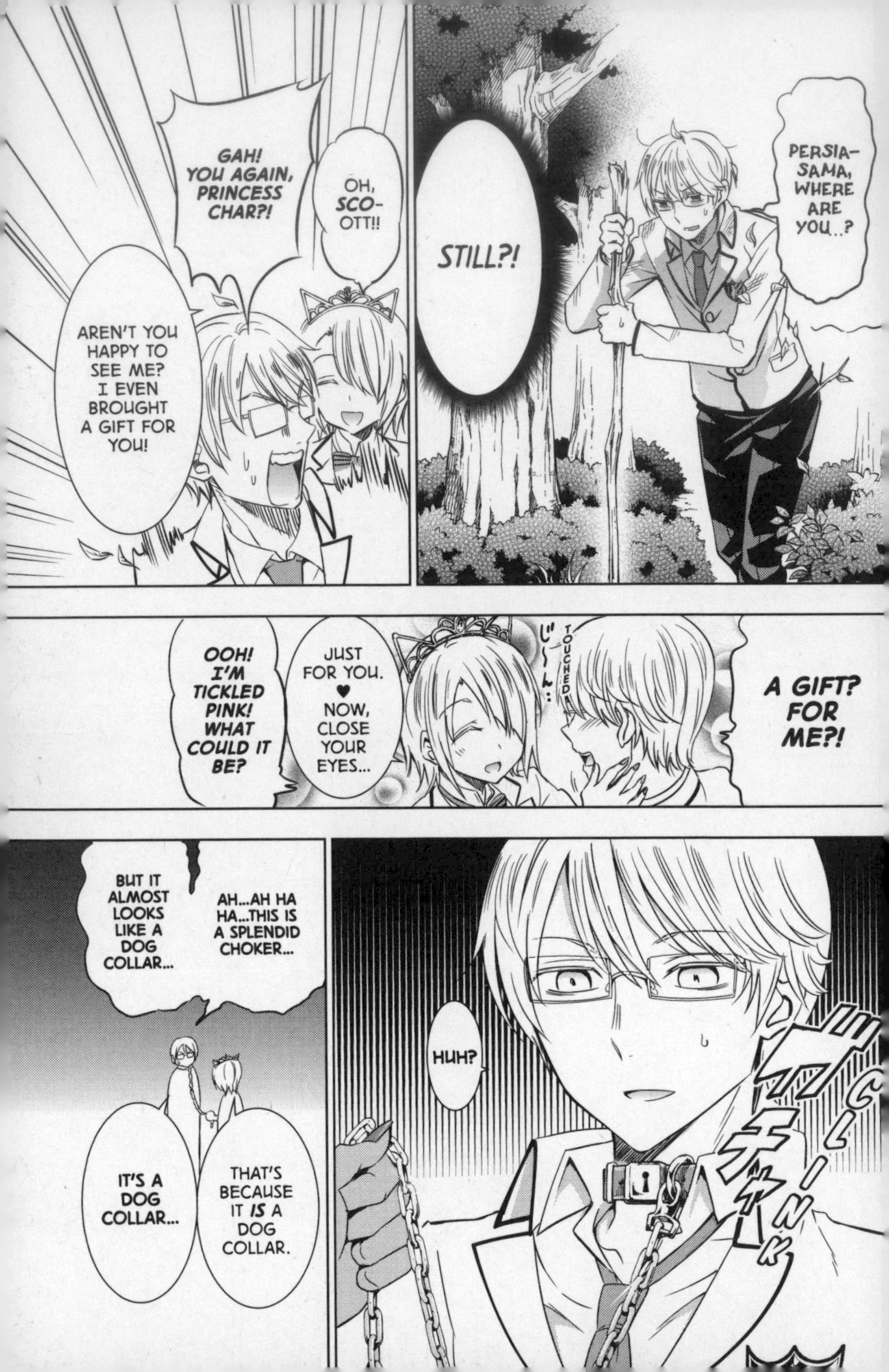
PERSIA-SAMA, WHERE ARE YOU...?
STILL?!
OH, SCO-OTT!!
GAH! YOU AGAIN, PRINCESS CHAR?!
AREN'T YOU HAPPY TO SEE ME? I EVEN BROUGHT A GIFT FOR YOU!
A GIFT? FOR ME?!
TOUCHED
JUST FOR YOU. ♥ NOW, CLOSE YOUR EYES...
OOH! I'M TICKLED PINK! WHAT COULD IT BE?
CLINK
HUH?
AH...AH HA HA...THIS IS A SPLENDID CHOKER...
BUT IT ALMOST LOOKS LIKE A DOG COLLAR...
THAT'S BECAUSE IT IS A DOG COLLAR.
IT'S A DOG COLLAR...

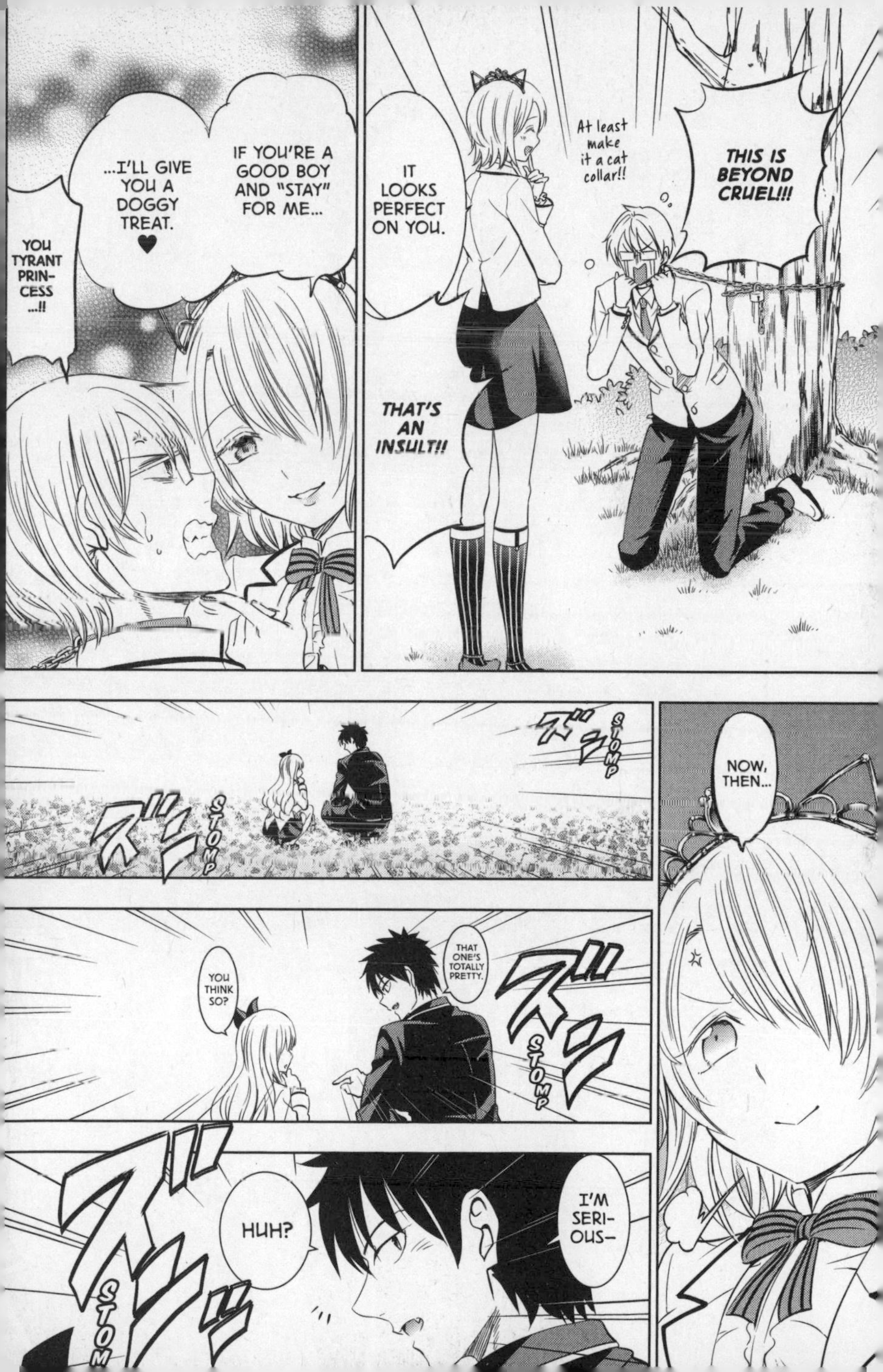
THIS IS BEYOND CRUEL!!!
At least make it a cat collar!!
IT LOOKS PERFECT ON YOU.
THAT'S AN INSULT!!
IF YOU'RE A GOOD BOY AND "STAY" FOR ME...
...I'LL GIVE YOU A DOGGY TREAT. ♥
YOU TYRANT PRINCESS ...!!
NOW, THEN...
STOMP
STOMP
THAT ONE'S TOTALLY PRETTY.
STOMP
YOU THINK SO?
I'M SERIOUS—
HUH?
STOM

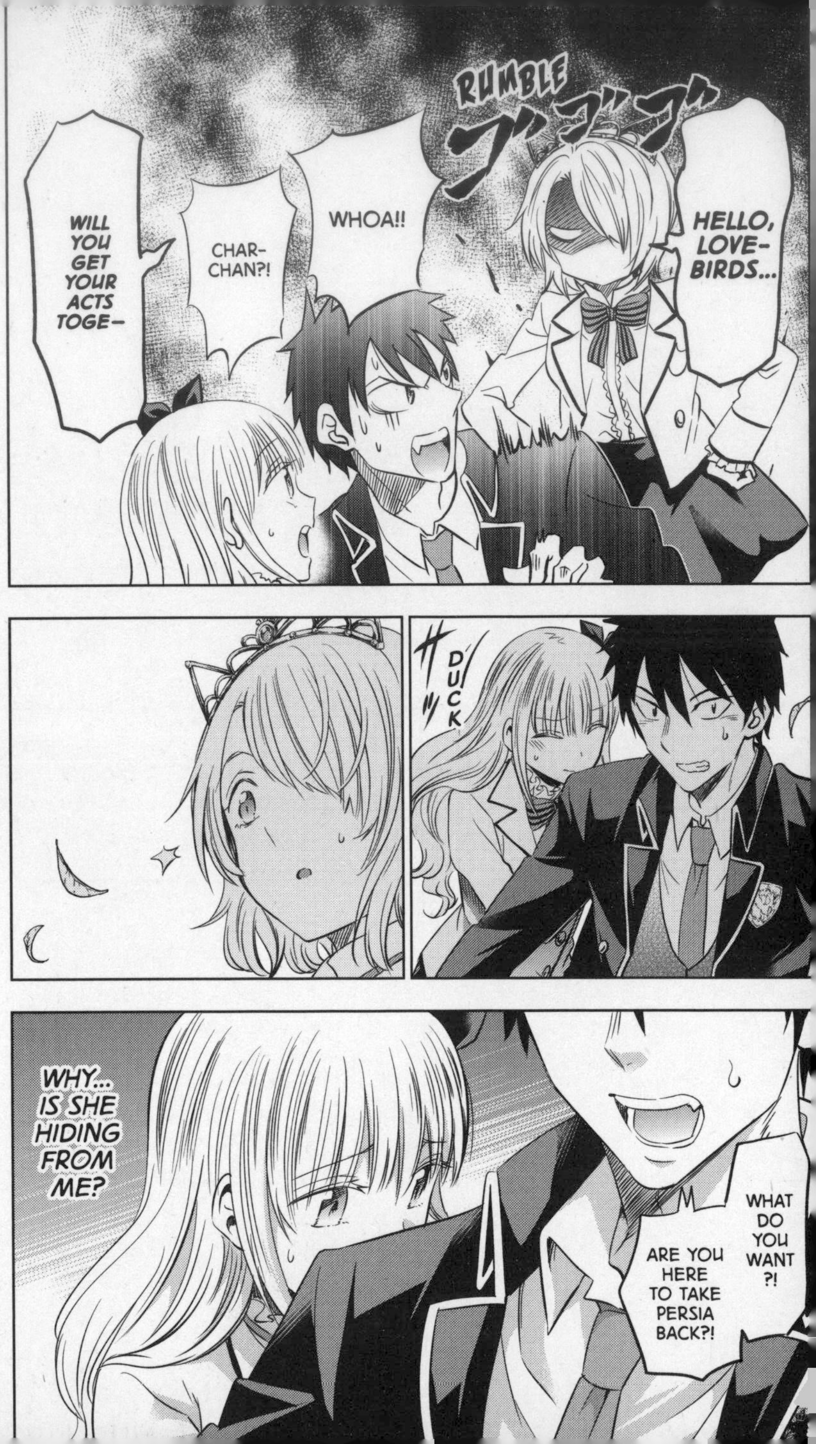
HELLO, LOVE-BIRDS...
RUMBLE
WHOA!!
CHAR-CHAN?!
WILL YOU GET YOUR ACTS TOGE—
DUCK
WHAT DO YOU WANT?!
ARE YOU HERE TO TAKE PERSIA BACK?!
WHY... IS SHE HIDING FROM ME?

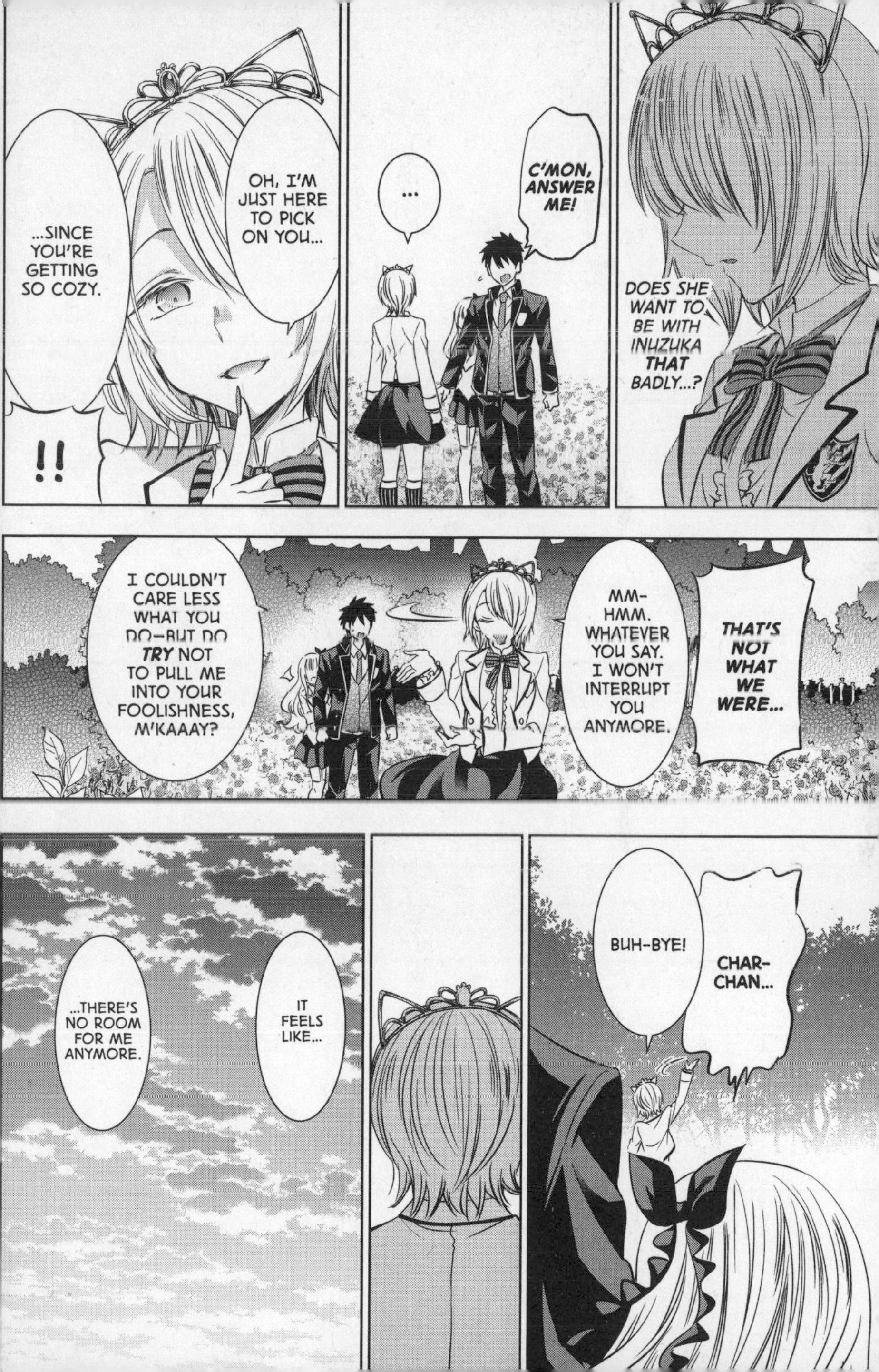
DOES SHE WANT TO BE WITH INUZUKA THAT BADLY...?
C'MON, ANSWER ME!
...
OH, I'M JUST HERE TO PICK ON YOU...
...SINCE YOU'RE GETTING SO COZY.
!!
THAT'S NOT WHAT WE WERE...
MM-HMM. WHATEVER YOU SAY. I WON'T INTERRUPT YOU ANYMORE.
I COULDN'T CARE LESS WHAT YOU DO—BUT DO TRY NOT TO PULL ME INTO YOUR FOOLISHNESS, M'KAAAY?
CHAR-CHAN...
BUH-BYE!
IT FEELS LIKE...
...THERE'S NO ROOM FOR ME ANYMORE.

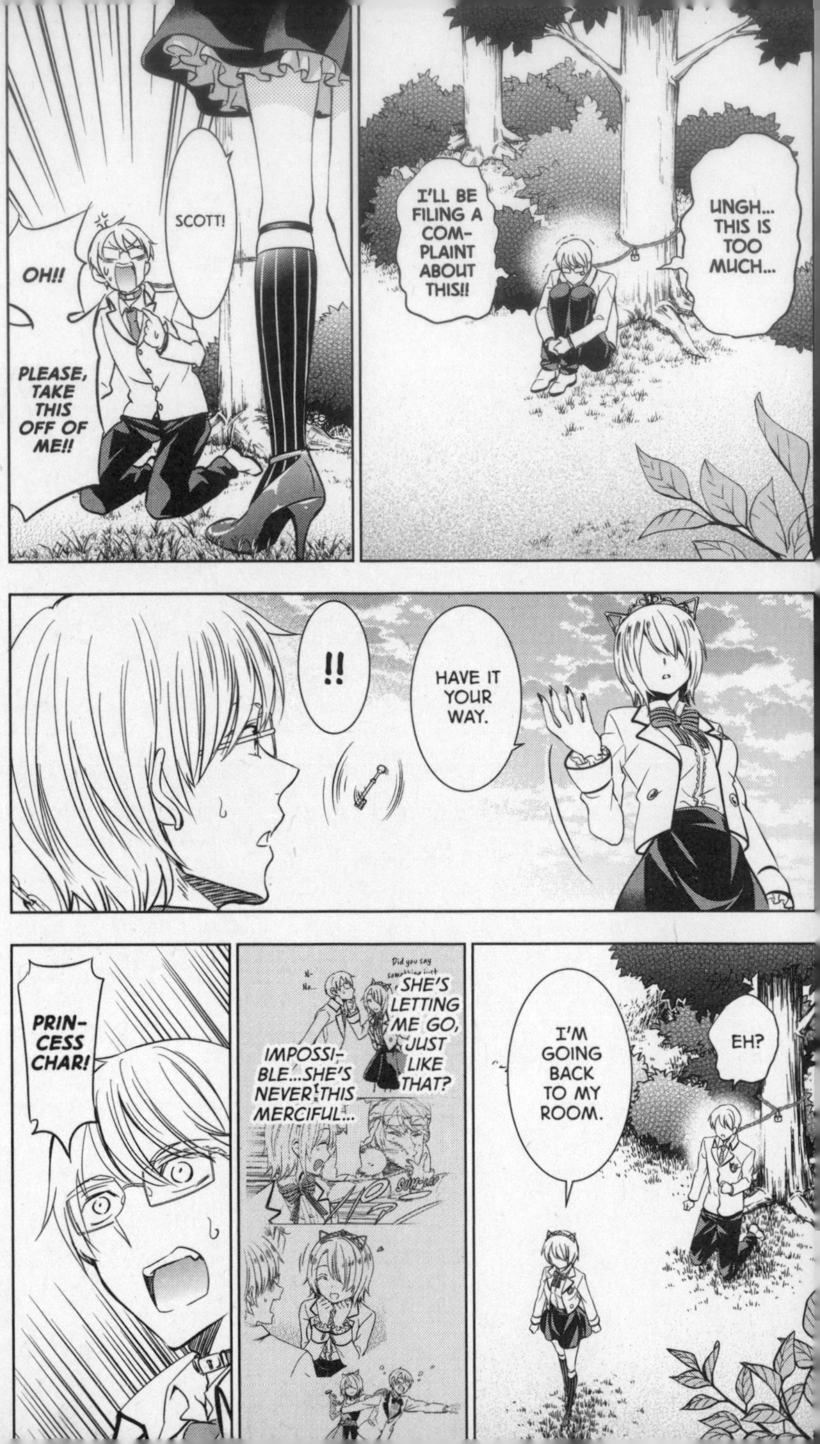
UNGH... THIS IS TOO MUCH...
I'LL BE FILING A COM-PLAINT ABOUT THIS!!
SCOTT!
OH!!
PLEASE, TAKE THIS OFF OF ME!!
HAVE IT YOUR WAY.
!!
EH?
I'M GOING BACK TO MY ROOM.
SHE'S LETTING ME GO, JUST LIKE THAT?
IMPOSSI-BLE...SHE'S NEVER THIS MERCIFUL...
PRIN-CESS CHAR!

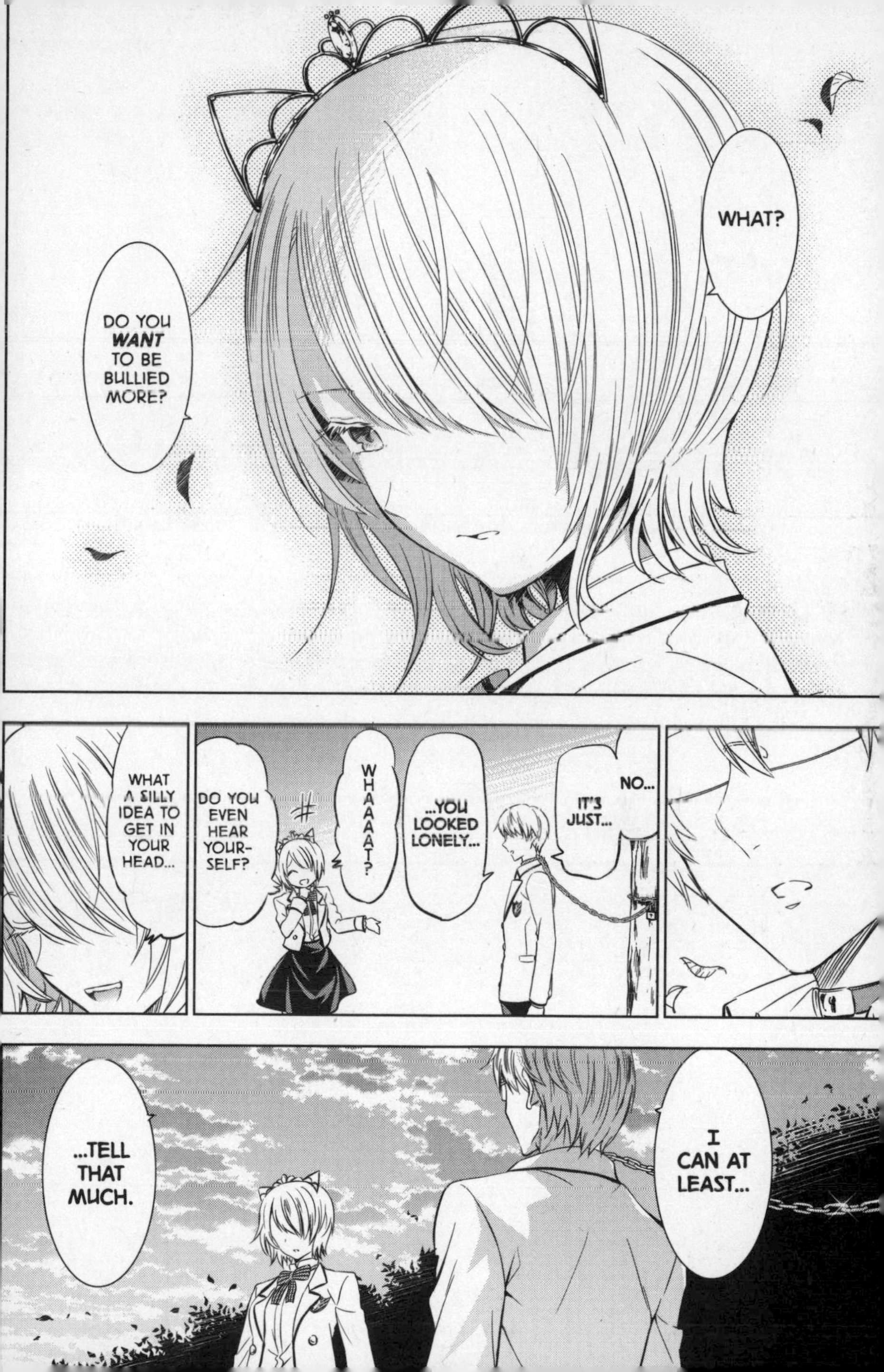
WHAT?
DO YOU *WANT* TO BE BULLIED MORE?
NO... IT'S JUST...
...YOU LOOKED LONELY...
WHAAAAT?
DO YOU EVEN HEAR YOUR-SELF?
WHAT A SILLY IDEA TO GET IN YOUR HEAD...
I CAN AT LEAST...
...TELL THAT MUCH.

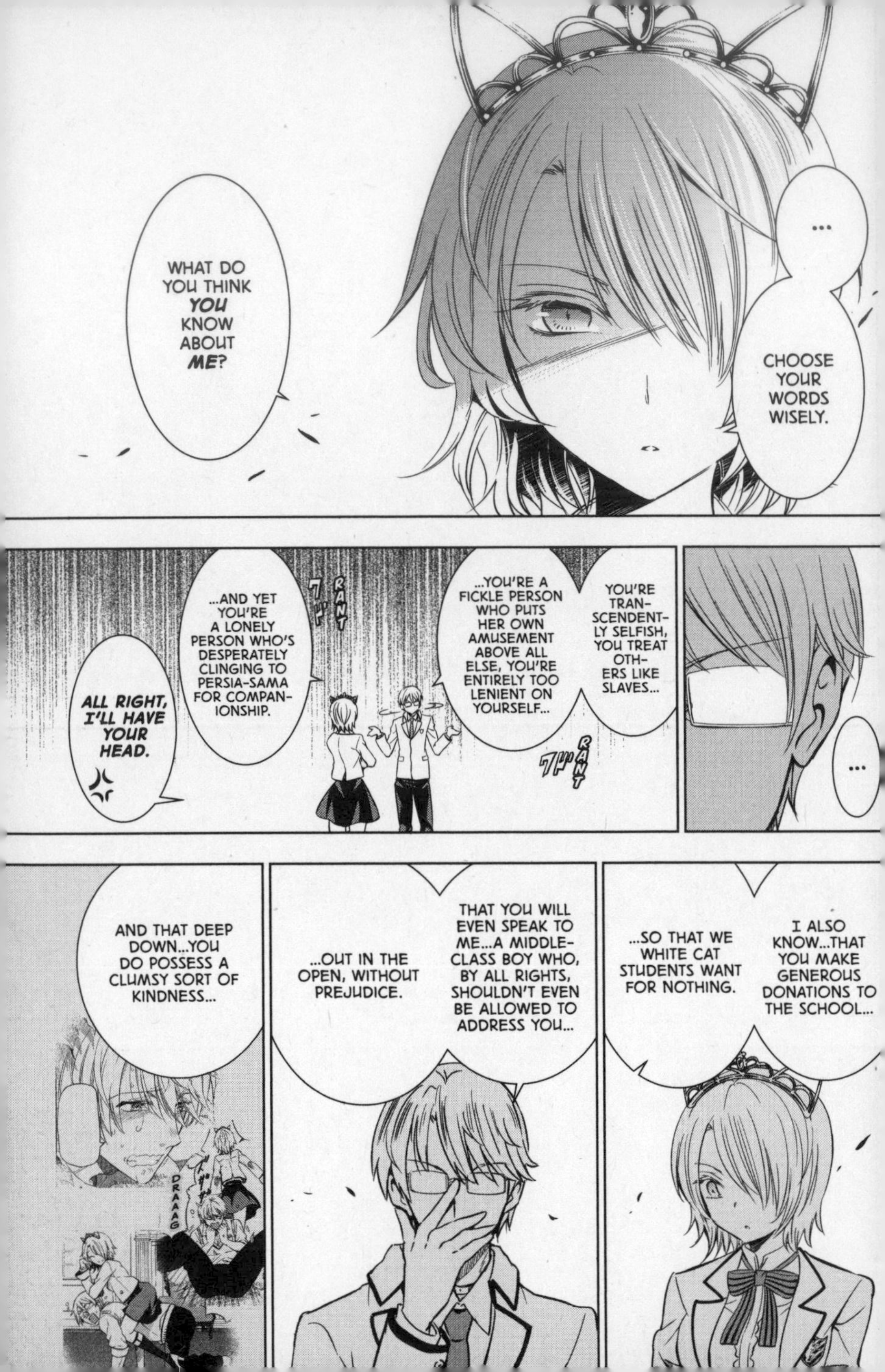
...
CHOOSE YOUR WORDS WISELY.
WHAT DO YOU THINK *YOU* KNOW ABOUT *ME*?
...
YOU'RE TRANSCENDENTLY SELFISH, YOU TREAT OTHERS LIKE SLAVES...
...YOU'RE A FICKLE PERSON WHO PUTS HER OWN AMUSEMENT ABOVE ALL ELSE, YOU'RE ENTIRELY TOO LENIENT ON YOURSELF...
RANT
RANT
...AND YET YOU'RE A LONELY PERSON WHO'S DESPERATELY CLINGING TO PERSIA-SAMA FOR COMPANIONSHIP.
ALL RIGHT, I'LL HAVE YOUR HEAD.
I ALSO KNOW...THAT YOU MAKE GENEROUS DONATIONS TO THE SCHOOL...
...SO THAT WE WHITE CAT STUDENTS WANT FOR NOTHING.
THAT YOU WILL EVEN SPEAK TO ME...A MIDDLE-CLASS BOY WHO, BY ALL RIGHTS, SHOULDN'T EVEN BE ALLOWED TO ADDRESS YOU...
...OUT IN THE OPEN, WITHOUT PREJUDICE.
AND THAT DEEP DOWN...YOU DO POSSESS A CLUMSY SORT OF KINDNESS...
DRAAAG

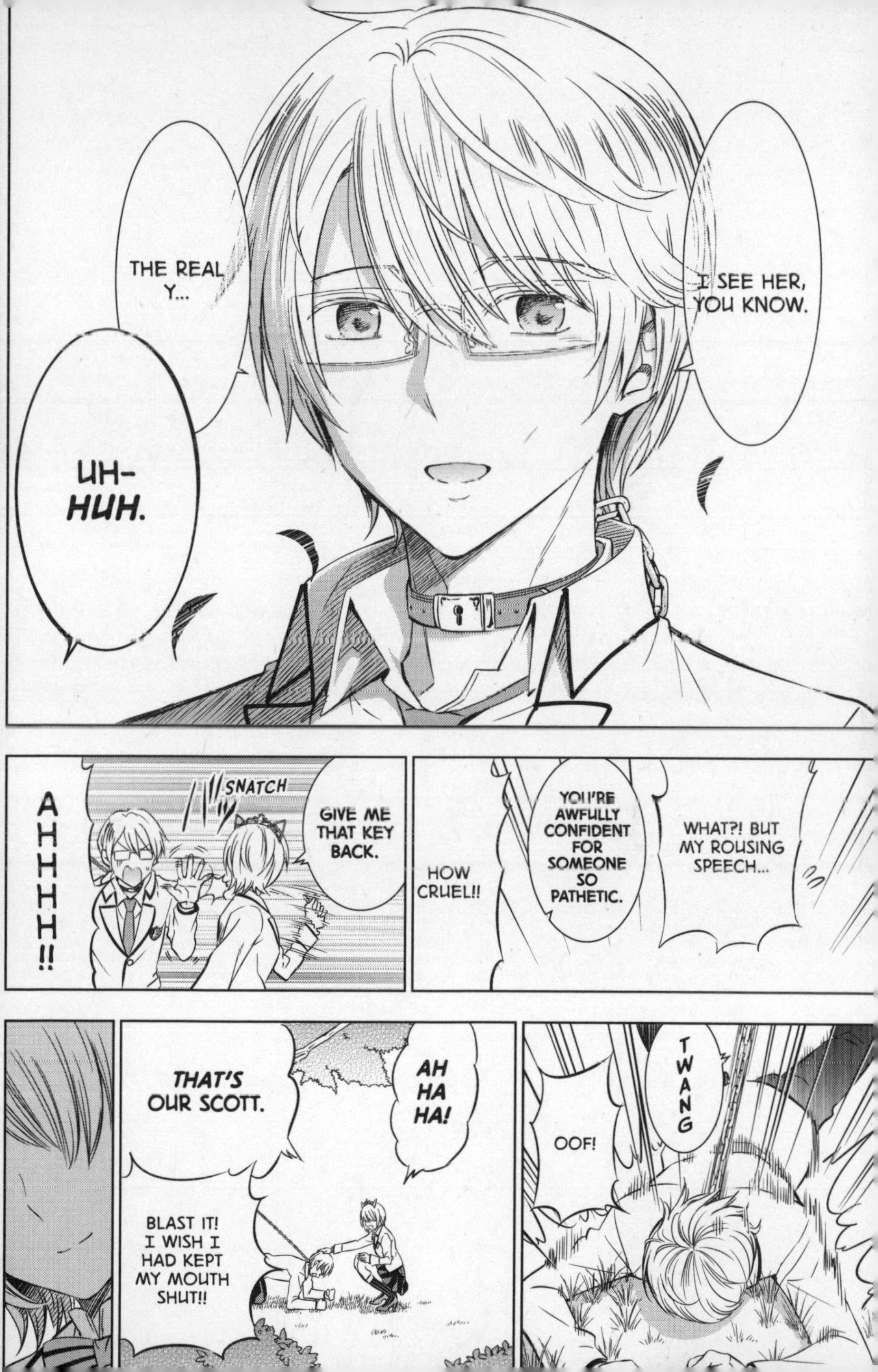
I SEE HER, YOU KNOW.
THE REAL Y...
UH-HUH.
WHAT?! BUT MY ROUSING SPEECH...
YOU'RE AWFULLY CONFIDENT FOR SOMEONE SO PATHETIC.
HOW CRUEL!!
GIVE ME THAT KEY BACK.
SNATCH
AHHHH!!
TWANG
OOF!
AH HA HA!
THAT'S OUR SCOTT.
BLAST IT! I WISH I HAD KEPT MY MOUTH SHUT!!

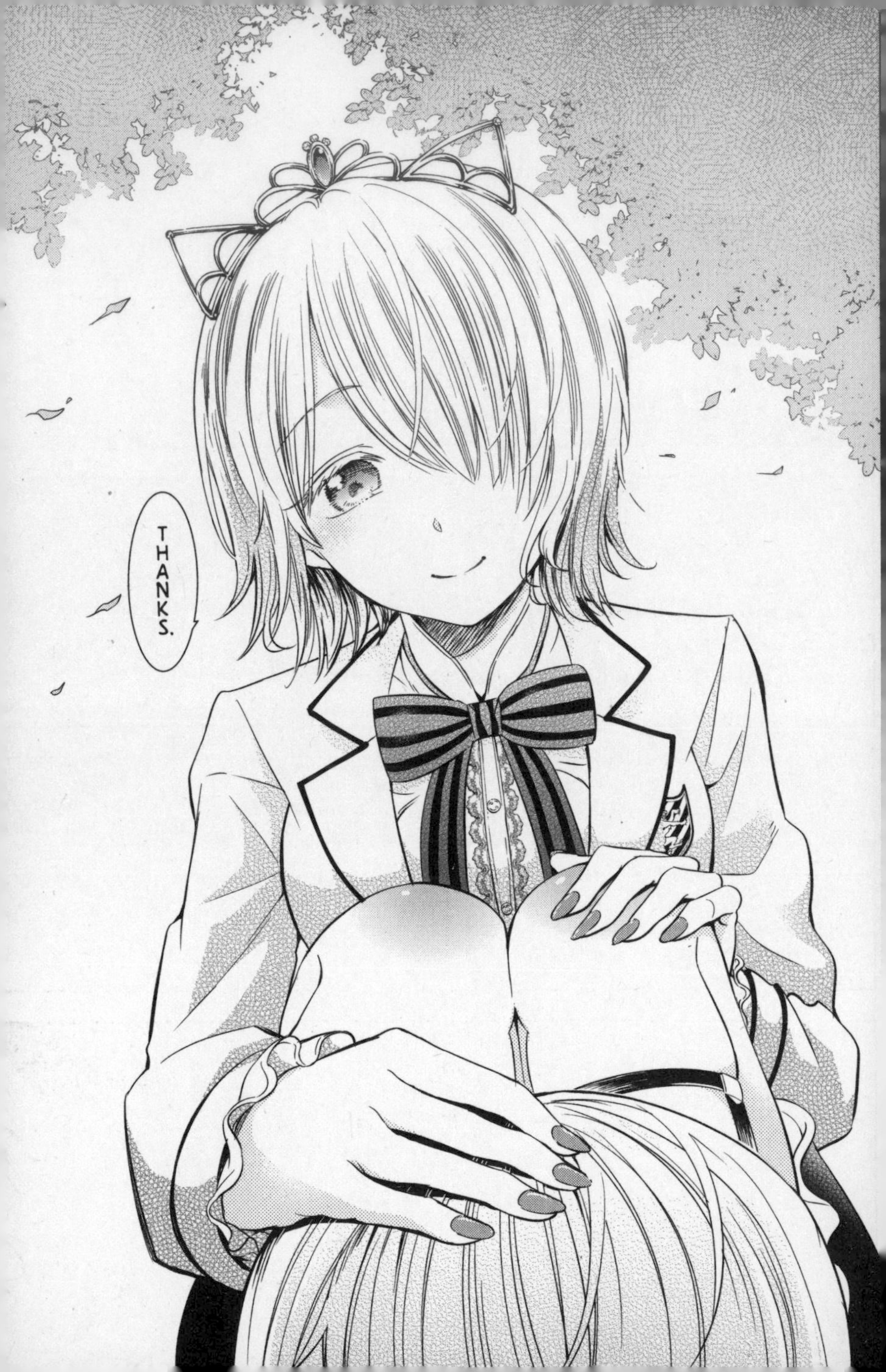
THANKS.

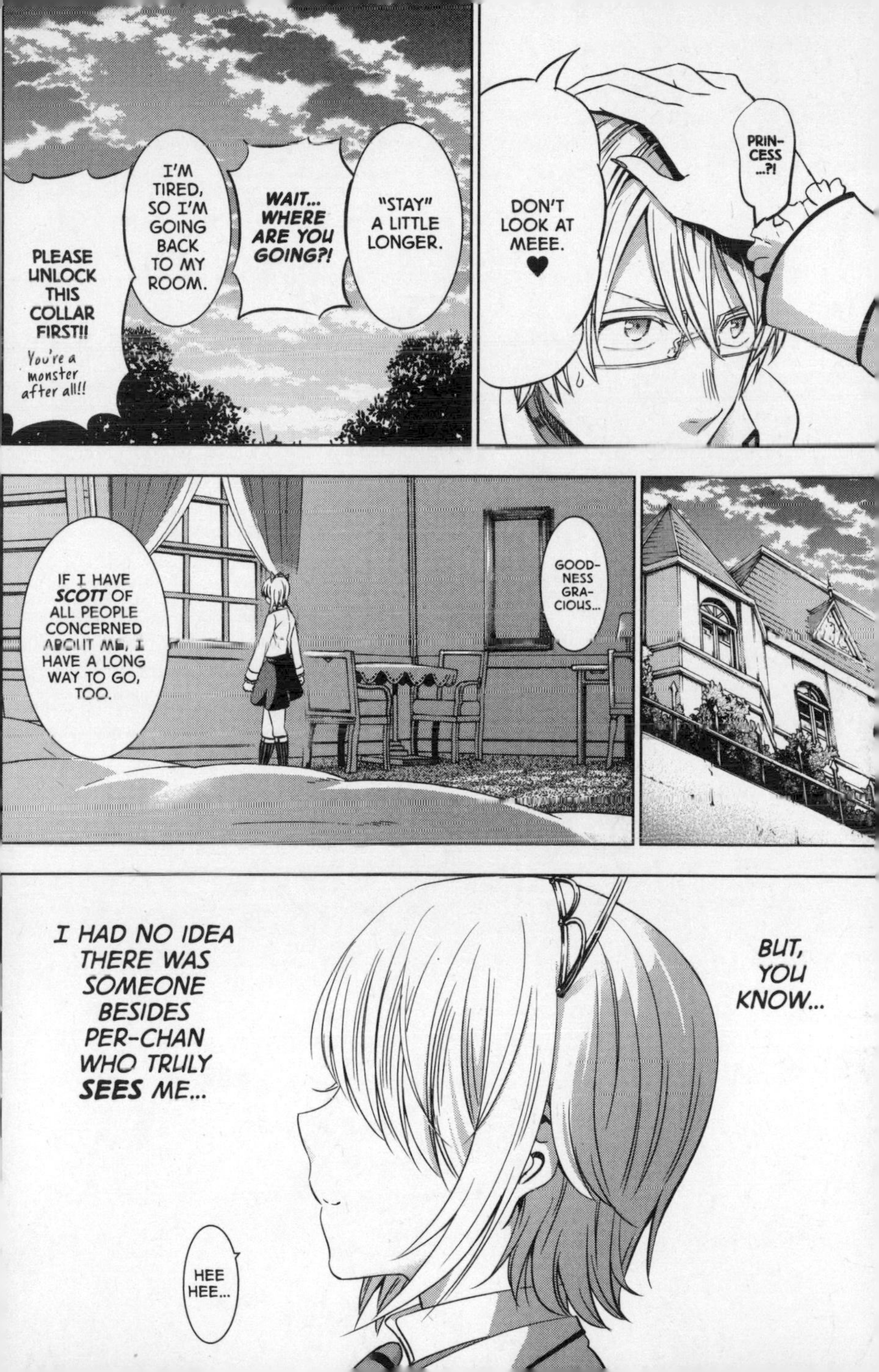
PRIN-CESS ...?!
DON'T LOOK AT MEEE. ♥
"STAY" A LITTLE LONGER.
WAIT... WHERE ARE YOU GOING?!
I'M TIRED, SO I'M GOING BACK TO MY ROOM.
PLEASE UNLOCK THIS COLLAR FIRST!!
You're a monster after all!!
GOOD-NESS GRA-CIOUS...
IF I HAVE SCOTT OF ALL PEOPLE CONCERNED ABOUT ME, I HAVE A LONG WAY TO GO, TOO.
BUT, YOU KNOW...
I HAD NO IDEA THERE WAS SOMEONE BESIDES PER-CHAN WHO TRULY SEES ME...
HEE HEE...

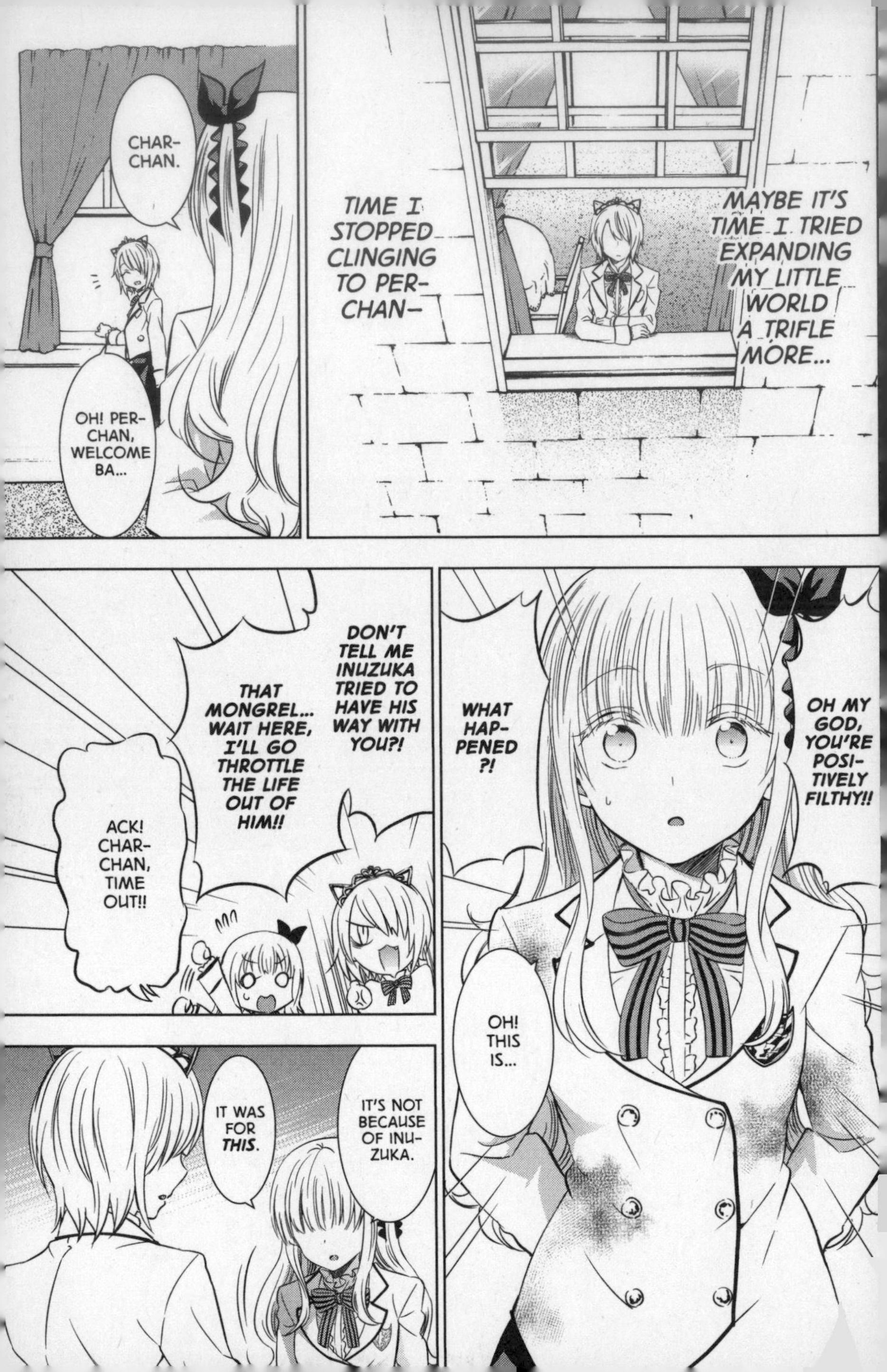
MAYBE IT'S TIME I TRIED EXPANDING MY LITTLE WORLD A TRIFLE MORE...
TIME I STOPPED CLINGING TO PER-CHAN—
CHAR-CHAN.
OH! PER-CHAN, WELCOME BA...
OH MY GOD, YOU'RE POSITIVELY FILTHY!!
WHAT HAPPENED?!
OH! THIS IS...
DON'T TELL ME INUZUKA TRIED TO HAVE HIS WAY WITH YOU?!
THAT MONGREL... WAIT HERE, I'LL GO THROTTLE THE LIFE OUT OF HIM!!
ACK! CHAR-CHAN, TIME OUT!!
IT'S NOT BECAUSE OF INUZUKA.
IT WAS FOR *THIS*.

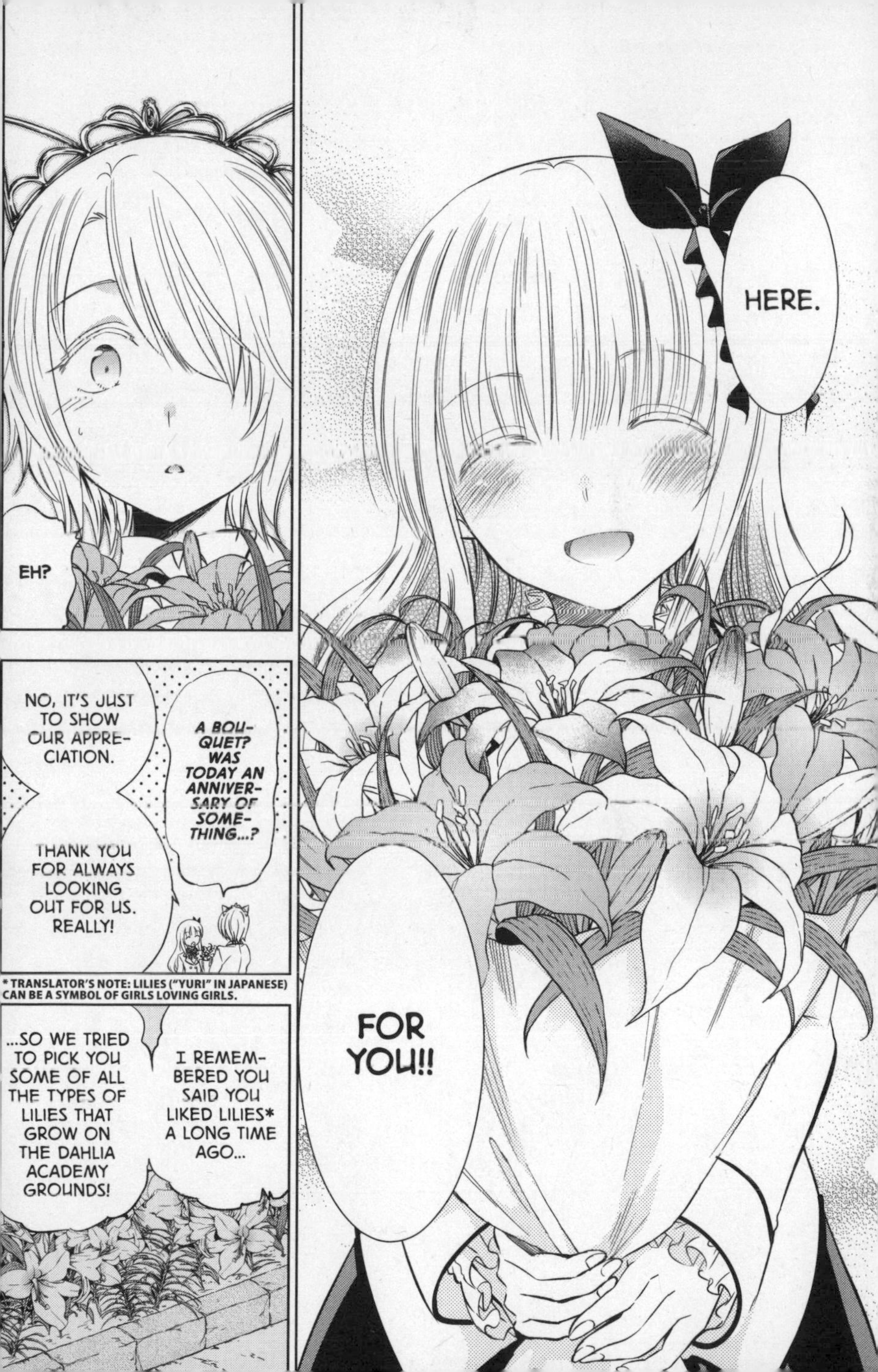
HERE.
FOR YOU!!
EH?
A BOUQUET? WAS TODAY AN ANNIVERSARY OF SOMETHING...?
NO, IT'S JUST TO SHOW OUR APPRECIATION.
THANK YOU FOR ALWAYS LOOKING OUT FOR US. REALLY!
* TRANSLATOR'S NOTE: LILIES ("YURI" IN JAPANESE) CAN BE A SYMBOL OF GIRLS LOVING GIRLS.
I REMEMBERED YOU SAID YOU LIKED LILIES* A LONG TIME AGO...
...SO WE TRIED TO PICK YOU SOME OF ALL THE TYPES OF LILIES THAT GROW ON THE DAHLIA ACADEMY GROUNDS!

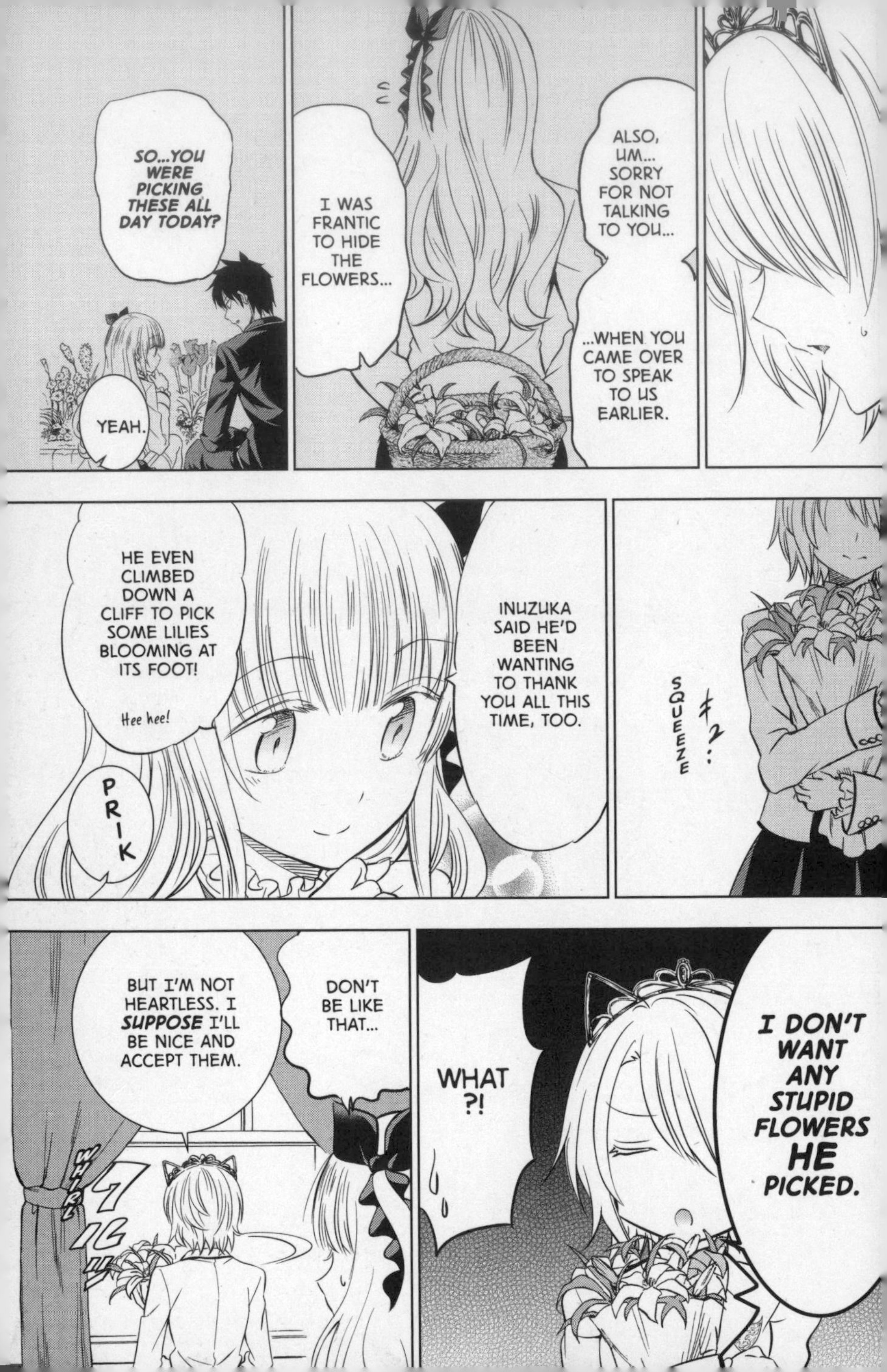
ALSO, UM... SORRY FOR NOT TALKING TO YOU...
...WHEN YOU CAME OVER TO SPEAK TO US EARLIER.
I WAS FRANTIC TO HIDE THE FLOWERS...
SO...YOU WERE PICKING THESE ALL DAY TODAY?
YEAH.
SQUEEZE
INUZUKA SAID HE'D BEEN WANTING TO THANK YOU ALL THIS TIME, TOO.
HE EVEN CLIMBED DOWN A CLIFF TO PICK SOME LILIES BLOOMING AT ITS FOOT!
Hee hee!
PRIK
I DON'T WANT ANY STUPID FLOWERS HE PICKED.
WHAT?!
DON'T BE LIKE THAT...
BUT I'M NOT HEARTLESS. I SUPPOSE I'LL BE NICE AND ACCEPT THEM.
WHIRL

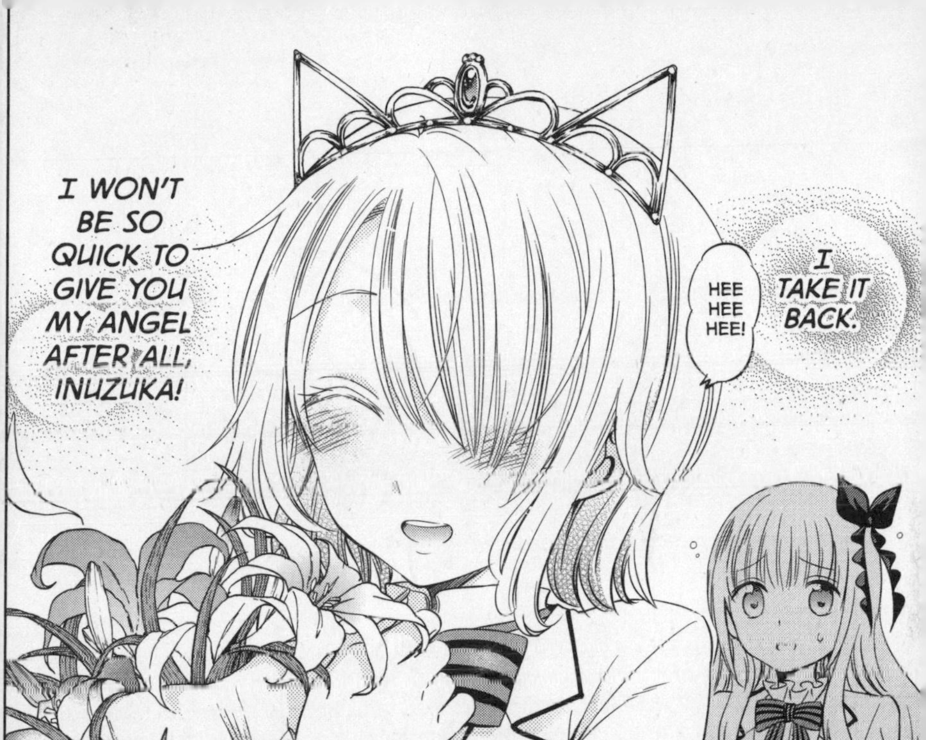
I TAKE IT BACK.
HEE HEE HEE!
I WON'T BE SO QUICK TO GIVE YOU MY ANGEL AFTER ALL, INUZUKA!

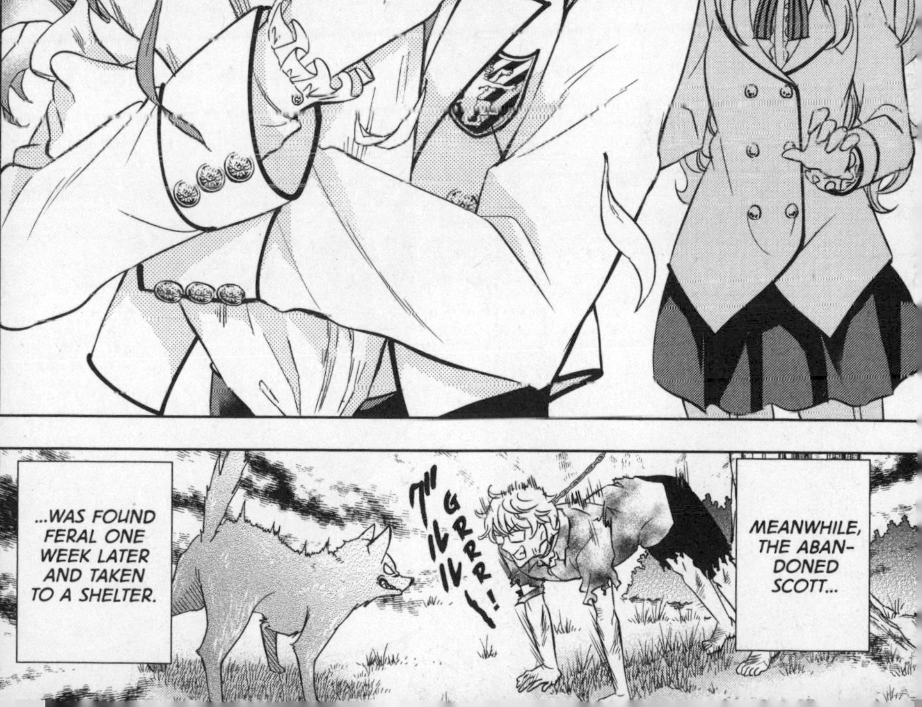
MEANWHILE, THE ABAN-DONED SCOTT...
グルル
GRRR!
...WAS FOUND FERAL ONE WEEK LATER AND TAKEN TO A SHELTER.

ACT 23:

ROMIO & SOMALI

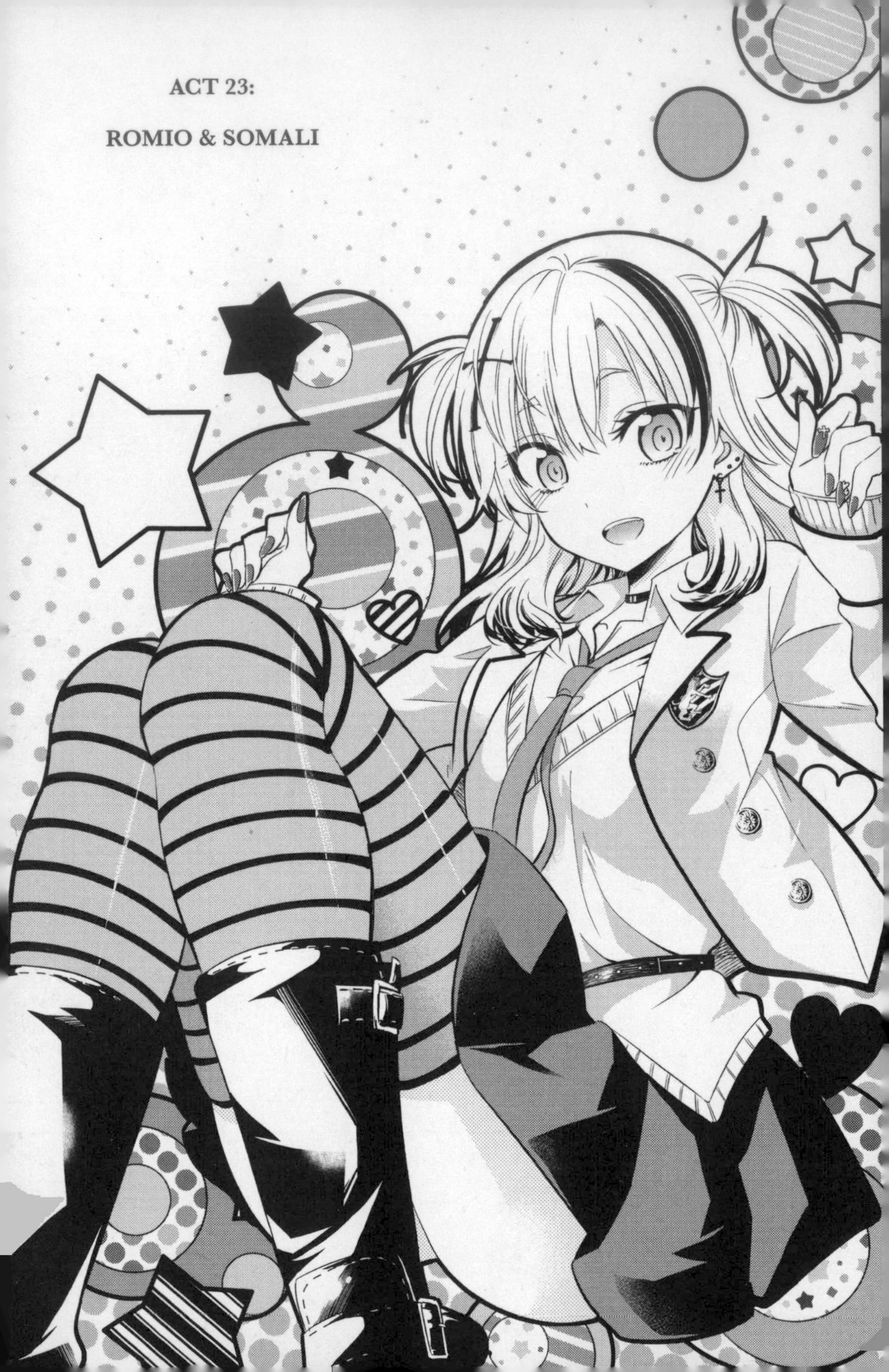

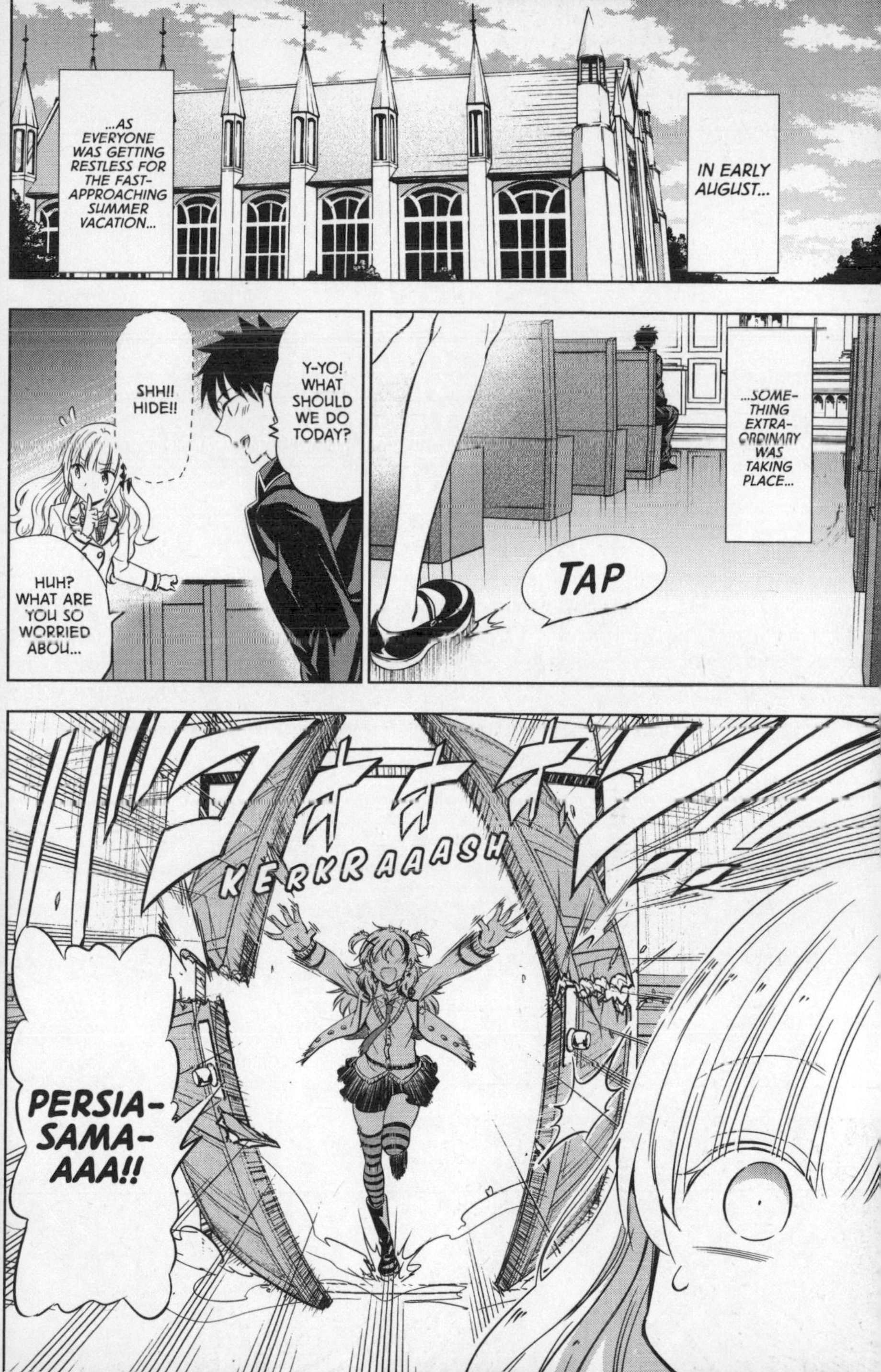
IN EARLY AUGUST...
...AS EVERYONE WAS GETTING RESTLESS FOR THE FAST-APPROACHING SUMMER VACATION...
...SOMETHING EXTRAORDINARY WAS TAKING PLACE...
TAP
Y-YO! WHAT SHOULD WE DO TODAY?
SHH!! HIDE!!
HUH? WHAT ARE YOU SO WORRIED ABOU...
KERKRAAAASH
PERSIA-SAMA-AAA!!

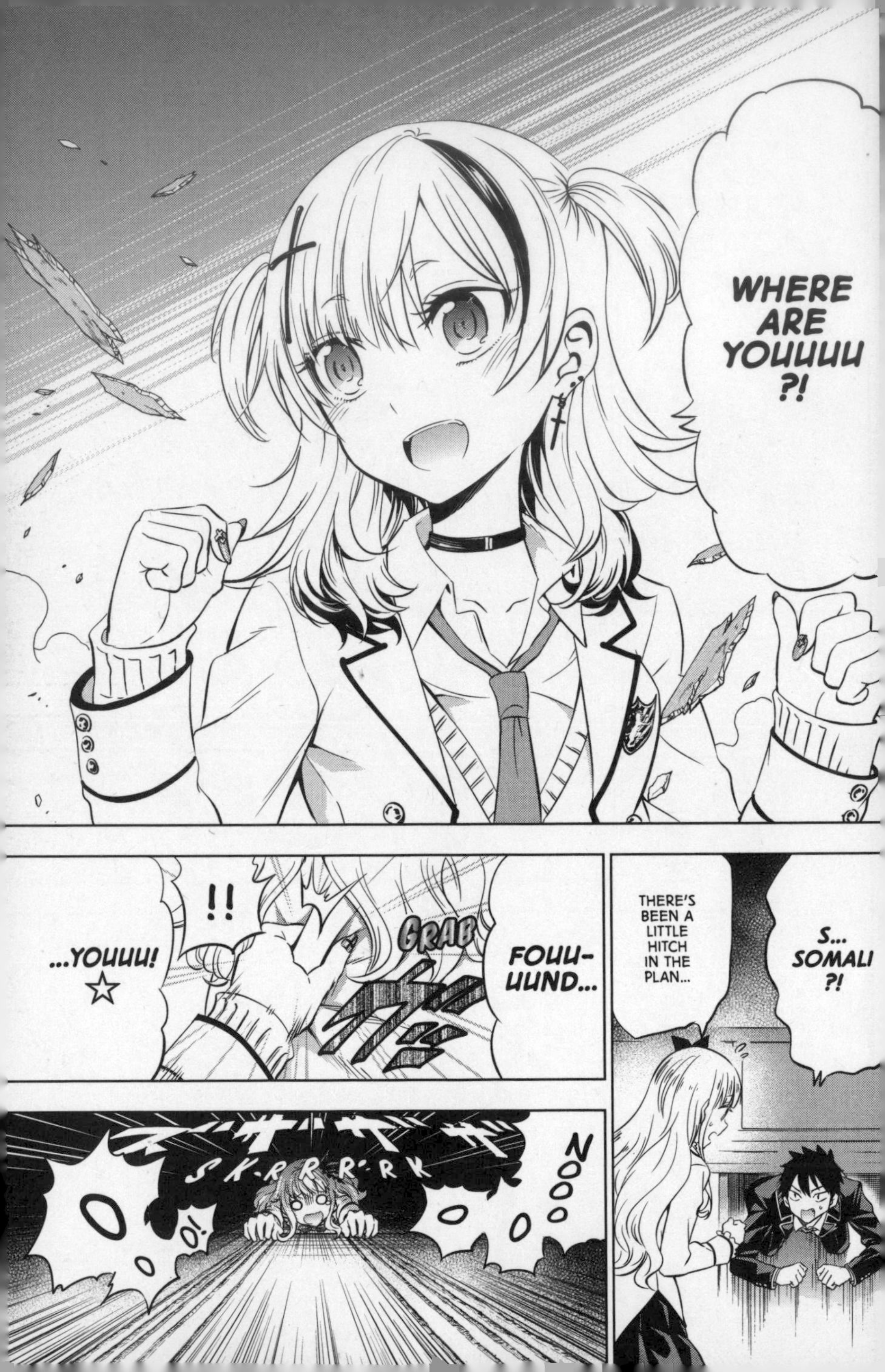
WHERE ARE YOUUUU ?!
S... SOMALI ?!
THERE'S BEEN A LITTLE HITCH IN THE PLAN...
FOUU-UUND...
GRAB
!!
...YOUUU! ☆
NOOOO
SKRRR-RK
O O O!

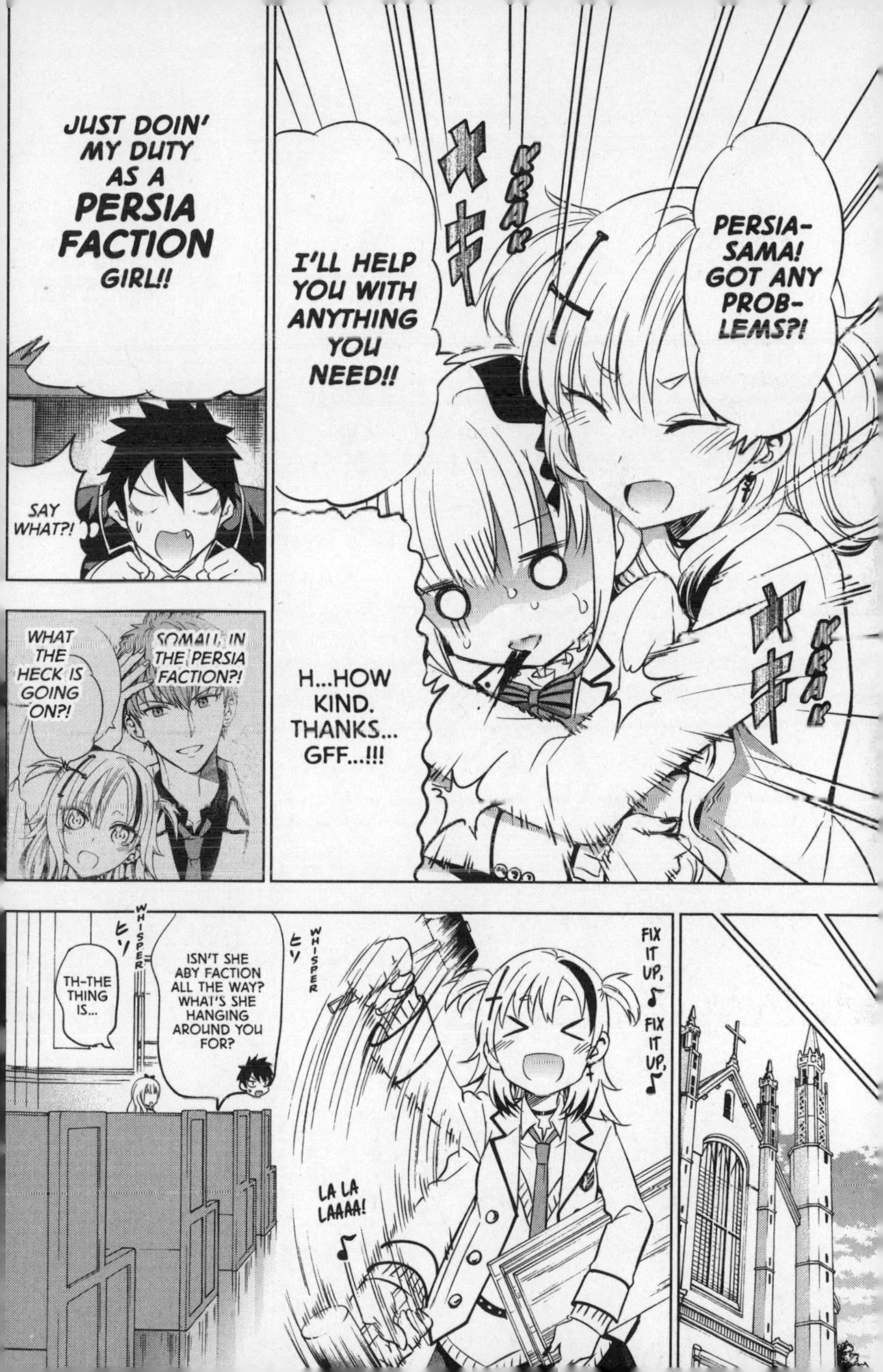
PERSIA-SAMA! GOT ANY PROB-LEMS?!
KRAK
I'LL HELP YOU WITH ANYTHING YOU NEED!!
KRAK
H...HOW KIND. THANKS... GFF...!!!
JUST DOIN' MY DUTY AS A PERSIA FACTION GIRL!!
SAY WHAT?!
SOMALI, IN THE PERSIA FACTION?!
WHAT THE HECK IS GOING ON?!
FIX IT UP, FIX IT UP,
LA LA LAAAA!
WHISPER
ISN'T SHE ABY FACTION ALL THE WAY? WHAT'S SHE HANGING AROUND YOU FOR?
WHISPER
TH-THE THING IS...

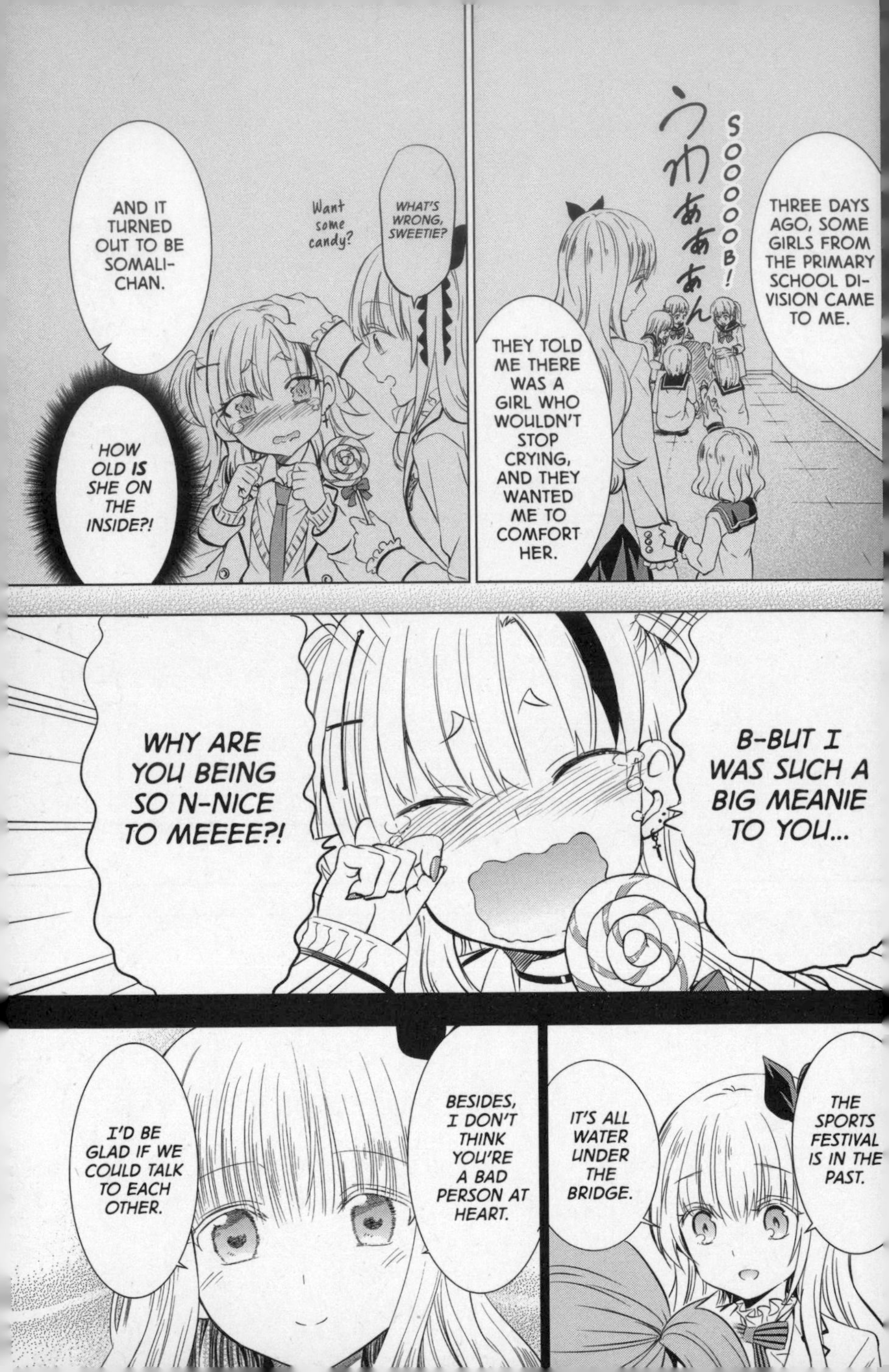
THREE DAYS AGO, SOME GIRLS FROM THE PRIMARY SCHOOL DIVISION CAME TO ME.
SOOOOOB!
うわあああん
THEY TOLD ME THERE WAS A GIRL WHO WOULDN'T STOP CRYING, AND THEY WANTED ME TO COMFORT HER.
WHAT'S WRONG, SWEETIE?
Want some candy?
AND IT TURNED OUT TO BE SOMALI-CHAN.
HOW OLD IS SHE ON THE INSIDE?!
B-BUT I WAS SUCH A BIG MEANIE TO YOU...
WHY ARE YOU BEING SO N-NICE TO MEEEE?!
THE SPORTS FESTIVAL IS IN THE PAST.
IT'S ALL WATER UNDER THE BRIDGE.
BESIDES, I DON'T THINK YOU'RE A BAD PERSON AT HEART.
I'D BE GLAD IF WE COULD TALK TO EACH OTHER.

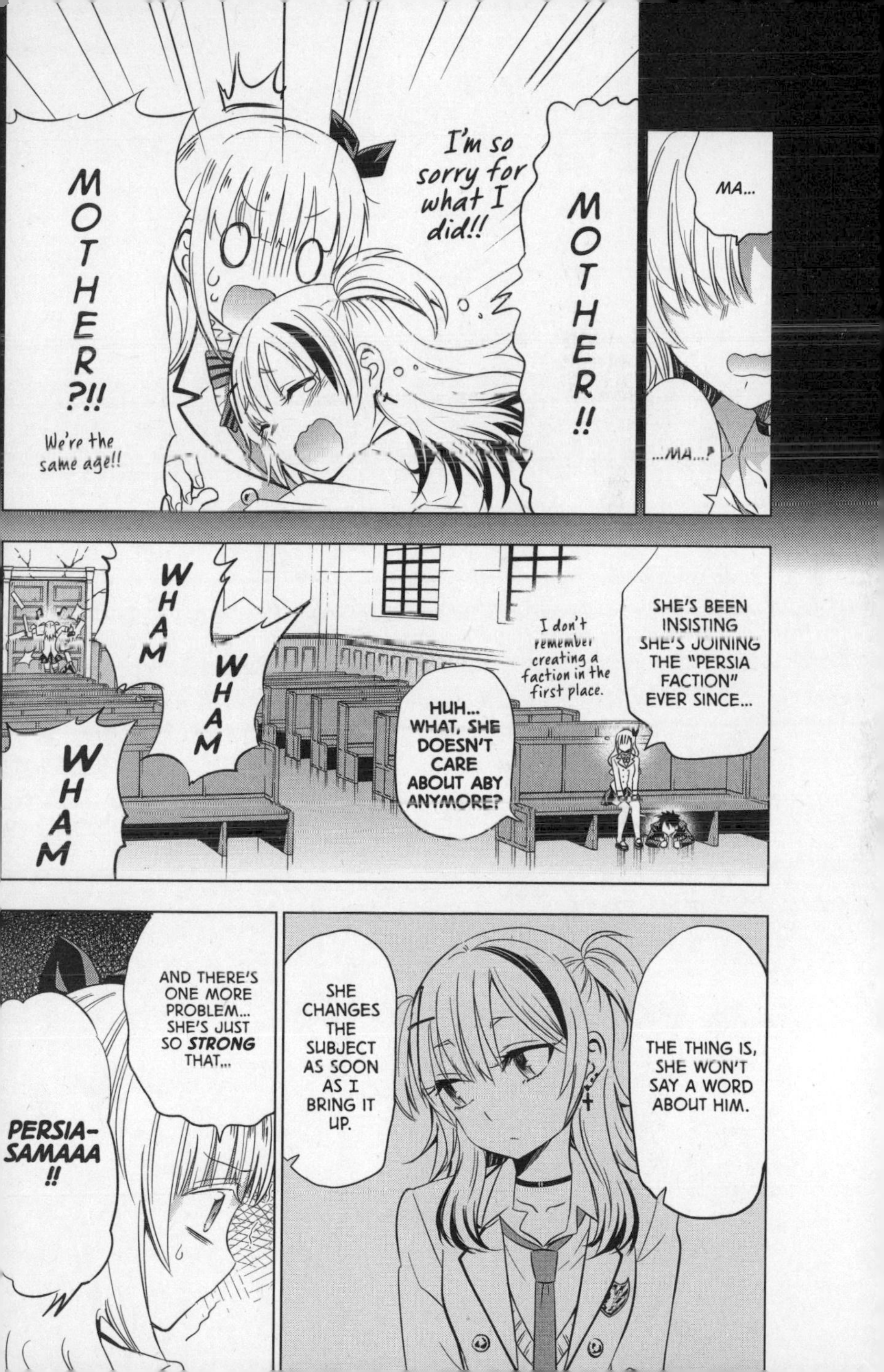
MA...
...MA...?
MOTHER!!
I'm so sorry for what I did!!
MOTHER?!!
We're the same age!!
SHE'S BEEN INSISTING SHE'S JOINING THE "PERSIA FACTION" EVER SINCE...
I don't remember creating a faction in the first place.
HUH... WHAT, SHE DOESN'T CARE ABOUT ABY ANYMORE?
WHAM
WHAM
WHAM
THE THING IS, SHE WON'T SAY A WORD ABOUT HIM.
SHE CHANGES THE SUBJECT AS SOON AS I BRING IT UP.
AND THERE'S ONE MORE PROBLEM... SHE'S JUST SO STRONG THAT...
PERSIA-SAMAAA!!

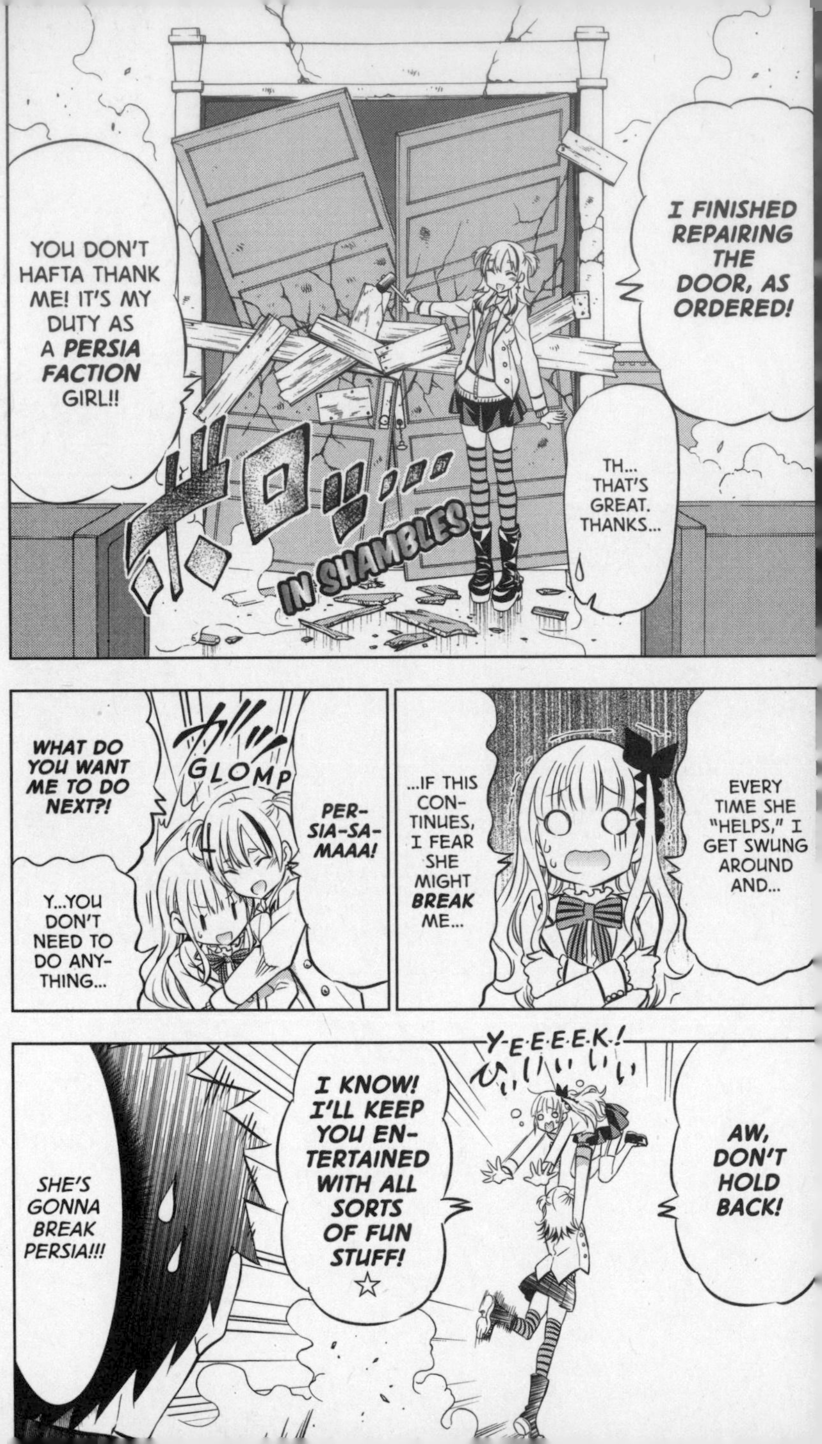
I FINISHED REPAIRING THE DOOR, AS ORDERED!
TH... THAT'S GREAT. THANKS...
YOU DON'T HAFTA THANK ME! IT'S MY DUTY AS A **PERSIA FACTION** GIRL!!
IN SHAMBLES
EVERY TIME SHE "HELPS," I GET SWUNG AROUND AND...
...IF THIS CONTINUES, I FEAR SHE MIGHT **BREAK** ME...
GLOMP
PER-SIA-SA-MAAA!
WHAT DO YOU WANT ME TO DO NEXT?!
Y...YOU DON'T NEED TO DO ANY-THING...
AW, DON'T HOLD BACK!
Y-E-E-E-K!
I KNOW! I'LL KEEP YOU EN-TERTAINED WITH ALL SORTS OF FUN STUFF! ☆
SHE'S GONNA BREAK PERSIA!!!

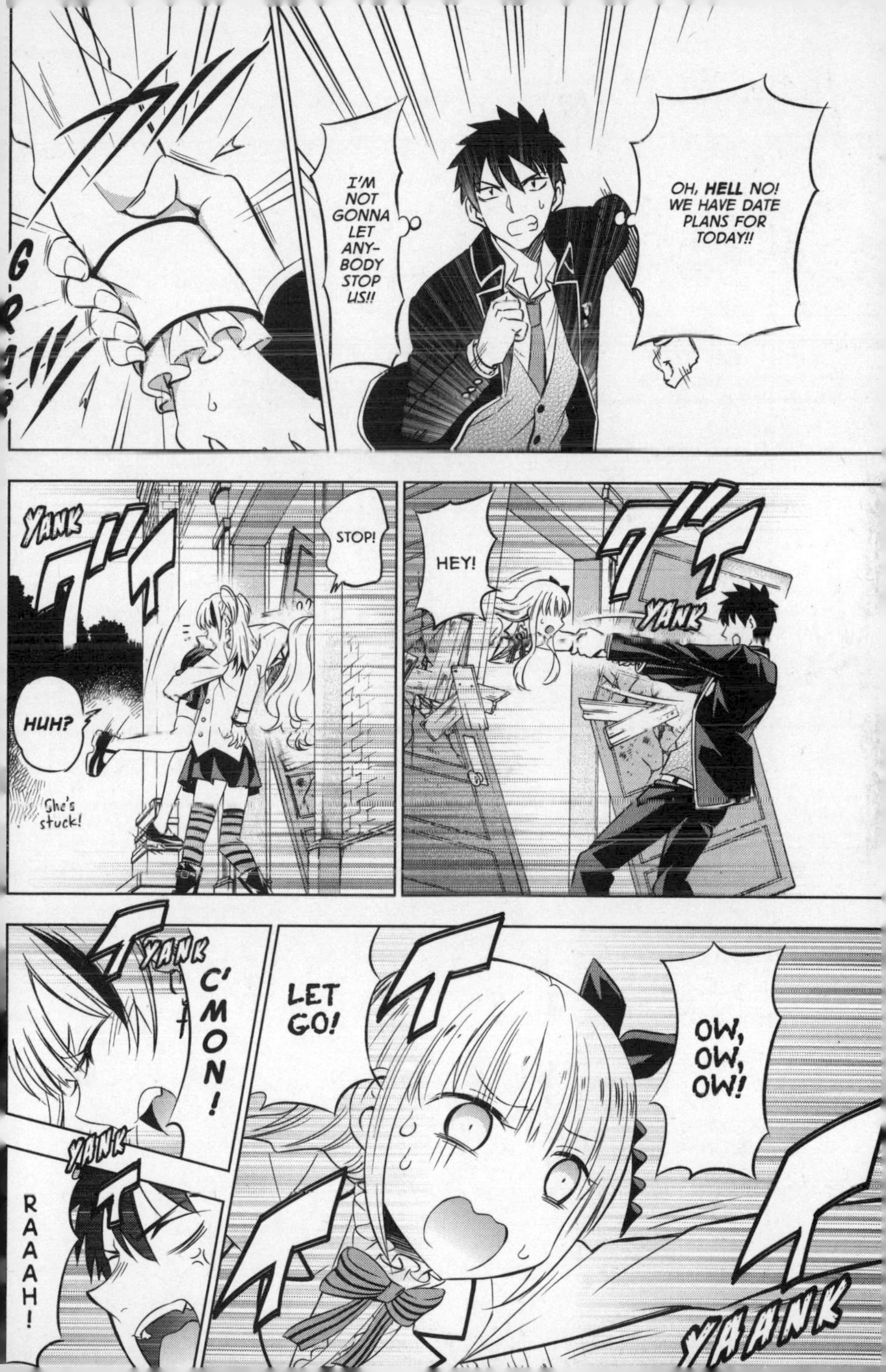
OH, HELL NO! WE HAVE DATE PLANS FOR TODAY!!
I'M NOT GONNA LET ANY-BODY STOP US!!
HEY!
YANK
STOP!
YANK
HUH?
She's stuck!
OW, OW, OW!
LET GO!
YAANK
YANK
C'MON!
YANK
RAAAAH!

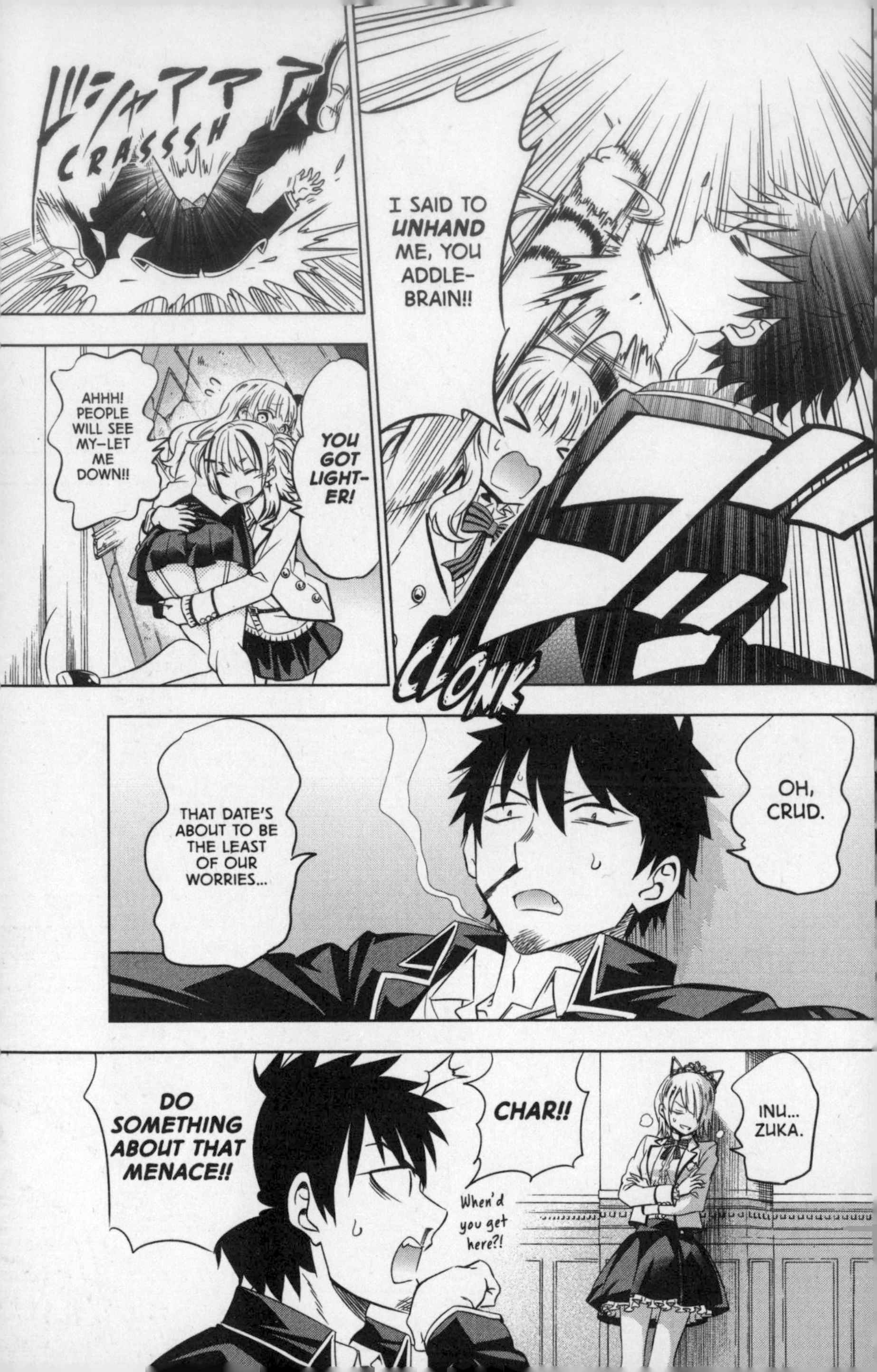
I SAID TO UNHAND ME, YOU ADDLE-BRAIN!!
CLONK
ドシャアアア
CRASSSH
YOU GOT LIGHTER!
AHHH! PEOPLE WILL SEE MY—LET ME DOWN!!
OH, CRUD.
THAT DATE'S ABOUT TO BE THE LEAST OF OUR WORRIES...
INU... ZUKA.
CHAR!!
DO SOMETHING ABOUT THAT MENACE!!
When'd you get here?!

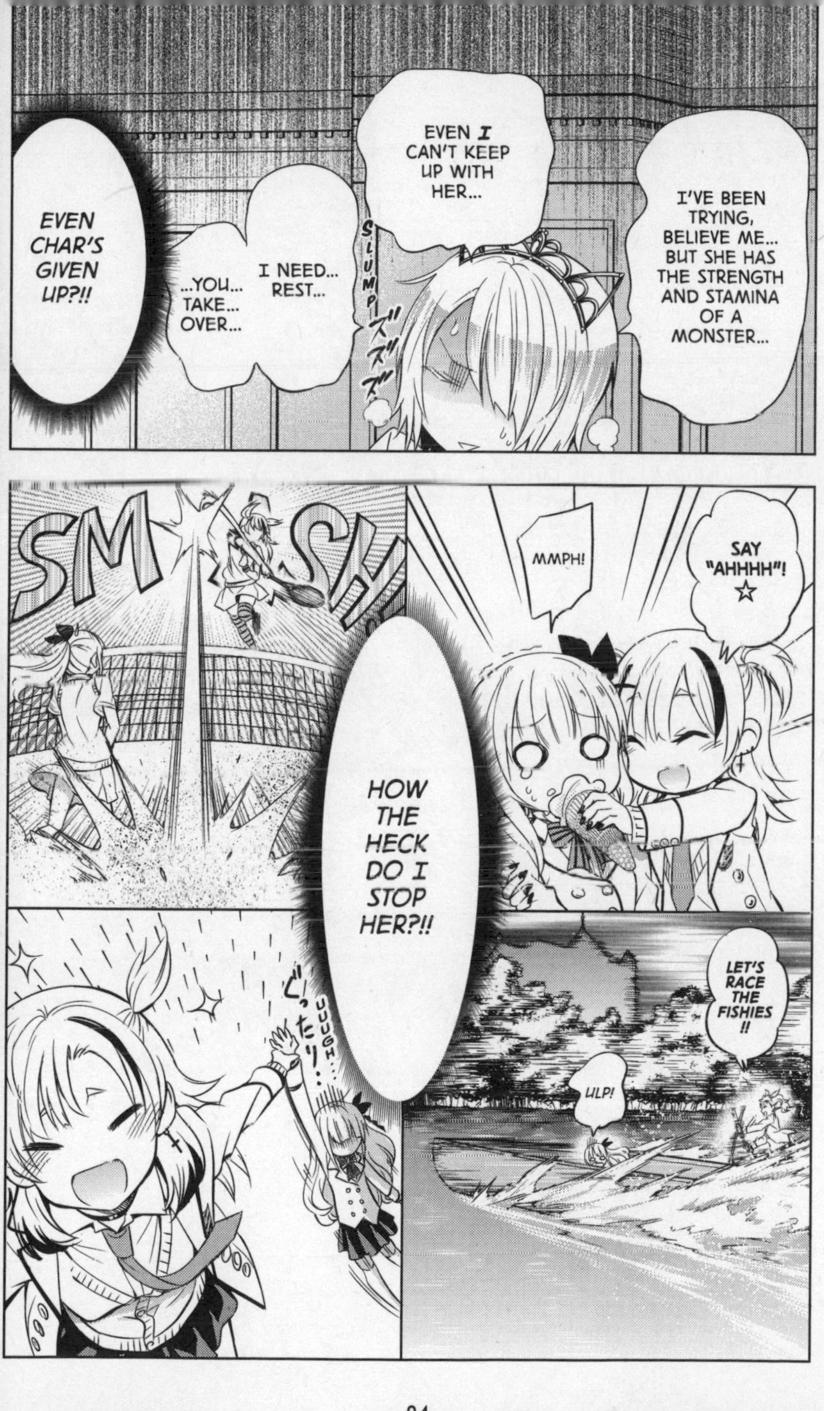
I'VE BEEN TRYING, BELIEVE ME... BUT SHE HAS THE STRENGTH AND STAMINA OF A MONSTER...
EVEN I CAN'T KEEP UP WITH HER...
SLUMP
ズズズ
I NEED... REST...
...YOU... TAKE... OVER...
EVEN CHAR'S GIVEN UP?!!
SAY "AHHHH"! ☆
MMPH!
SM SH
HOW THE HECK DO I STOP HER?!!
LET'S RACE THE FISHIES!!
ULP!
ぐったり…
UUUGH…

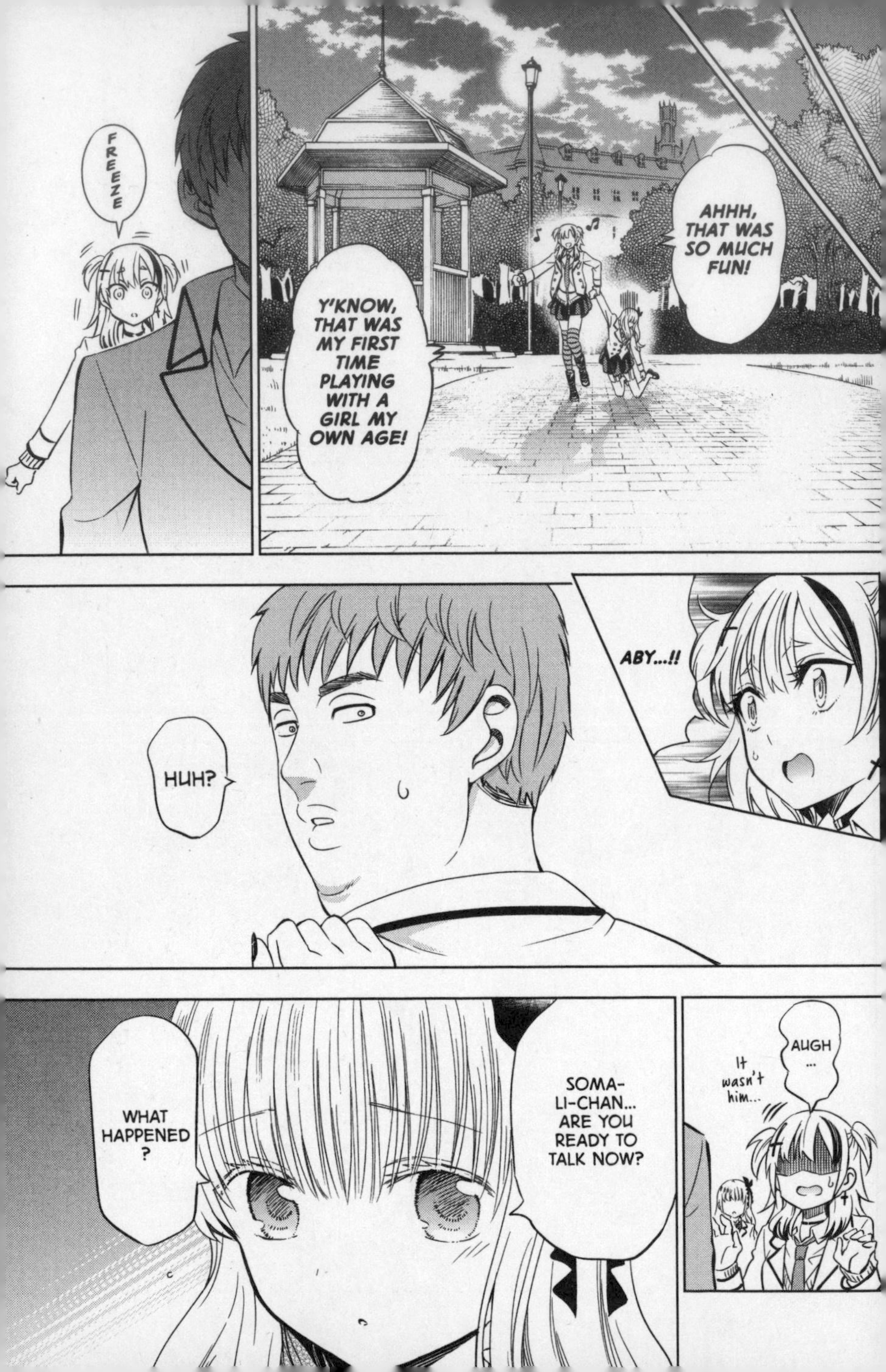
AHHH, THAT WAS SO MUCH FUN!
Y'KNOW, THAT WAS MY FIRST TIME PLAYING WITH A GIRL MY OWN AGE!
FREEZE
ABY...!!
HUH?
AUGH...
It wasn't him...
SOMA-LI-CHAN... ARE YOU READY TO TALK NOW?
WHAT HAPPENED?

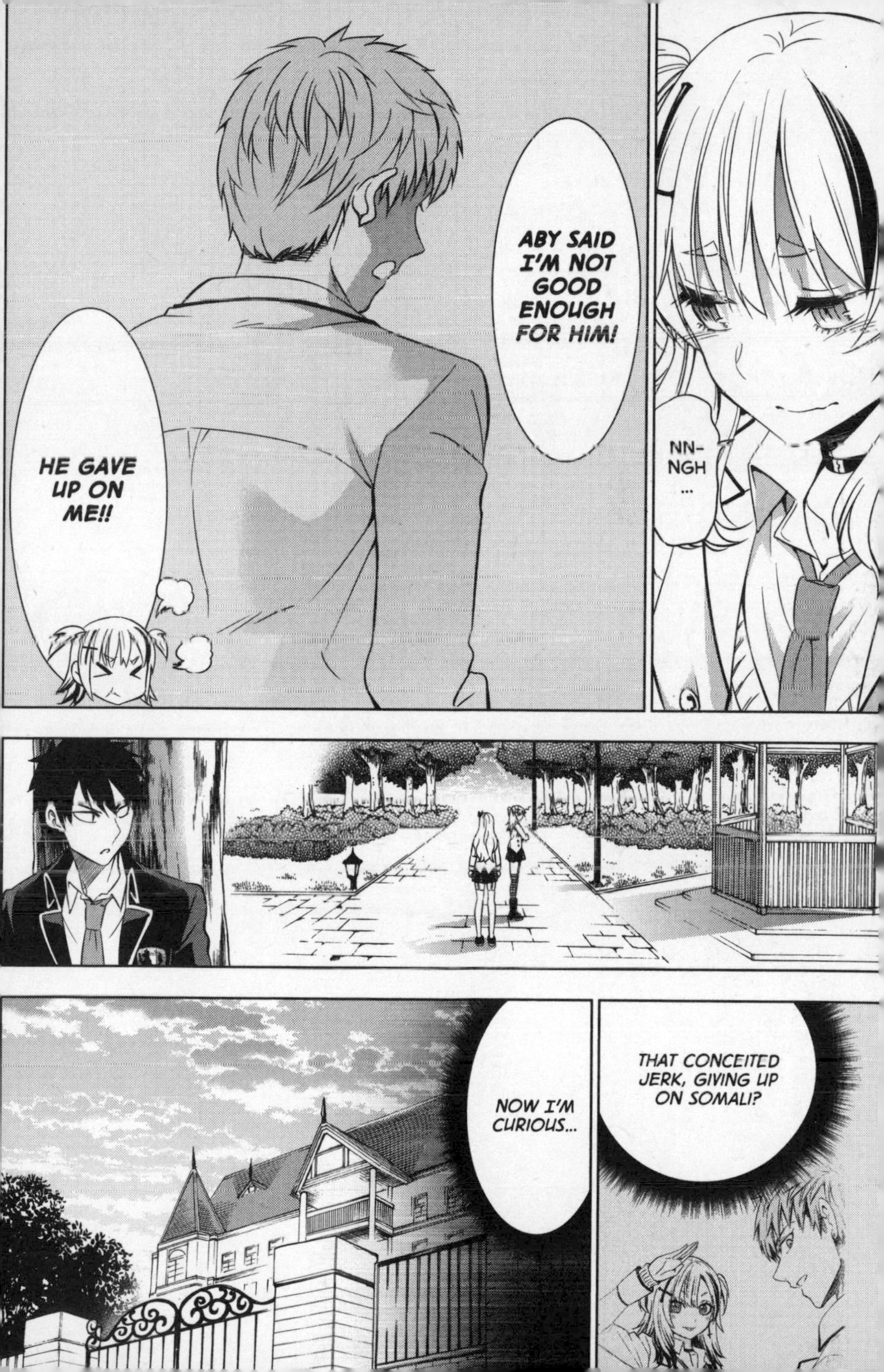
NN-NGH ...
ABY SAID I'M NOT GOOD ENOUGH FOR HIM!
HE GAVE UP ON ME!!
THAT CONCEITED JERK, GIVING UP ON SOMALI?
NOW I'M CURIOUS...

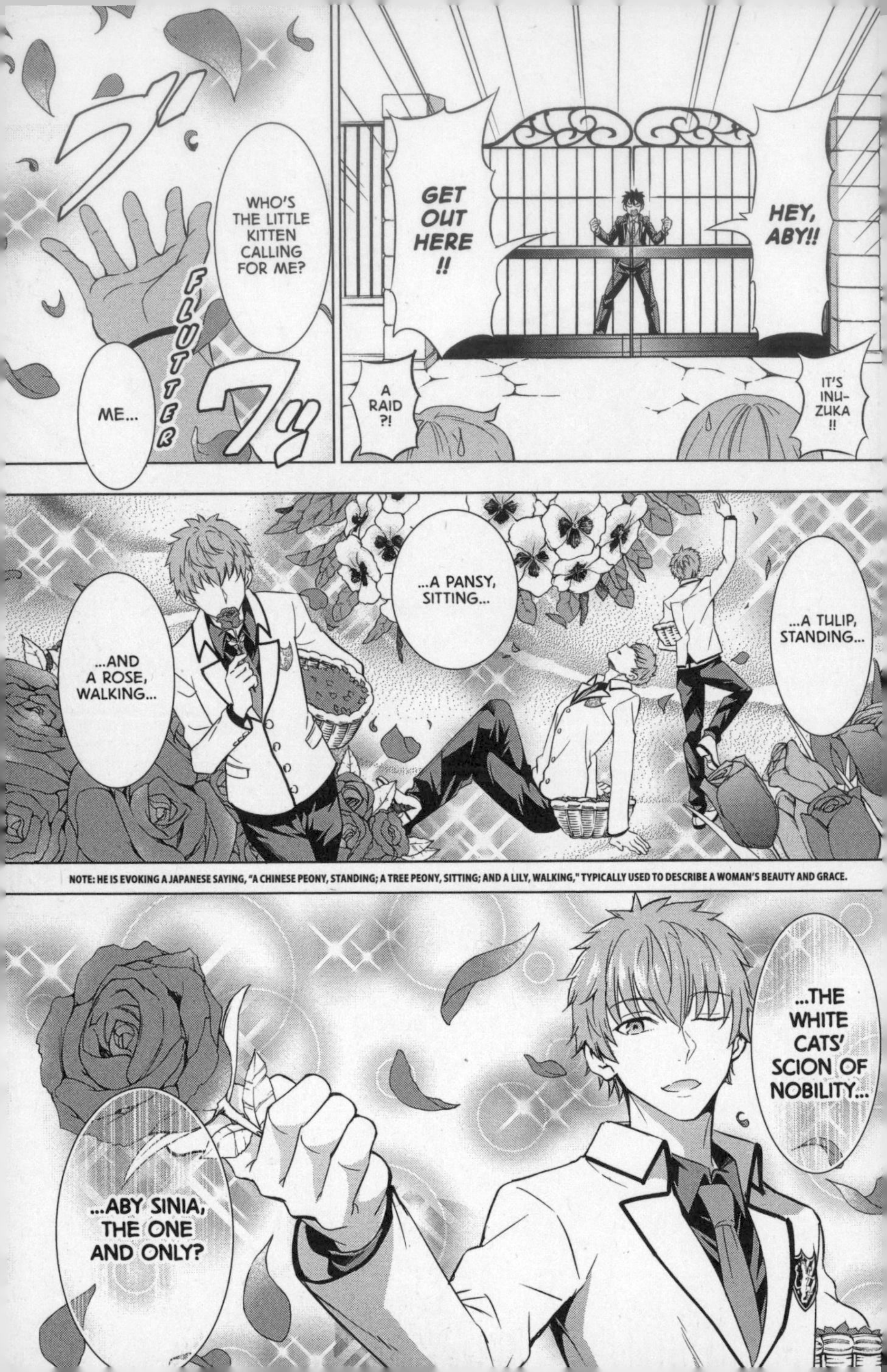
HEY, ABY!!
GET OUT HERE!!
IT'S INUZUKA!!
A RAID?!
WHO'S THE LITTLE KITTEN CALLING FOR ME?
FLUTTER
ME...
...A TULIP, STANDING...
...A PANSY, SITTING...
...AND A ROSE, WALKING...
...THE WHITE CATS' SCION OF NOBILITY...
...ABY SINIA, THE ONE AND ONLY?

NOTE: HE IS EVOKING A JAPANESE SAYING, "A CHINESE PEONY, STANDING; A TREE PEONY, SITTING; AND A LILY, WALKING," TYPICALLY USED TO DESCRIBE A WOMAN'S BEAUTY AND GRACE.

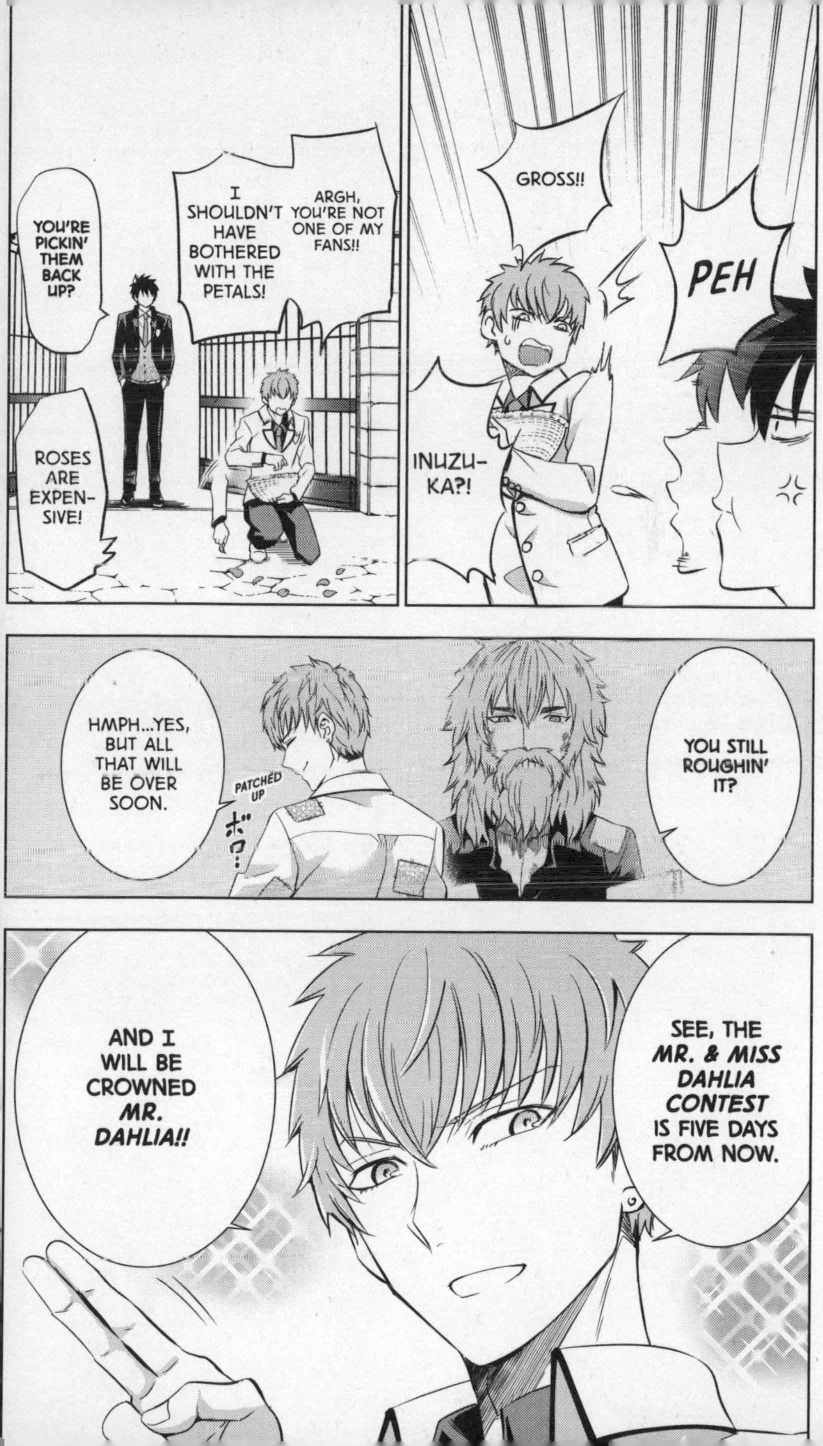
PEH
GROSS!!
INUZUKA?!
ARGH, YOU'RE NOT ONE OF MY FANS!!
I SHOULDN'T HAVE BOTHERED WITH THE PETALS!
YOU'RE PICKIN' THEM BACK UP?
ROSES ARE EXPEN-SIVE!
YOU STILL ROUGHIN' IT?
PATCHED UP
ボロ…
HMPH...YES, BUT ALL THAT WILL BE OVER SOON.
SEE, THE *MR. & MISS DAHLIA CONTEST* IS FIVE DAYS FROM NOW.
AND I WILL BE CROWNED *MR. DAHLIA!!*

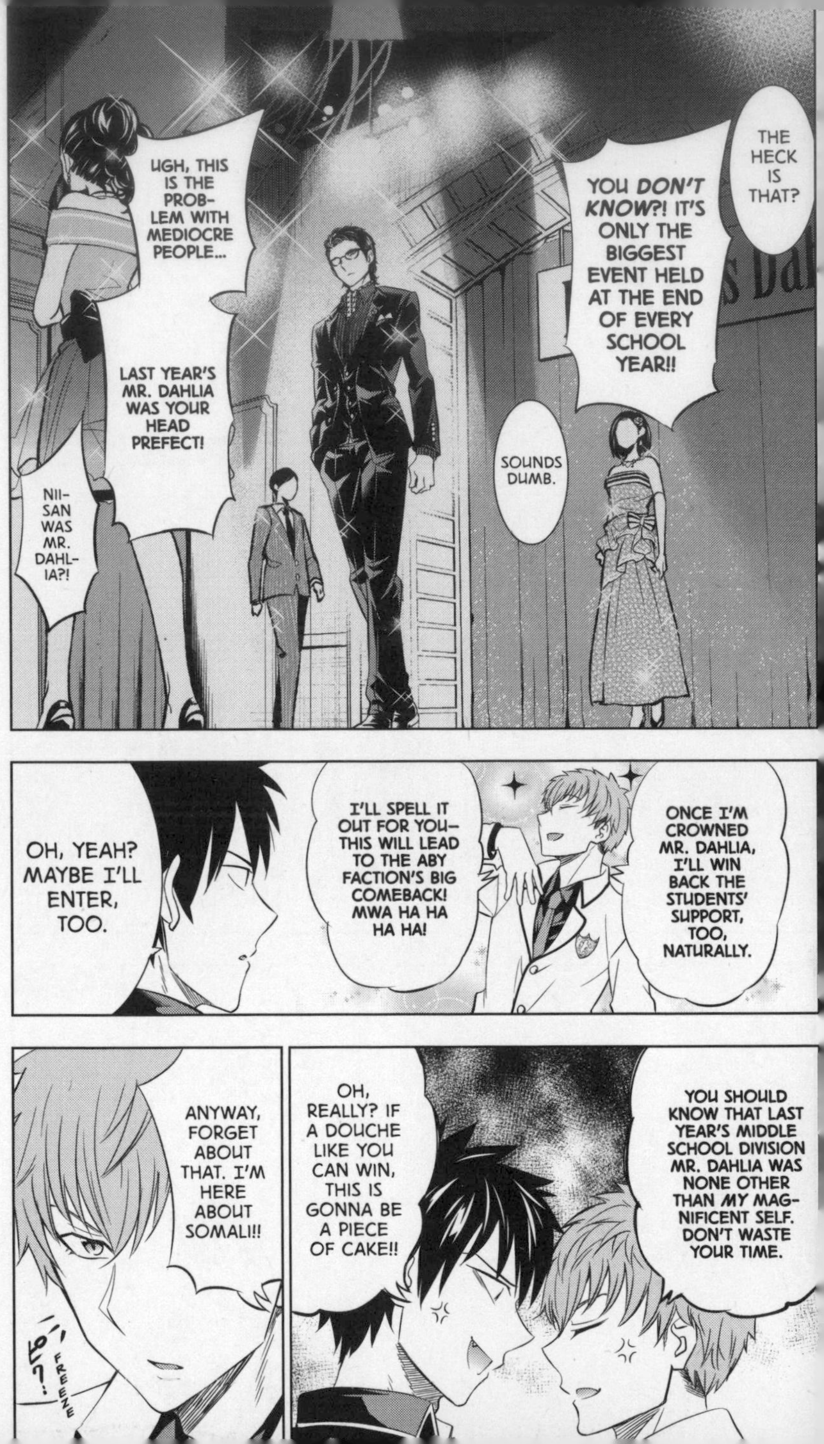
THE HECK IS THAT?
YOU *DON'T KNOW*?! IT'S ONLY THE BIGGEST EVENT HELD AT THE END OF EVERY SCHOOL YEAR!!
SOUNDS DUMB.
UGH, THIS IS THE PROB-LEM WITH MEDIOCRE PEOPLE...
LAST YEAR'S MR. DAHLIA WAS YOUR HEAD PREFECT!
NII-SAN WAS MR. DAHL-IA?!
ONCE I'M CROWNED MR. DAHLIA, I'LL WIN BACK THE STUDENTS' SUPPORT, TOO, NATURALLY.
I'LL SPELL IT OUT FOR YOU— THIS WILL LEAD TO THE ABY FACTION'S BIG COMEBACK! MWA HA HA HA HA!
OH, YEAH? MAYBE I'LL ENTER, TOO.
YOU SHOULD KNOW THAT LAST YEAR'S MIDDLE SCHOOL DIVISION MR. DAHLIA WAS NONE OTHER THAN *MY* MAG-NIFICENT SELF. DON'T WASTE YOUR TIME.
OH, REALLY? IF A DOUCHE LIKE YOU CAN WIN, THIS IS GONNA BE A PIECE OF CAKE!!
ANYWAY, FORGET ABOUT THAT. I'M HERE ABOUT SOMALI!!
FREEZE

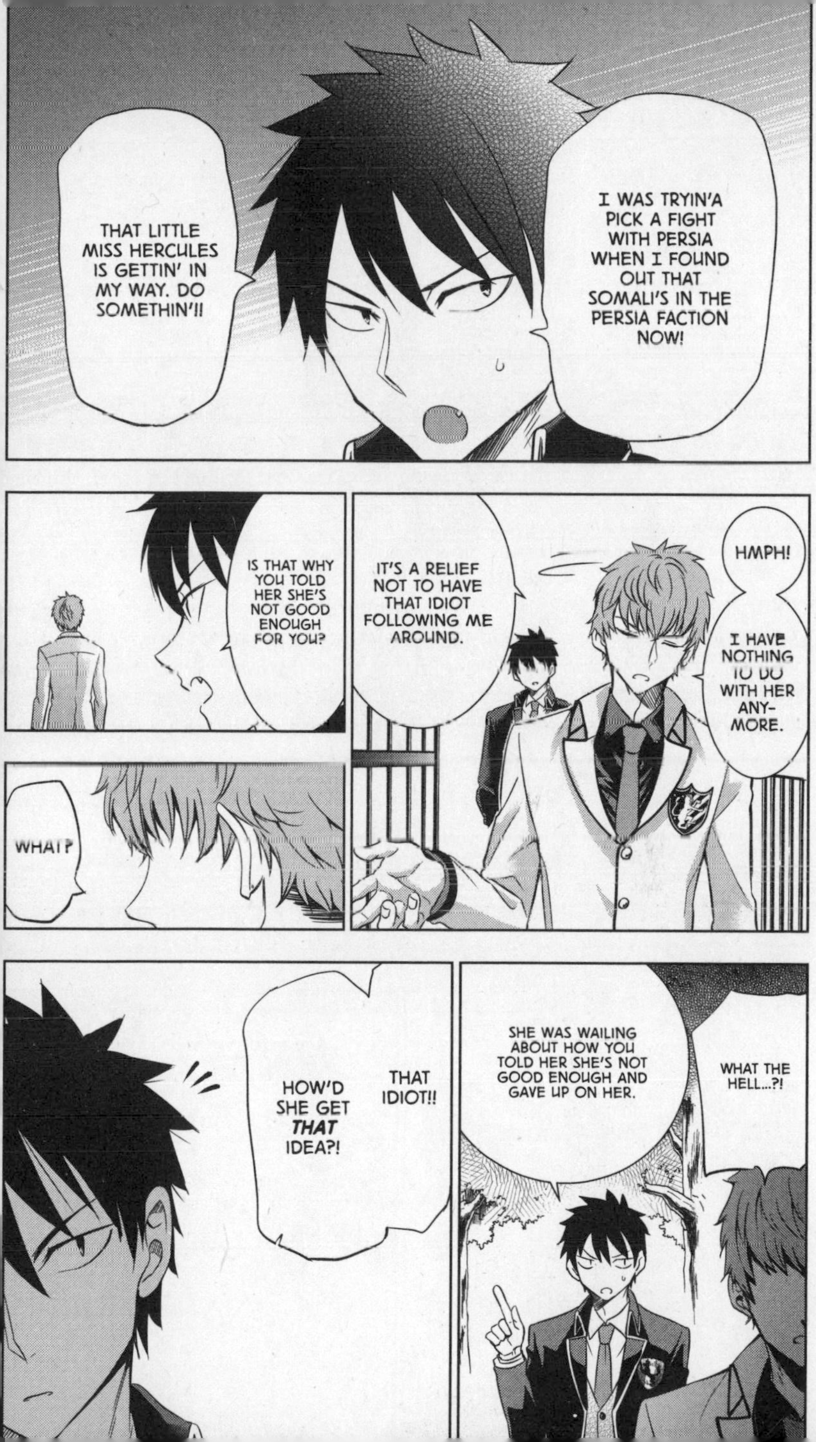
I WAS TRYIN'A PICK A FIGHT WITH PERSIA WHEN I FOUND OUT THAT SOMALI'S IN THE PERSIA FACTION NOW!
THAT LITTLE MISS HERCULES IS GETTIN' IN MY WAY. DO SOMETHIN'!!
HMPH!
I HAVE NOTHING TO DO WITH HER ANYMORE.
IT'S A RELIEF NOT TO HAVE THAT IDIOT FOLLOWING ME AROUND.
IS THAT WHY YOU TOLD HER SHE'S NOT GOOD ENOUGH FOR YOU?
WHAT?
WHAT THE HELL...?!
SHE WAS WAILING ABOUT HOW YOU TOLD HER SHE'S NOT GOOD ENOUGH AND GAVE UP ON HER.
THAT IDIOT!!
HOW'D SHE GET *THAT* IDEA?!

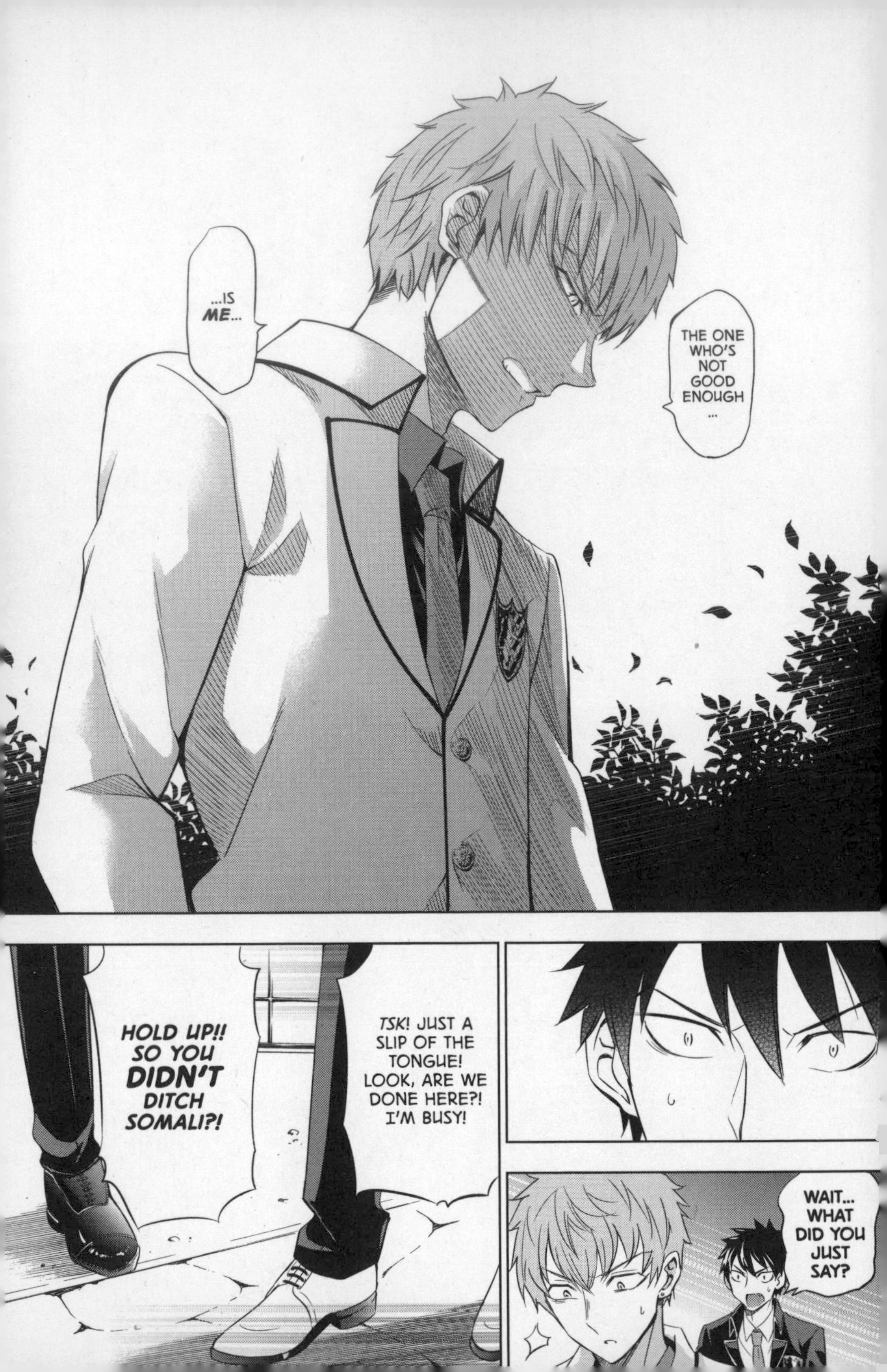
THE ONE WHO'S NOT GOOD ENOUGH ...
...IS ME...
WAIT... WHAT DID YOU JUST SAY?
HOLD UP!! SO YOU DIDN'T DITCH SOMALI?!
TSK! JUST A SLIP OF THE TONGUE! LOOK, ARE WE DONE HERE?! I'M BUSY!

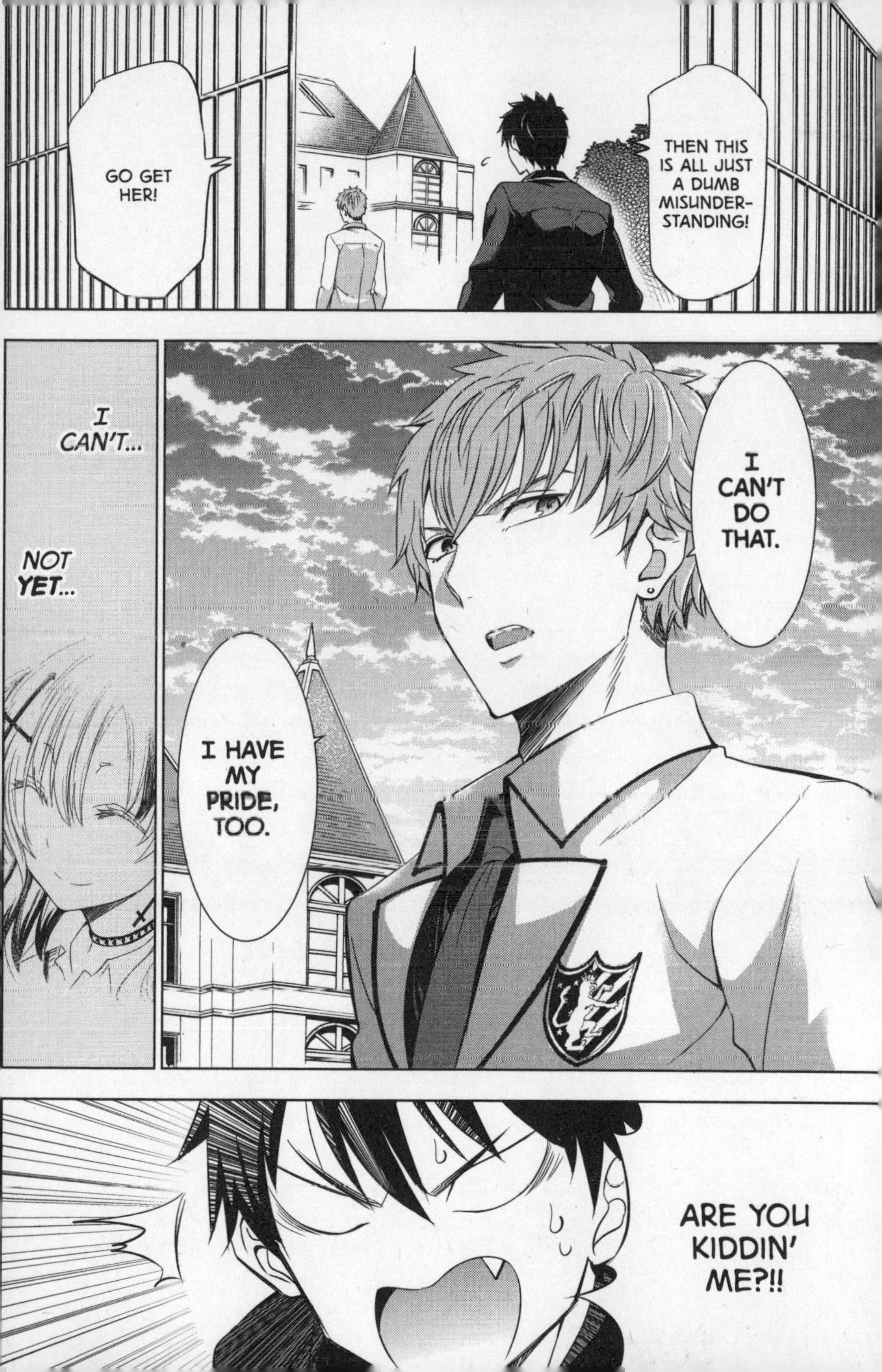
THEN THIS IS ALL JUST A DUMB MISUNDERSTANDING!
GO GET HER!
I CAN'T DO THAT.
I HAVE MY PRIDE, TOO.
I CAN'T...
NOT YET...
ARE YOU KIDDIN' ME?!!

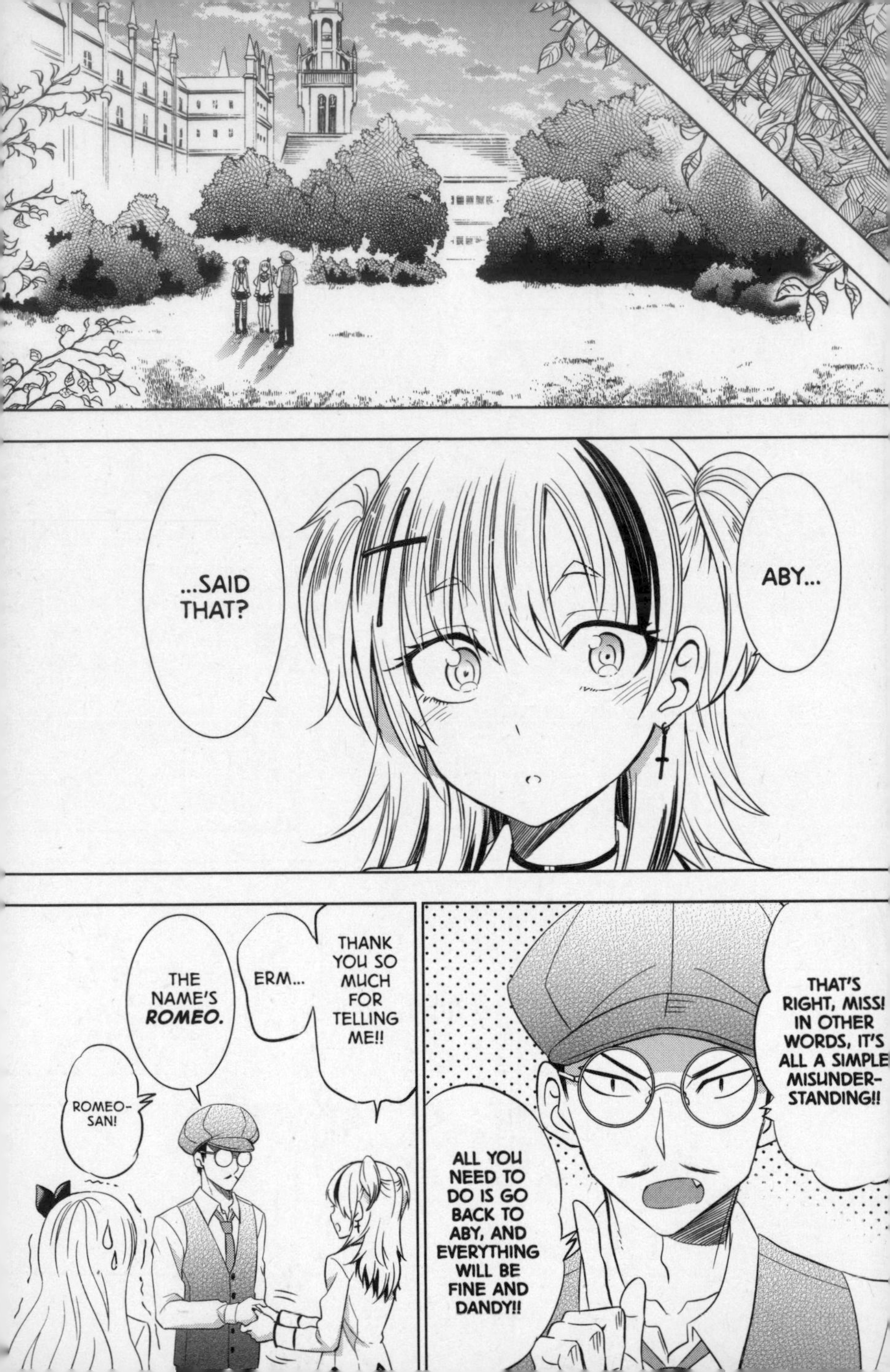
ABY...
...SAID THAT?
THAT'S RIGHT, MISS! IN OTHER WORDS, IT'S ALL A SIMPLE MISUNDER-STANDING!!
ALL YOU NEED TO DO IS GO BACK TO ABY, AND EVERYTHING WILL BE FINE AND DANDY!!
THANK YOU SO MUCH FOR TELLING ME!!
ERM...
THE NAME'S *ROMEO.*
ROMEO-SAN!

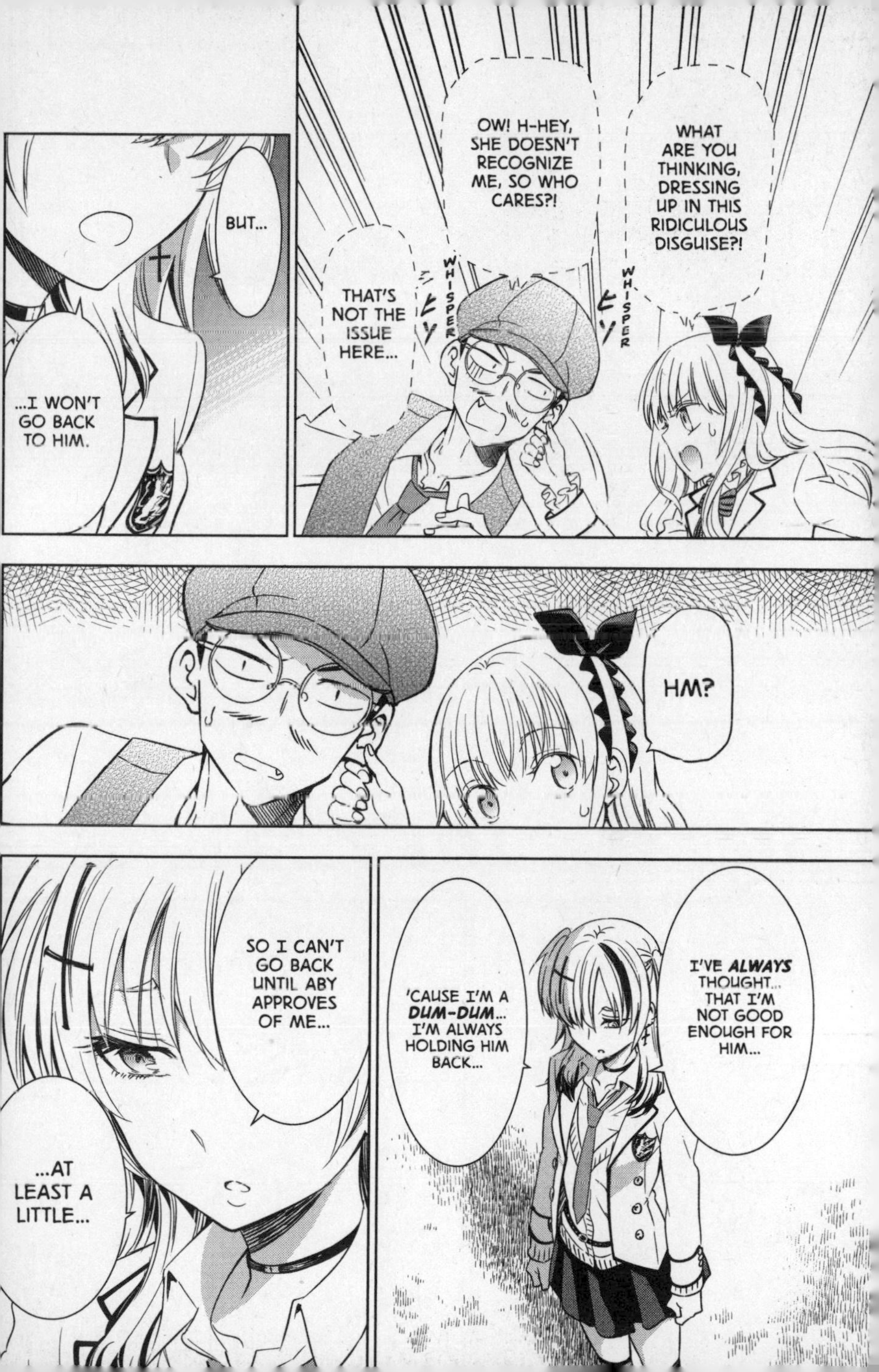
WHAT ARE YOU THINKING, DRESSING UP IN THIS RIDICULOUS DISGUISE?!
WHISPER
OW! H-HEY, SHE DOESN'T RECOGNIZE ME, SO WHO CARES?!
WHISPER
THAT'S NOT THE ISSUE HERE...
BUT...
...I WON'T GO BACK TO HIM.
HM?
I'VE *ALWAYS* THOUGHT... THAT I'M NOT GOOD ENOUGH FOR HIM...
'CAUSE I'M A *DUM-DUM*... I'M ALWAYS HOLDING HIM BACK...
SO I CAN'T GO BACK UNTIL ABY APPROVES OF ME...
...AT LEAST A LITTLE...

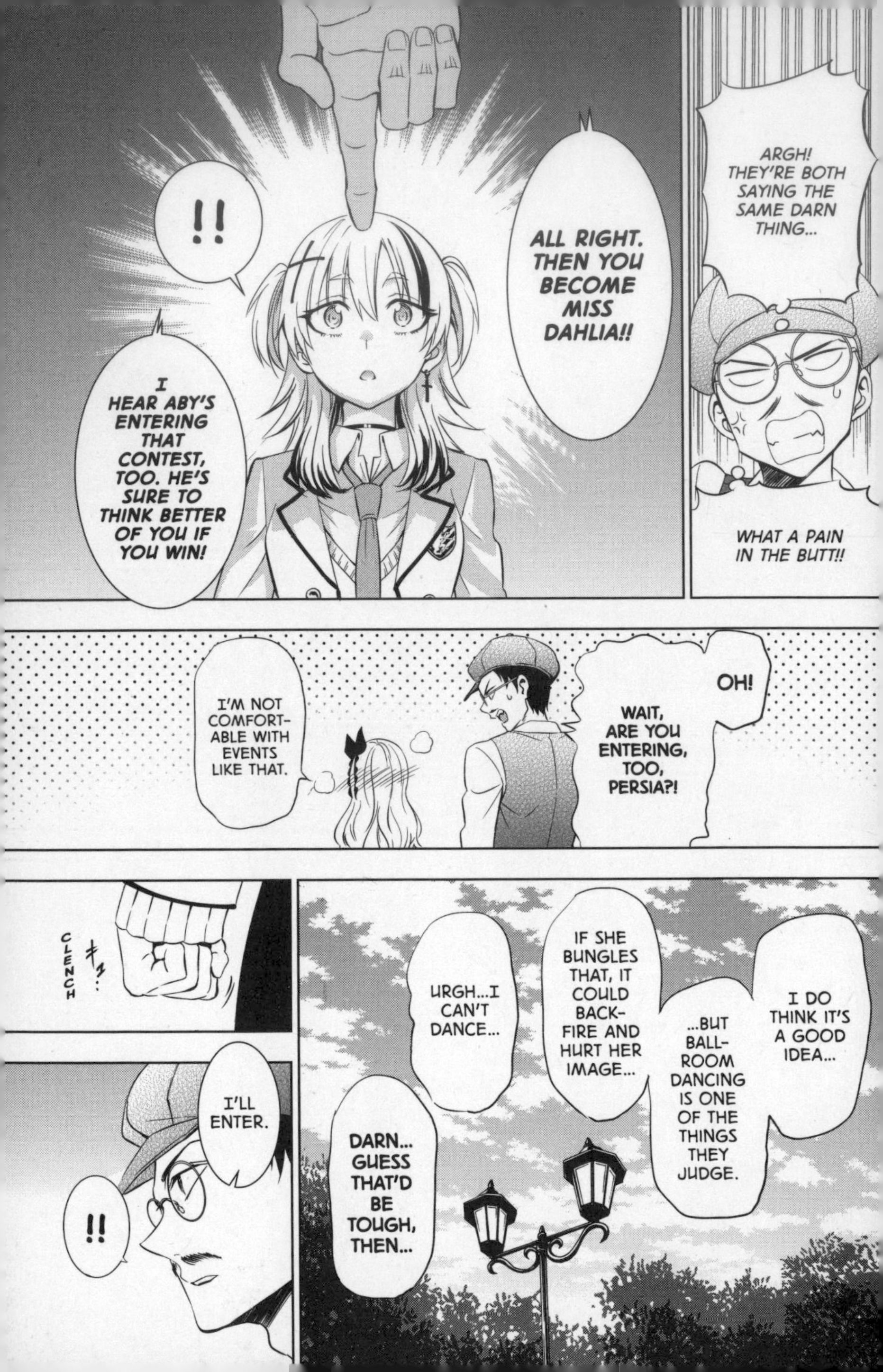
ARGH! THEY'RE BOTH SAYING THE SAME DARN THING...
WHAT A PAIN IN THE BUTT!!
ALL RIGHT. THEN YOU BECOME MISS DAHLIA!!
!!
I HEAR ABY'S ENTERING THAT CONTEST, TOO. HE'S SURE TO THINK BETTER OF YOU IF YOU WIN!
OH!
WAIT, ARE YOU ENTERING, TOO, PERSIA?!
I'M NOT COMFORTABLE WITH EVENTS LIKE THAT.
I DO THINK IT'S A GOOD IDEA...
...BUT BALLROOM DANCING IS ONE OF THE THINGS THEY JUDGE.
IF SHE BUNGLES THAT, IT COULD BACKFIRE AND HURT HER IMAGE...
URGH...I CAN'T DANCE...
DARN... GUESS THAT'D BE TOUGH, THEN...
CLENCH
I'LL ENTER.
!!

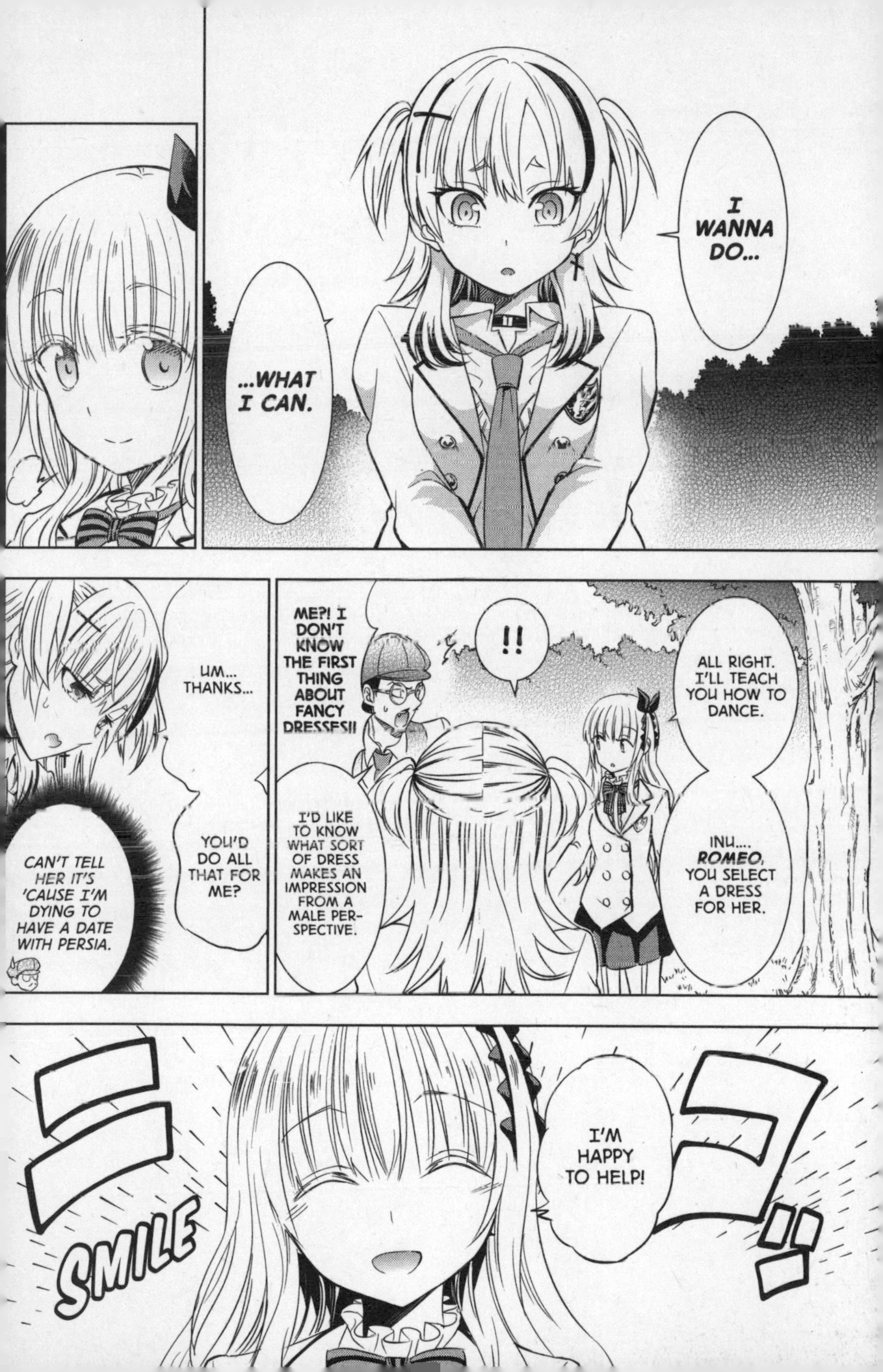
I WANNA DO...
...WHAT I CAN.
ALL RIGHT. I'LL TEACH YOU HOW TO DANCE.
INU.... *ROMEO*, YOU SELECT A DRESS FOR HER.
!!
ME?! I DON'T KNOW THE FIRST THING ABOUT FANCY DRESSES!!
I'D LIKE TO KNOW WHAT SORT OF DRESS MAKES AN IMPRESSION FROM A MALE PERSPECTIVE.
UM... THANKS...
YOU'D DO ALL THAT FOR ME?
CAN'T TELL HER IT'S 'CAUSE I'M DYING TO HAVE A DATE WITH PERSIA.
I'M HAPPY TO HELP!
ニコッ
SMILE

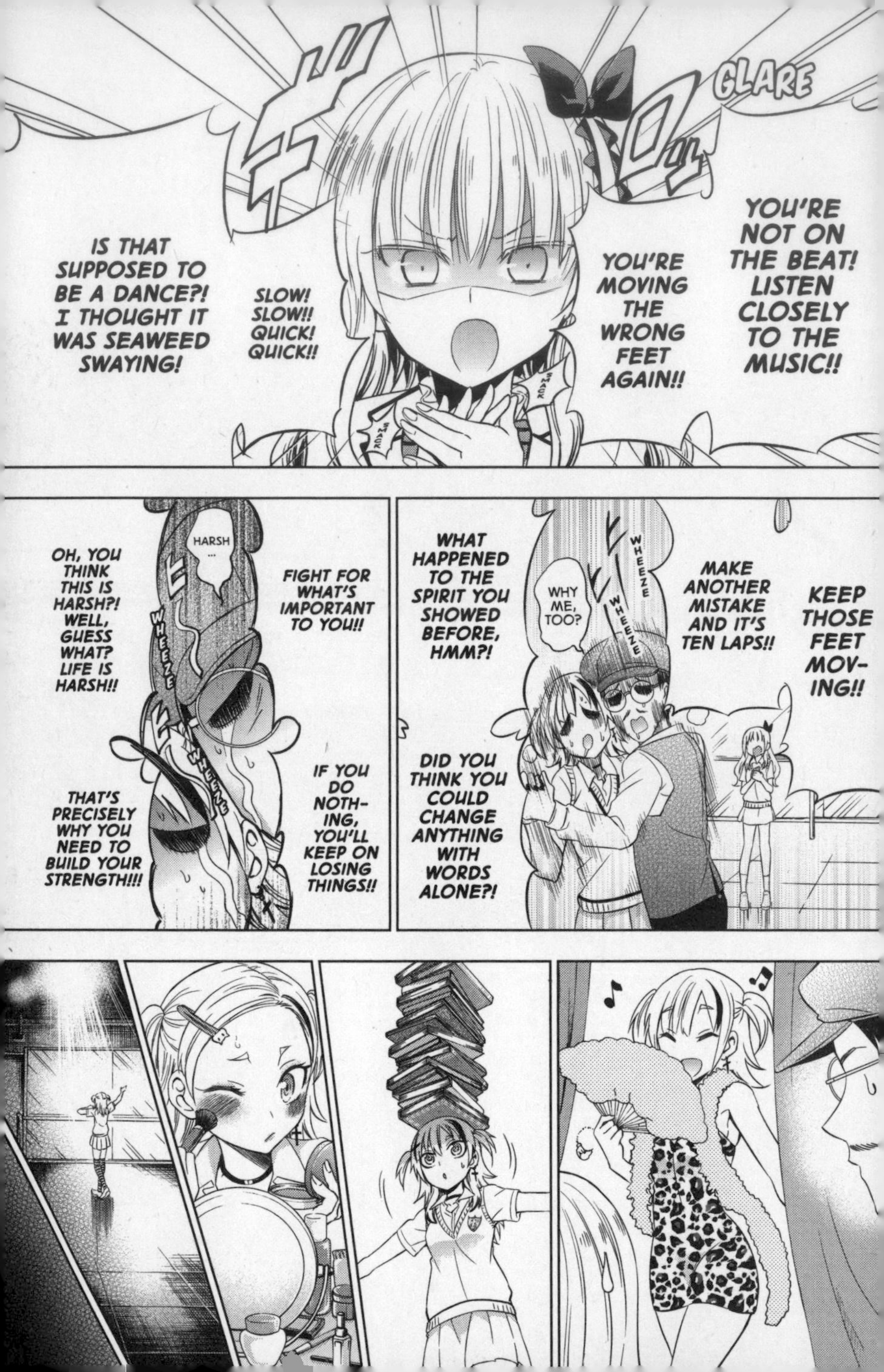

GLARE
YOU'RE NOT ON THE BEAT! LISTEN CLOSELY TO THE MUSIC!!
YOU'RE MOVING THE WRONG FEET AGAIN!!
SLOW! SLOW!! QUICK! QUICK!!
IS THAT SUPPOSED TO BE A DANCE?! I THOUGHT IT WAS SEAWEED SWAYING!
KEEP THOSE FEET MOV-ING!!
MAKE ANOTHER MISTAKE AND IT'S TEN LAPS!!
WHEEZE
WHEEZE
WHY ME, TOO?
WHAT HAPPENED TO THE SPIRIT YOU SHOWED BEFORE, HMM?!
DID YOU THINK YOU COULD CHANGE ANYTHING WITH WORDS ALONE?!
FIGHT FOR WHAT'S IMPORTANT TO YOU!!
HARSH...
OH, YOU THINK THIS IS HARSH?! WELL, GUESS WHAT? LIFE IS HARSH!!
WHEEZE
WHEEZE
IF YOU DO NOTH-ING, YOU'LL KEEP ON LOSING THINGS!!
THAT'S PRECISELY WHY YOU NEED TO BUILD YOUR STRENGTH!!!

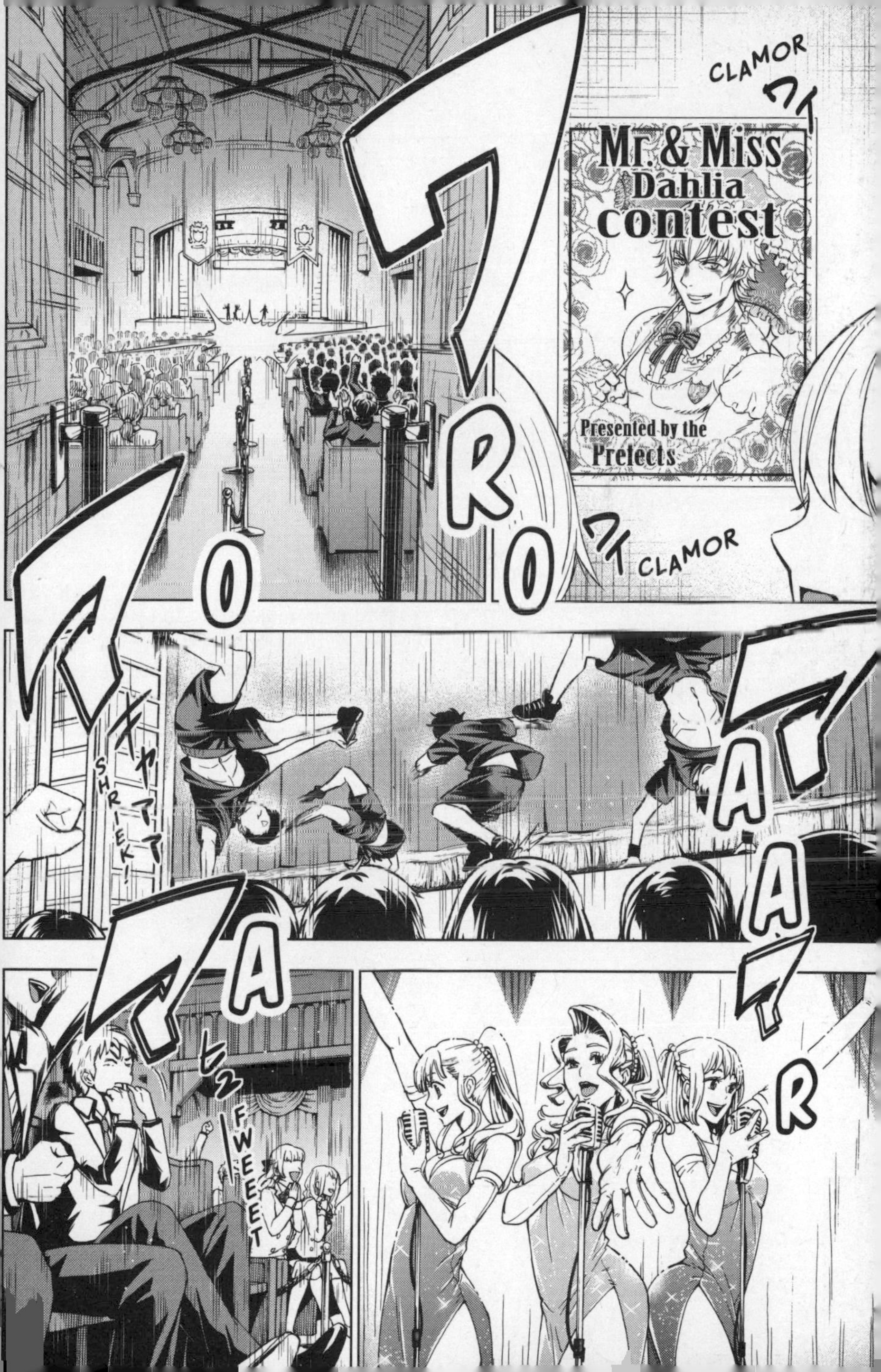
ワイ CLAMOR
Mr. & Miss Dahlia contest
Presented by the Prefects
ワイ CLAMOR
ROOAAAR
キャァァ SHRIEK!
ピュ~ FWEEET

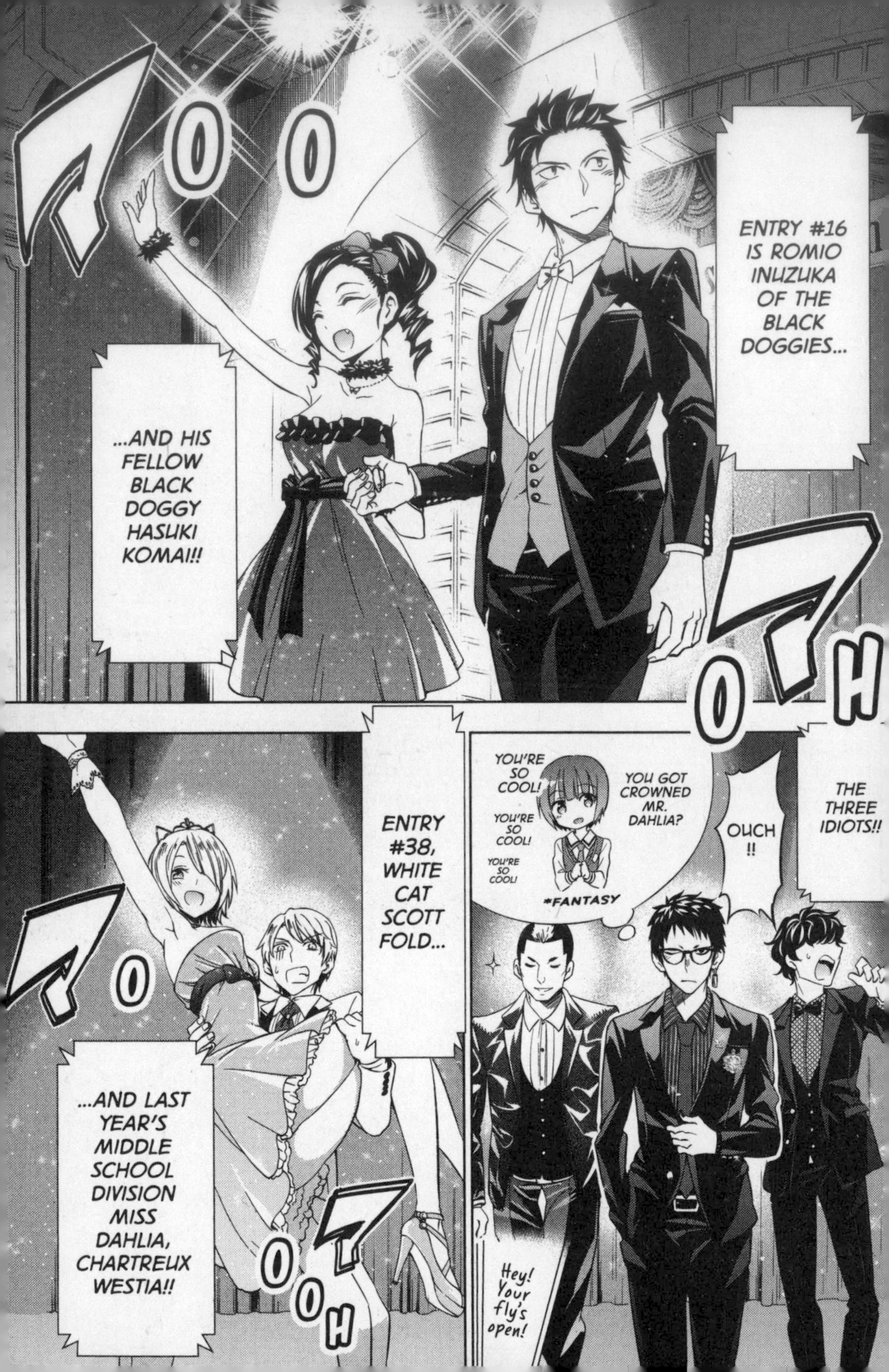
ENTRY #16 IS ROMIO INUZUKA OF THE BLACK DOGGIES...
...AND HIS FELLOW BLACK DOGGY HASUKI KOMAI!!
OOOH
THE THREE IDIOTS!!
OUCH!!
YOU GOT CROWNED MR. DAHLIA?
YOU'RE SO COOL!
YOU'RE SO COOL!
YOU'RE SO COOL!
*FANTASY
Hey! Your fly's open!
ENTRY #38, WHITE CAT SCOTT FOLD...
...AND LAST YEAR'S MIDDLE SCHOOL DIVISION MISS DAHLIA, CHARTREUX WESTIA!!
OOOH

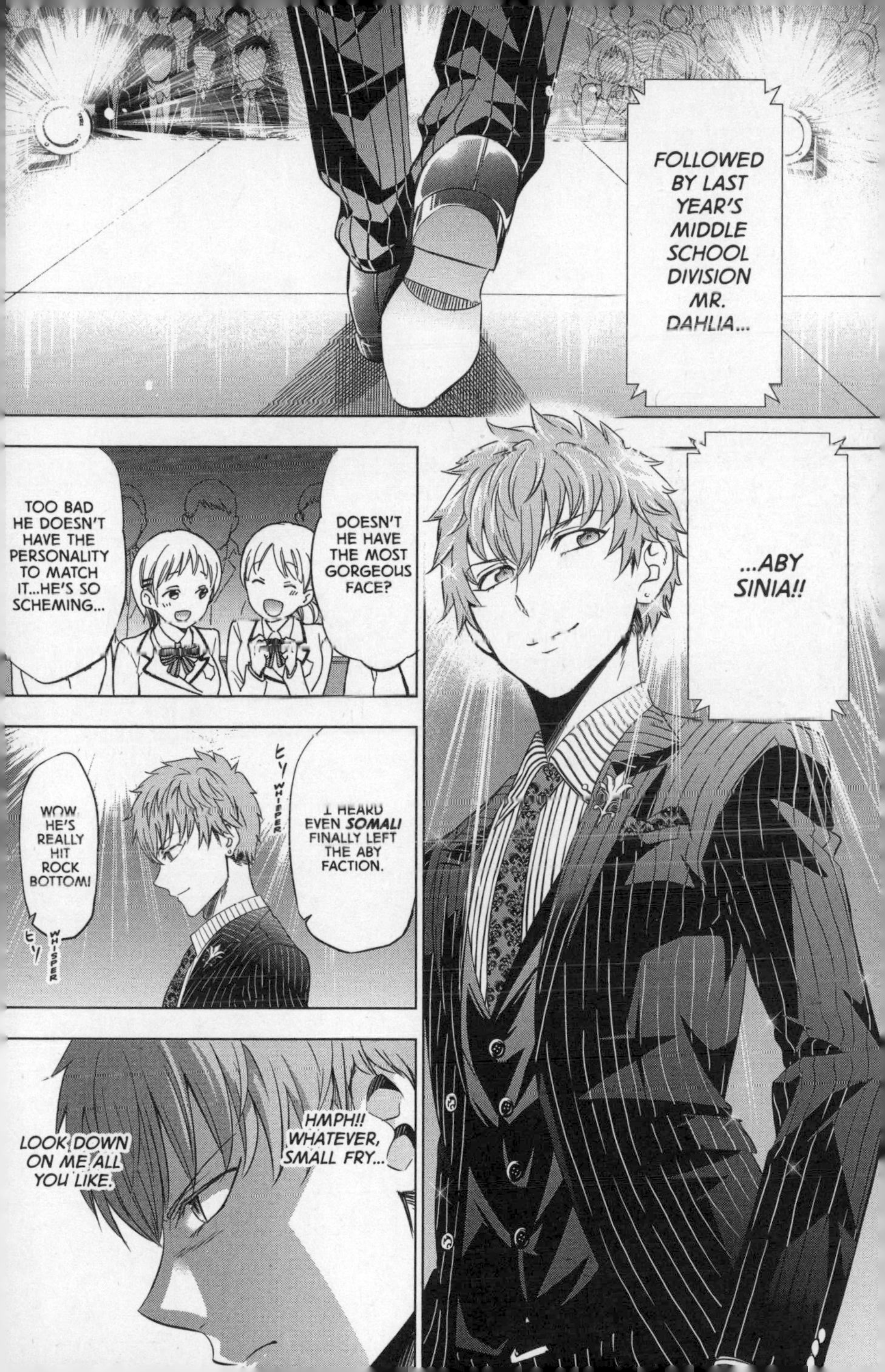
FOLLOWED BY LAST YEAR'S MIDDLE SCHOOL DIVISION MR. DAHLIA...
...ABY SINIA!!
DOESN'T HE HAVE THE MOST GORGEOUS FACE?
TOO BAD HE DOESN'T HAVE THE PERSONALITY TO MATCH IT...HE'S SO SCHEMING...
ヒソ WHISPER
I HEARD EVEN *SOMALI* FINALLY LEFT THE ABY FACTION.
WOW, HE'S REALLY HIT ROCK BOTTOM!
ヒソ WHISPER
HMPH!! WHATEVER, SMALL FRY...
LOOK DOWN ON ME ALL YOU LIKE.

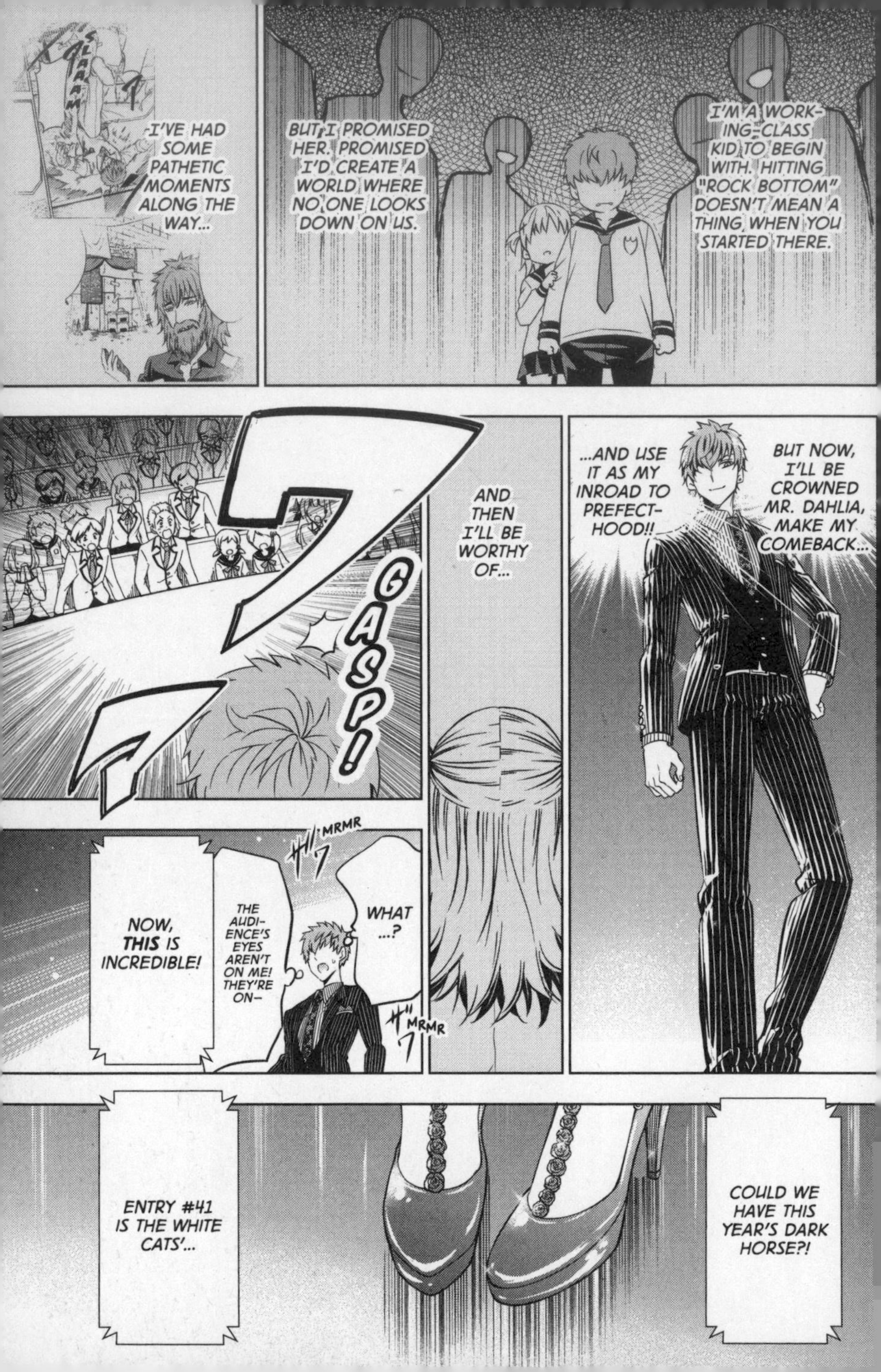
I'M A WORKING-CLASS KID TO BEGIN WITH. HITTING "ROCK BOTTOM" DOESN'T MEAN A THING WHEN YOU STARTED THERE.
BUT, I PROMISED HER. PROMISED I'D CREATE A WORLD WHERE NO ONE LOOKS DOWN ON US.
I'VE HAD SOME PATHETIC MOMENTS ALONG THE WAY...
BUT NOW, I'LL BE CROWNED MR. DAHLIA, MAKE MY COMEBACK...
...AND USE IT AS MY INROAD TO PREFECT-HOOD!!
AND THEN I'LL BE WORTHY OF...
GASP!
MRMR
WHAT ...?
THE AUDIENCE'S EYES AREN'T ON ME! THEY'RE ON–
NOW, THIS IS INCREDIBLE!
MRMR
COULD WE HAVE THIS YEAR'S DARK HORSE?!
ENTRY #41 IS THE WHITE CATS'...

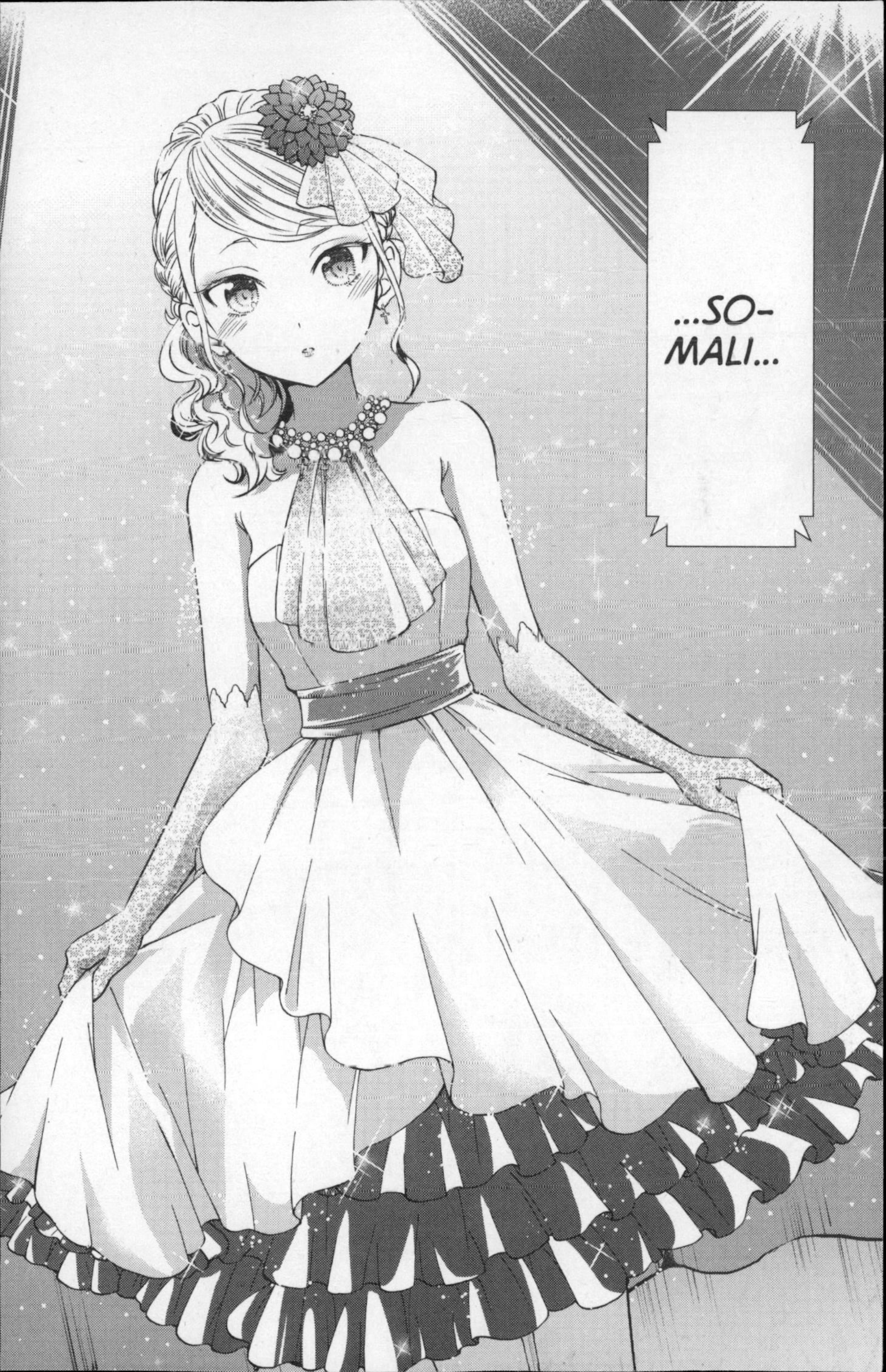
...SO-
MALI...

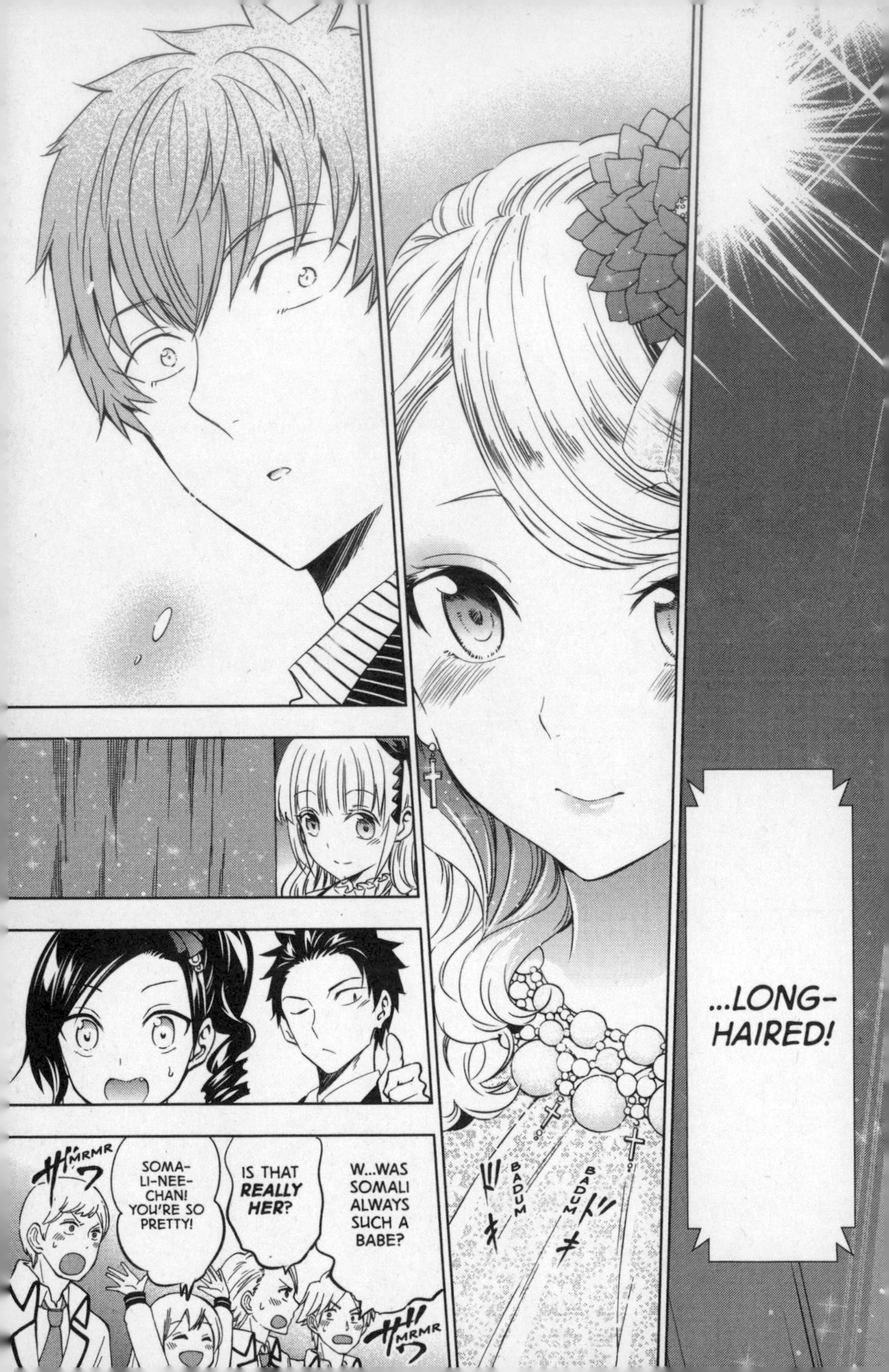

...LONG-HAIRED!
BADUM
BADUM
W...WAS SOMALI ALWAYS SUCH A BABE?
IS THAT REALLY HER?
SOMA-LI-NEE-CHAN! YOU'RE SO PRETTY!
MRMR
MRMR

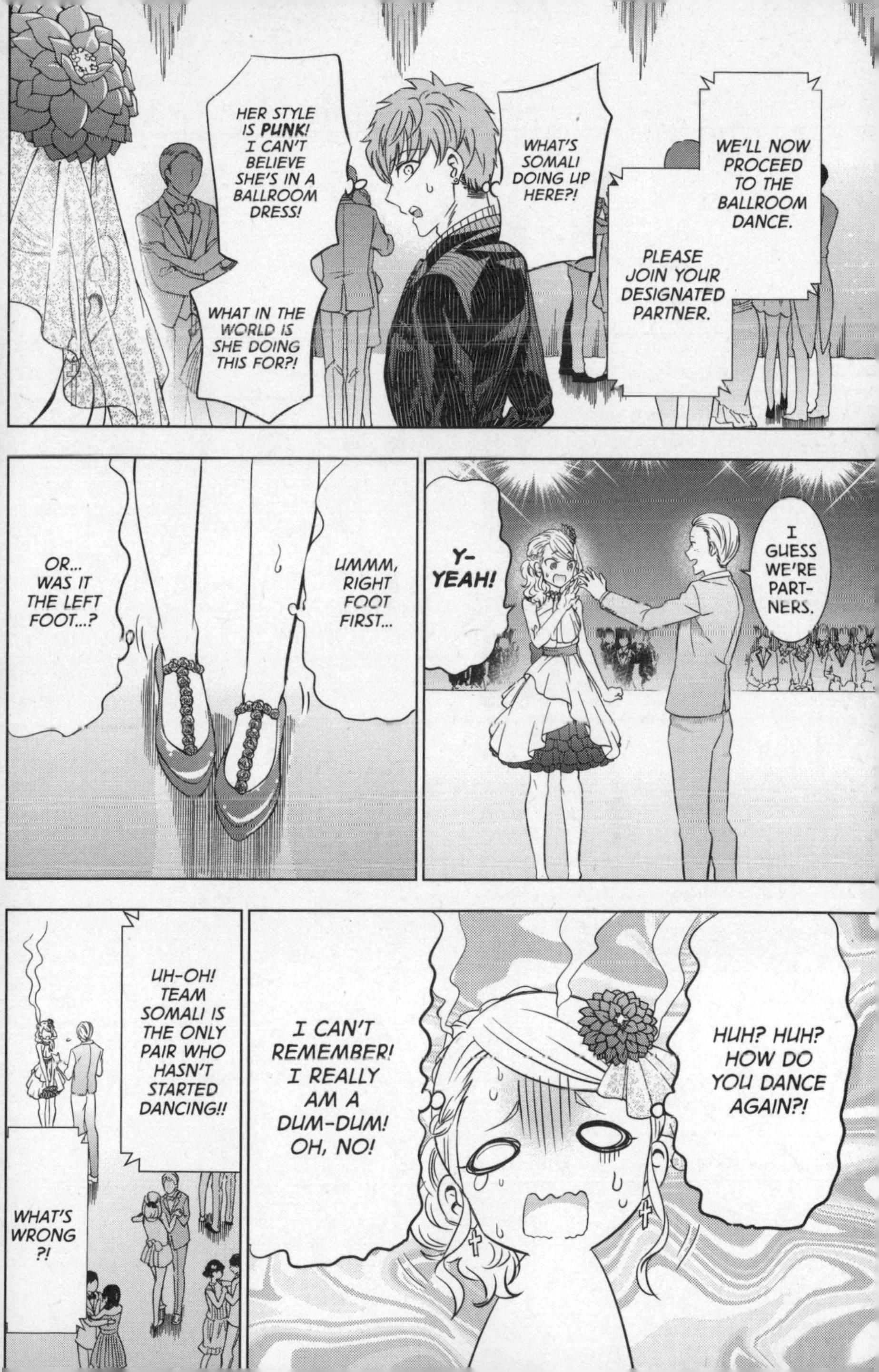
WE'LL NOW PROCEED TO THE BALLROOM DANCE.
PLEASE JOIN YOUR DESIGNATED PARTNER.
WHAT'S SOMALI DOING UP HERE?!
HER STYLE IS **PUNK**! I CAN'T BELIEVE SHE'S IN A BALLROOM DRESS!
WHAT IN THE WORLD IS SHE DOING THIS FOR?!
I GUESS WE'RE PART-NERS.
Y-YEAH!
UMMM, RIGHT FOOT FIRST...
OR... WAS IT THE LEFT FOOT...?
HUH? HUH? HOW DO YOU DANCE AGAIN?!
I CAN'T REMEMBER! I REALLY AM A DUM-DUM! OH, NO!
UH-OH! TEAM SOMALI IS THE ONLY PAIR WHO HASN'T STARTED DANCING!!
WHAT'S WRONG ?!

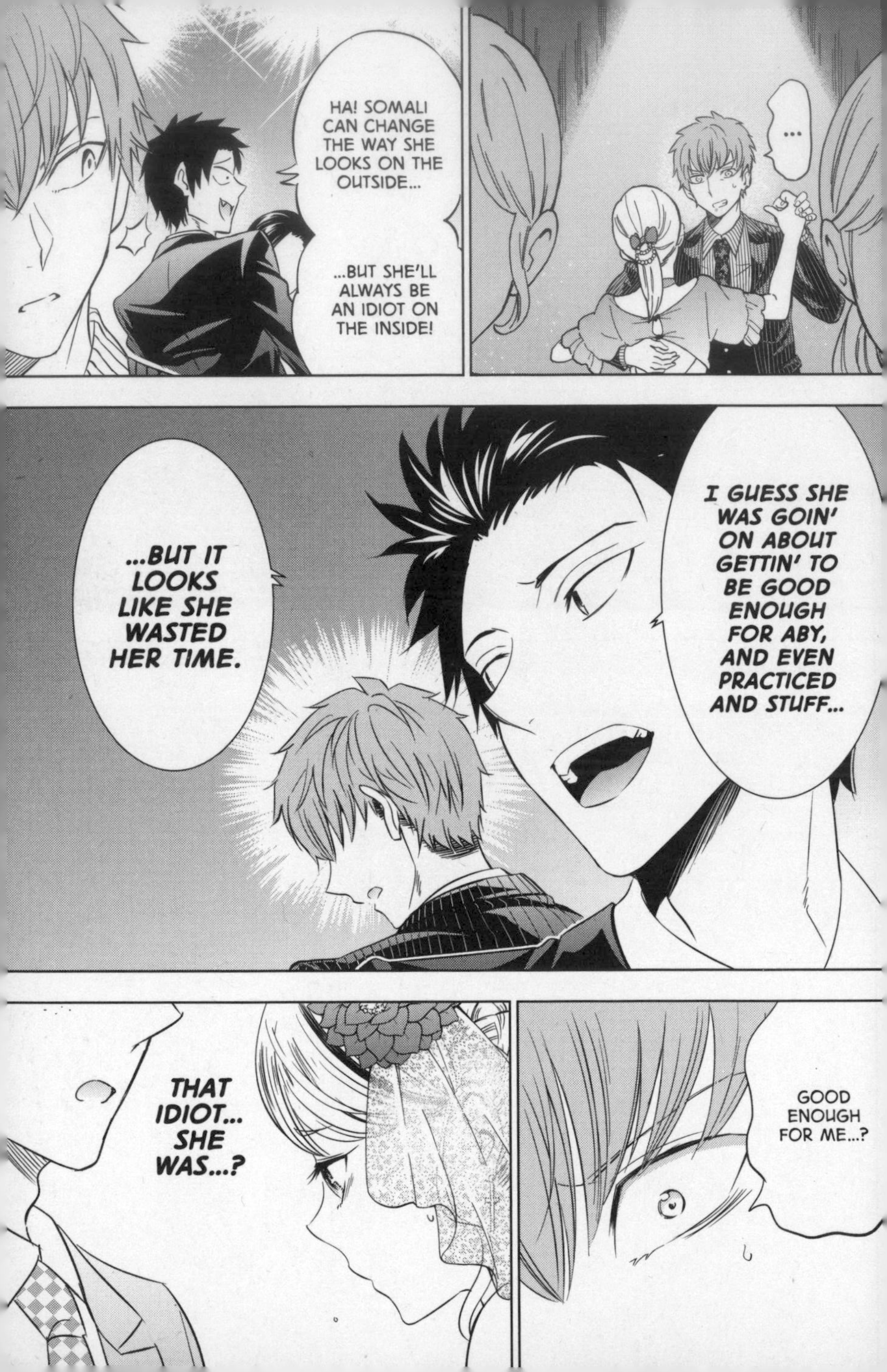
...
HA! SOMALI CAN CHANGE THE WAY SHE LOOKS ON THE OUTSIDE...
...BUT SHE'LL ALWAYS BE AN IDIOT ON THE INSIDE!
I GUESS SHE WAS GOIN' ON ABOUT GETTIN' TO BE GOOD ENOUGH FOR ABY, AND EVEN PRACTICED AND STUFF...
...BUT IT LOOKS LIKE SHE WASTED HER TIME.
GOOD ENOUGH FOR ME...?
THAT IDIOT... SHE WAS...?

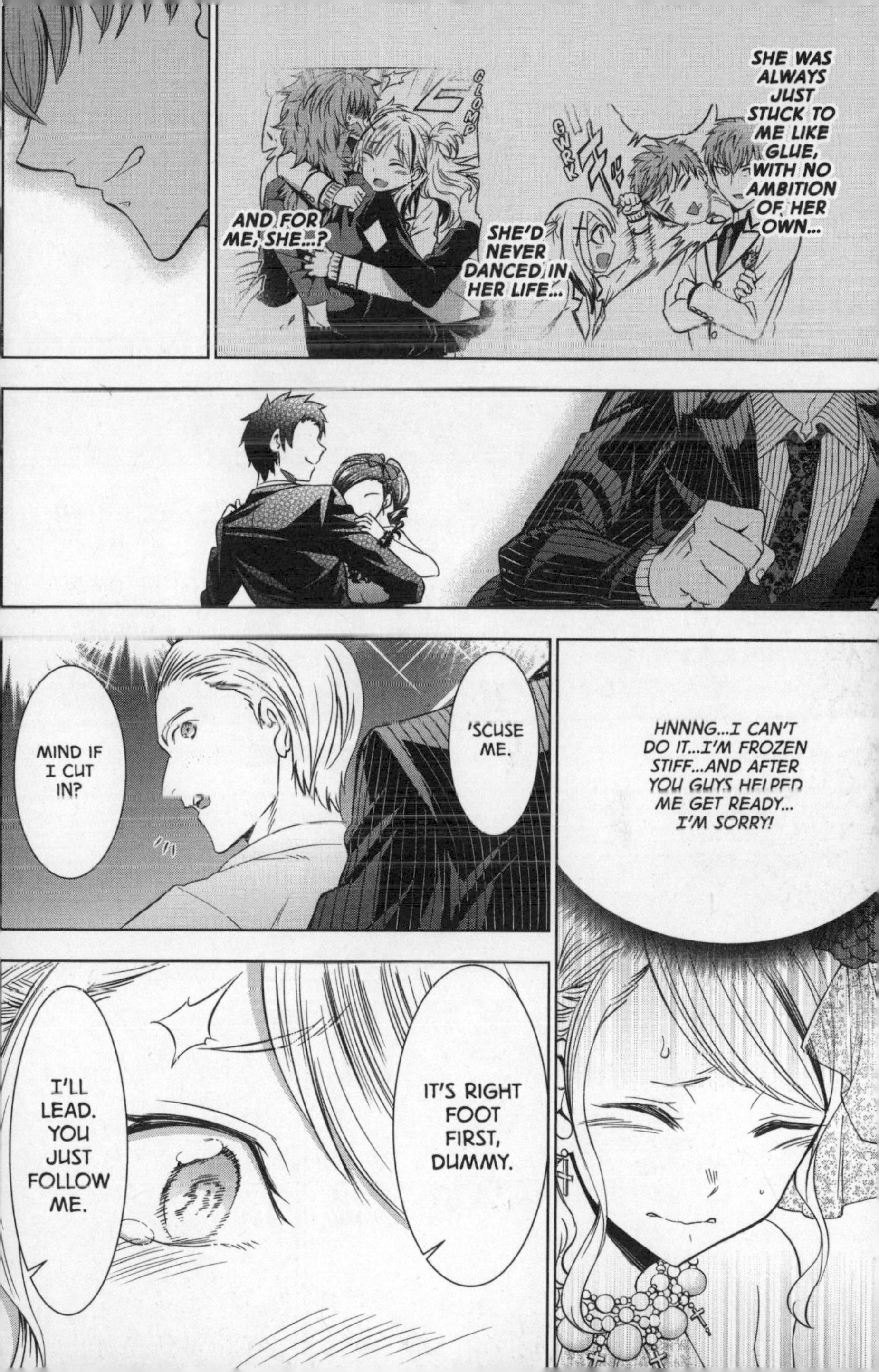
SHE WAS ALWAYS JUST STUCK TO ME LIKE GLUE, WITH NO AMBITION OF HER OWN...
GWRK
SHE'D NEVER DANCED IN HER LIFE...
GLOMP
AND FOR ME, SHE...?
HNNNG...I CAN'T DO IT...I'M FROZEN STIFF...AND AFTER YOU GUYS HELPED ME GET READY... I'M SORRY!
'SCUSE ME.
MIND IF I CUT IN?
IT'S RIGHT FOOT FIRST, DUMMY.
I'LL LEAD. YOU JUST FOLLOW ME.

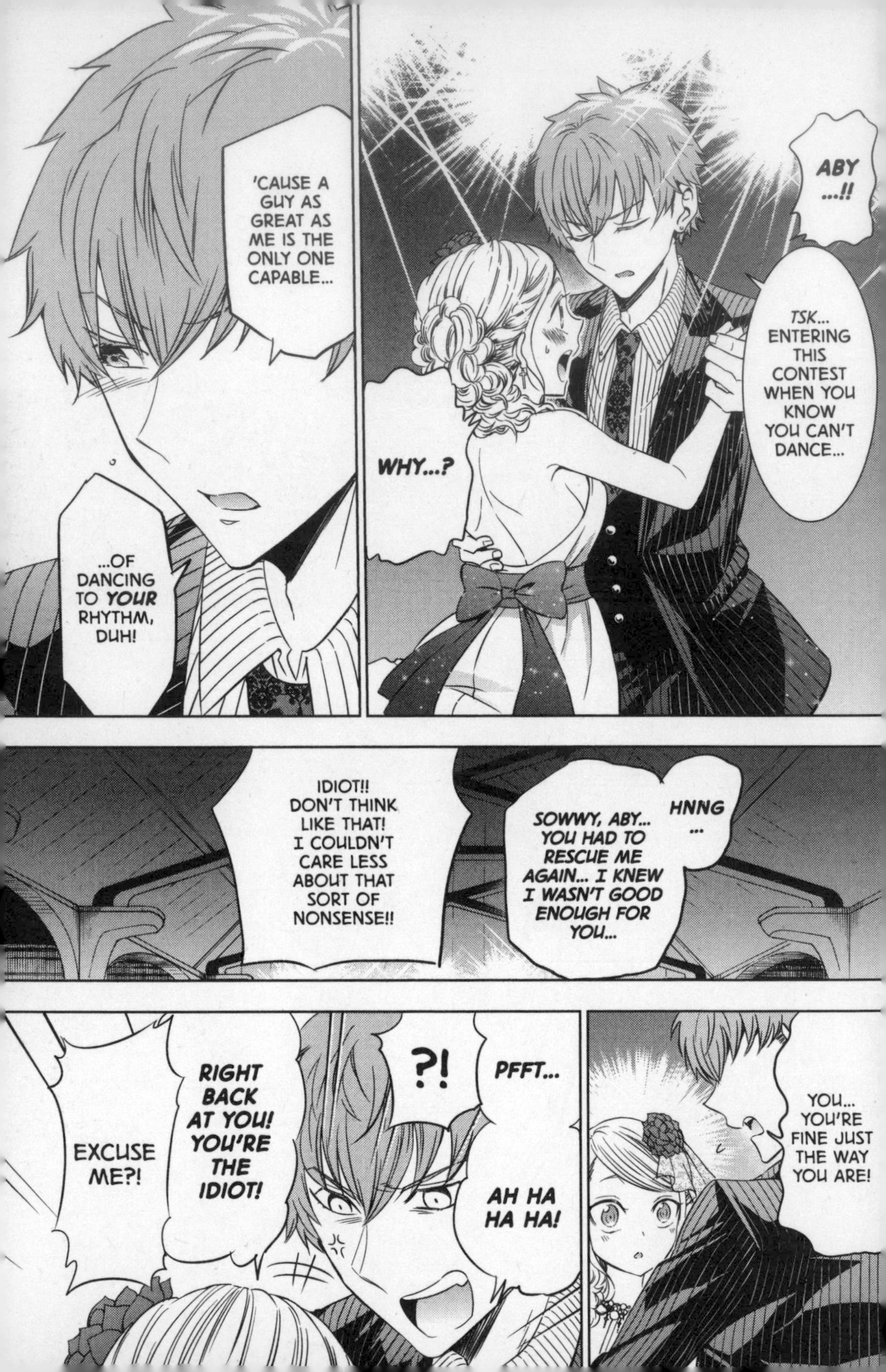
ABY ...!!
TSK... ENTERING THIS CONTEST WHEN YOU KNOW YOU CAN'T DANCE...
WHY...?
'CAUSE A GUY AS GREAT AS ME IS THE ONLY ONE CAPABLE...
...OF DANCING TO *YOUR* RHYTHM, DUH!
HNNG ...
SOWWY, ABY... YOU HAD TO RESCUE ME AGAIN... I KNEW I WASN'T GOOD ENOUGH FOR YOU...
IDIOT!! DON'T THINK LIKE THAT! I COULDN'T CARE LESS ABOUT THAT SORT OF NONSENSE!!
YOU... YOU'RE FINE JUST THE WAY YOU ARE!
PFFT...
AH HA HA HA!
?!
RIGHT BACK AT YOU! YOU'RE THE IDIOT!
EXCUSE ME?!

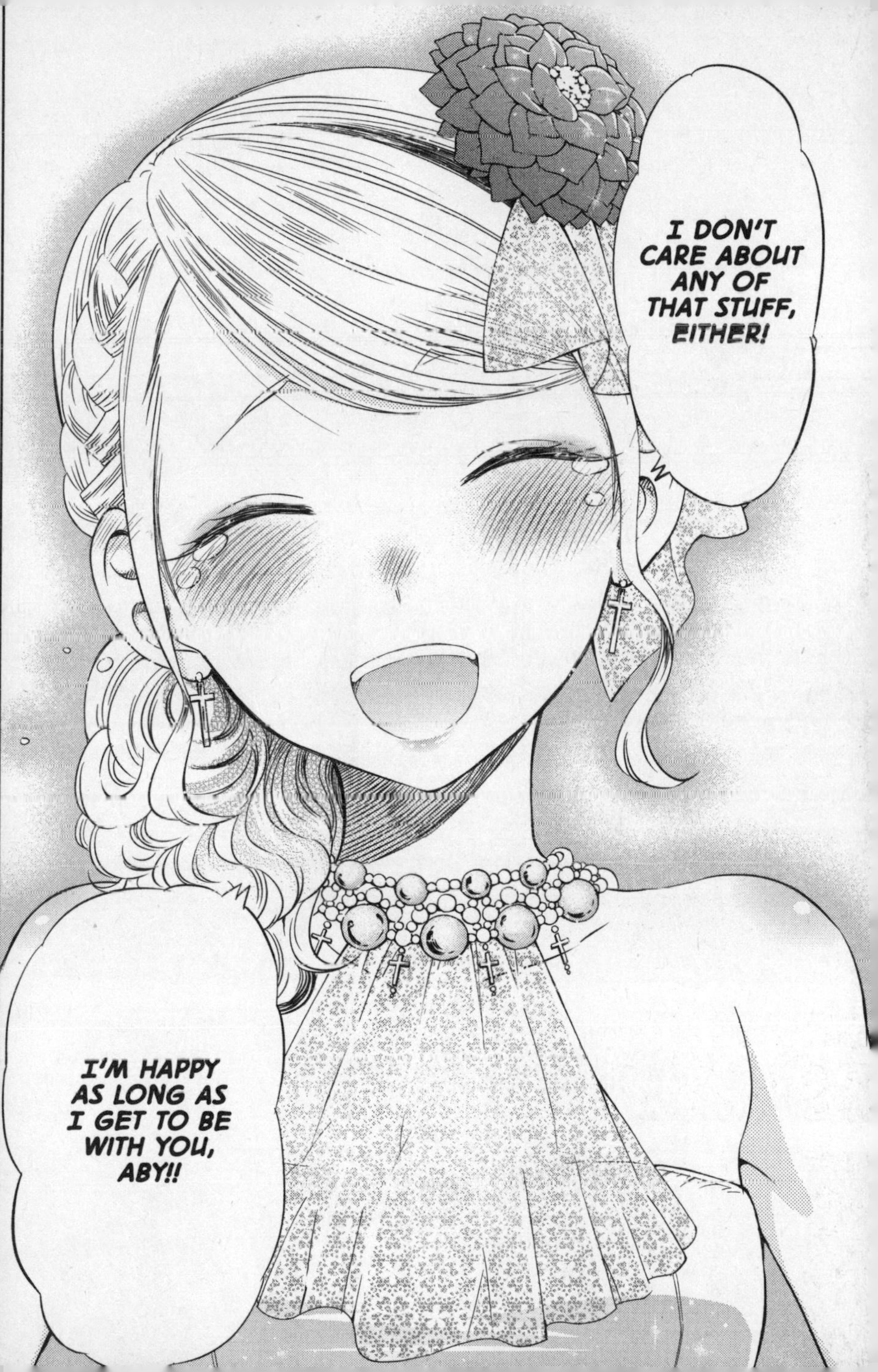
I DON'T CARE ABOUT ANY OF THAT STUFF, EITHER!
I'M HAPPY AS LONG AS I GET TO BE WITH YOU, ABY!!

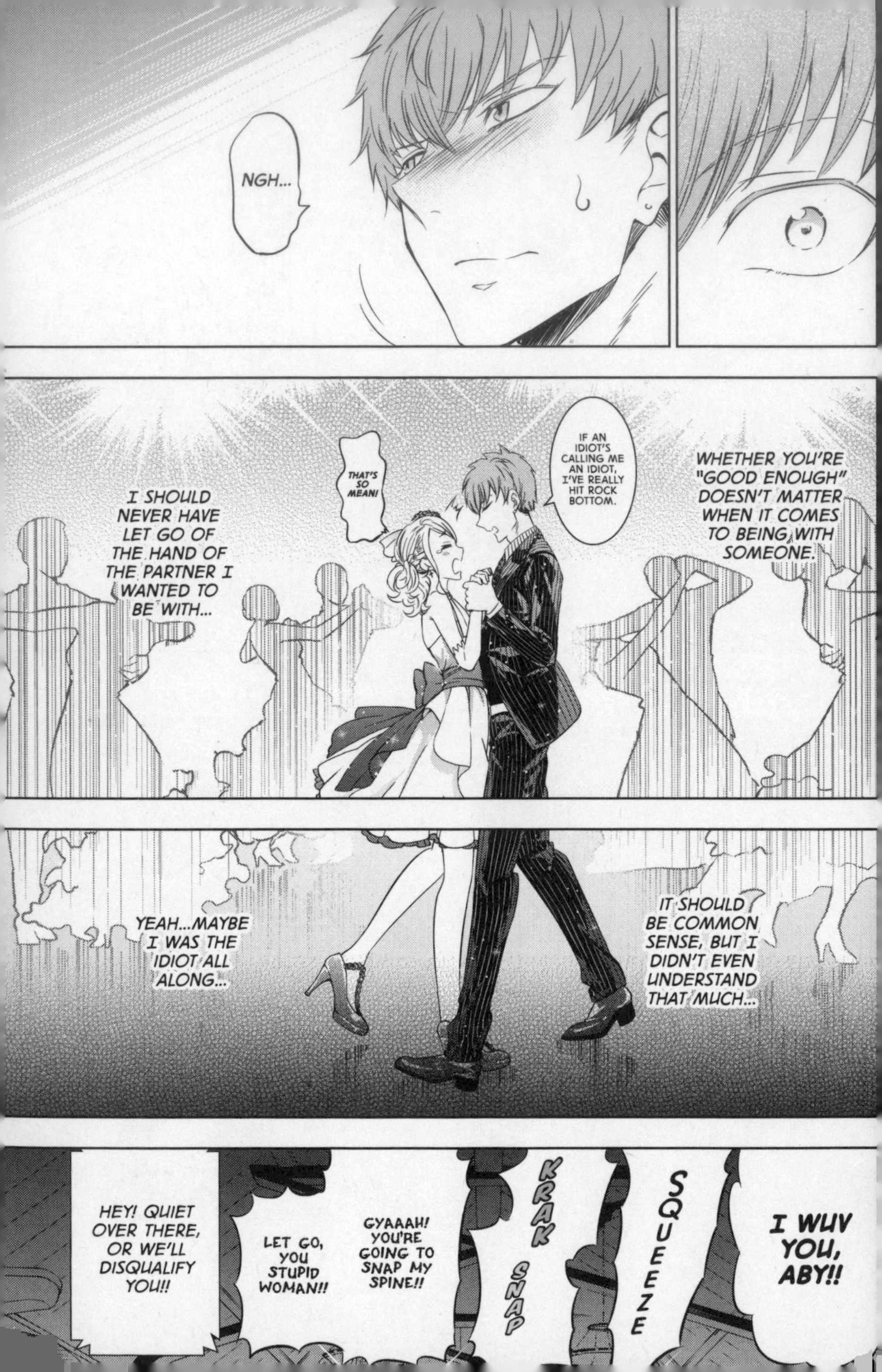

NGH...
WHETHER YOU'RE "GOOD ENOUGH" DOESN'T MATTER WHEN IT COMES TO BEING WITH SOMEONE.
IF AN IDIOT'S CALLING ME AN IDIOT, I'VE REALLY HIT ROCK BOTTOM.
THAT'S SO MEAN!
I SHOULD NEVER HAVE LET GO OF THE HAND OF THE PARTNER I WANTED TO BE WITH...
IT SHOULD BE COMMON SENSE, BUT I DIDN'T EVEN UNDERSTAND THAT MUCH...
YEAH...MAYBE I WAS THE IDIOT ALL ALONG...
I WUV YOU, ABY!!
SQUEEZE
KRAK
SNAP
GYAAAH! YOU'RE GOING TO SNAP MY SPINE!!
LET GO, YOU STUPID WOMAN!!
HEY! QUIET OVER THERE, OR WE'LL DISQUALIFY YOU!!

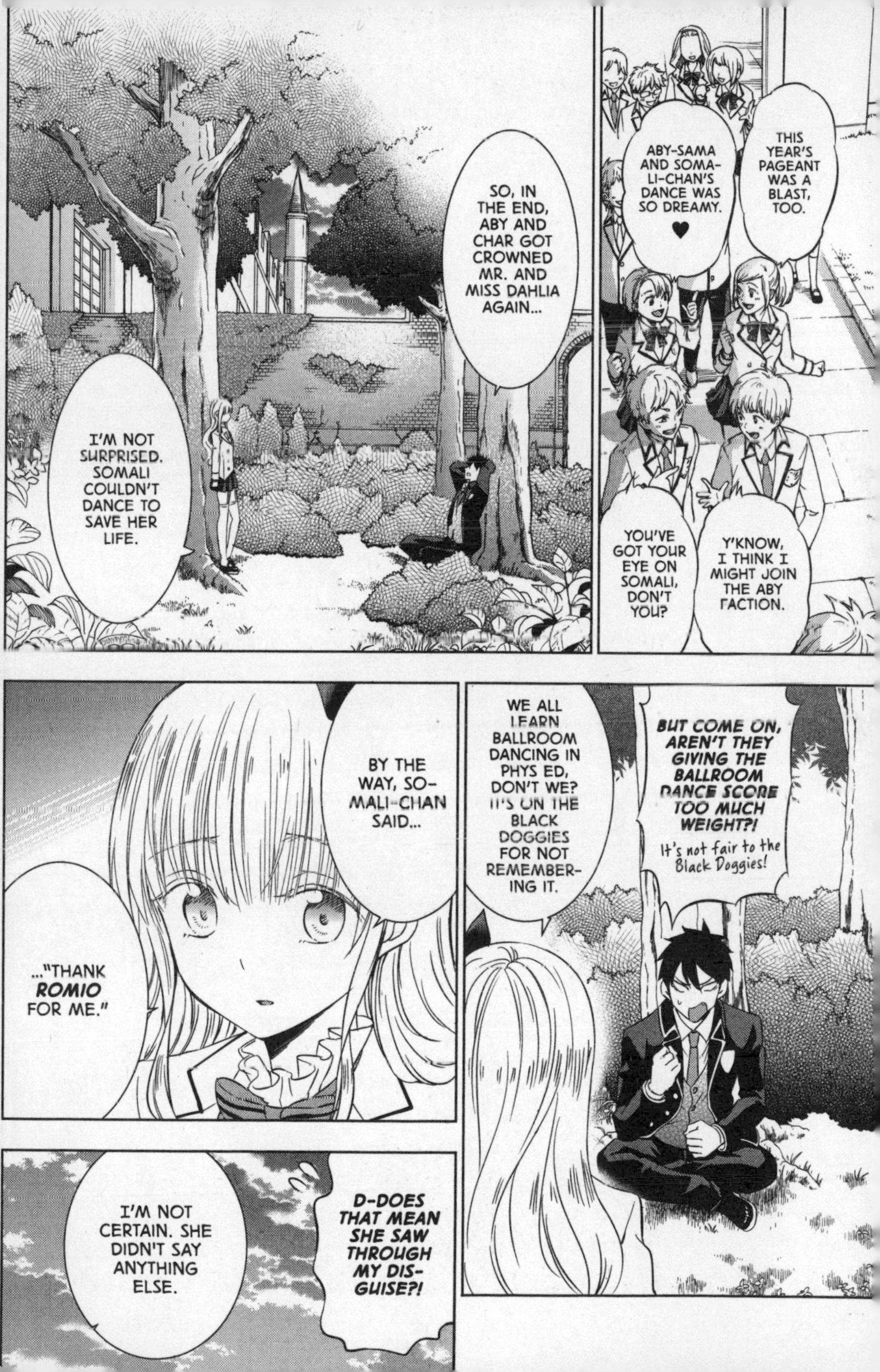
THIS YEAR'S PAGEANT WAS A BLAST, TOO.
ABY-SAMA AND SOMALI-CHAN'S DANCE WAS SO DREAMY. ♥
Y'KNOW, I THINK I MIGHT JOIN THE ABY FACTION.
YOU'VE GOT YOUR EYE ON SOMALI, DON'T YOU?
SO, IN THE END, ABY AND CHAR GOT CROWNED MR. AND MISS DAHLIA AGAIN...
I'M NOT SURPRISED. SOMALI COULDN'T DANCE TO SAVE HER LIFE.
BUT COME ON, AREN'T THEY GIVING THE BALLROOM DANCE SCORE TOO MUCH WEIGHT?!
It's not fair to the Black Doggies!
WE ALL LEARN BALLROOM DANCING IN PHYS ED, DON'T WE? IT'S ON THE BLACK DOGGIES FOR NOT REMEMBERING IT.
BY THE WAY, SO-MALI-CHAN SAID...
..."THANK ROMIO FOR ME."
D-DOES THAT MEAN SHE SAW THROUGH MY DIS-GUISE?!
I'M NOT CERTAIN. SHE DIDN'T SAY ANYTHING ELSE.

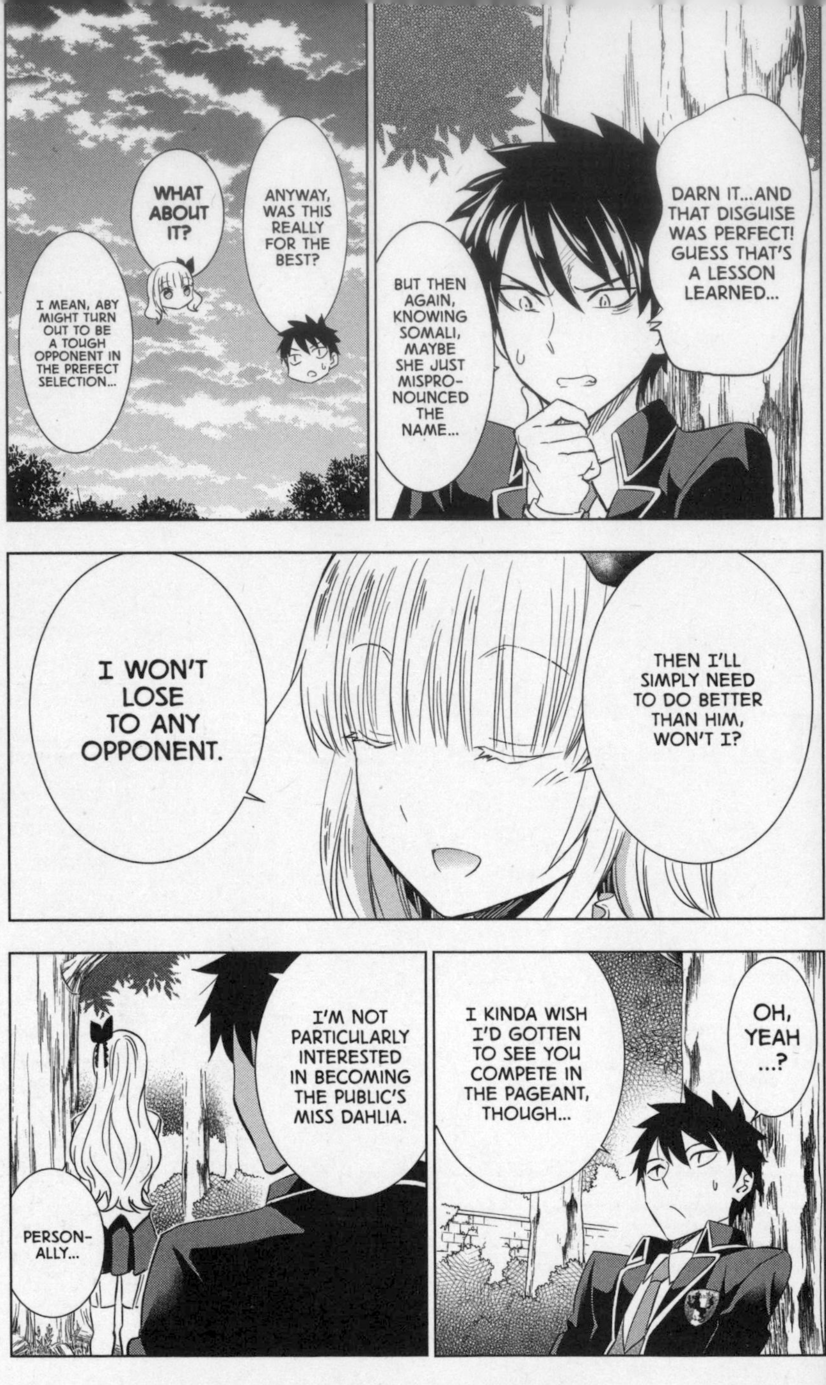
DARN IT...AND THAT DISGUISE WAS PERFECT! GUESS THAT'S A LESSON LEARNED...
BUT THEN AGAIN, KNOWING SOMALI, MAYBE SHE JUST MISPRO-NOUNCED THE NAME...
ANYWAY, WAS THIS REALLY FOR THE BEST?
WHAT ABOUT IT?
I MEAN, ABY MIGHT TURN OUT TO BE A TOUGH OPPONENT IN THE PREFECT SELECTION...
THEN I'LL SIMPLY NEED TO DO BETTER THAN HIM, WON'T I?
I WON'T LOSE TO ANY OPPONENT.
OH, YEAH ...?
I KINDA WISH I'D GOTTEN TO SEE YOU COMPETE IN THE PAGEANT, THOUGH...
I'M NOT PARTICULARLY INTERESTED IN BECOMING THE PUBLIC'S MISS DAHLIA.
PERSON-ALLY...

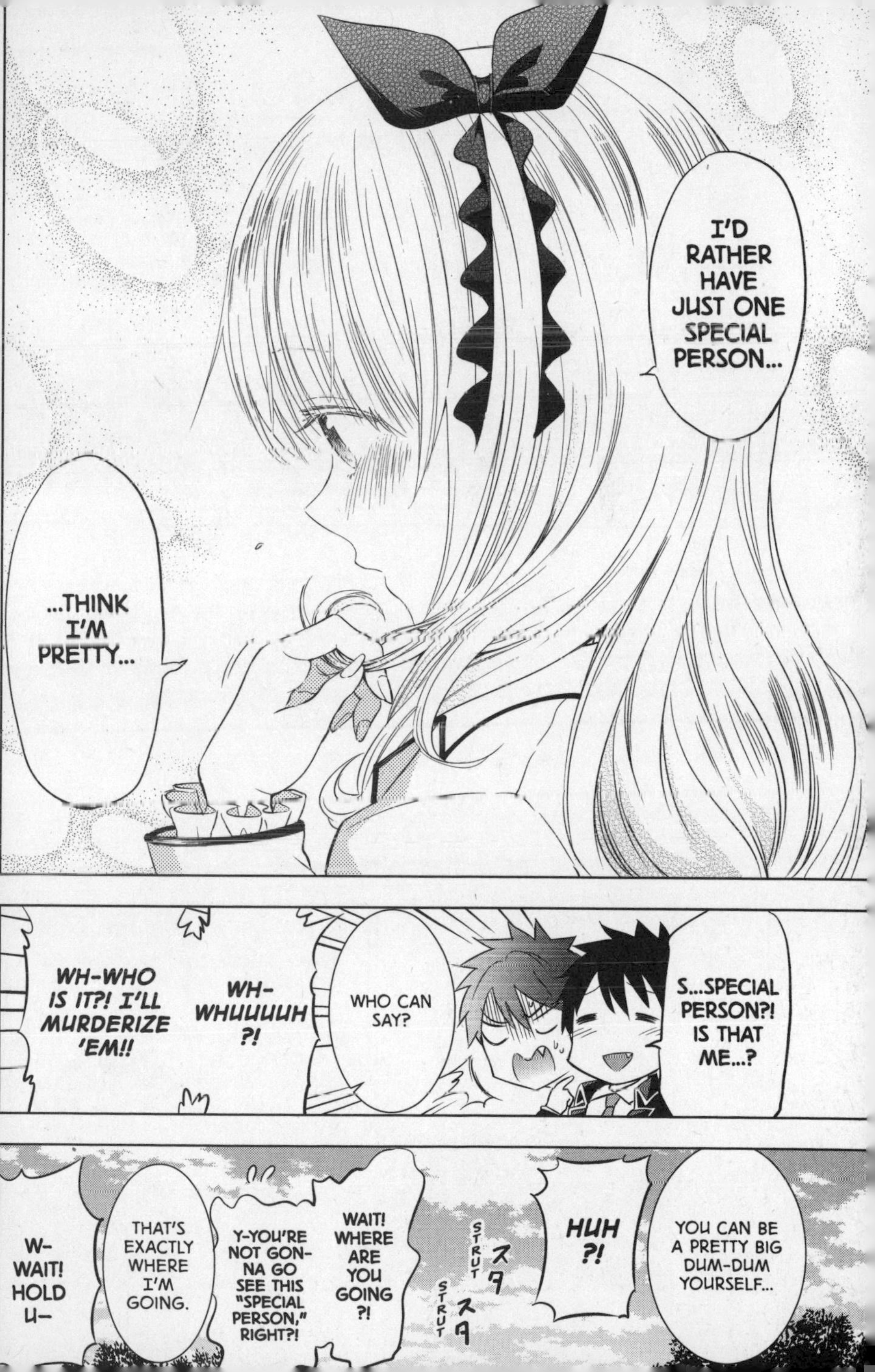
I'D RATHER HAVE JUST ONE SPECIAL PERSON...
...THINK I'M PRETTY...
S...SPECIAL PERSON?! IS THAT ME...?
WHO CAN SAY?
WH-WHUUUUH?!
WH-WHO IS IT?! I'LL MURDERIZE 'EM!!
YOU CAN BE A PRETTY BIG DUM-DUM YOURSELF...
HUH?!
STRUT スタ
STRUT スタ
WAIT! WHERE ARE YOU GOING?!
Y-YOU'RE NOT GON-NA GO SEE THIS "SPECIAL PERSON," RIGHT?!
THAT'S EXACTLY WHERE I'M GOING.
W-WAIT! HOLD U—

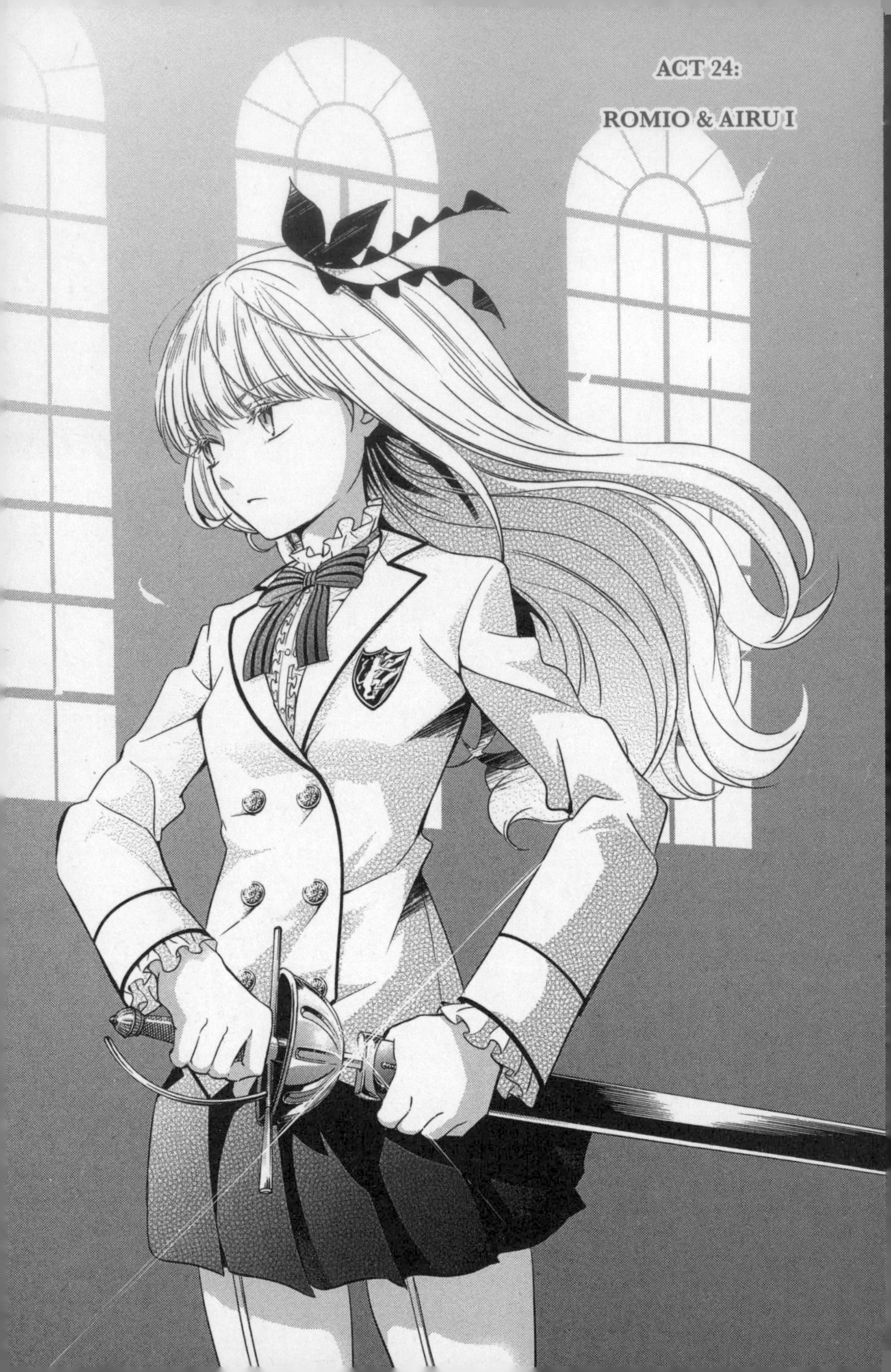
ACT 24:
ROMIO & AIRU I

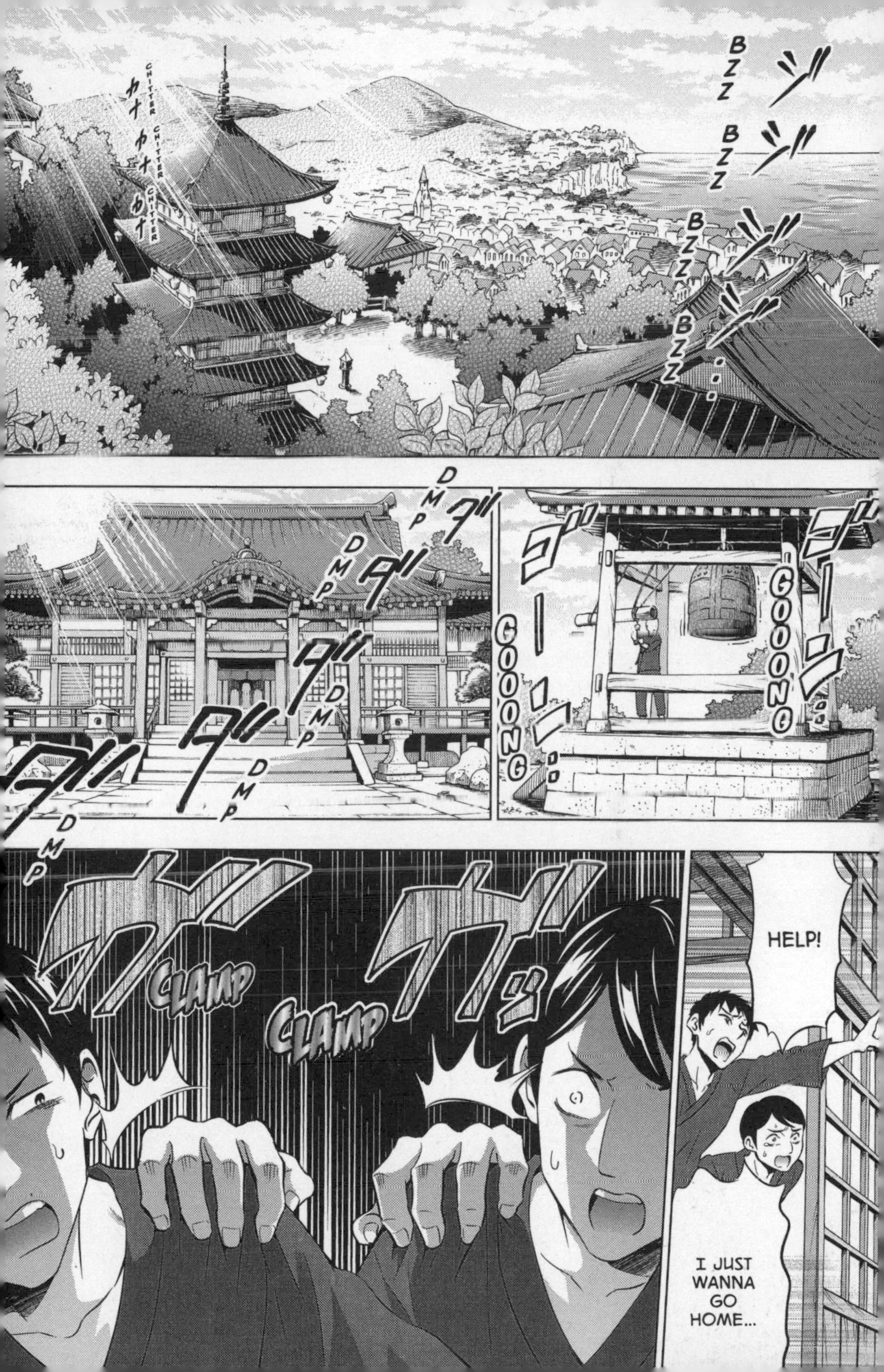
BZZ BZZ BZZ BZZ
CHITTER CHITTER CHITTER
GOOONG
GOOONG
DMP DMP DMP DMP DMP
HELP!
I JUST WANNA GO HOME...
CLAMP
CLAMP

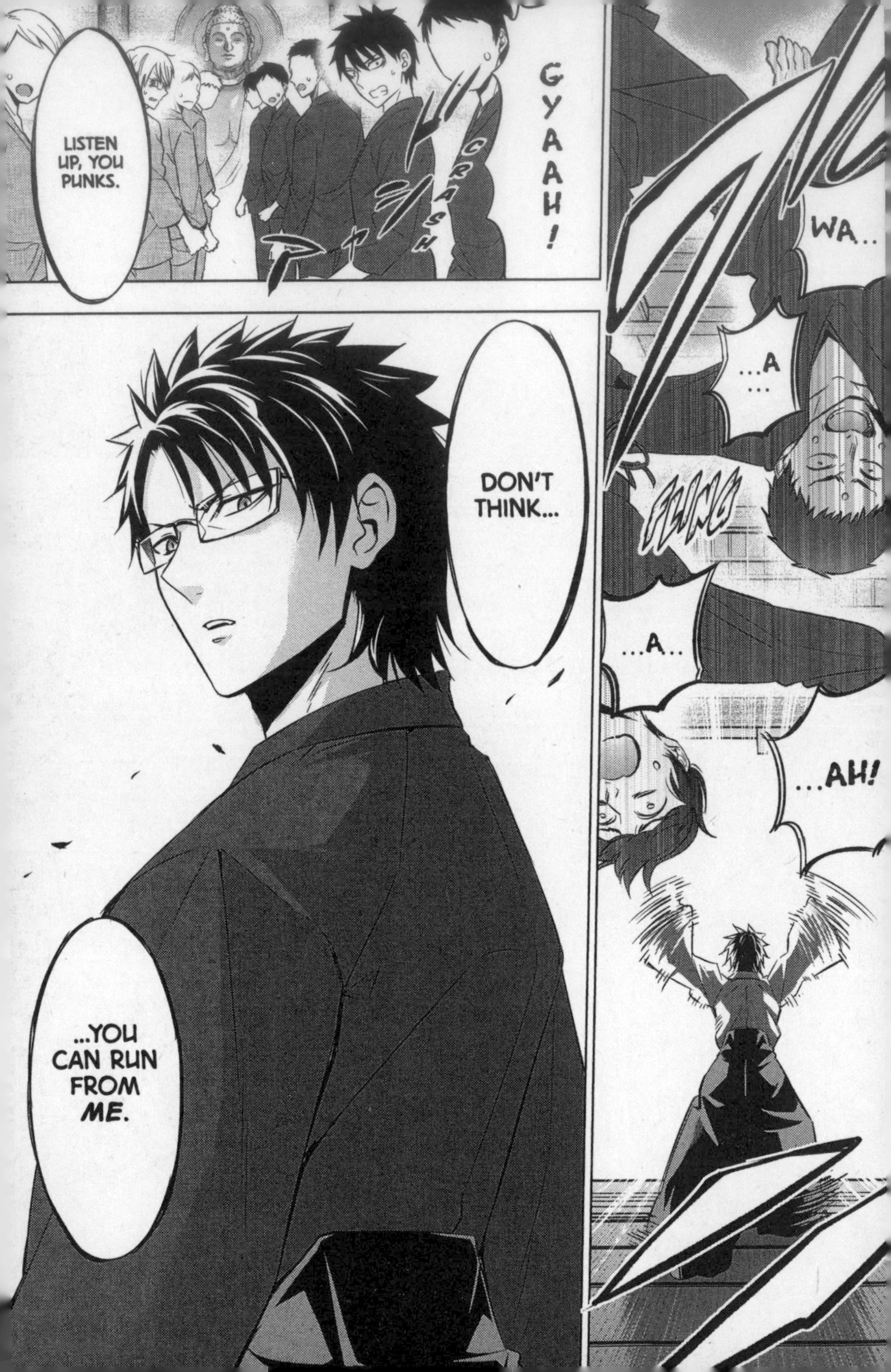
WA...
...A...
FLING
...A...
...AH!
GYAAH!
CRASH
LISTEN UP, YOU PUNKS.
DON'T THINK...
...YOU CAN RUN FROM *ME*.

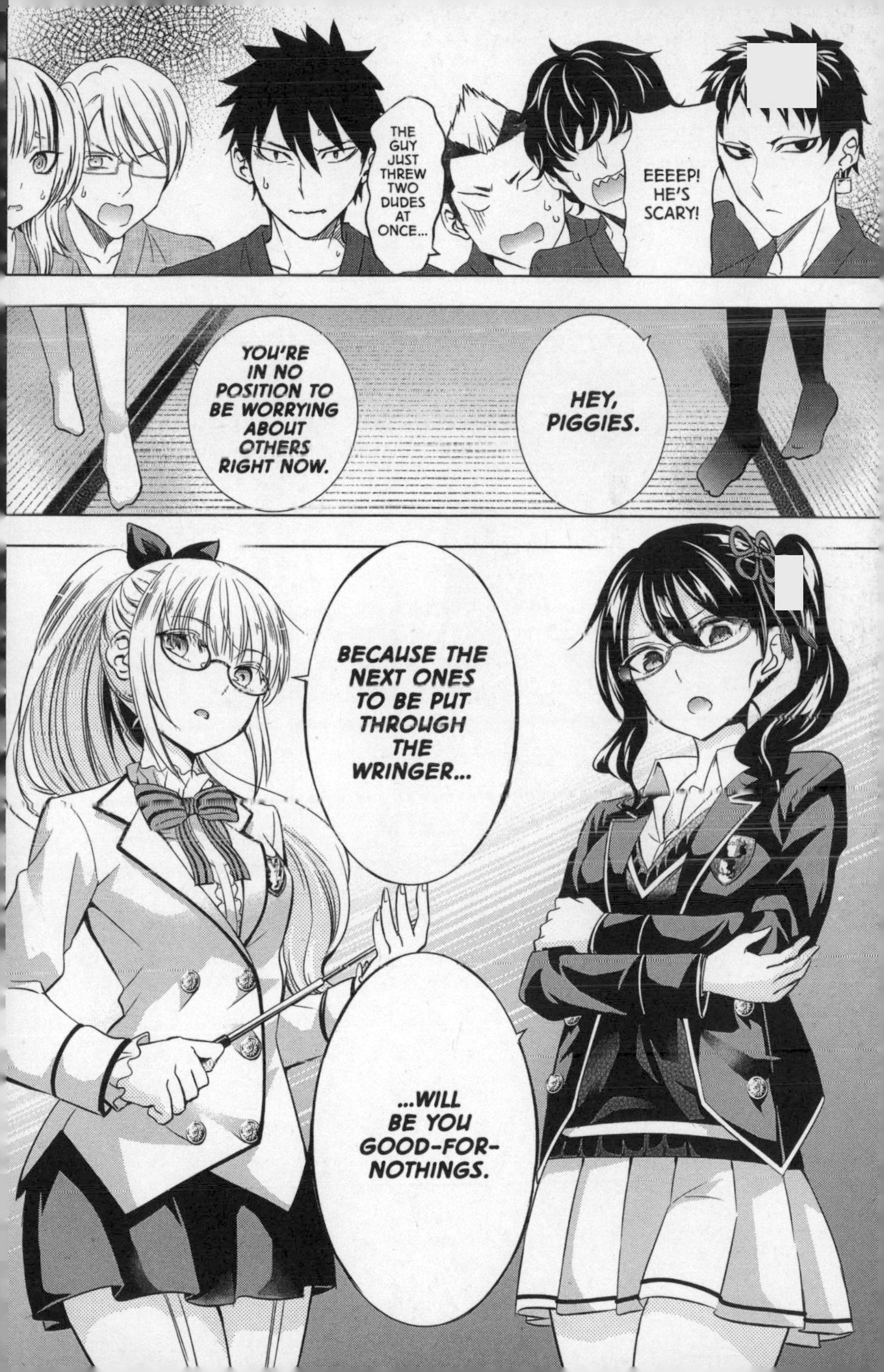
EEEEP! HE'S SCARY!
THE GUY JUST THREW TWO DUDES AT ONCE...
HEY, PIGGIES.
YOU'RE IN NO POSITION TO BE WORRYING ABOUT OTHERS RIGHT NOW.
BECAUSE THE NEXT ONES TO BE PUT THROUGH THE WRINGER...
...WILL BE YOU GOOD-FOR-NOTHINGS.

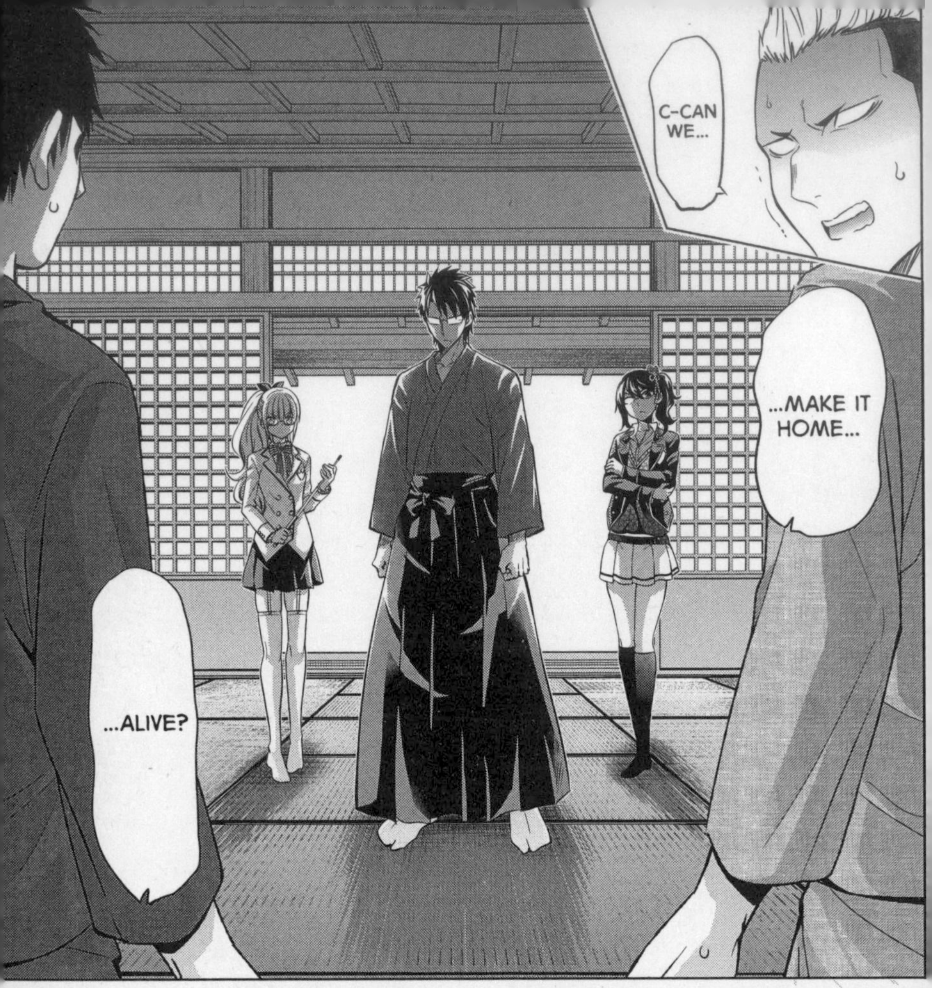
C-CAN WE...
...MAKE IT HOME...
...ALIVE?

THE SUMMER SCHOOL FROM HELL

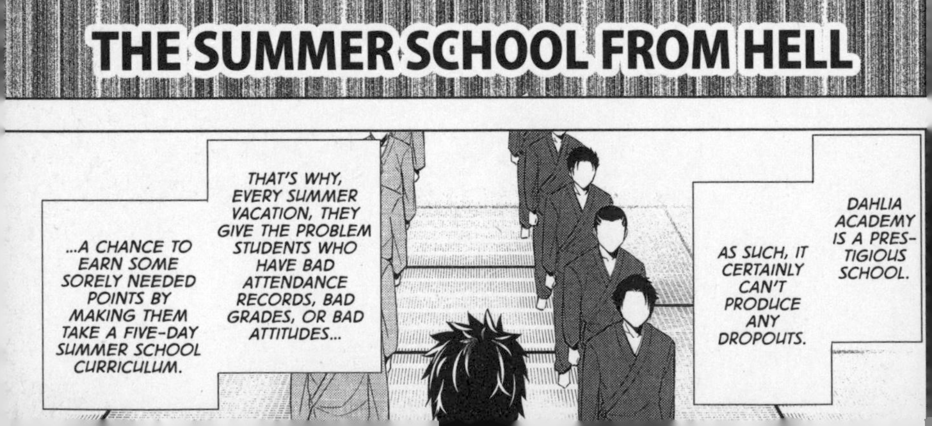
DAHLIA ACADEMY IS A PRES-TIGIOUS SCHOOL.
AS SUCH, IT CERTAINLY CAN'T PRODUCE ANY DROPOUTS.
THAT'S WHY, EVERY SUMMER VACATION, THEY GIVE THE PROBLEM STUDENTS WHO HAVE BAD ATTENDANCE RECORDS, BAD GRADES, OR BAD ATTITUDES...
...A CHANCE TO EARN SOME SORELY NEEDED POINTS BY MAKING THEM TAKE A FIVE-DAY SUMMER SCHOOL CURRICULUM.

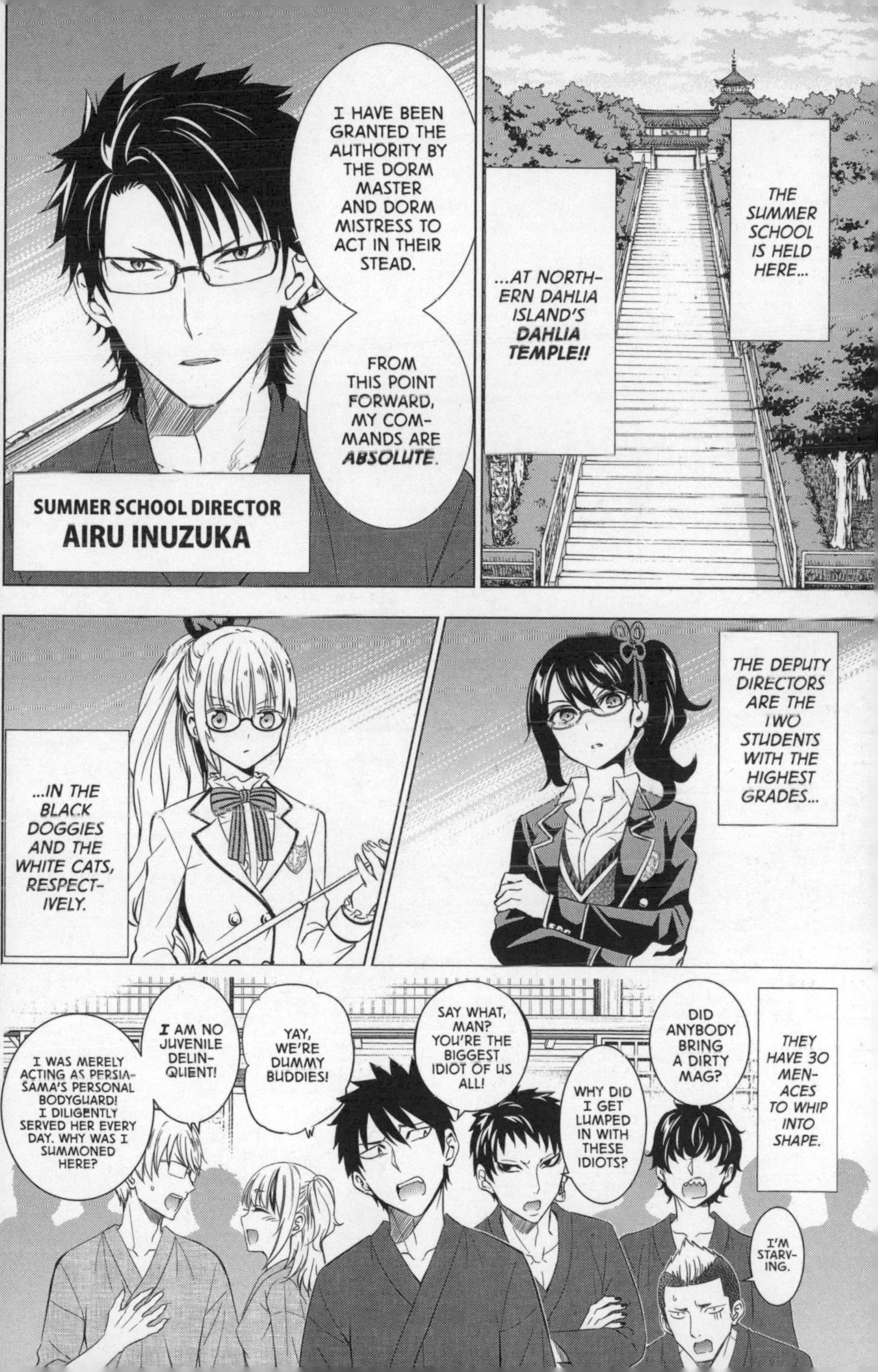
THE SUMMER SCHOOL IS HELD HERE...
...AT NORTHERN DAHLIA ISLAND'S DAHLIA TEMPLE!!
I HAVE BEEN GRANTED THE AUTHORITY BY THE DORM MASTER AND DORM MISTRESS TO ACT IN THEIR STEAD.
FROM THIS POINT FORWARD, MY COMMANDS ARE ABSOLUTE.
SUMMER SCHOOL DIRECTOR AIRU INUZUKA
THE DEPUTY DIRECTORS ARE THE TWO STUDENTS WITH THE HIGHEST GRADES...
...IN THE BLACK DOGGIES AND THE WHITE CATS, RESPECTIVELY.
THEY HAVE 30 MENACES TO WHIP INTO SHAPE.
DID ANYBODY BRING A DIRTY MAG?
I'M STARVING.
WHY DID I GET LUMPED IN WITH THESE IDIOTS?
SAY WHAT, MAN? YOU'RE THE BIGGEST IDIOT OF US ALL!
YAY, WE'RE DUMMY BUDDIES!
I AM NO JUVENILE DELINQUENT!
I WAS MERELY ACTING AS PERSIA-SAMA'S PERSONAL BODYGUARD! I DILIGENTLY SERVED HER EVERY DAY. WHY WAS I SUMMONED HERE?

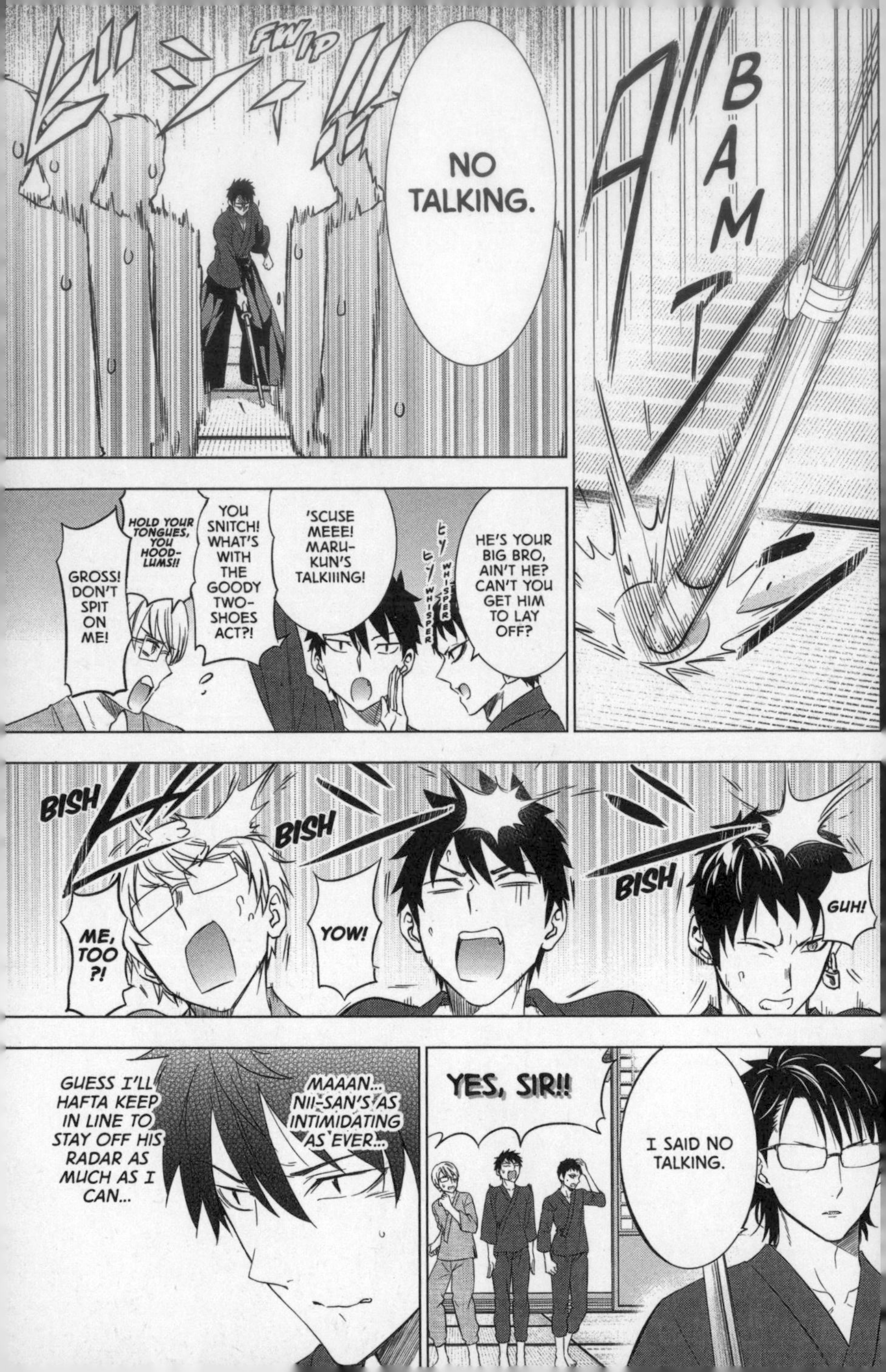
B A M
NO TALKING.
FWIP
HE'S YOUR BIG BRO, AIN'T HE? CAN'T YOU GET HIM TO LAY OFF?
WHISPER WHISPER
'SCUSE MEEE! MARU-KUN'S TALKIIING!
YOU SNITCH! WHAT'S WITH THE GOODY TWO-SHOES ACT?!
HOLD YOUR TONGUES, YOU HOOD-LUMS!!
GROSS! DON'T SPIT ON ME!
GUH!
BISH
YOW!
BISH
BISH
ME, TOO ?!
I SAID NO TALKING.
YES, SIR!!
MAAAN... NII-SAN'S AS INTIMIDATING AS EVER...
GUESS I'LL HAFTA KEEP IN LINE TO STAY OFF HIS RADAR AS MUCH AS I CAN...

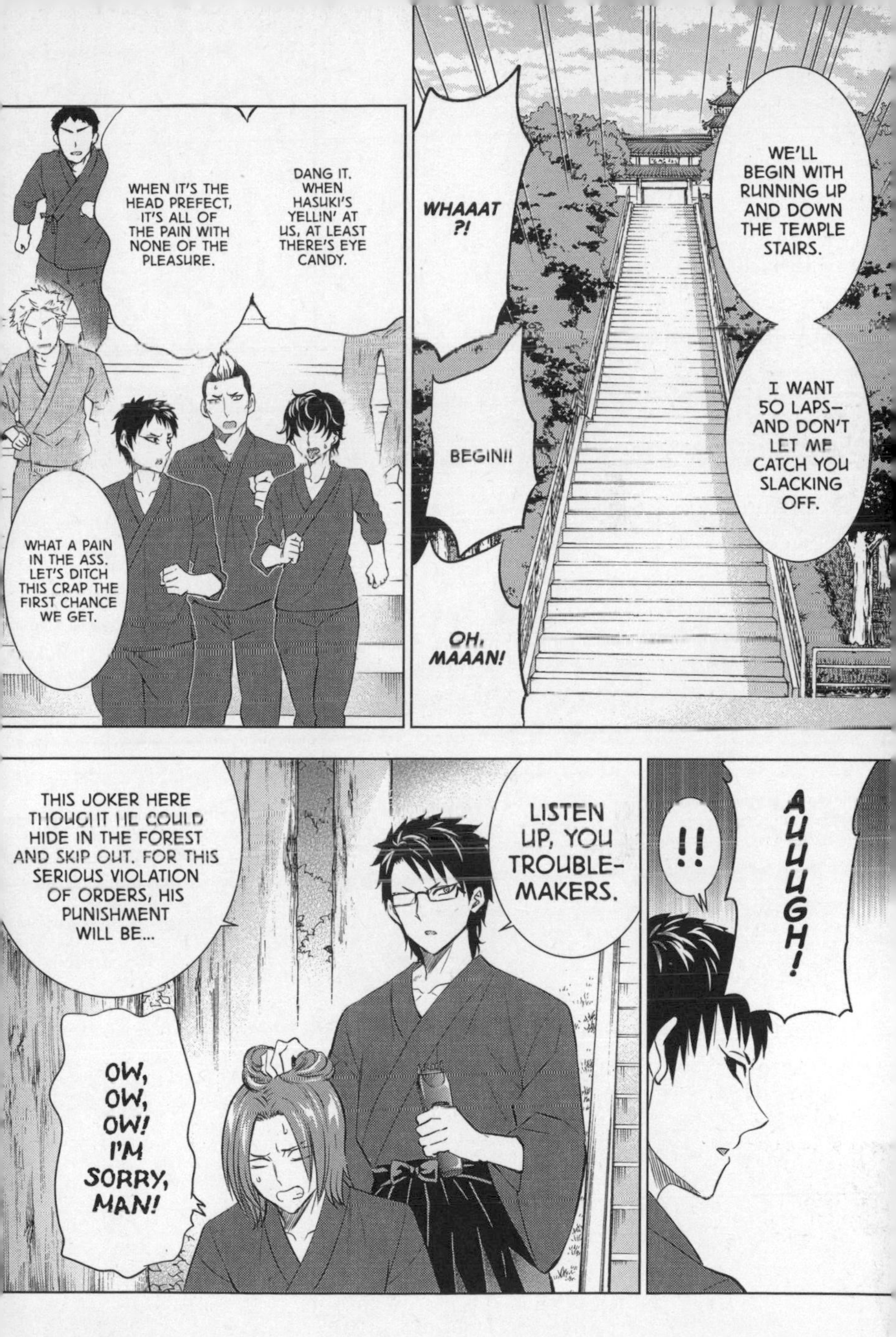
WE'LL BEGIN WITH RUNNING UP AND DOWN THE TEMPLE STAIRS.
I WANT 50 LAPS—AND DON'T LET ME CATCH YOU SLACKING OFF.
WHAAAT?!
BEGIN!!
OH, MAAAN!
DANG IT. WHEN HASUKI'S YELLIN' AT US, AT LEAST THERE'S EYE CANDY.
WHEN IT'S THE HEAD PREFECT, IT'S ALL OF THE PAIN WITH NONE OF THE PLEASURE.
WHAT A PAIN IN THE ASS. LET'S DITCH THIS CRAP THE FIRST CHANCE WE GET.
AUUUGH!
!!
LISTEN UP, YOU TROUBLE-MAKERS.
THIS JOKER HERE THOUGHT HE COULD HIDE IN THE FOREST AND SKIP OUT. FOR THIS SERIOUS VIOLATION OF ORDERS, HIS PUNISHMENT WILL BE...
OW, OW, OW! I'M SORRY, MAN!

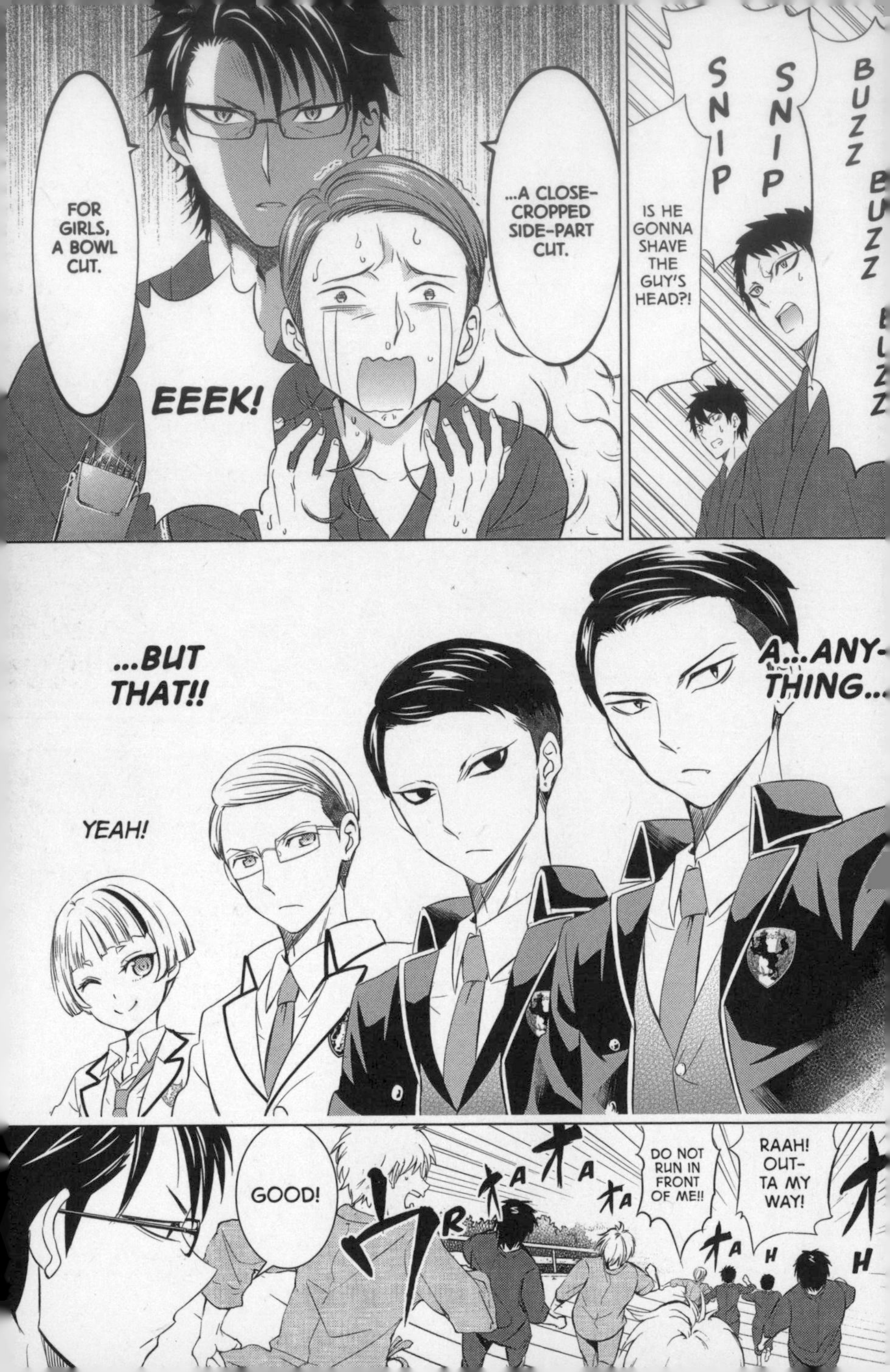
SNIP SNIP
BUZZ BUZZ BUZZ
IS HE GONNA SHAVE THE GUY'S HEAD?!
...A CLOSE-CROPPED SIDE-PART CUT.
FOR GIRLS, A BOWL CUT.
EEEK!
A...ANY-THING...
...BUT THAT!!
YEAH!
RAAH! OUTTA MY WAY!
DO NOT RUN IN FRONT OF ME!!
GOOD!

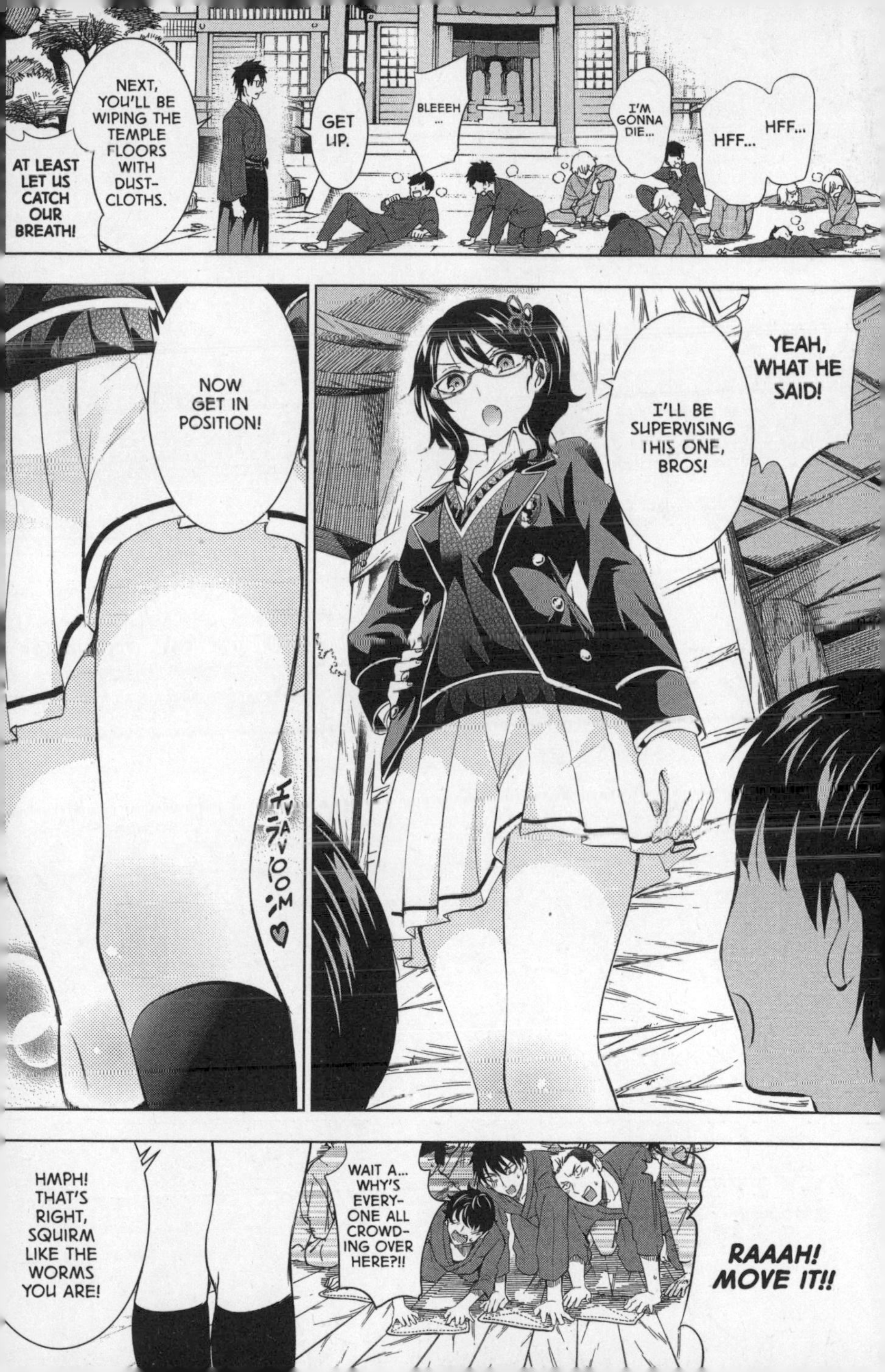

HFF... HFF...
I'M GONNA DIE...
BLEEEH ...
GET UP.
NEXT, YOU'LL BE WIPING THE TEMPLE FLOORS WITH DUST-CLOTHS.
AT LEAST LET US CATCH OUR BREATH!
YEAH, WHAT HE SAID!
I'LL BE SUPERVISING THIS ONE, BROS!
NOW GET IN POSITION!
チラ～ッ♥
VAVOOM
RAAAH! MOVE IT!!
WAIT A... WHY'S EVERYONE ALL CROWDING OVER HERE?!!
HMPH! THAT'S RIGHT, SQUIRM LIKE THE WORMS YOU ARE!

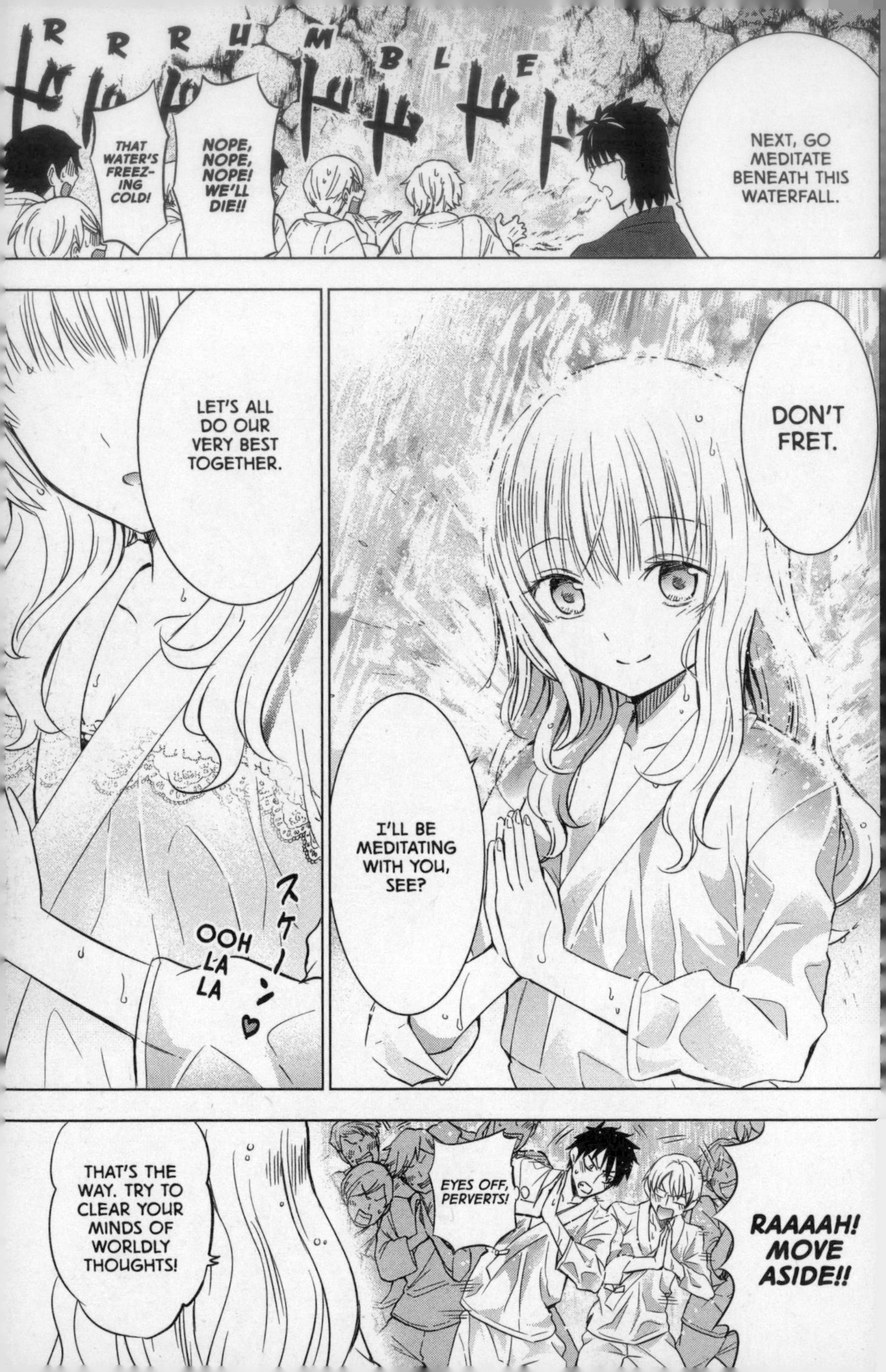
NEXT, GO MEDITATE BENEATH THIS WATERFALL.
RRRUMBLE
NOPE, NOPE, NOPE! WE'LL DIE!!
THAT WATER'S FREEZ-ING COLD!
DON'T FRET.
I'LL BE MEDITATING WITH YOU, SEE?
LET'S ALL DO OUR VERY BEST TOGETHER.
OOH LA LA
RAAAAH! MOVE ASIDE!!
EYES OFF, PERVERTS!
THAT'S THE WAY. TRY TO CLEAR YOUR MINDS OF WORLDLY THOUGHTS!

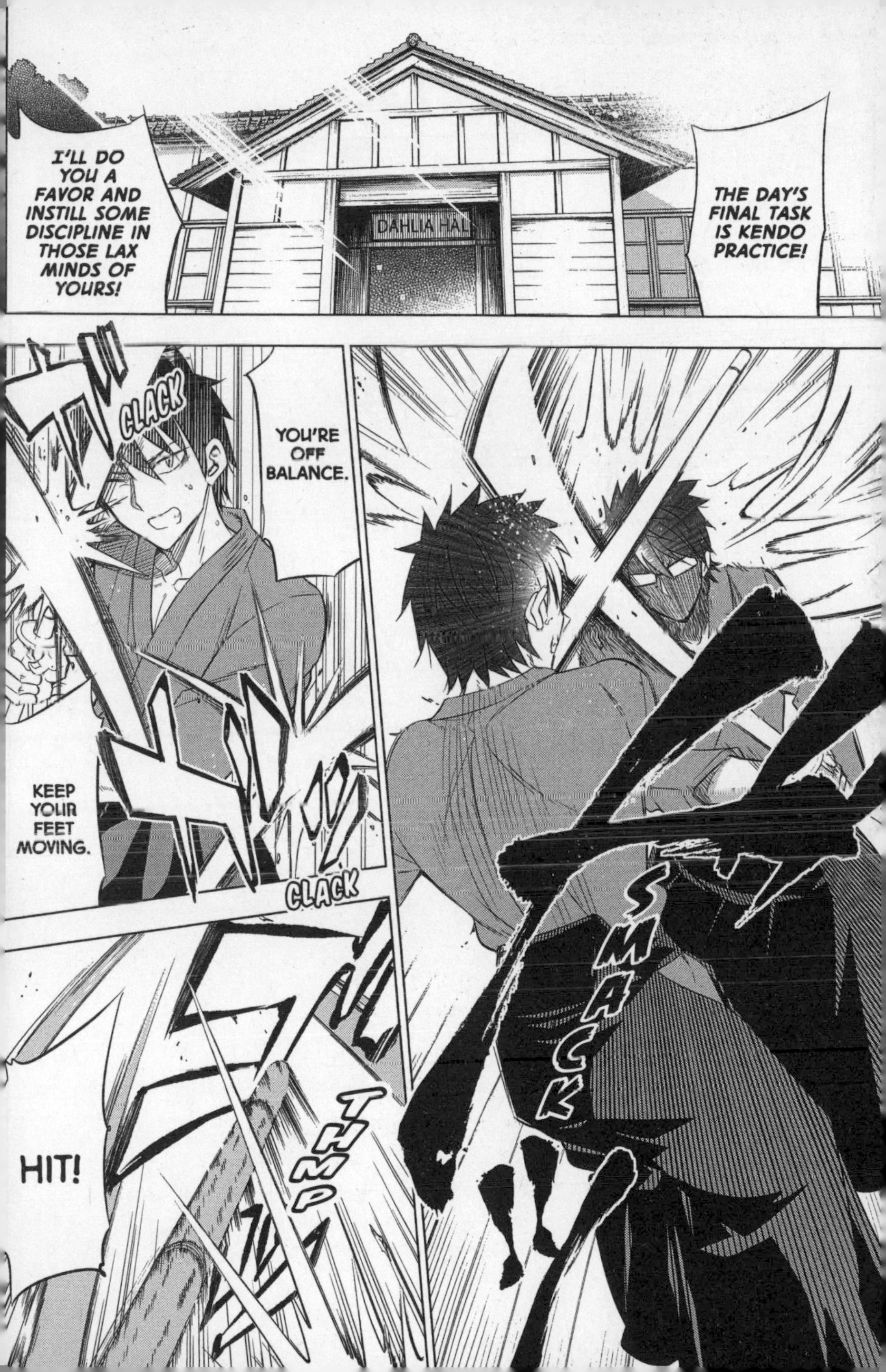
THE DAY'S FINAL TASK IS KENDO PRACTICE!
DAHLIA HAL
I'LL DO YOU A FAVOR AND INSTILL SOME DISCIPLINE IN THOSE LAX MINDS OF YOURS!
SMACK
CLACK
YOU'RE OFF BALANCE.
KEEP YOUR FEET MOVING.
CLACK
THMP
HIT!

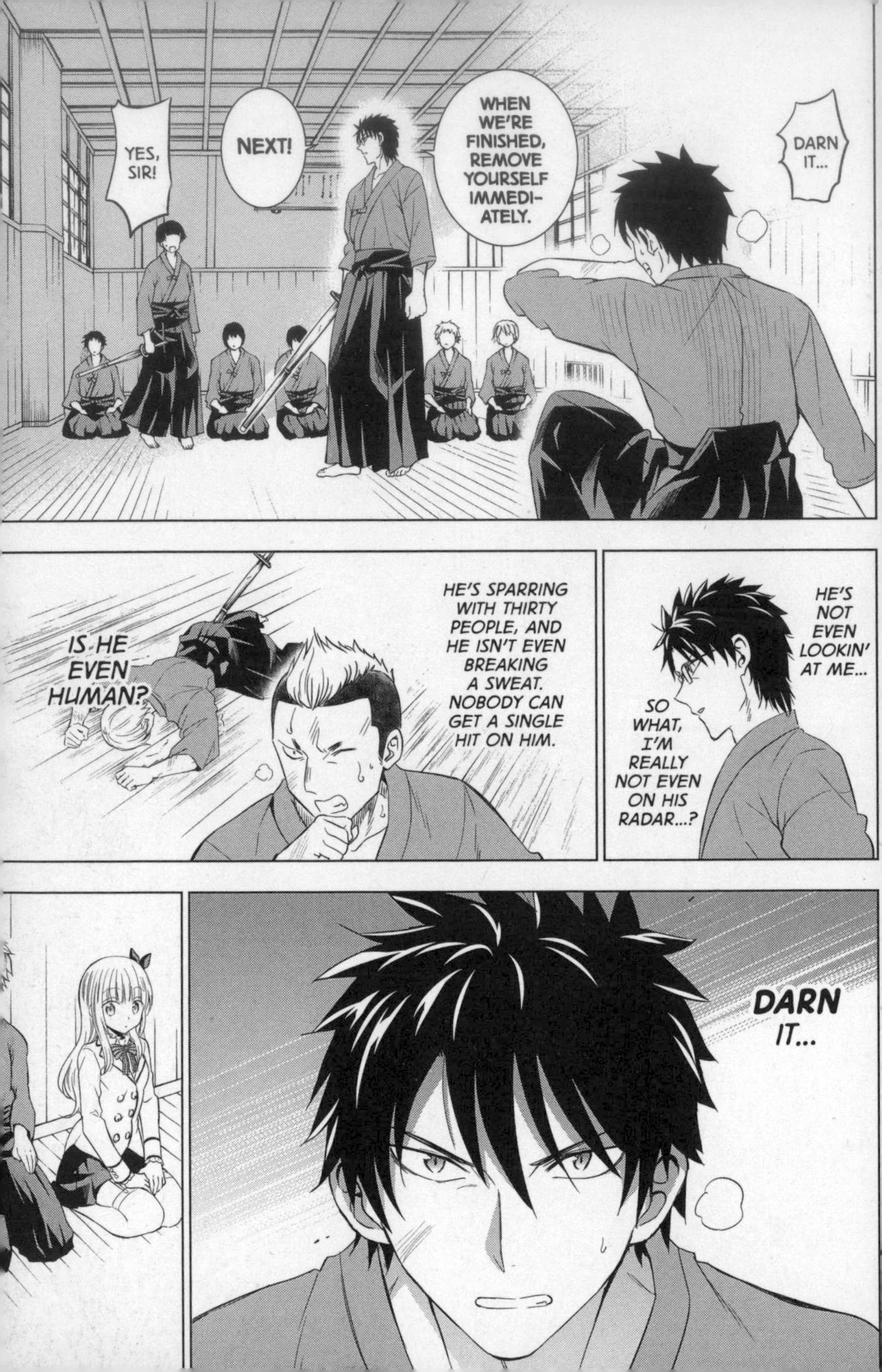
DARN IT...
WHEN WE'RE FINISHED, REMOVE YOURSELF IMMEDI-ATELY.
NEXT!
YES, SIR!
HE'S NOT EVEN LOOKIN' AT ME...
SO WHAT, I'M REALLY NOT EVEN ON HIS RADAR...?
HE'S SPARRING WITH THIRTY PEOPLE, AND HE ISN'T EVEN BREAKING A SWEAT. NOBODY CAN GET A SINGLE HIT ON HIM.
IS HE EVEN HUMAN?
DARN IT...

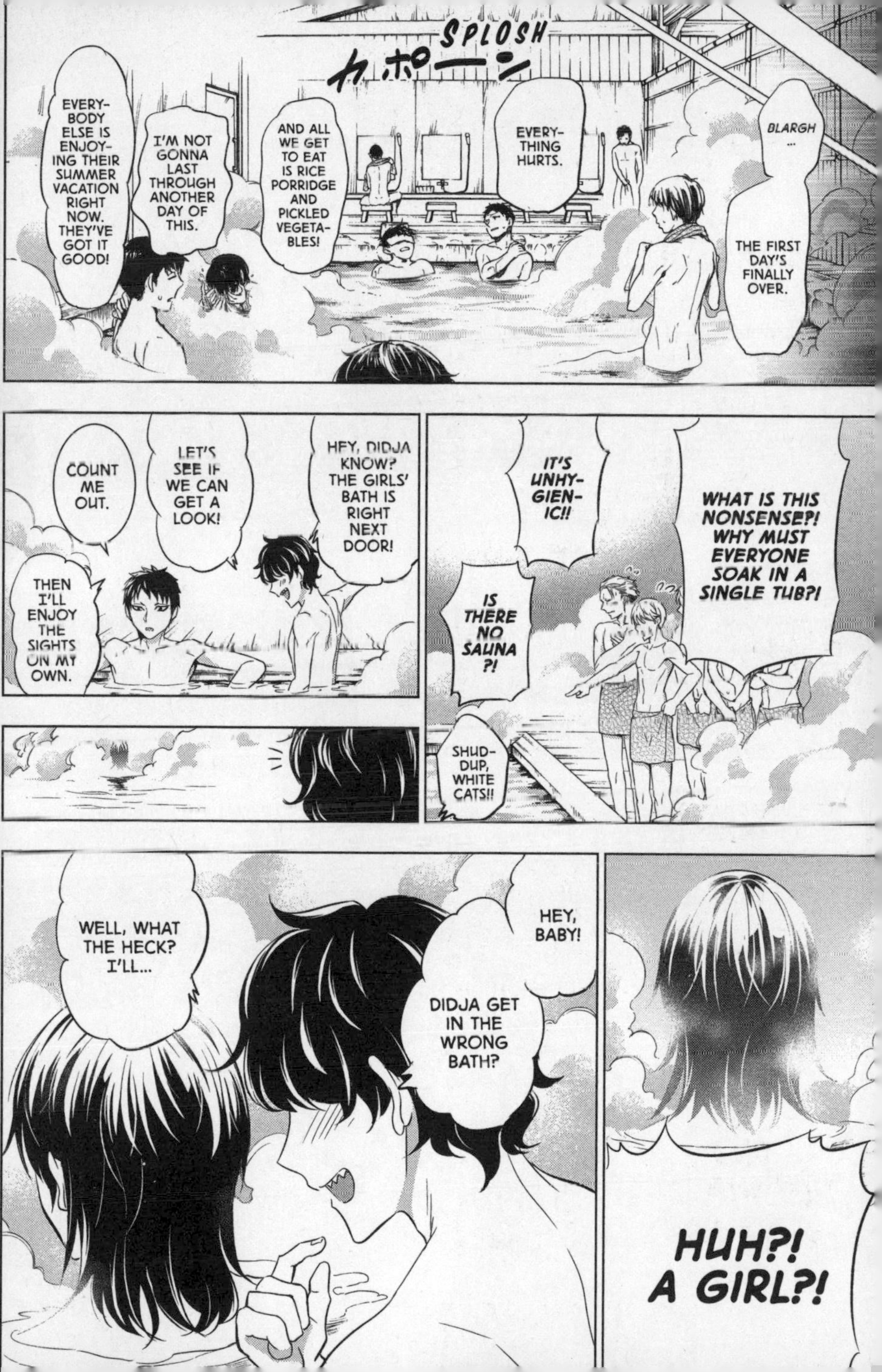
SPLOSH
カポーン
BLARGH ...
THE FIRST DAY'S FINALLY OVER.
EVERYTHING HURTS.
AND ALL WE GET TO EAT IS RICE PORRIDGE AND PICKLED VEGETABLES!
I'M NOT GONNA LAST THROUGH ANOTHER DAY OF THIS.
EVERYBODY ELSE IS ENJOYING THEIR SUMMER VACATION RIGHT NOW. THEY'VE GOT IT GOOD!
WHAT IS THIS NONSENSE?! WHY MUST EVERYONE SOAK IN A SINGLE TUB?!
IT'S UNHYGIENIC!!
IS THERE NO SAUNA?!
SHUDDUP, WHITE CATS!!
HEY, DIDJA KNOW? THE GIRLS' BATH IS RIGHT NEXT DOOR!
LET'S SEE IF WE CAN GET A LOOK!
COUNT ME OUT.
THEN I'LL ENJOY THE SIGHTS ON MY OWN.
HUH?! A GIRL?!
HEY, BABY!
DIDJA GET IN THE WRONG BATH?
WELL, WHAT THE HECK? I'LL...

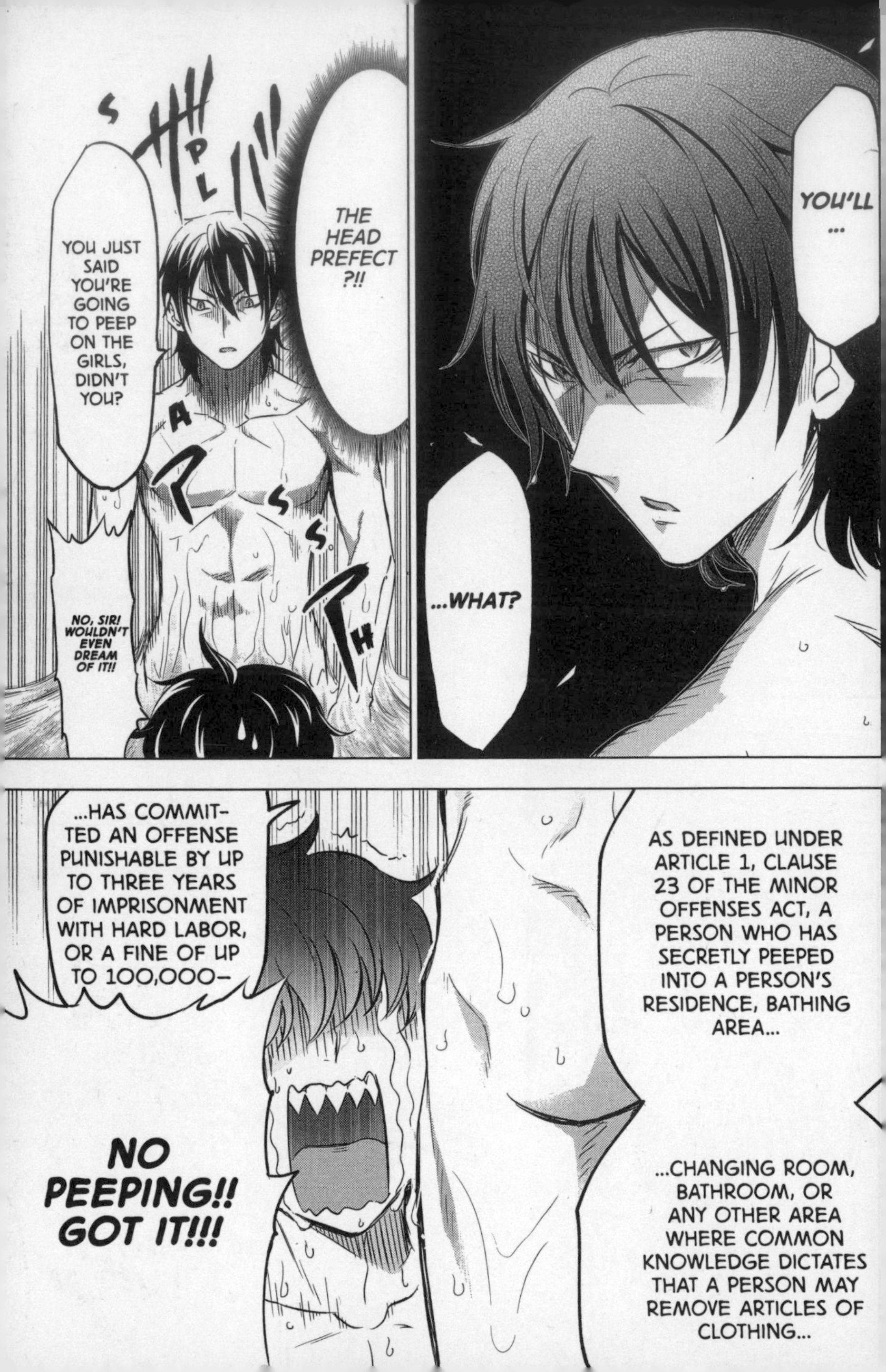
YOU'LL ...
...WHAT?
SPLASSH
THE HEAD PREFECT ?!!
YOU JUST SAID YOU'RE GOING TO PEEP ON THE GIRLS, DIDN'T YOU?
NO, SIR! WOULDN'T EVEN DREAM OF IT!!
AS DEFINED UNDER ARTICLE 1, CLAUSE 23 OF THE MINOR OFFENSES ACT, A PERSON WHO HAS SECRETLY PEEPED INTO A PERSON'S RESIDENCE, BATHING AREA...
...CHANGING ROOM, BATHROOM, OR ANY OTHER AREA WHERE COMMON KNOWLEDGE DICTATES THAT A PERSON MAY REMOVE ARTICLES OF CLOTHING...
...HAS COMMIT-TED AN OFFENSE PUNISHABLE BY UP TO THREE YEARS OF IMPRISONMENT WITH HARD LABOR, OR A FINE OF UP TO 100,000–
NO PEEPING!! GOT IT!!!

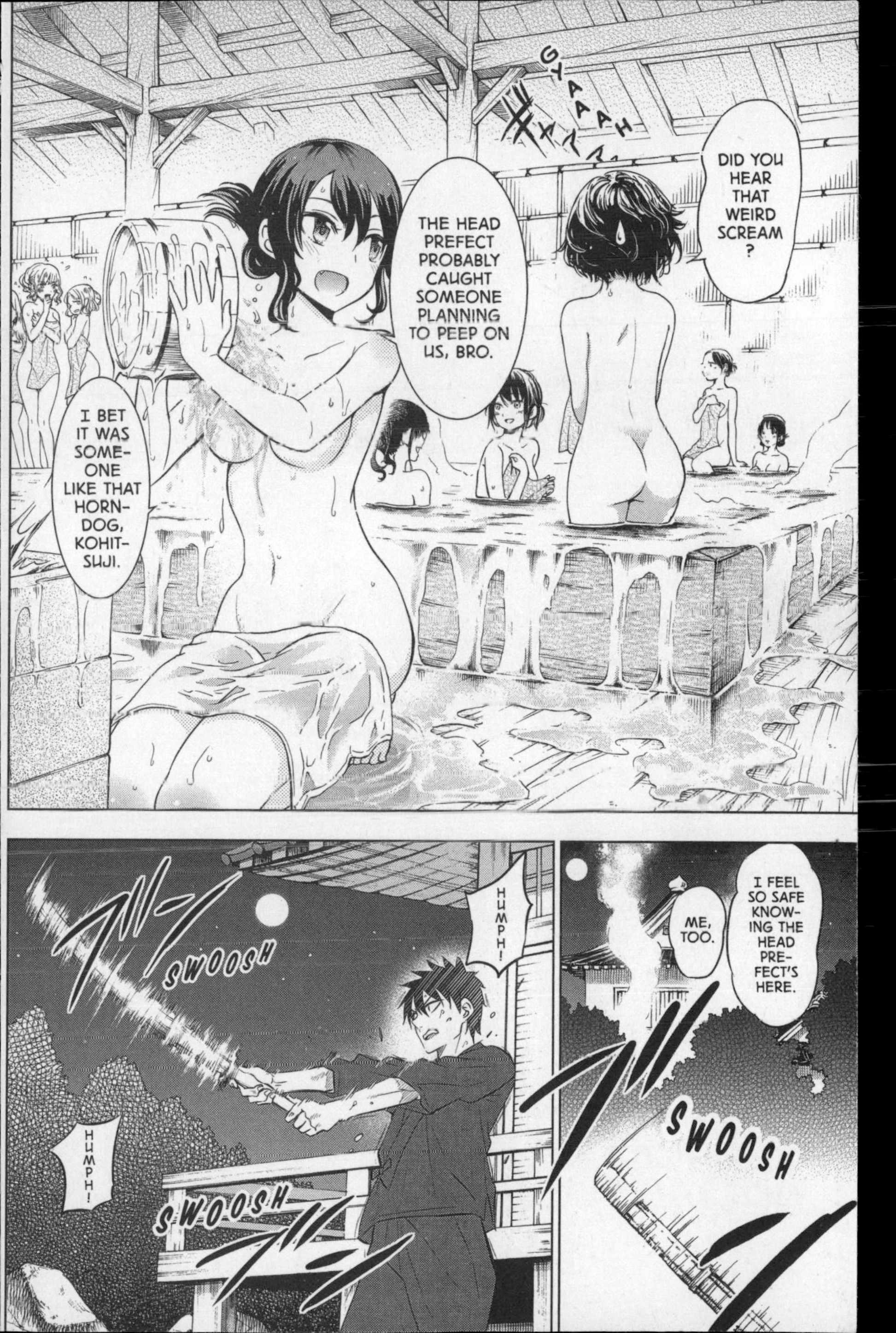
GYAAAAH
DID YOU HEAR THAT WEIRD SCREAM?
THE HEAD PREFECT PROBABLY CAUGHT SOMEONE PLANNING TO PEEP ON US, BRO.
I BET IT WAS SOMEONE LIKE THAT HORNDOG, KOHITSUJI.
I FEEL SO SAFE KNOWING THE HEAD PREFECT'S HERE.
ME, TOO.
SWOOSH
HUMPH!
SWOOSH
HUMPH!
SWOOSH

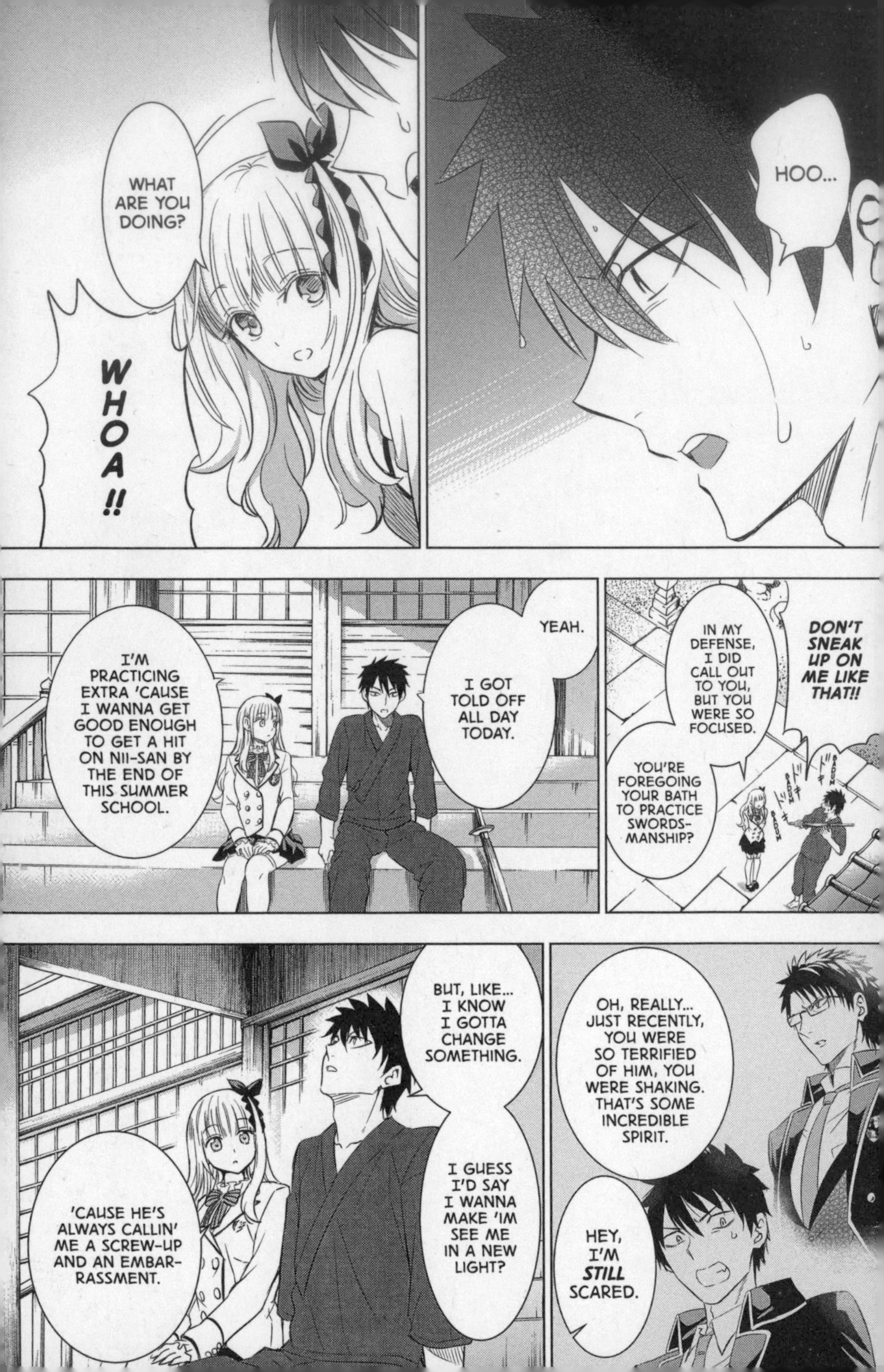
HOO...
WHAT ARE YOU DOING?
WHOA!!
DON'T SNEAK UP ON ME LIKE THAT!!
IN MY DEFENSE, I DID CALL OUT TO YOU, BUT YOU WERE SO FOCUSED.
BADUM BADUM BADUM
YOU'RE FOREGOING YOUR BATH TO PRACTICE SWORDS-MANSHIP?
YEAH.
I GOT TOLD OFF ALL DAY TODAY.
I'M PRACTICING EXTRA 'CAUSE I WANNA GET GOOD ENOUGH TO GET A HIT ON NII-SAN BY THE END OF THIS SUMMER SCHOOL.
OH, REALLY... JUST RECENTLY, YOU WERE SO TERRIFIED OF HIM, YOU WERE SHAKING. THAT'S SOME INCREDIBLE SPIRIT.
HEY, I'M STILL SCARED.
BUT, LIKE... I KNOW I GOTTA CHANGE SOMETHING.
I GUESS I'D SAY I WANNA MAKE 'IM SEE ME IN A NEW LIGHT?
'CAUSE HE'S ALWAYS CALLIN' ME A SCREW-UP AND AN EMBAR-RASSMENT.

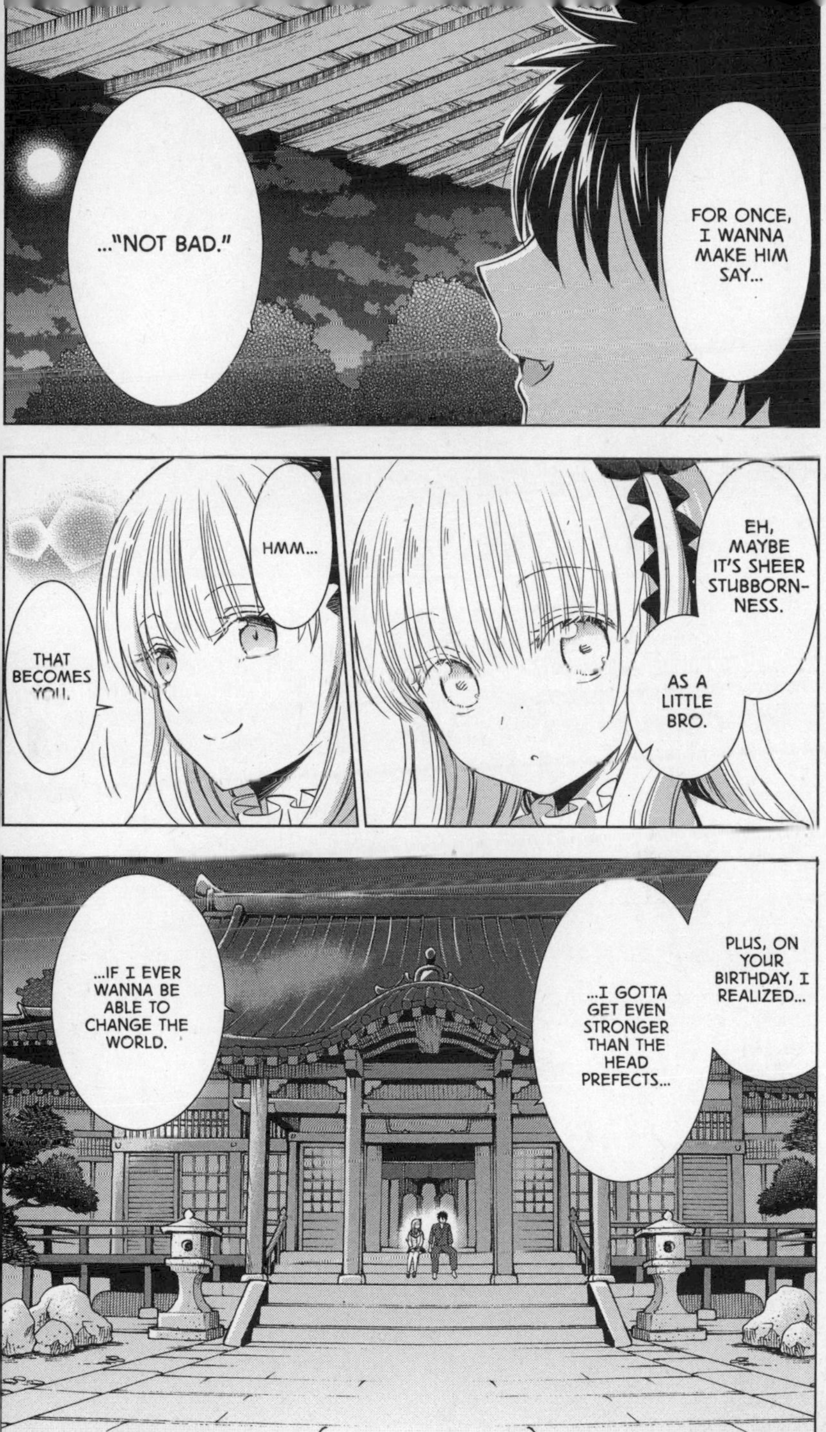
FOR ONCE, I WANNA MAKE HIM SAY...
..."NOT BAD."
EH, MAYBE IT'S SHEER STUBBORN-NESS.
AS A LITTLE BRO.
HMM...
THAT BECOMES YOU.
PLUS, ON YOUR BIRTHDAY, I REALIZED...
...I GOTTA GET EVEN STRONGER THAN THE HEAD PREFECTS...
...IF I EVER WANNA BE ABLE TO CHANGE THE WORLD.

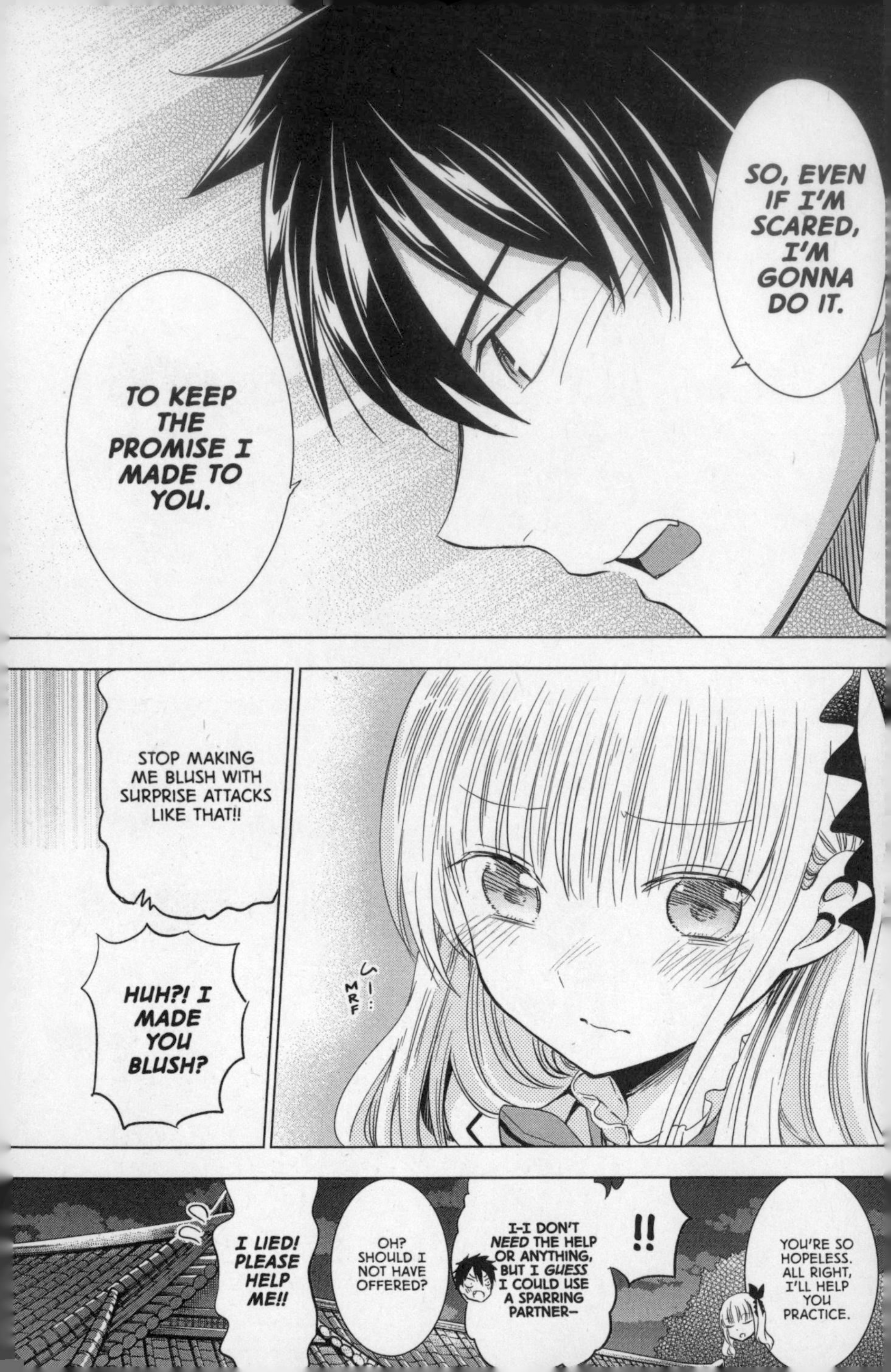
SO, EVEN IF I'M SCARED, I'M GONNA DO IT.
TO KEEP THE PROMISE I MADE TO YOU.
MRF
STOP MAKING ME BLUSH WITH SURPRISE ATTACKS LIKE THAT!!
HUH?! I MADE YOU BLUSH?
YOU'RE SO HOPELESS. ALL RIGHT, I'LL HELP YOU PRACTICE.
!!
I-I DON'T *NEED* THE HELP OR ANYTHING, BUT I *GUESS* I COULD USE A SPARRING PARTNER—
OH? SHOULD I NOT HAVE OFFERED?
I LIED! PLEASE HELP ME!!

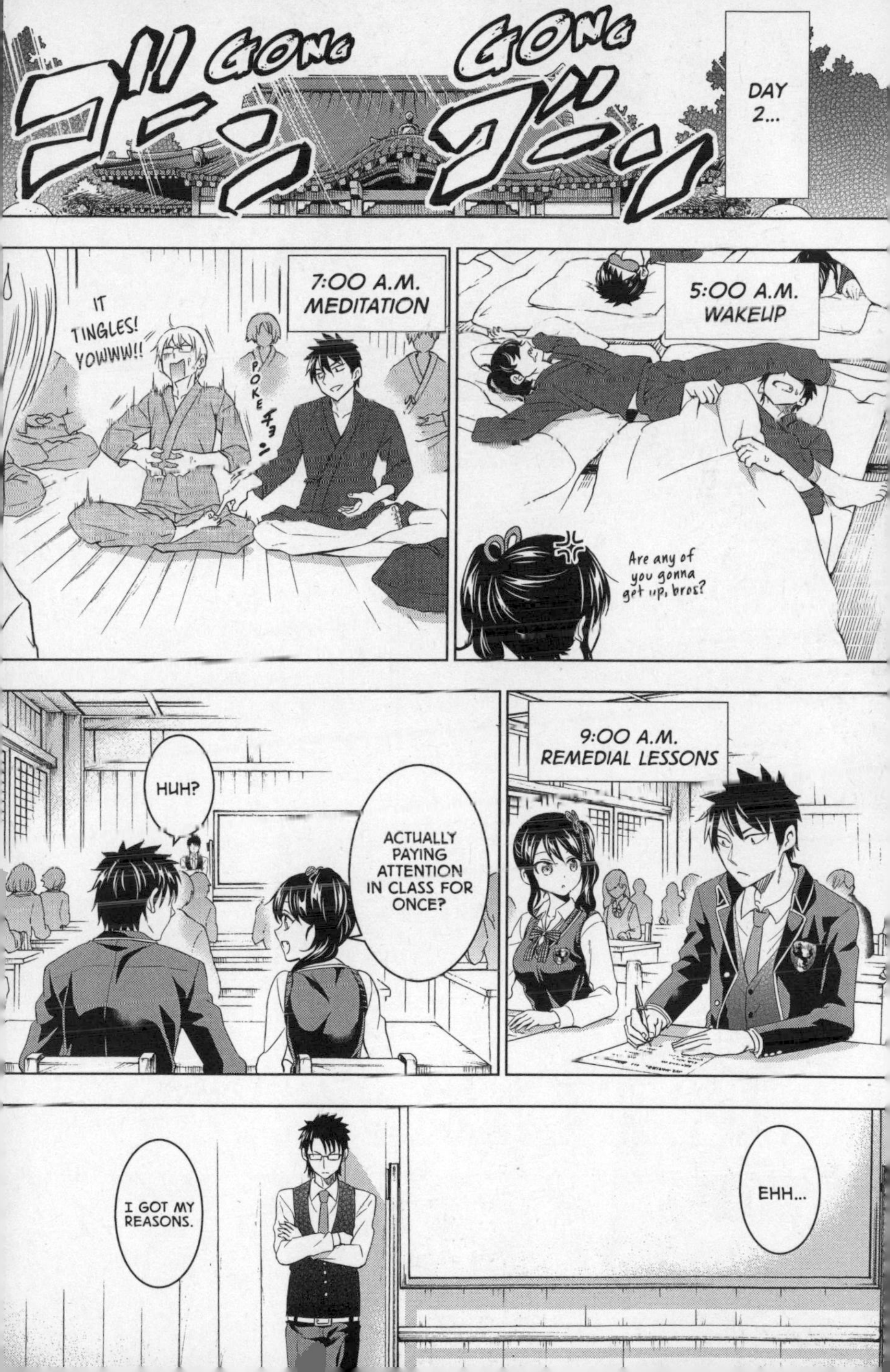
DAY 2...
GONG
GONG
5:00 A.M. WAKEUP
Are any of you gonna get up, bros?
7:00 A.M. MEDITATION
POKE
IT TINGLES! YOWWW!!
9:00 A.M. REMEDIAL LESSONS
ACTUALLY PAYING ATTENTION IN CLASS FOR ONCE?
HUH?
EHH...
I GOT MY REASONS.

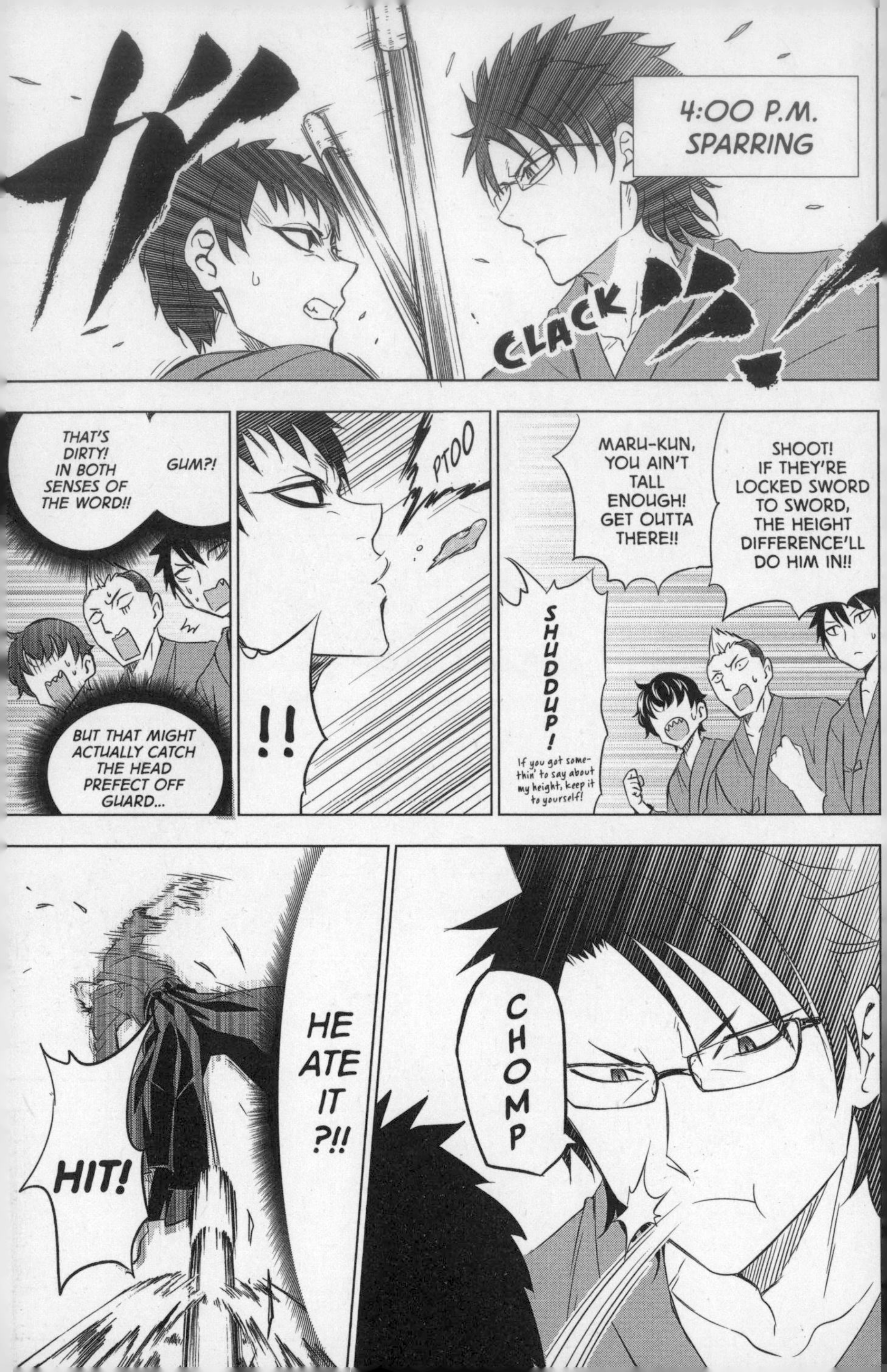
4:00 P.M. SPARRING
CLACK
SHOOT! IF THEY'RE LOCKED SWORD TO SWORD, THE HEIGHT DIFFERENCE'LL DO HIM IN!!
MARU-KUN, YOU AIN'T TALL ENOUGH! GET OUTTA THERE!!
SHUDDUP!
If you got somethin' to say about my height, keep it to yourself!
PTOO
!!
GUM?!
THAT'S DIRTY! IN BOTH SENSES OF THE WORD!!
BUT THAT MIGHT ACTUALLY CATCH THE HEAD PREFECT OFF GUARD...
CHOMP
HE ATE IT ?!!
HIT!

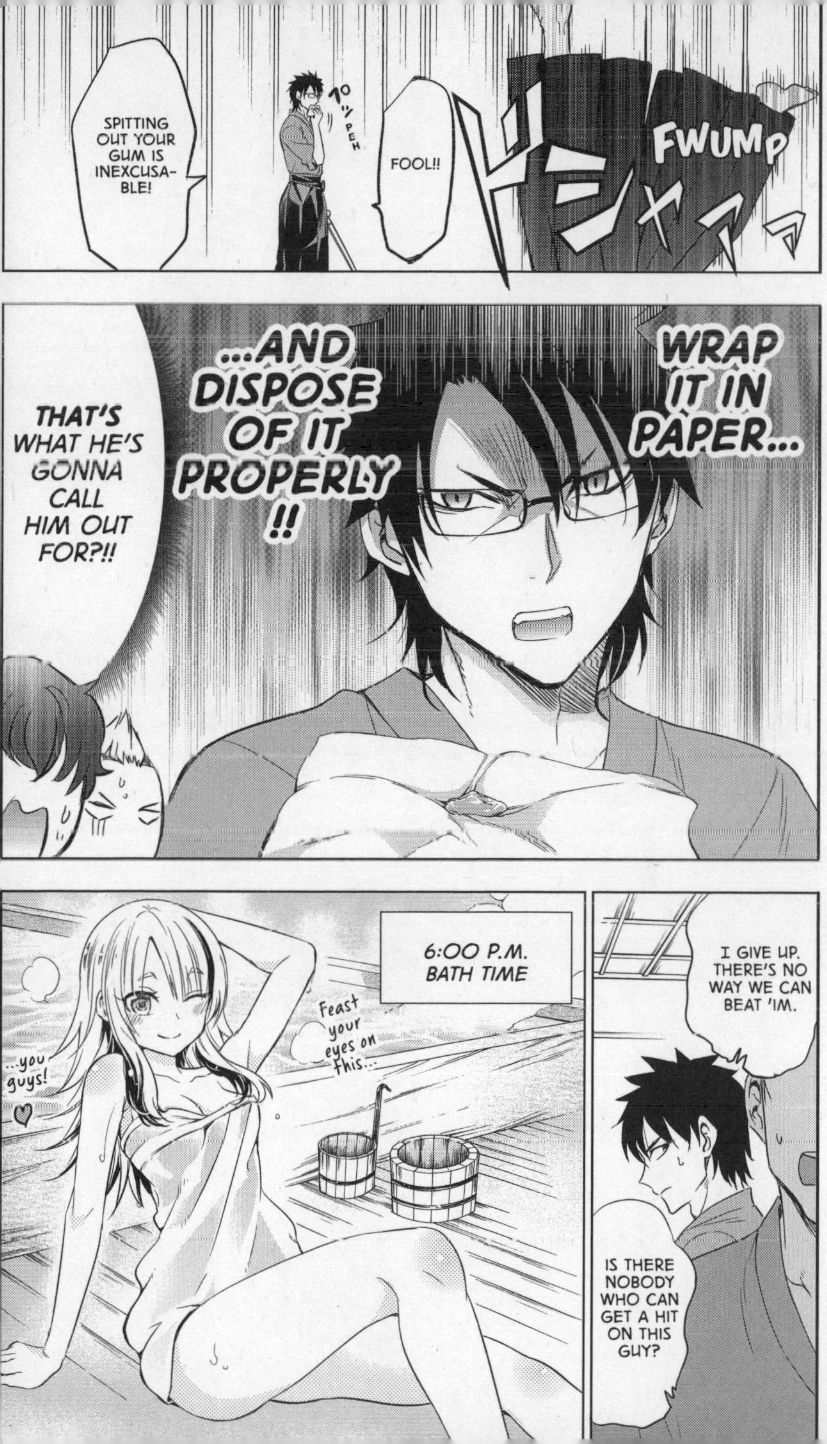
FWUMP
FOOL!!
PEH
SPITTING OUT YOUR GUM IS INEXCUSA-BLE!
WRAP IT IN PAPER...
...AND DISPOSE OF IT PROPERLY!!
THAT'S WHAT HE'S GONNA CALL HIM OUT FOR?!!
I GIVE UP. THERE'S NO WAY WE CAN BEAT 'IM.
IS THERE NOBODY WHO CAN GET A HIT ON THIS GUY?
6:00 P.M. BATH TIME
Feast your eyes on this...
...you guys! ♥

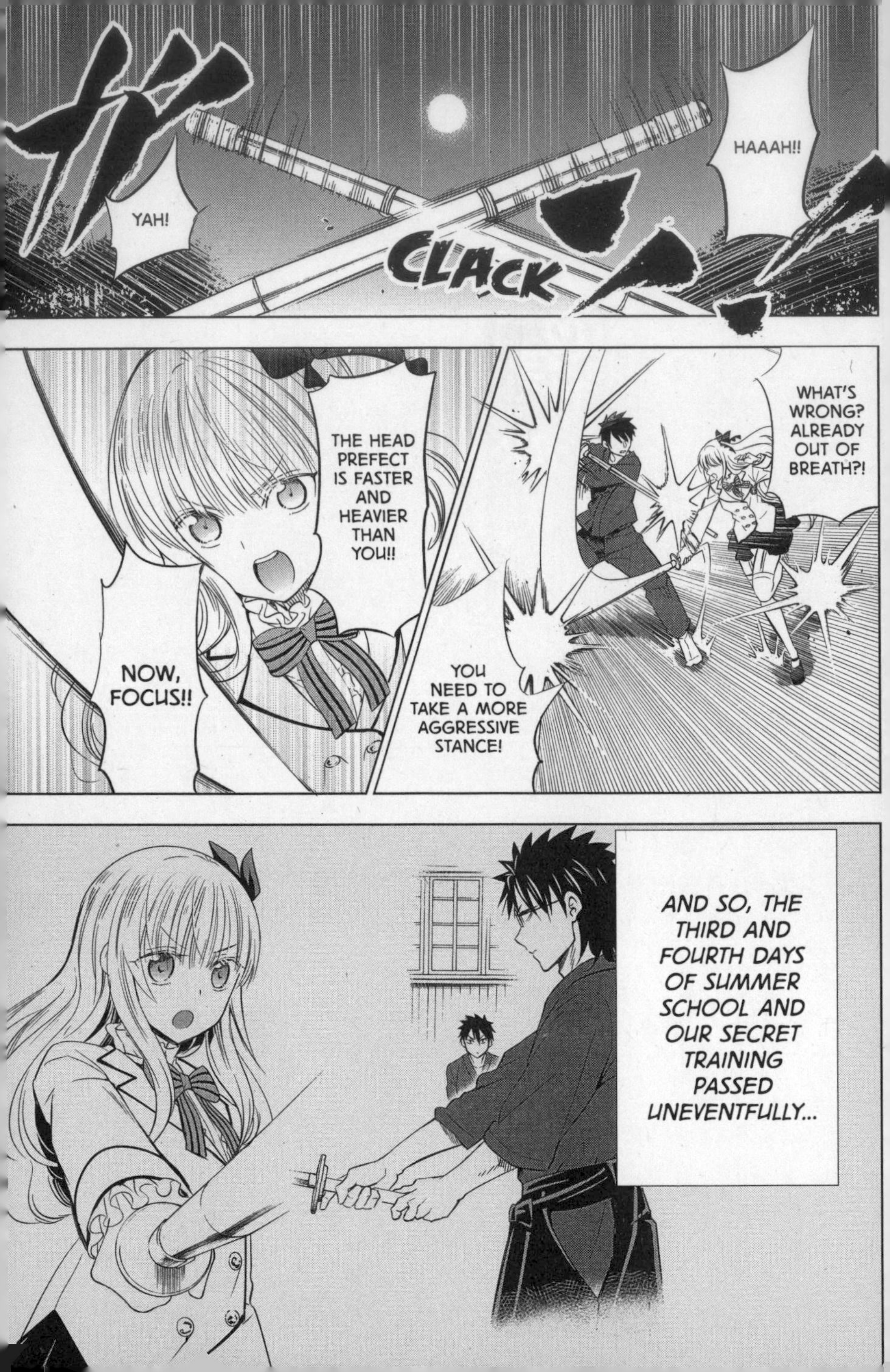
HAAAH!!
CLACK
YAH!
WHAT'S WRONG? ALREADY OUT OF BREATH?!
YOU NEED TO TAKE A MORE AGGRESSIVE STANCE!
THE HEAD PREFECT IS FASTER AND HEAVIER THAN YOU!!
NOW, FOCUS!!
AND SO, THE THIRD AND FOURTH DAYS OF SUMMER SCHOOL AND OUR SECRET TRAINING PASSED UNEVENTFULLY...

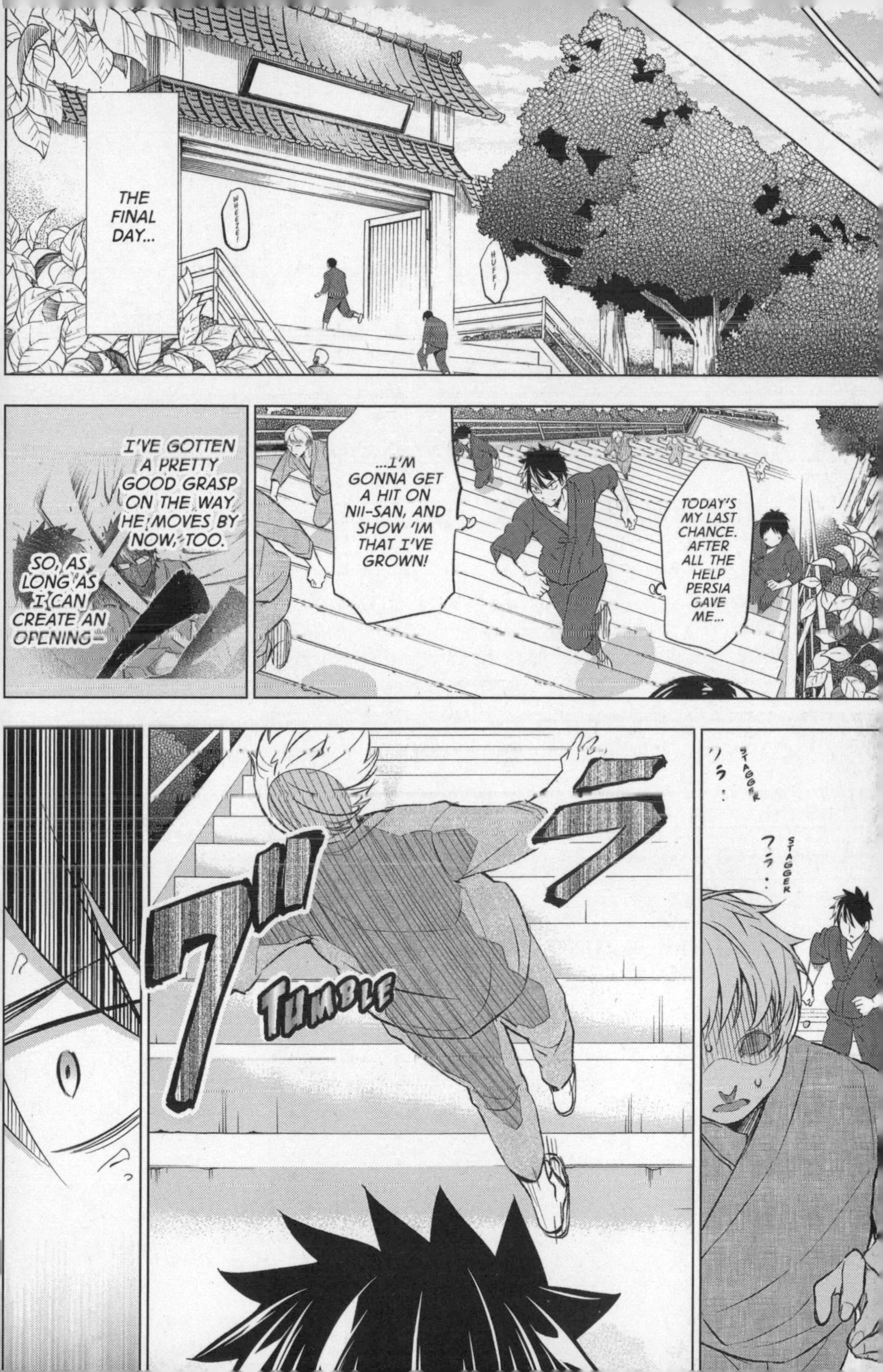
HUFF!
WHEEZE!
THE FINAL DAY...
TODAY'S MY LAST CHANCE. AFTER ALL THE HELP PERSIA GAVE ME...
...I'M GONNA GET A HIT ON NII-SAN, AND SHOW 'IM THAT I'VE GROWN!
I'VE GOTTEN A PRETTY GOOD GRASP ON THE WAY HE MOVES BY NOW, TOO.
SO, AS LONG AS I CAN CREATE AN OPENING–
フラ!
STAGGER
フラ..
STAGGER
TUMBLE

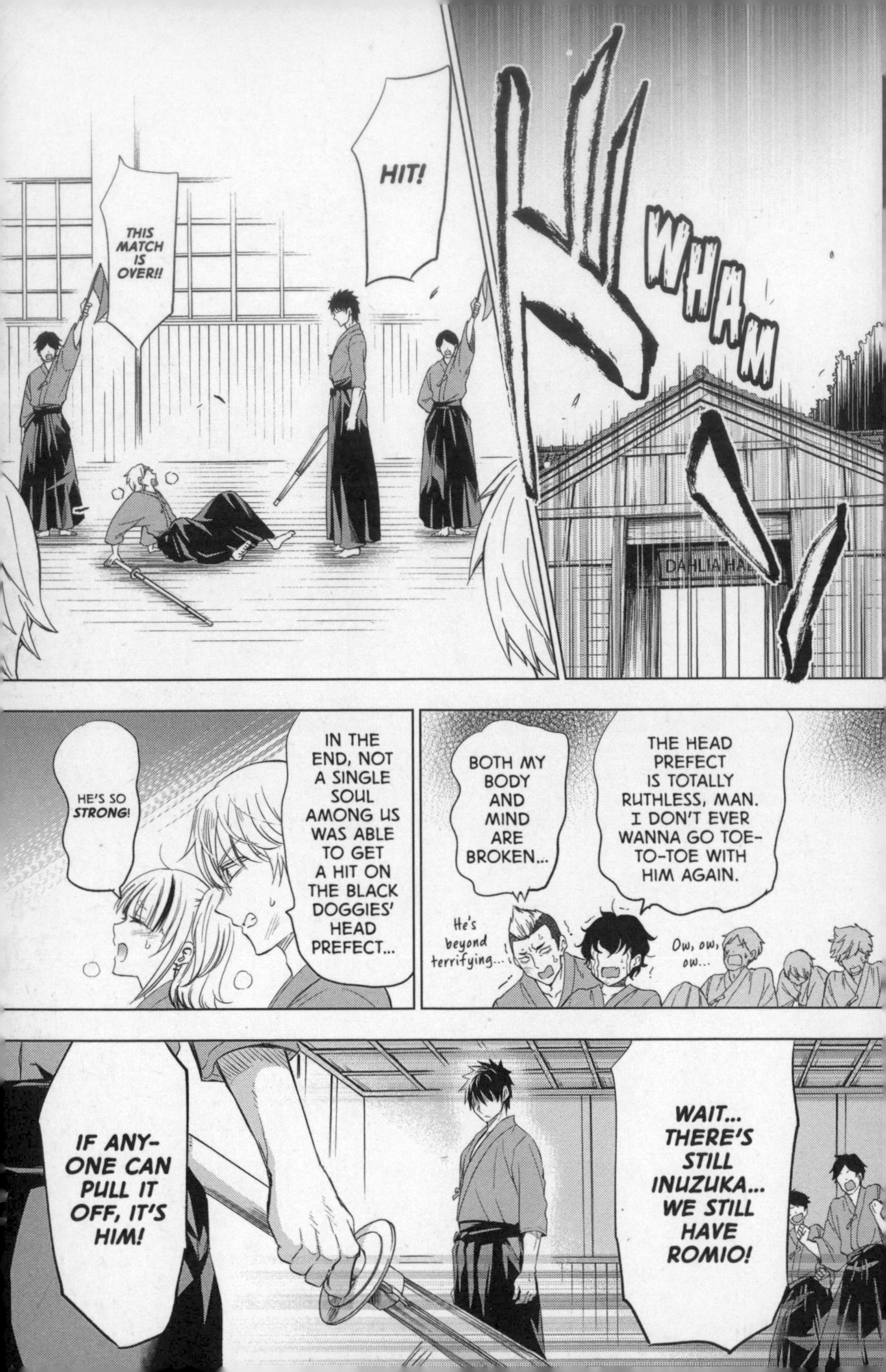

WHAM
DAHLIA HA
HIT!
THIS MATCH IS OVER!!
THE HEAD PREFECT IS TOTALLY RUTHLESS, MAN. I DON'T EVER WANNA GO TOE-TO-TOE WITH HIM AGAIN.
BOTH MY BODY AND MIND ARE BROKEN...
He's beyond terrifying...
Ow, ow, ow...
IN THE END, NOT A SINGLE SOUL AMONG US WAS ABLE TO GET A HIT ON THE BLACK DOGGIES' HEAD PREFECT...
HE'S SO STRONG!
WAIT... THERE'S STILL INUZUKA... WE STILL HAVE ROMIO!
IF ANY-ONE CAN PULL IT OFF, IT'S HIM!

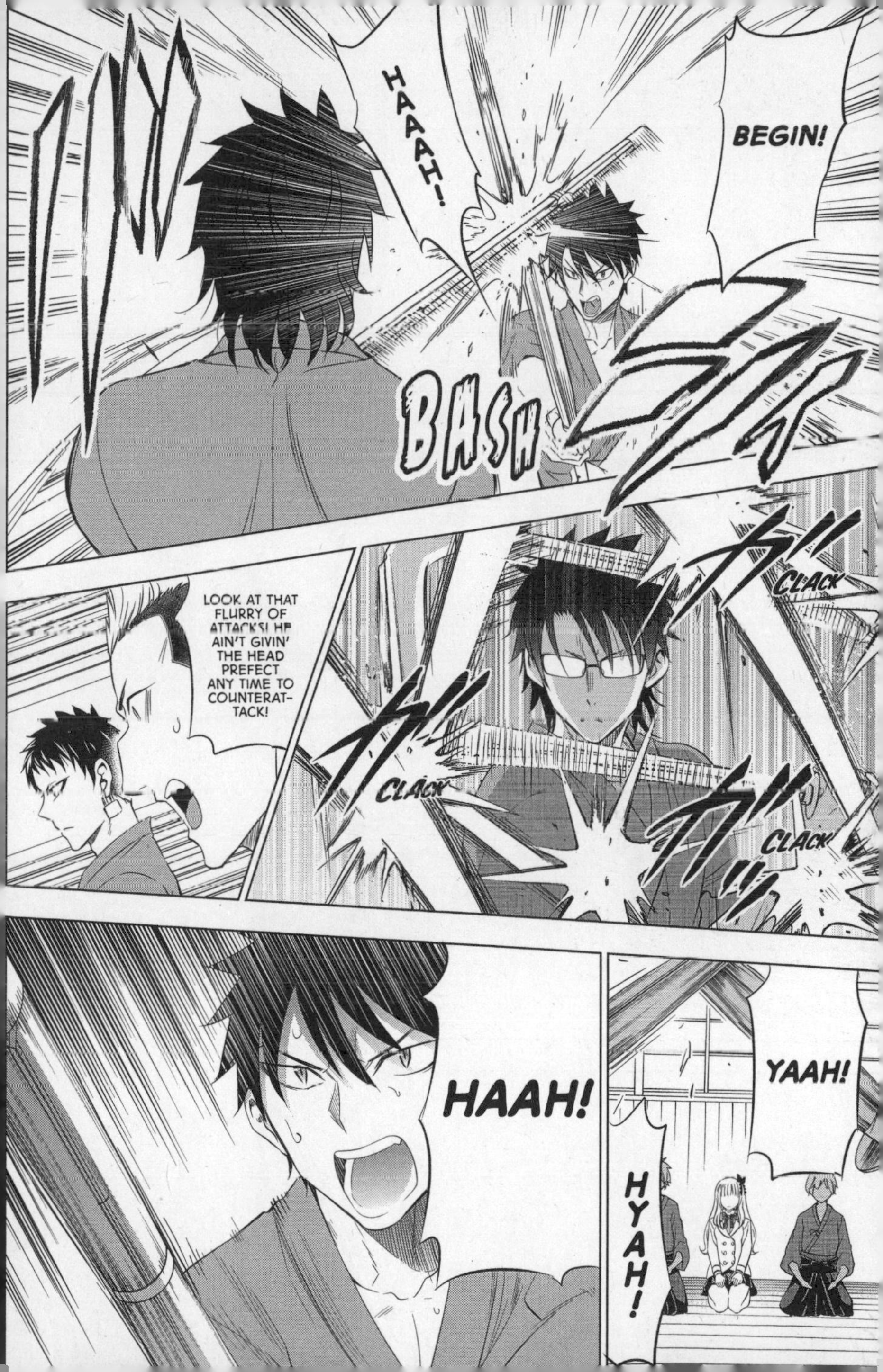
BEGIN!
HAAAAH!
BASH
CLACK
CLACK
CLACK
LOOK AT THAT FLURRY OF ATTACKS! HE AIN'T GIVIN' THE HEAD PREFECT ANY TIME TO COUNTERAT-TACK!
YAAH!
HYAAH!
HAAH!

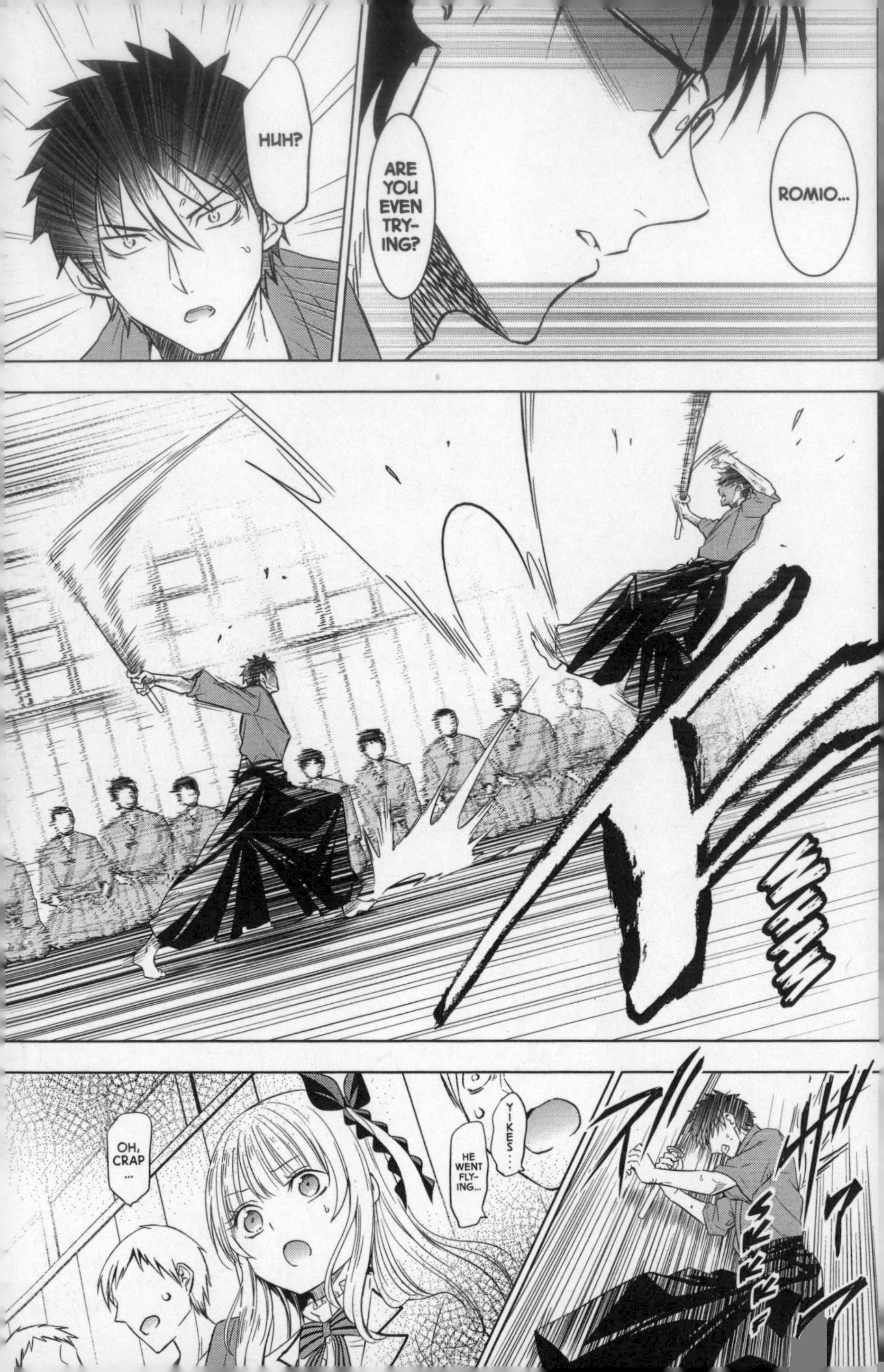
ROMIO...
ARE YOU EVEN TRY-ING?
HUH?
WHAM
YIKES...
HE WENT FLY-ING...
OH, CRAP...

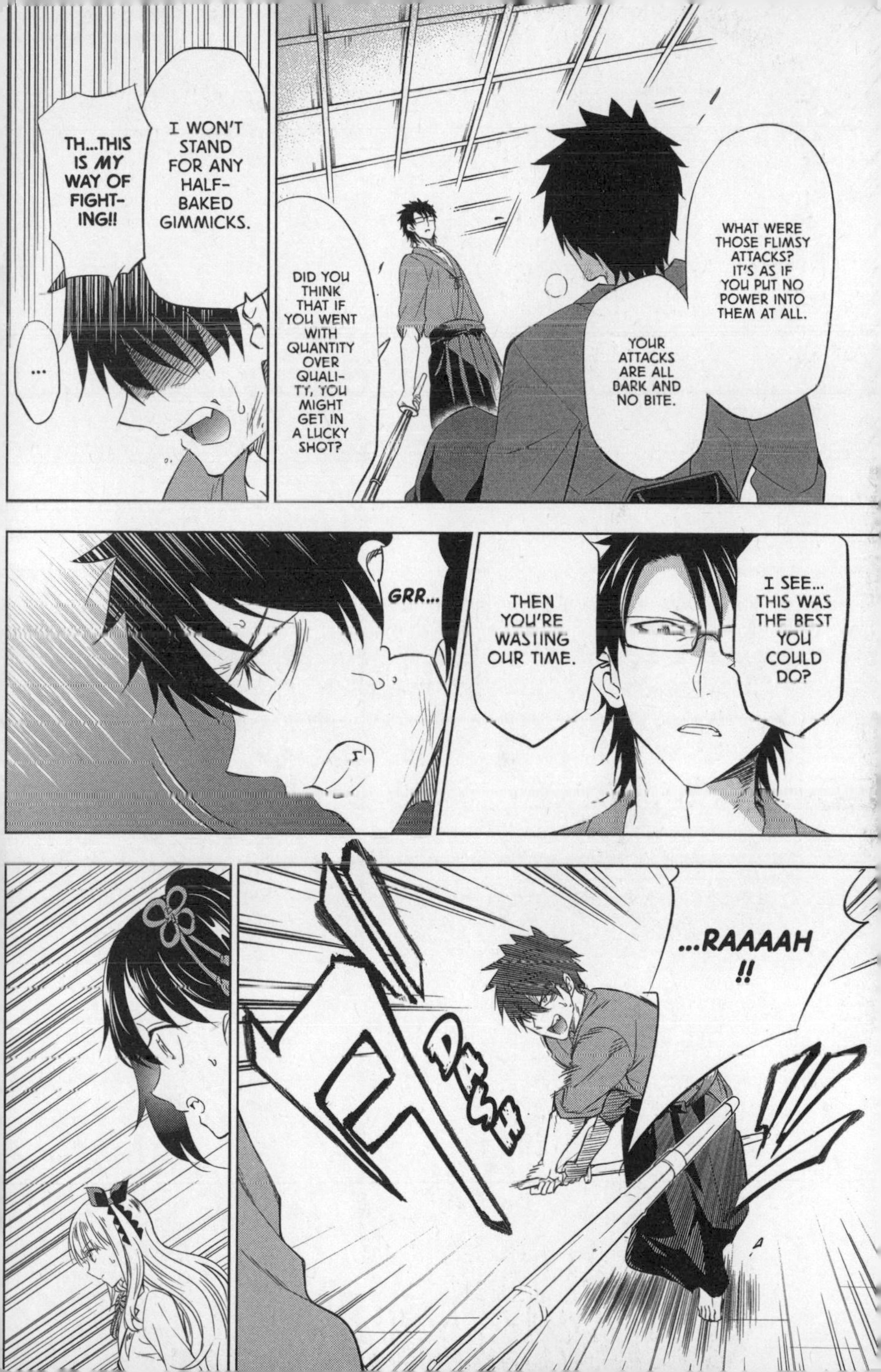
WHAT WERE THOSE FLIMSY ATTACKS? IT'S AS IF YOU PUT NO POWER INTO THEM AT ALL.
YOUR ATTACKS ARE ALL BARK AND NO BITE.
DID YOU THINK THAT IF YOU WENT WITH QUANTITY OVER QUALITY, YOU MIGHT GET IN A LUCKY SHOT?
I WON'T STAND FOR ANY HALF-BAKED GIMMICKS.
TH...THIS IS *MY* WAY OF FIGHTING!!
...
I SEE... THIS WAS THE BEST YOU COULD DO?
THEN YOU'RE WASTING OUR TIME.
GRR...
...RAAAAH!!
DASH

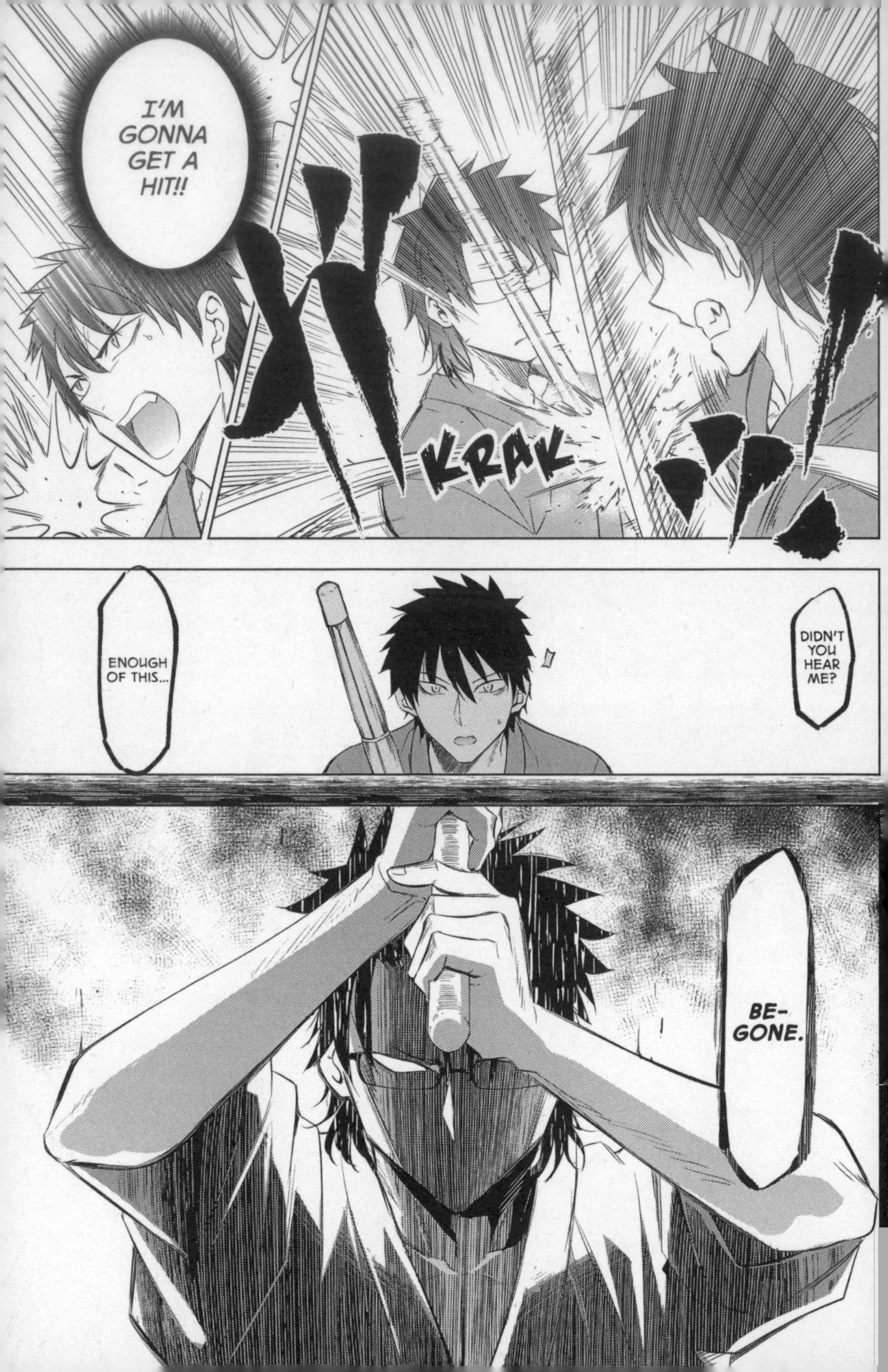
I'M GONNA GET A HIT!!
KRAK
DIDN'T YOU HEAR ME?
ENOUGH OF THIS...
BE-GONE.

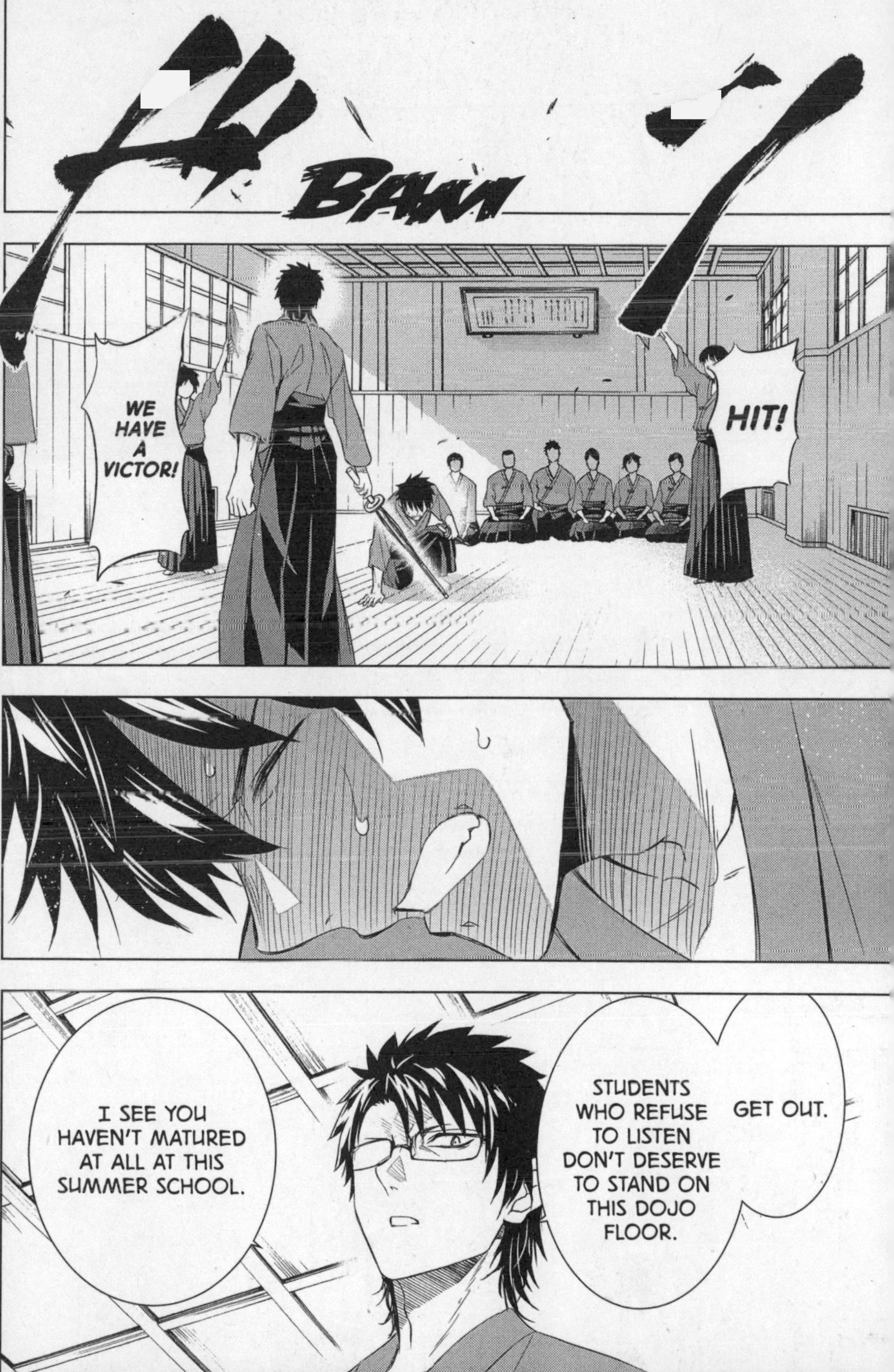
BAM
HIT!
WE HAVE A VICTOR!
GET OUT.
STUDENTS WHO REFUSE TO LISTEN DON'T DESERVE TO STAND ON THIS DOJO FLOOR.
I SEE YOU HAVEN'T MATURED AT ALL AT THIS SUMMER SCHOOL.

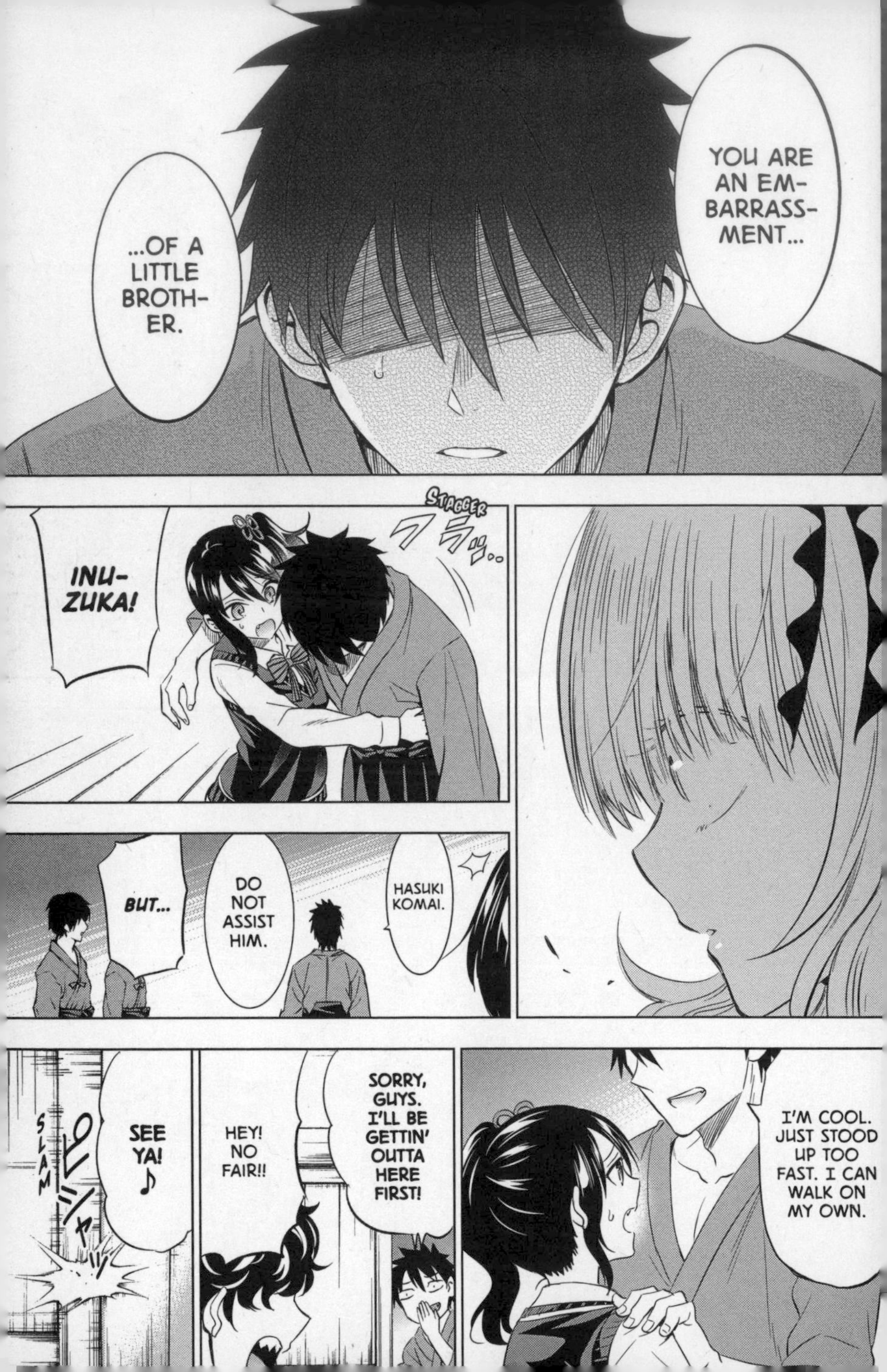
YOU ARE AN EM-BARRASS-MENT...
...OF A LITTLE BROTH-ER.
STAGGER
INU-ZUKA!
HASUKI KOMAI.
DO NOT ASSIST HIM.
BUT...
I'M COOL. JUST STOOD UP TOO FAST. I CAN WALK ON MY OWN.
SORRY, GUYS. I'LL BE GETTIN' OUTTA HERE FIRST!
HEY! NO FAIR!!
SEE YA! ♪
SLAM

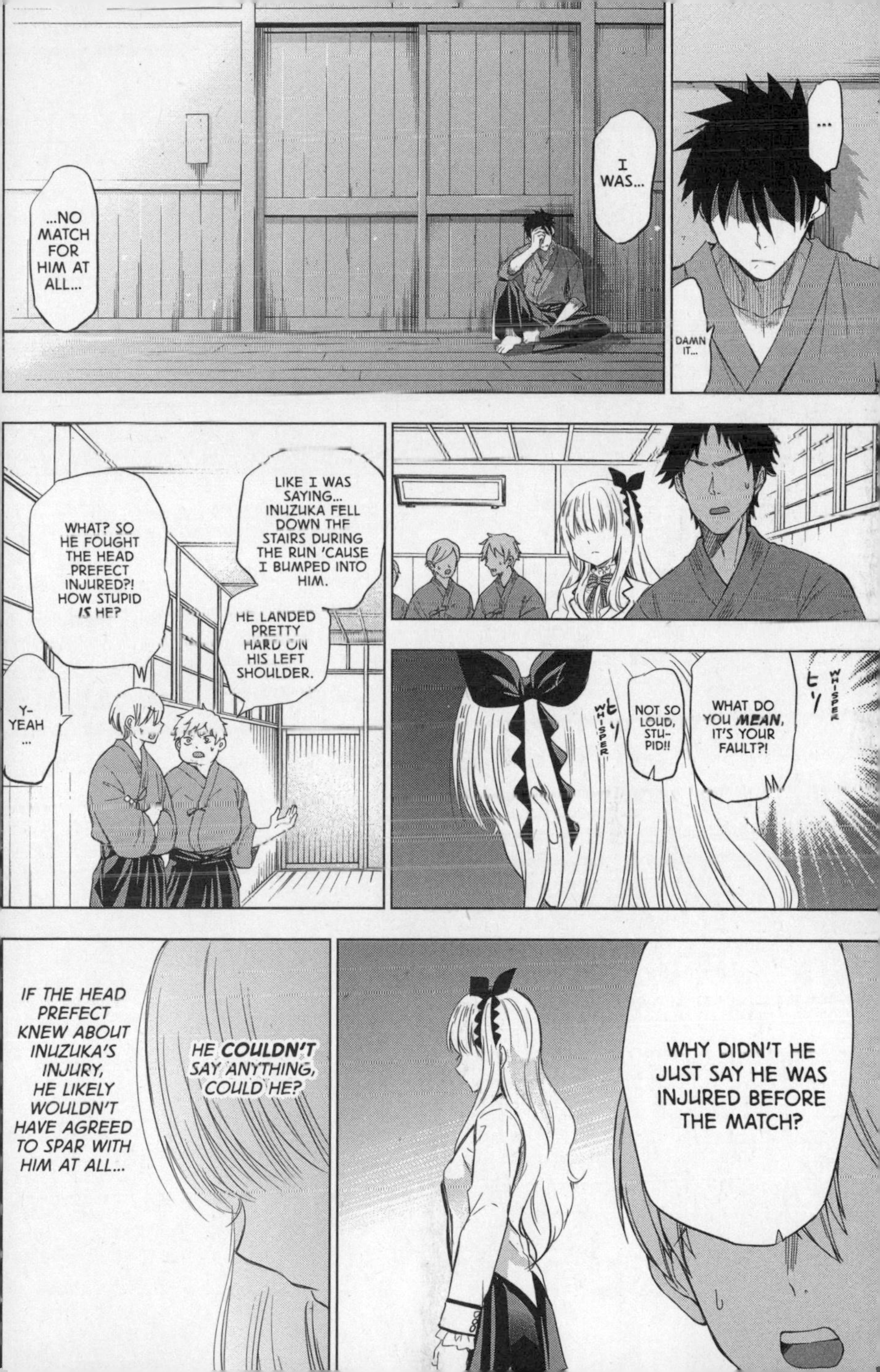
...
DAMN IT...
I WAS...
...NO MATCH FOR HIM AT ALL...
ヒソ WHISPER
WHAT DO YOU MEAN, IT'S YOUR FAULT?!
ヒソ WHISPER
NOT SO LOUD, STUPID!!
LIKE I WAS SAYING... INUZUKA FELL DOWN THE STAIRS DURING THE RUN 'CAUSE I BUMPED INTO HIM.
HE LANDED PRETTY HARD ON HIS LEFT SHOULDER.
WHAT? SO HE FOUGHT THE HEAD PREFECT INJURED?! HOW STUPID IS HE?
Y-YEAH ...
WHY DIDN'T HE JUST SAY HE WAS INJURED BEFORE THE MATCH?
HE COULDN'T SAY ANYTHING, COULD HE?
IF THE HEAD PREFECT KNEW ABOUT INUZUKA'S INJURY, HE LIKELY WOULDN'T HAVE AGREED TO SPAR WITH HIM AT ALL...

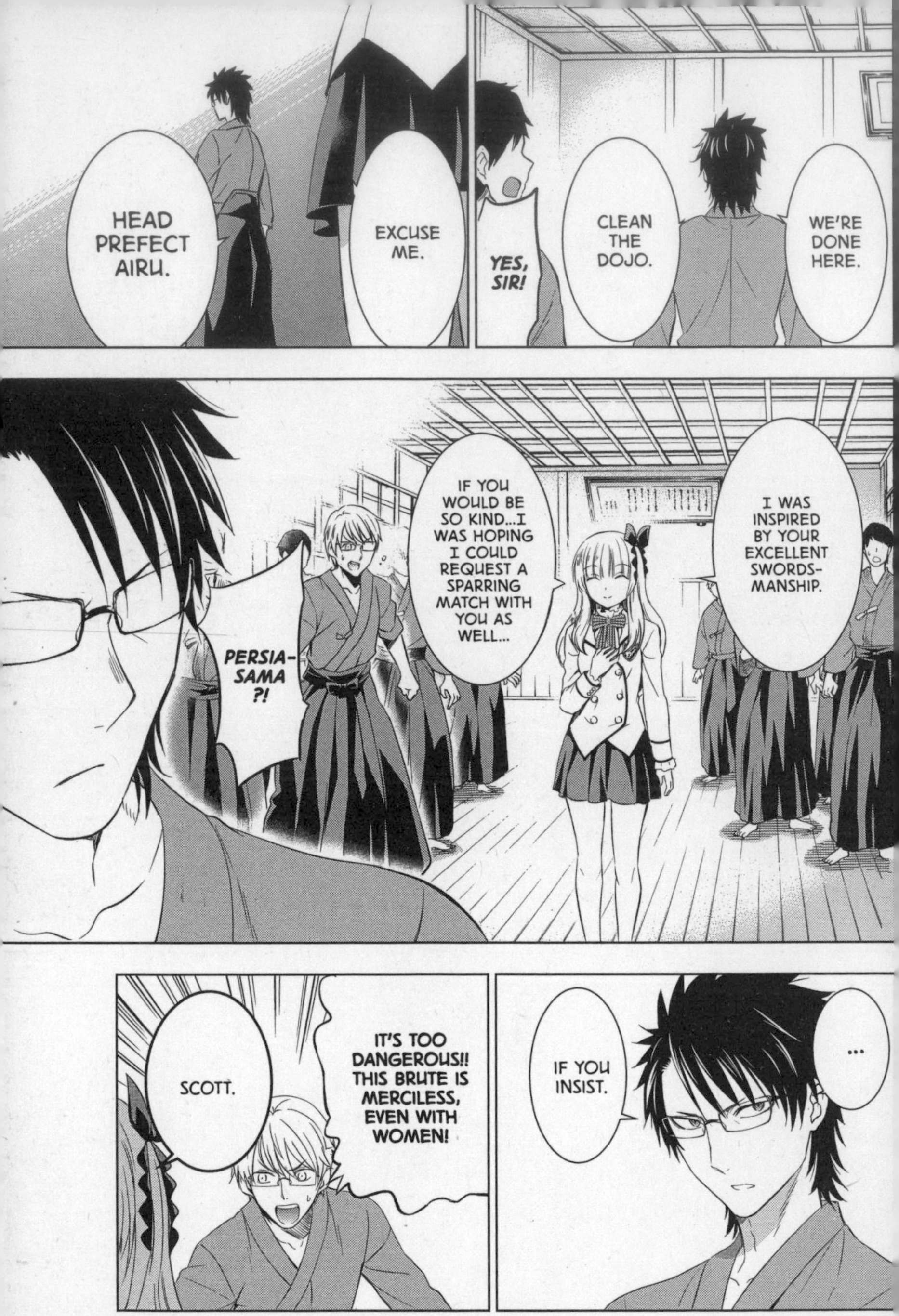
WE'RE DONE HERE.
CLEAN THE DOJO.
YES, SIR!
EXCUSE ME.
HEAD PREFECT AIRU.
I WAS INSPIRED BY YOUR EXCELLENT SWORDS-MANSHIP.
IF YOU WOULD BE SO KIND...I WAS HOPING I COULD REQUEST A SPARRING MATCH WITH YOU AS WELL...
PERSIA-SAMA ?!
...
IF YOU INSIST.
IT'S TOO DANGEROUS!! THIS BRUTE IS MERCILESS, EVEN WITH WOMEN!
SCOTT.

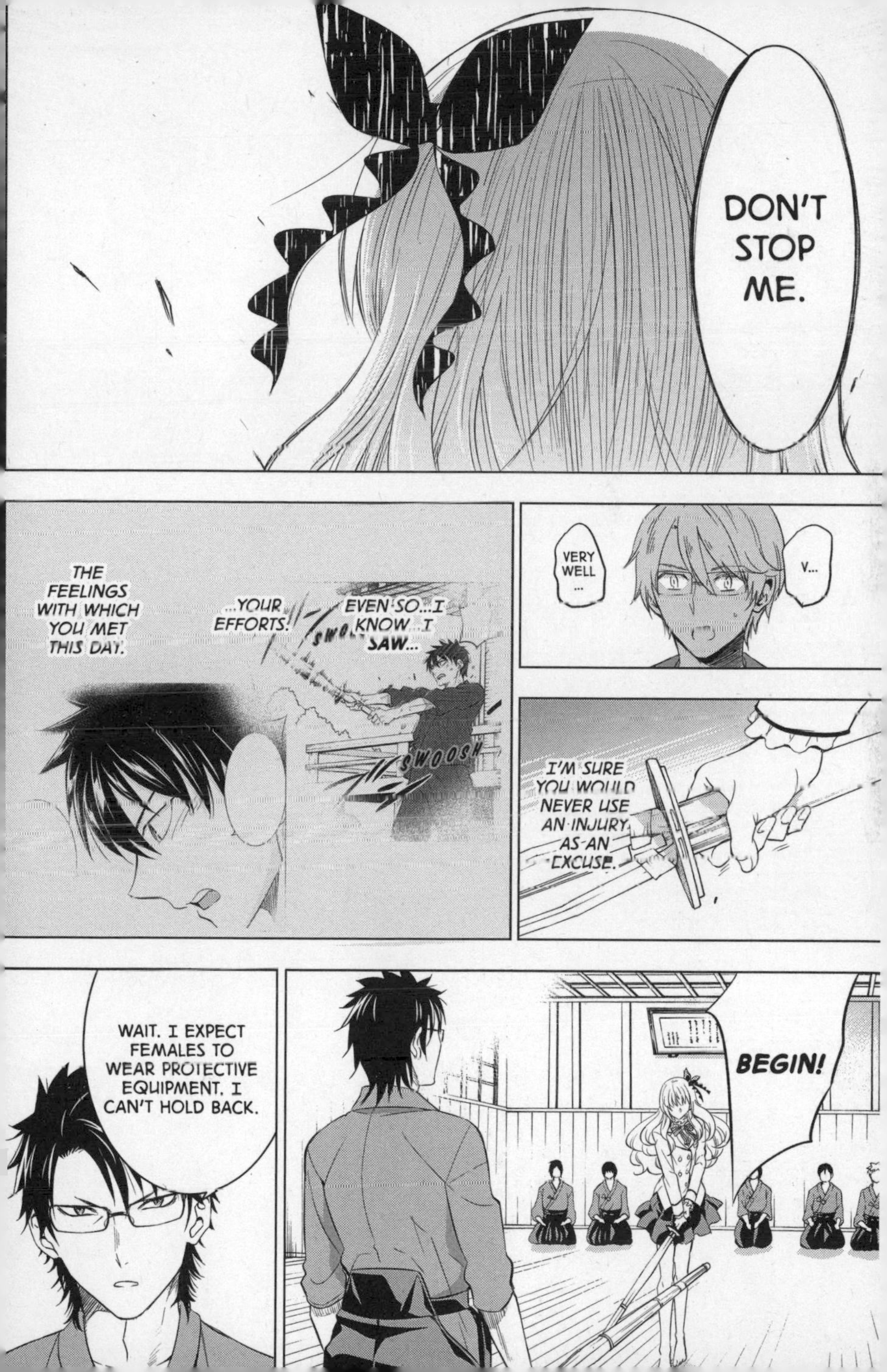
DON'T STOP ME.
V...
VERY WELL ...
I'M SURE YOU WOULD NEVER USE AN INJURY AS AN EXCUSE.
EVEN SO...I KNOW...I SAW...
...YOUR EFFORTS!
SWOOSH
THE FEELINGS WITH WHICH YOU MET THIS DAY.
BEGIN!
WAIT. I EXPECT FEMALES TO WEAR PROTECTIVE EQUIPMENT. I CAN'T HOLD BACK.

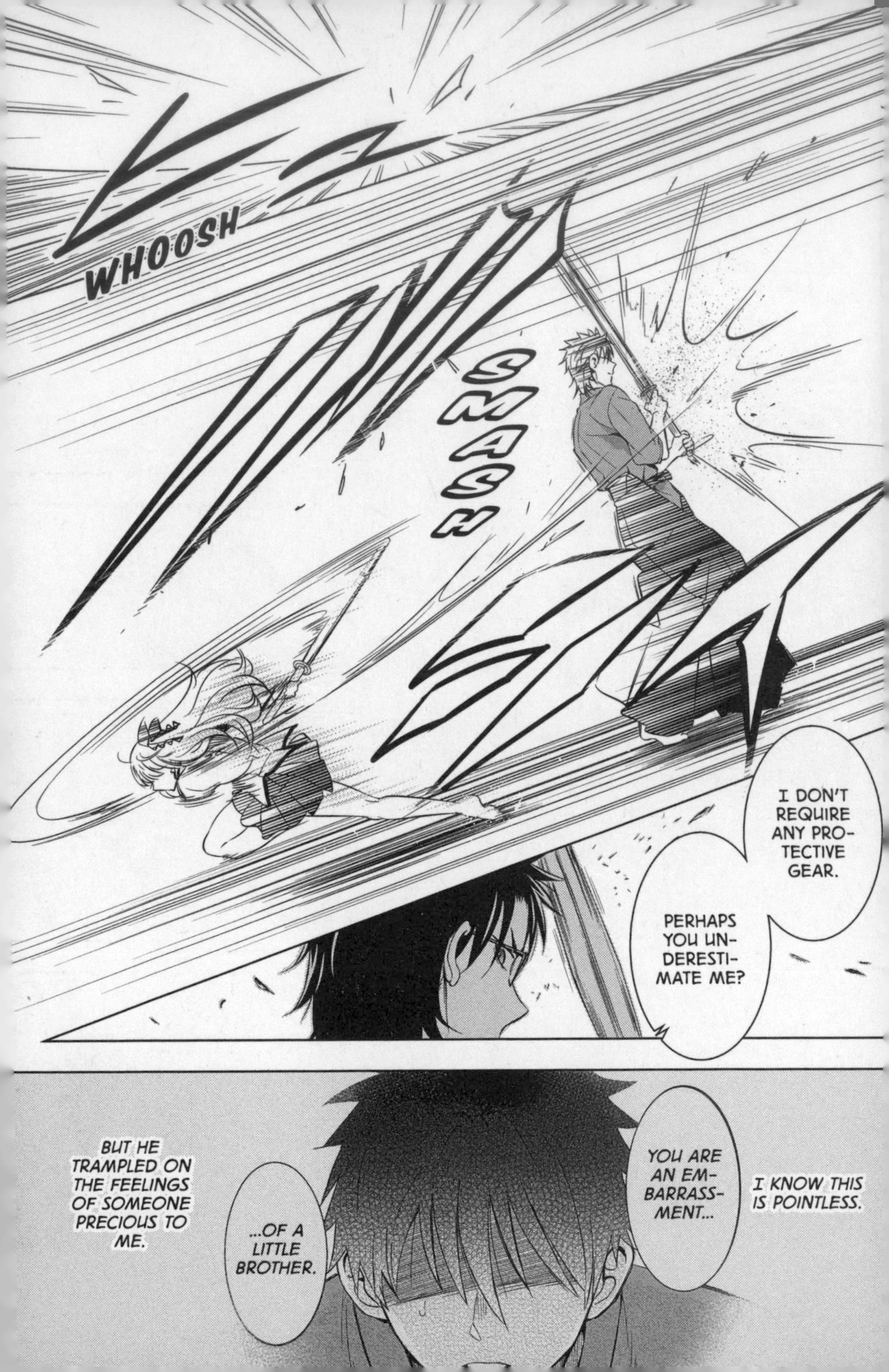
WHOOSH
SMASH
I DON'T REQUIRE ANY PRO-TECTIVE GEAR.
PERHAPS YOU UN-DERESTI-MATE ME?
I KNOW THIS IS POINTLESS.
YOU ARE AN EM-BARRASS-MENT...
...OF A LITTLE BROTHER.
BUT HE TRAMPLED ON THE FEELINGS OF SOMEONE PRECIOUS TO ME.

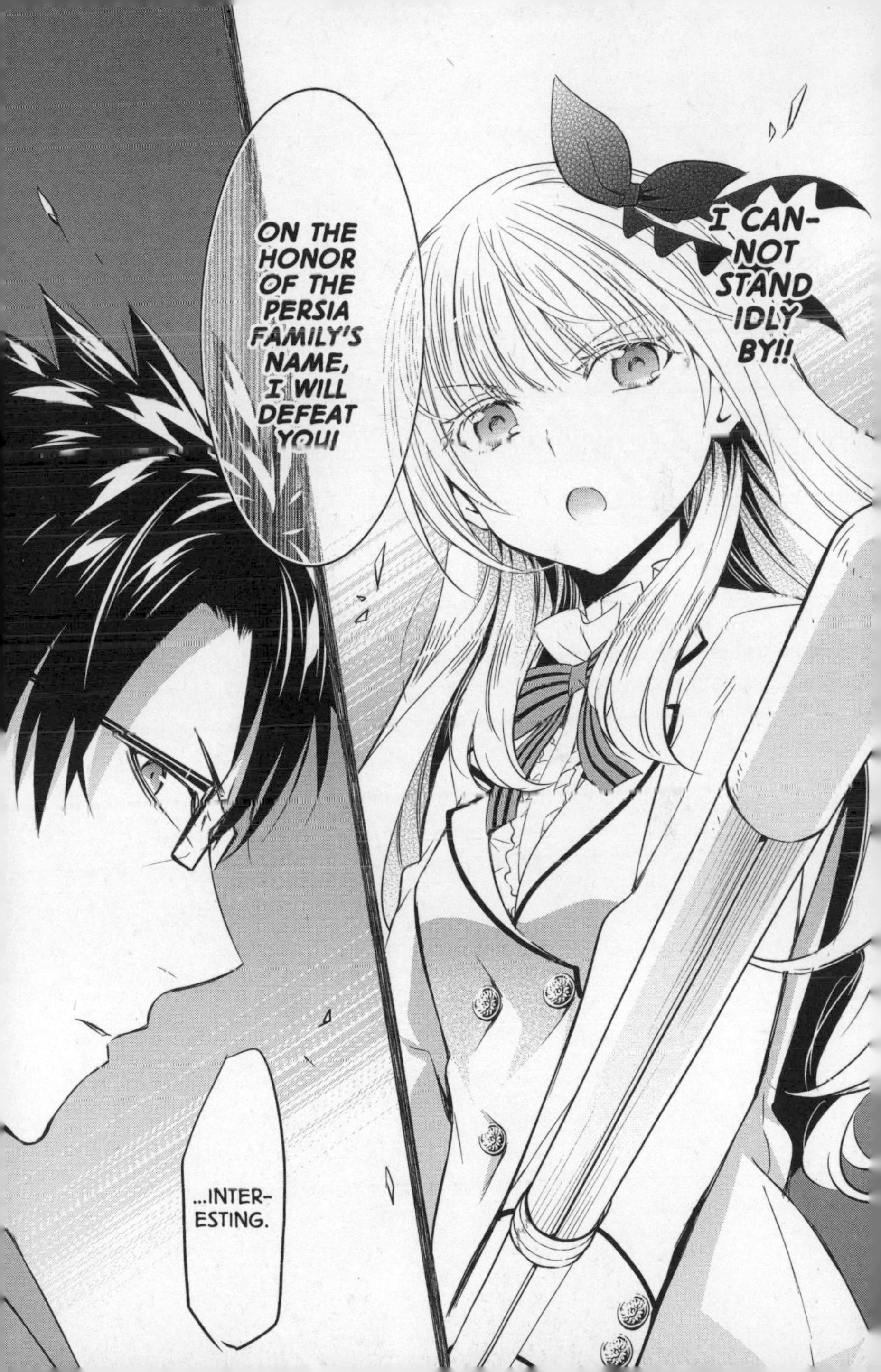
I CAN-NOT STAND IDLY BY!!
ON THE HONOR OF THE PERSIA FAMILY'S NAME, I WILL DEFEAT YOU!
...INTER-ESTING.

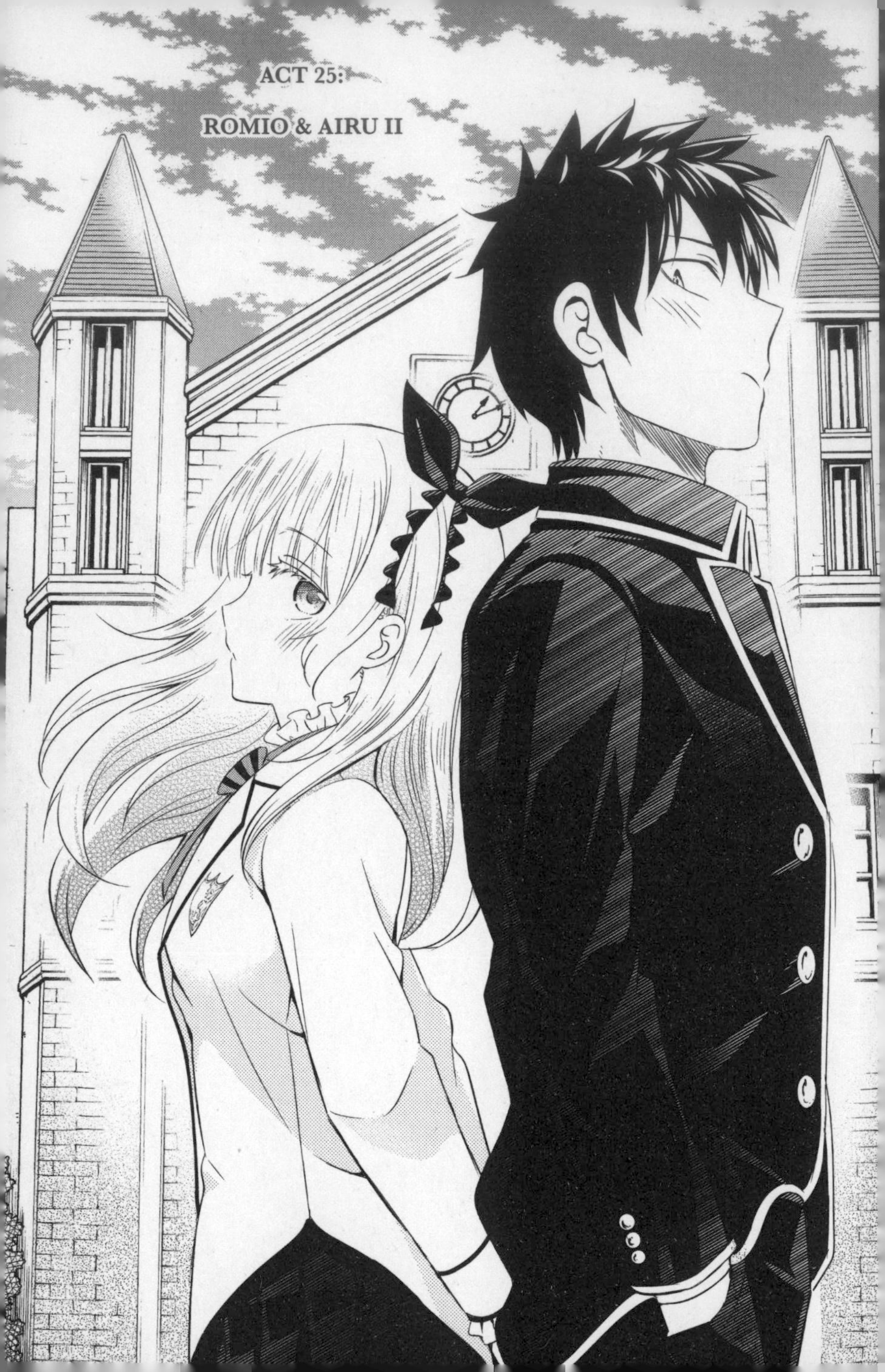
ACT 25:
ROMIO & AIRU II

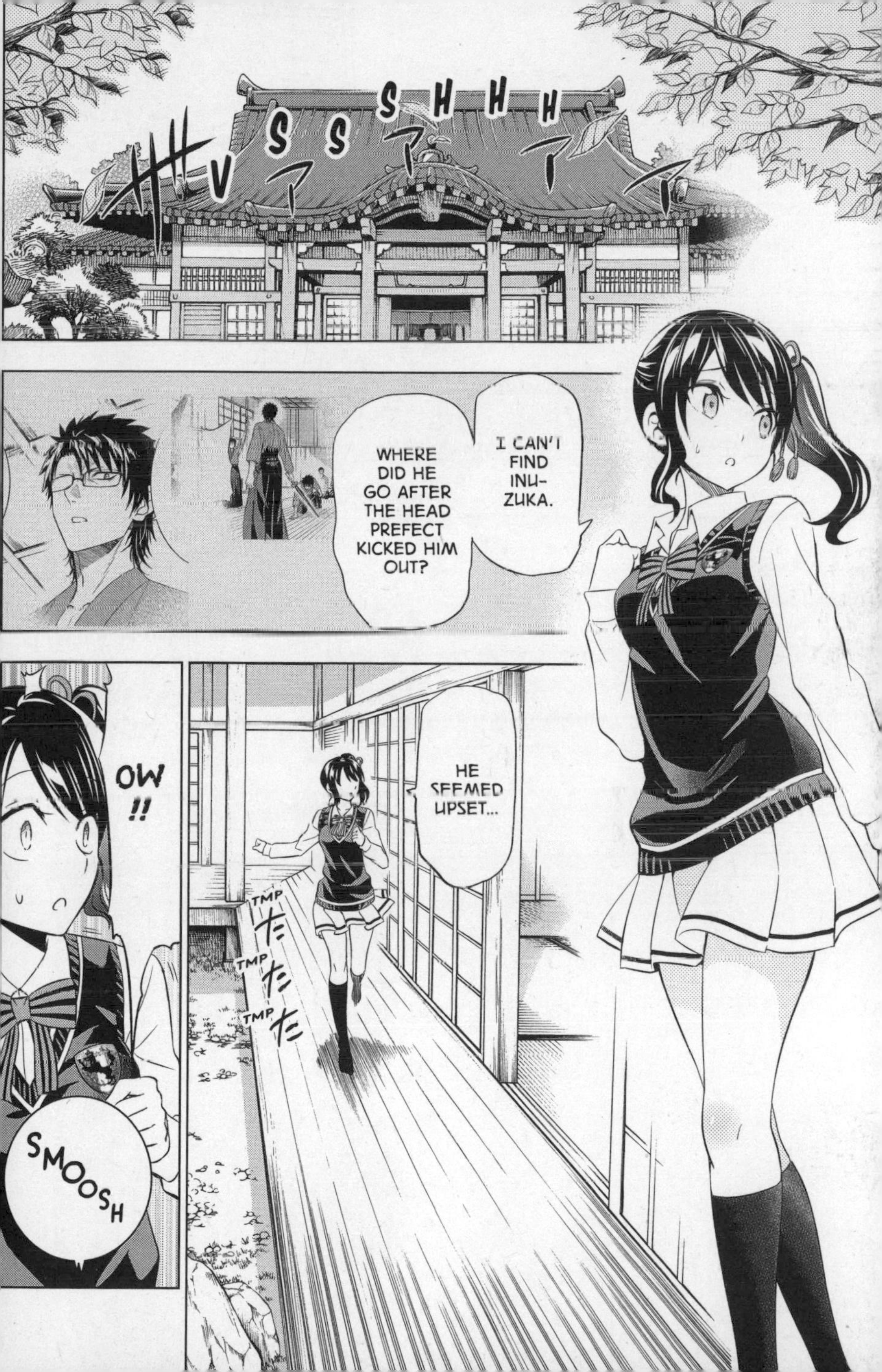
VSSSHHH
I CAN'T FIND INU-ZUKA.
WHERE DID HE GO AFTER THE HEAD PREFECT KICKED HIM OUT?
HE SEEMED UPSET...
TMP TMP TMP
OW!!
SMOOSH

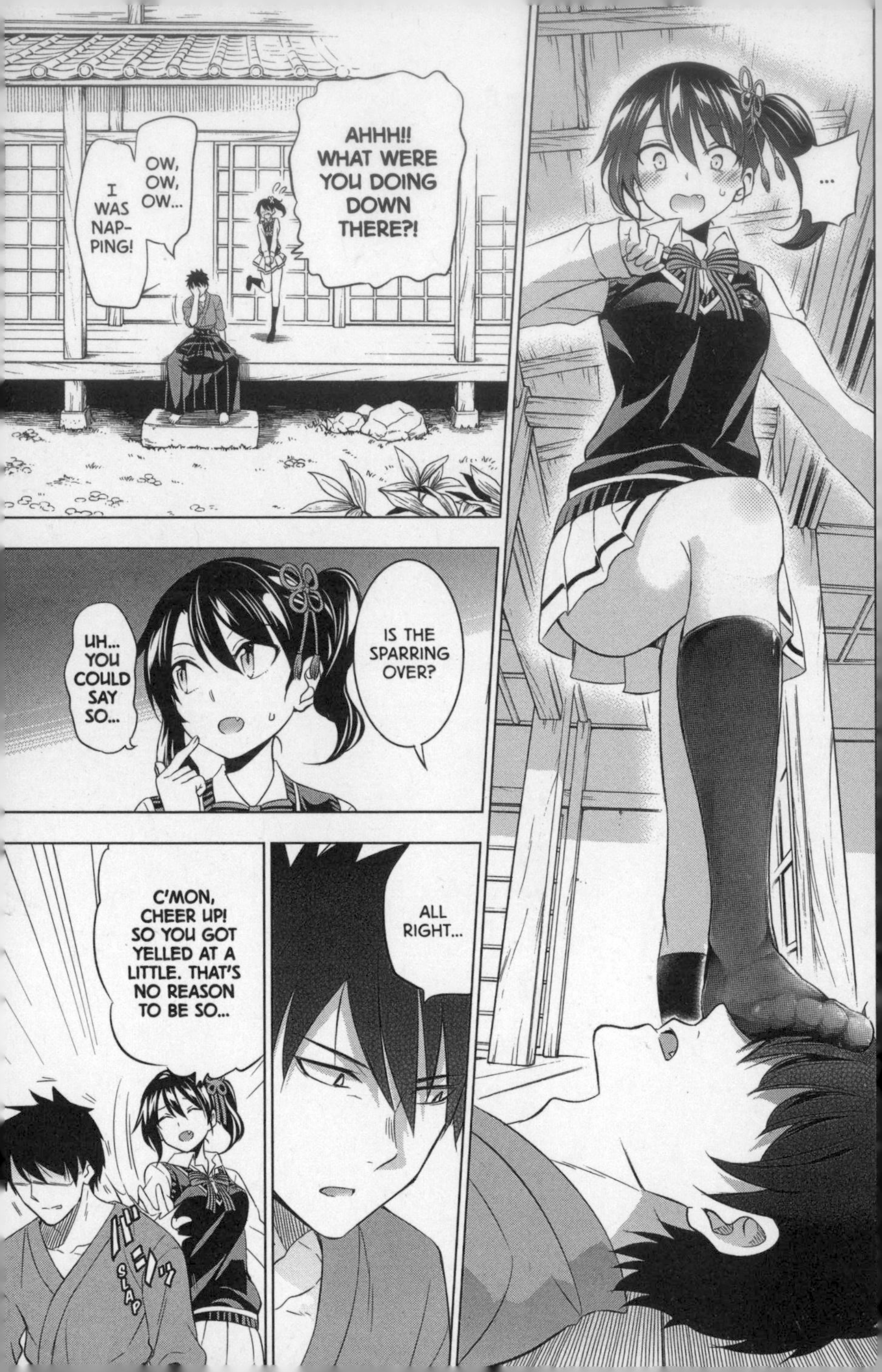
...
AHHH!! WHAT WERE YOU DOING DOWN THERE?!
OW, OW, OW...
I WAS NAP-PING!
IS THE SPARRING OVER?
UH... YOU COULD SAY SO...
ALL RIGHT...
C'MON, CHEER UP! SO YOU GOT YELLED AT A LITTLE. THAT'S NO REASON TO BE SO...
SLAP

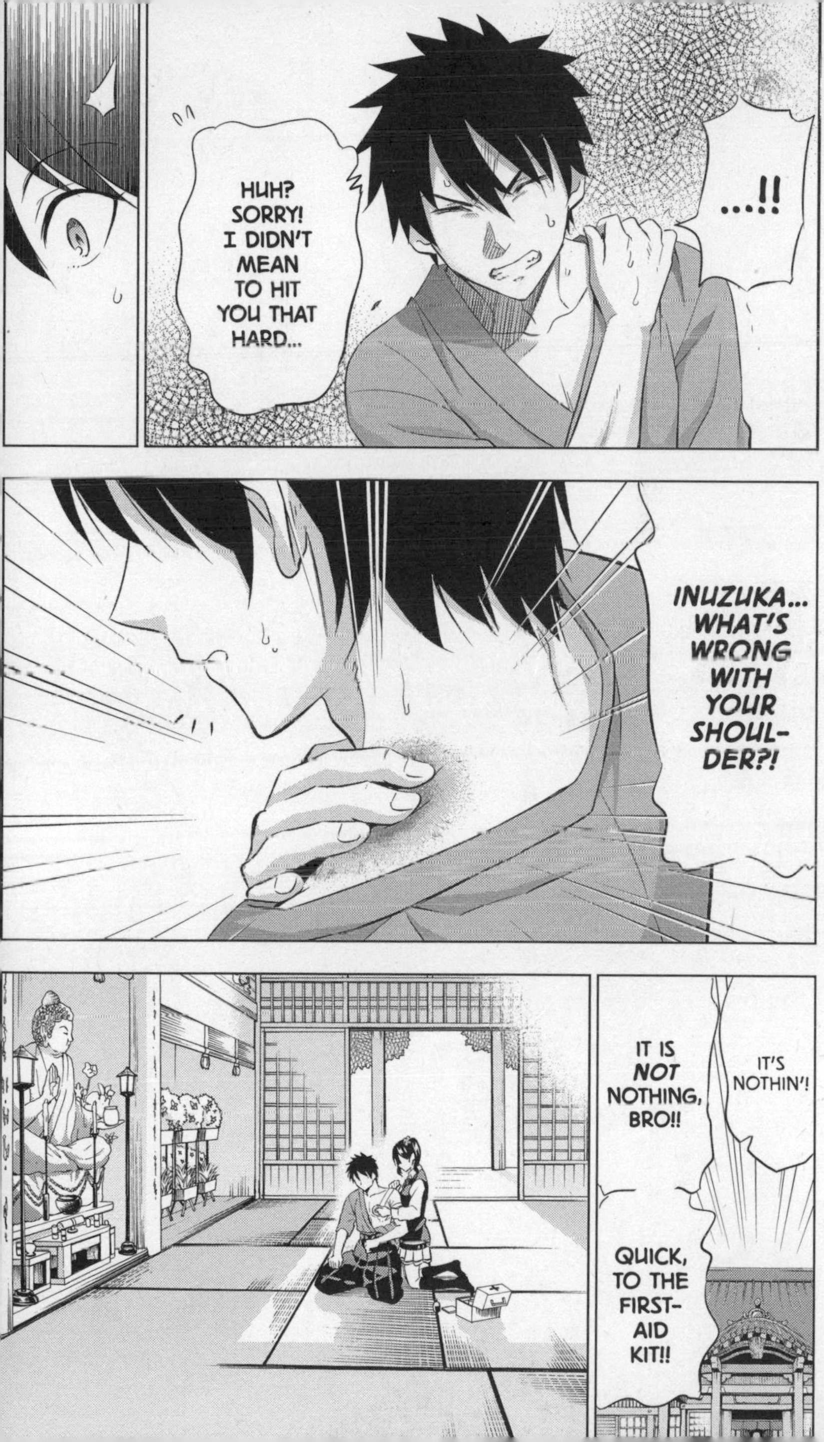
...!!
HUH? SORRY! I DIDN'T MEAN TO HIT YOU THAT HARD...
INUZUKA... WHAT'S WRONG WITH YOUR SHOULDER?!
IT'S NOTHIN'!
IT IS NOT NOTHING, BRO!!
QUICK, TO THE FIRST-AID KIT!!

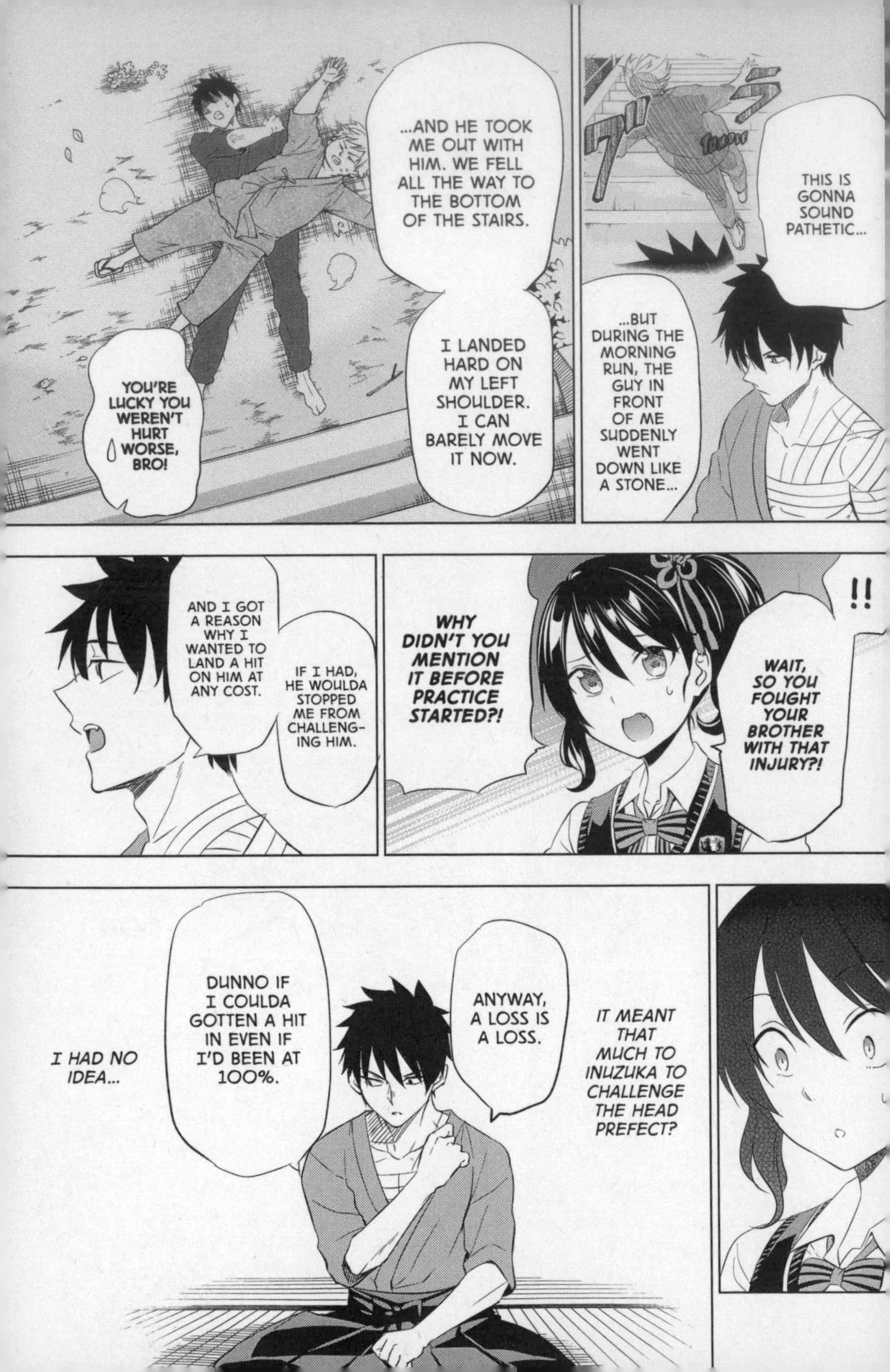
THIS IS GONNA SOUND PATHETIC...
...BUT DURING THE MORNING RUN, THE GUY IN FRONT OF ME SUDDENLY WENT DOWN LIKE A STONE...
...AND HE TOOK ME OUT WITH HIM. WE FELL ALL THE WAY TO THE BOTTOM OF THE STAIRS.
I LANDED HARD ON MY LEFT SHOULDER. I CAN BARELY MOVE IT NOW.
YOU'RE LUCKY YOU WEREN'T HURT WORSE, BRO!
!!
WAIT, SO YOU FOUGHT YOUR BROTHER WITH THAT INJURY?!
WHY DIDN'T YOU MENTION IT BEFORE PRACTICE STARTED?!
IF I HAD, HE WOULDA STOPPED ME FROM CHALLENG-ING HIM.
AND I GOT A REASON WHY I WANTED TO LAND A HIT ON HIM AT ANY COST.
IT MEANT THAT MUCH TO INUZUKA TO CHALLENGE THE HEAD PREFECT?
ANYWAY, A LOSS IS A LOSS.
DUNNO IF I COULDA GOTTEN A HIT IN EVEN IF I'D BEEN AT 100%.
I HAD NO IDEA...

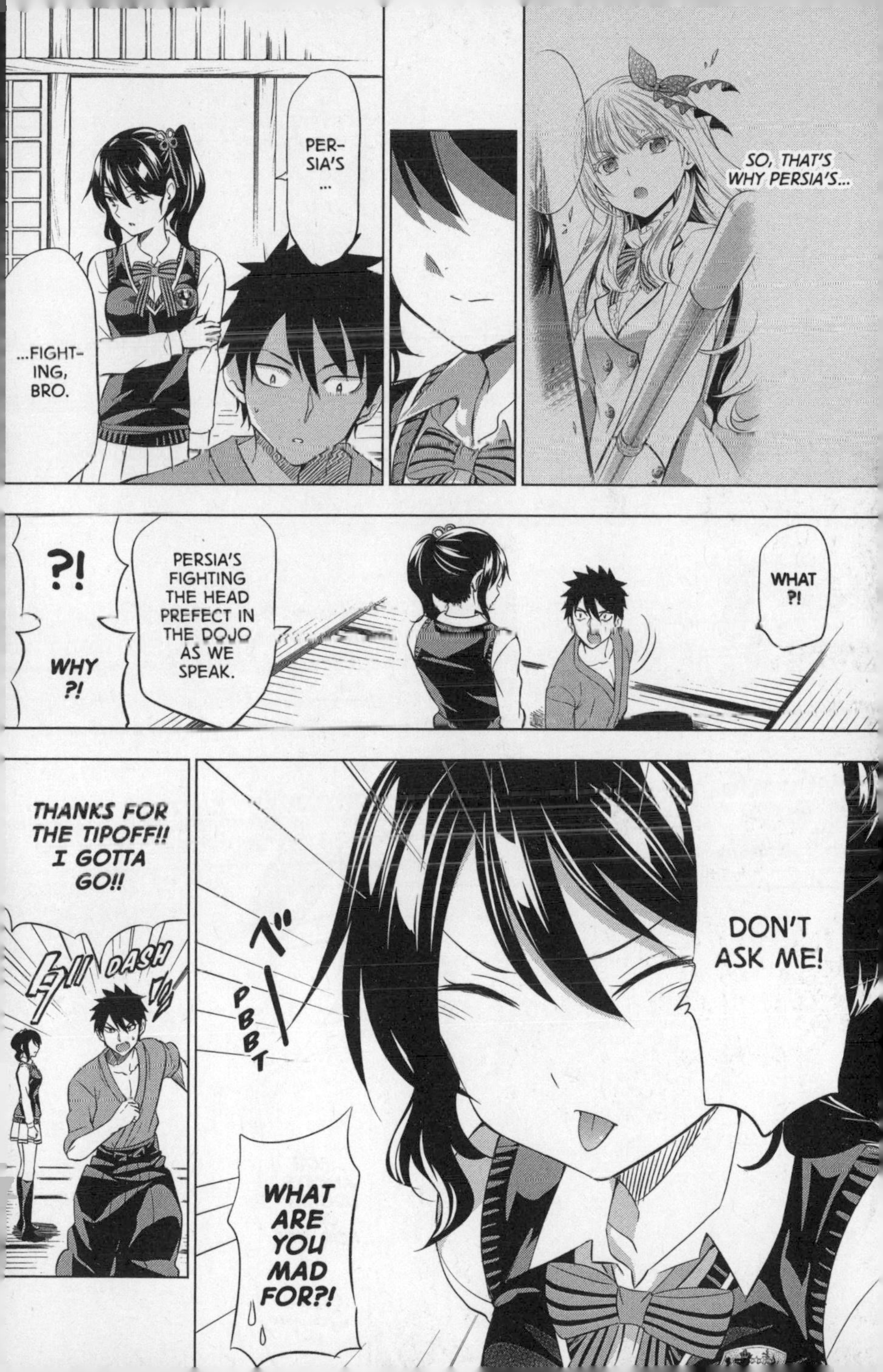
SO, THAT'S WHY PERSIA'S...
PER-SIA'S ...
...FIGHT-ING, BRO.
WHAT ?!
PERSIA'S FIGHTING THE HEAD PREFECT IN THE DOJO AS WE SPEAK.
?!
WHY ?!
DON'T ASK ME!
べー
PBBT
WHAT ARE YOU MAD FOR?!
THANKS FOR THE TIPOFF!! I GOTTA GO!!
DASH

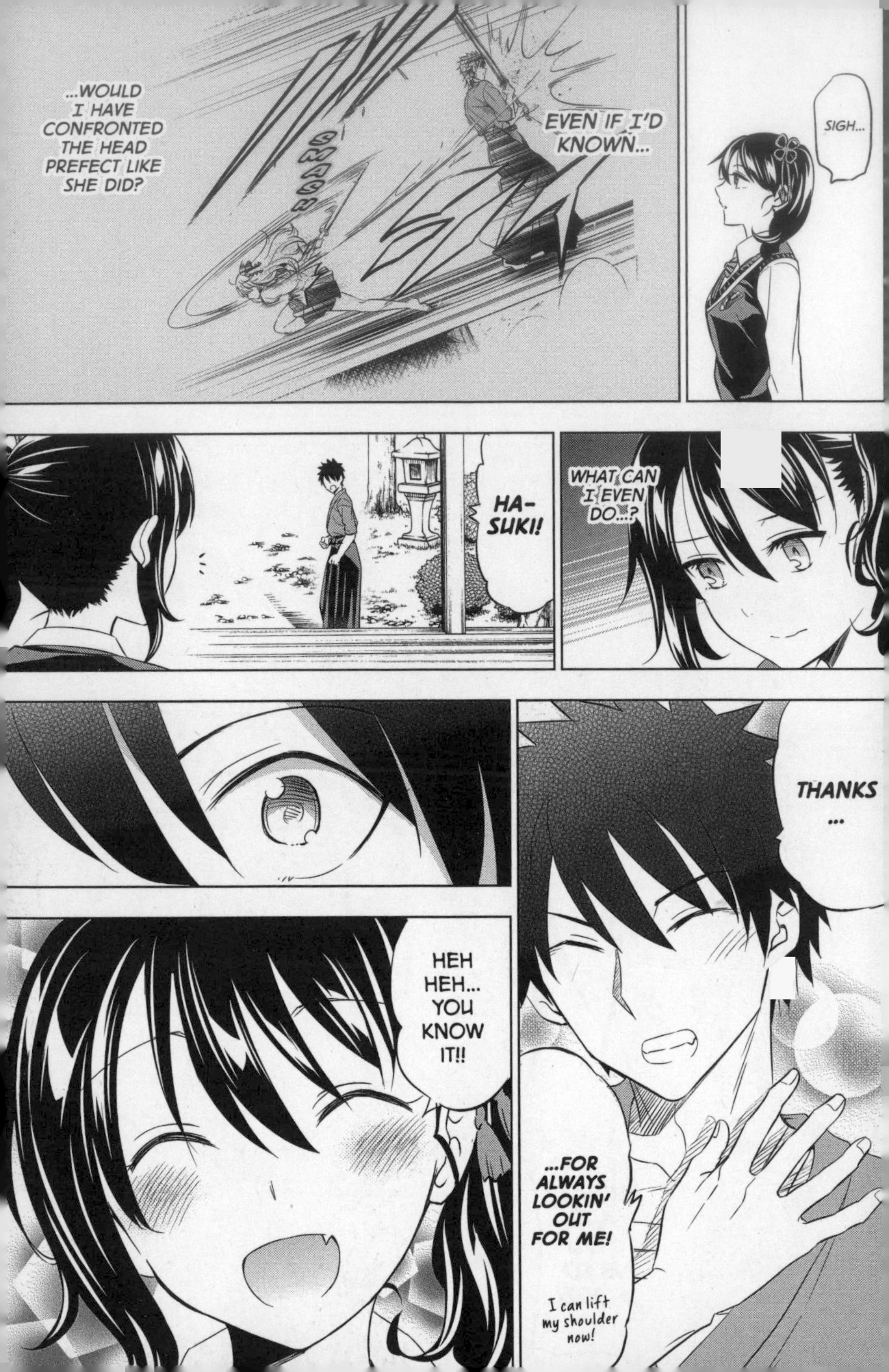

SIGH...
EVEN IF I'D KNOWN...
...WOULD I HAVE CONFRONTED THE HEAD PREFECT LIKE SHE DID?
SMASH
WHAT CAN I EVEN DO...?
HA-SUKI!
THANKS...
...FOR ALWAYS LOOKIN' OUT FOR ME!
I can lift my shoulder now!
HEH HEH... YOU KNOW IT!!

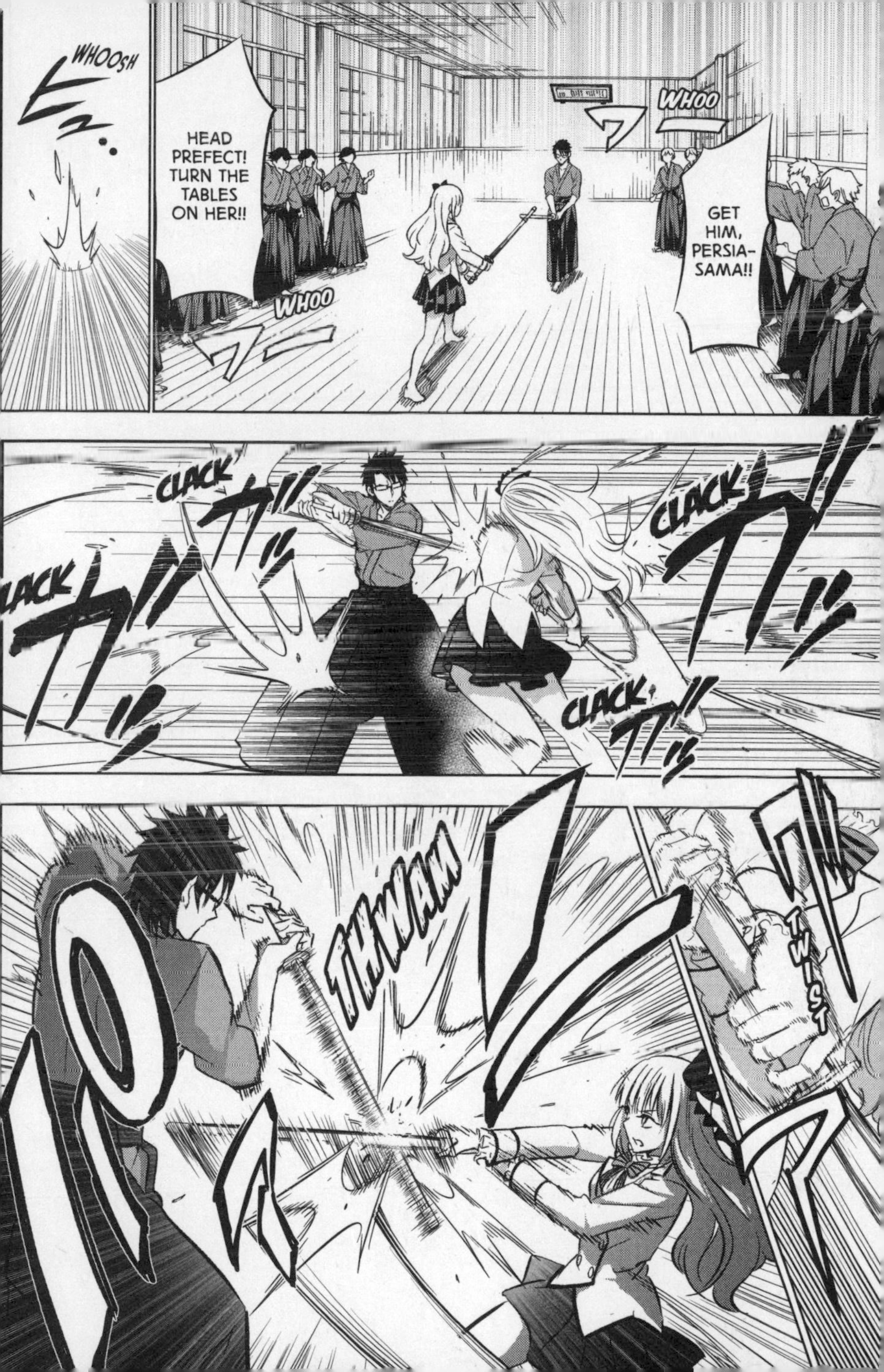
WHOO
GET HIM, PERSIA-SAMA!!
HEAD PREFECT! TURN THE TABLES ON HER!!
WHOO
WHOOSH
CLACK
CLACK
CLACK
CLACK
TWIST
THWAM

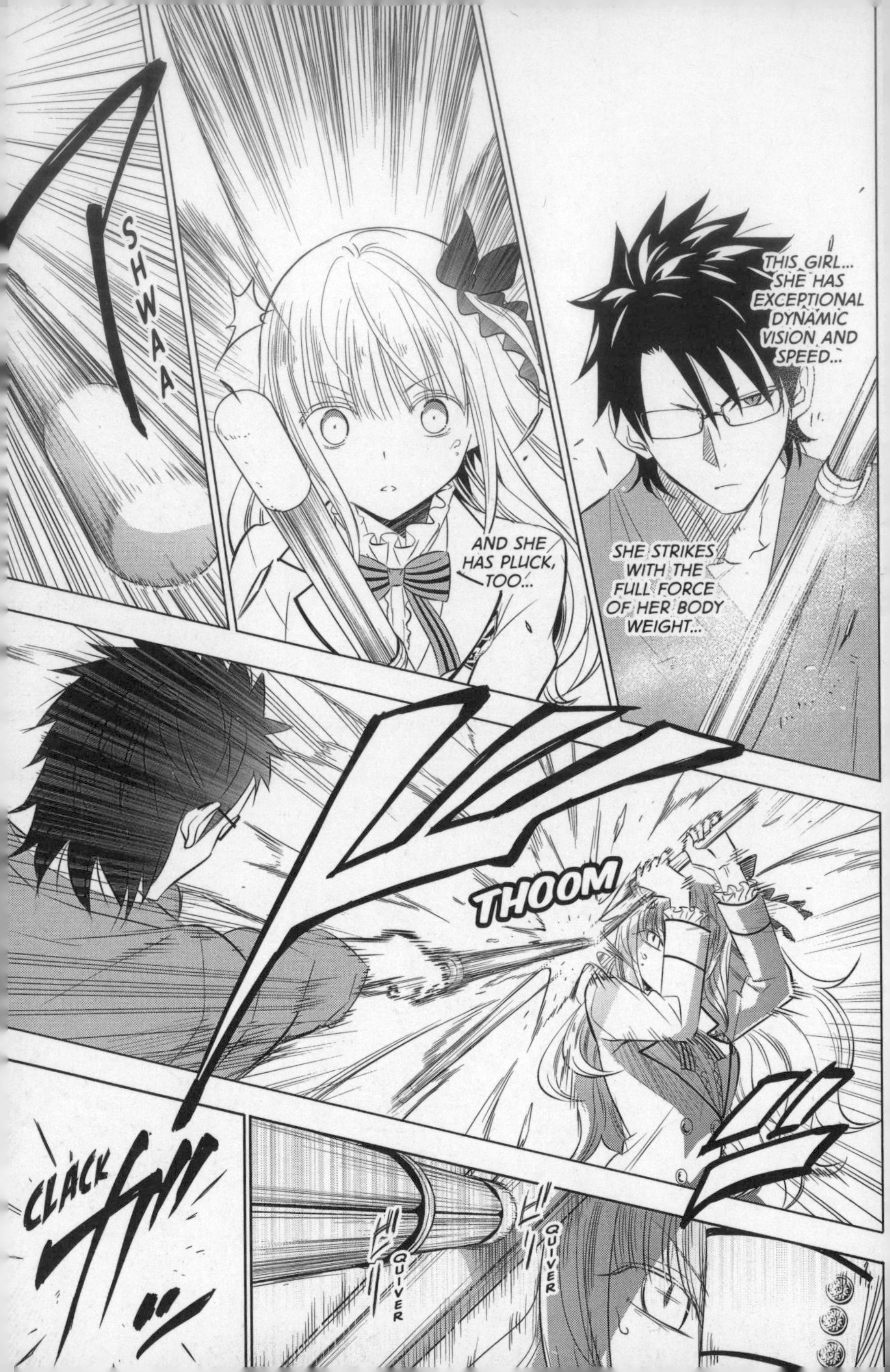
THIS GIRL... SHE HAS EXCEPTIONAL DYNAMIC VISION AND SPEED...
SHE STRIKES WITH THE FULL FORCE OF HER BODY WEIGHT...
AND SHE HAS PLUCK, TOO...
SHWAA
THOOM
QUIVER
QUIVER
CLACK

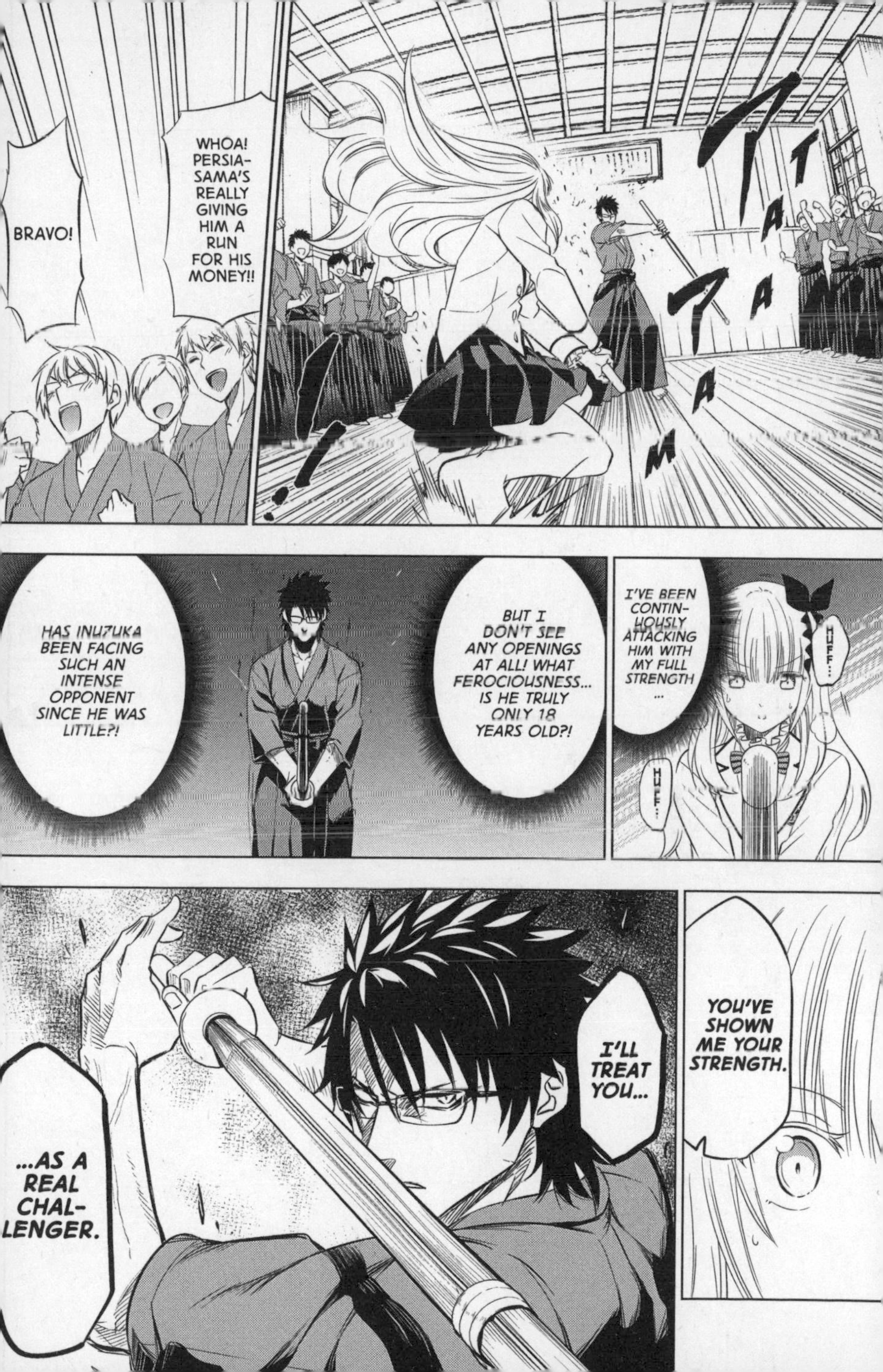
WHOA! PERSIA-SAMA'S REALLY GIVING HIM A RUN FOR HIS MONEY!!
BRAVO!
I'VE BEEN CONTIN-UOUSLY ATTACKING HIM WITH MY FULL STRENGTH ...
HUFF...
HUFF...
BUT I DON'T SEE ANY OPENINGS AT ALL! WHAT FEROCIOUSNESS... IS HE TRULY ONLY 18 YEARS OLD?!
HAS INUZUKA BEEN FACING SUCH AN INTENSE OPPONENT SINCE HE WAS LITTLE?!
YOU'VE SHOWN ME YOUR STRENGTH.
I'LL TREAT YOU...
...AS A REAL CHAL-LENGER.

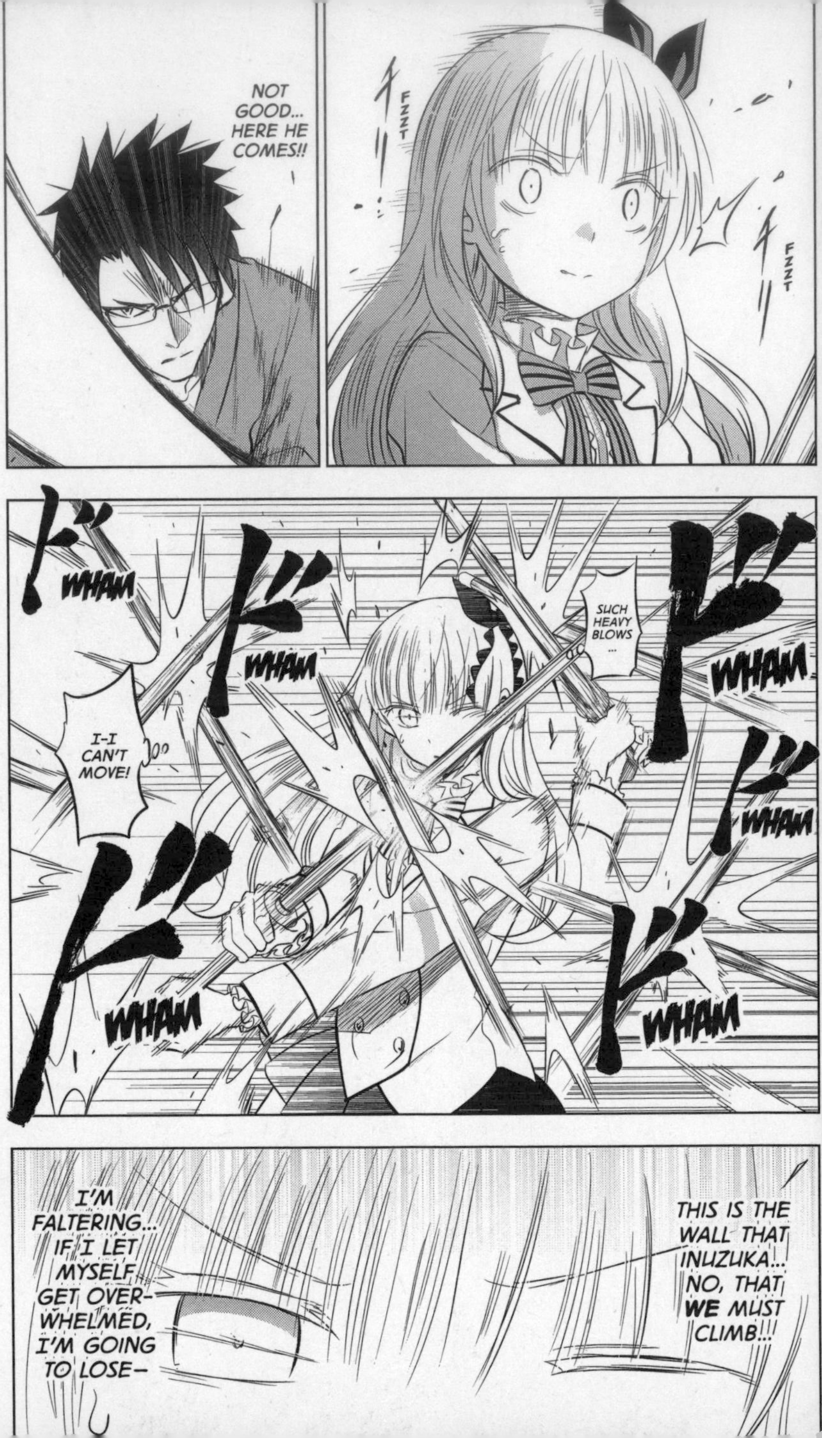
FZZT
FZZT
NOT GOOD... HERE HE COMES!!
SUCH HEAVY BLOWS ...
WHAM
WHAM
WHAM
WHAM
WHAM
WHAM
I-I CAN'T MOVE!
THIS IS THE WALL THAT INUZUKA... NO, THAT WE MUST CLIMB!!
I'M FALTERING... IF I LET MYSELF GET OVER-WHELMED, I'M GOING TO LOSE—

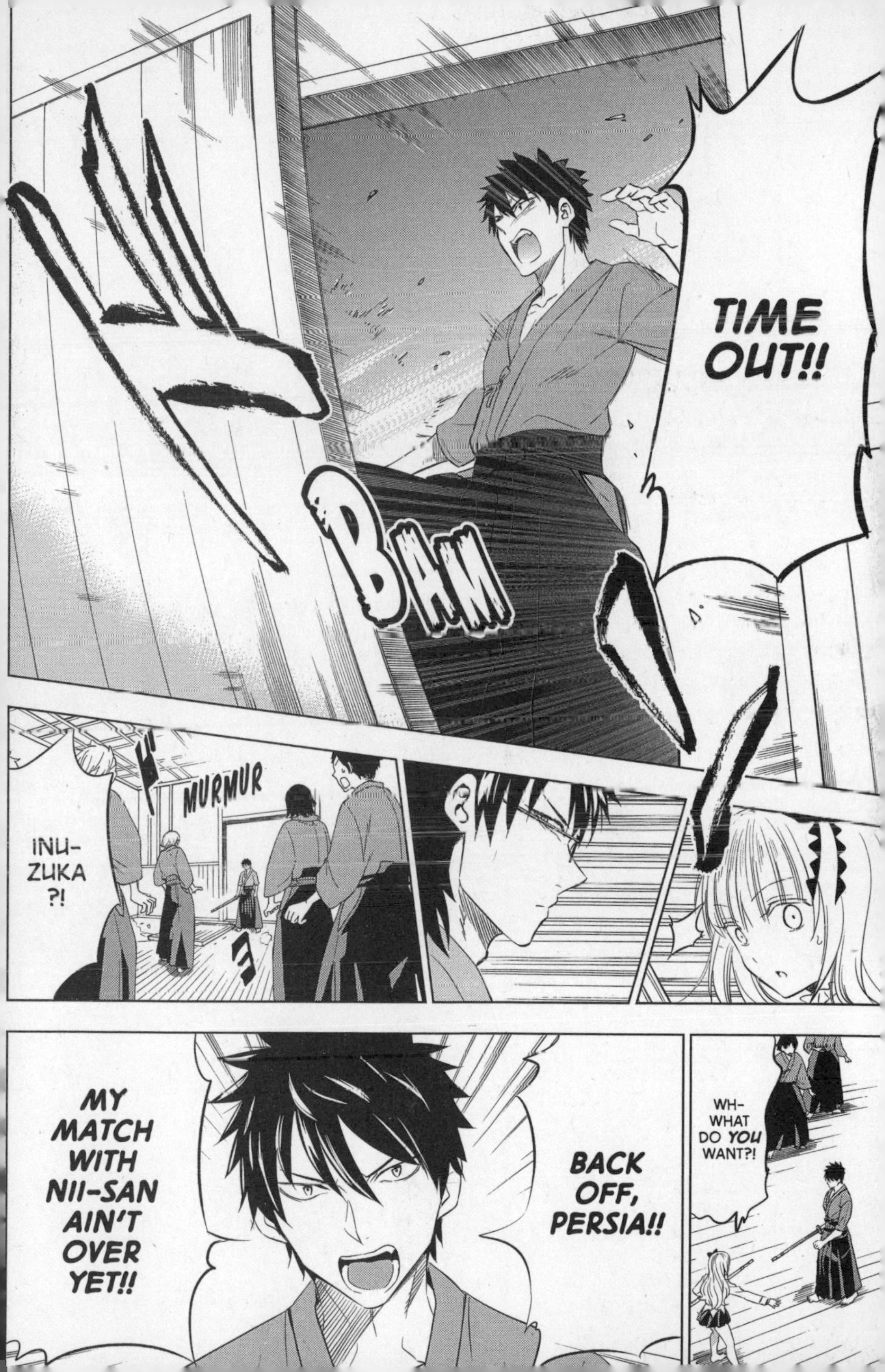
TIME OUT!!
BAM
MURMUR
INU-ZUKA ?!
WH- WHAT DO YOU WANT?!
BACK OFF, PERSIA!!
MY MATCH WITH NII-SAN AIN'T OVER YET!!

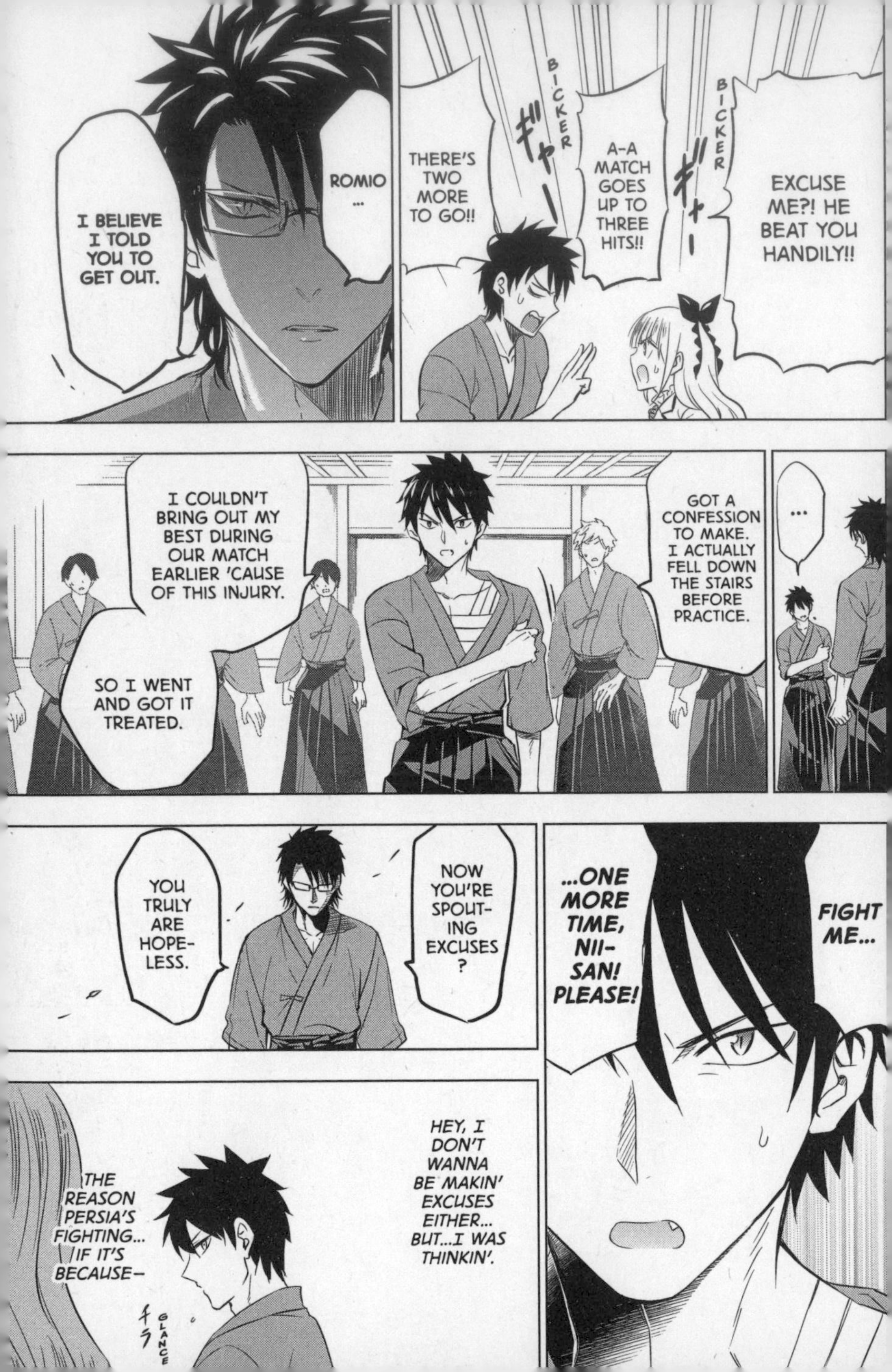
EXCUSE ME?! HE BEAT YOU HANDILY!!
BICKER
ギャー
A-A MATCH GOES UP TO THREE HITS!!
BICKER
ギャー
THERE'S TWO MORE TO GO!!
ROMIO ...
I BELIEVE I TOLD YOU TO GET OUT.
...
GOT A CONFESSION TO MAKE. I ACTUALLY FELL DOWN THE STAIRS BEFORE PRACTICE.
I COULDN'T BRING OUT MY BEST DURING OUR MATCH EARLIER 'CAUSE OF THIS INJURY.
SO I WENT AND GOT IT TREATED.
FIGHT ME...
...ONE MORE TIME, NII-SAN! PLEASE!
NOW YOU'RE SPOUT-ING EXCUSES?
YOU TRULY ARE HOPE-LESS.
HEY, I DON'T WANNA BE MAKIN' EXCUSES EITHER... BUT...I WAS THINKIN'.
THE REASON PERSIA'S FIGHTING... IF IT'S BECAUSE—
チラ
GLANCE

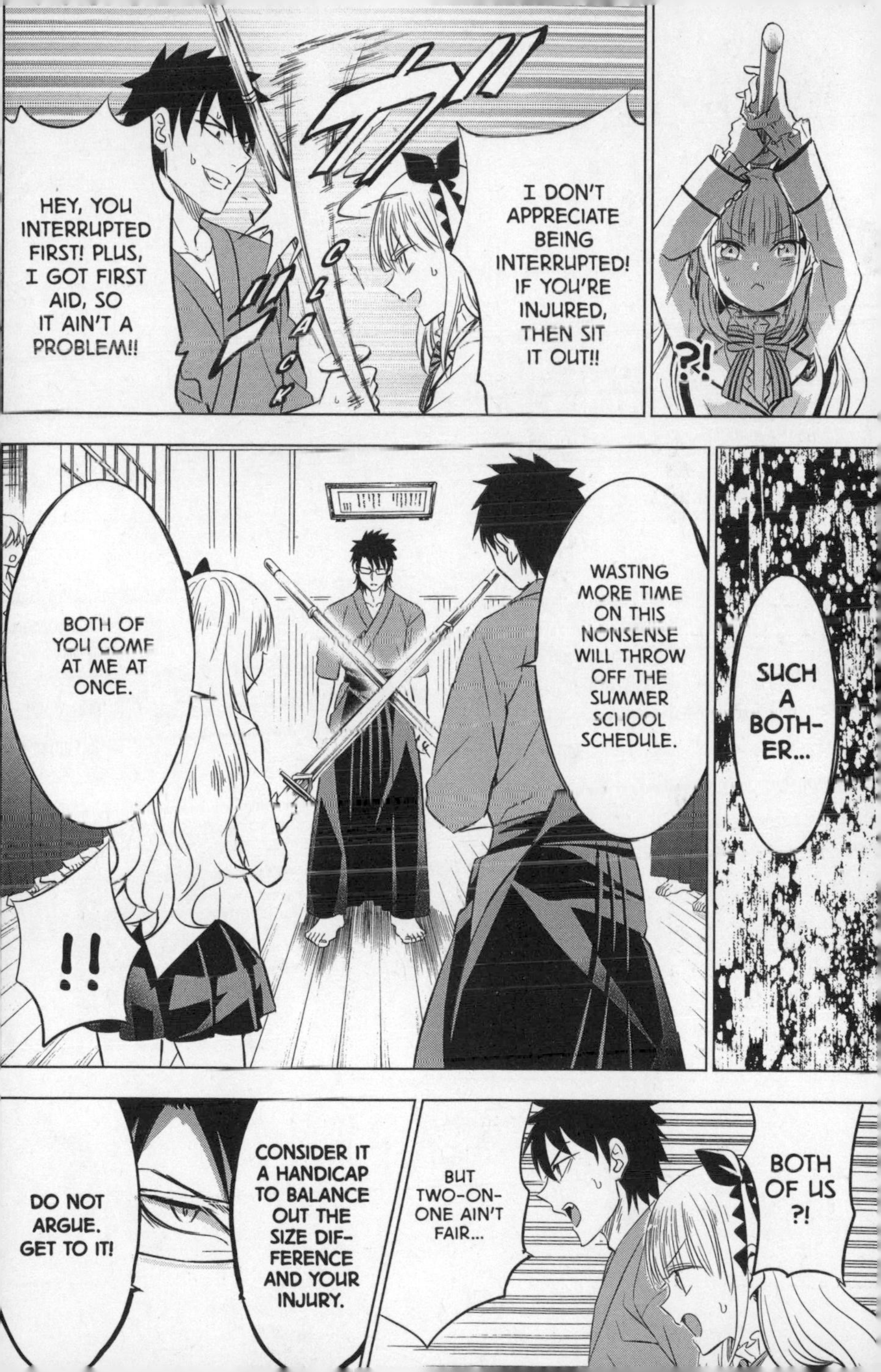
?!
I DON'T APPRECIATE BEING INTERRUPTED! IF YOU'RE INJURED, THEN SIT IT OUT!!
CLACK
HEY, YOU INTERRUPTED FIRST! PLUS, I GOT FIRST AID, SO IT AIN'T A PROBLEM!!
SUCH A BOTH-ER...
WASTING MORE TIME ON THIS NONSENSE WILL THROW OFF THE SUMMER SCHOOL SCHEDULE.
BOTH OF YOU COME AT ME AT ONCE.
!!
BOTH OF US ?!
BUT TWO-ON-ONE AIN'T FAIR...
CONSIDER IT A HANDICAP TO BALANCE OUT THE SIZE DIF-FERENCE AND YOUR INJURY.
DO NOT ARGUE. GET TO IT!

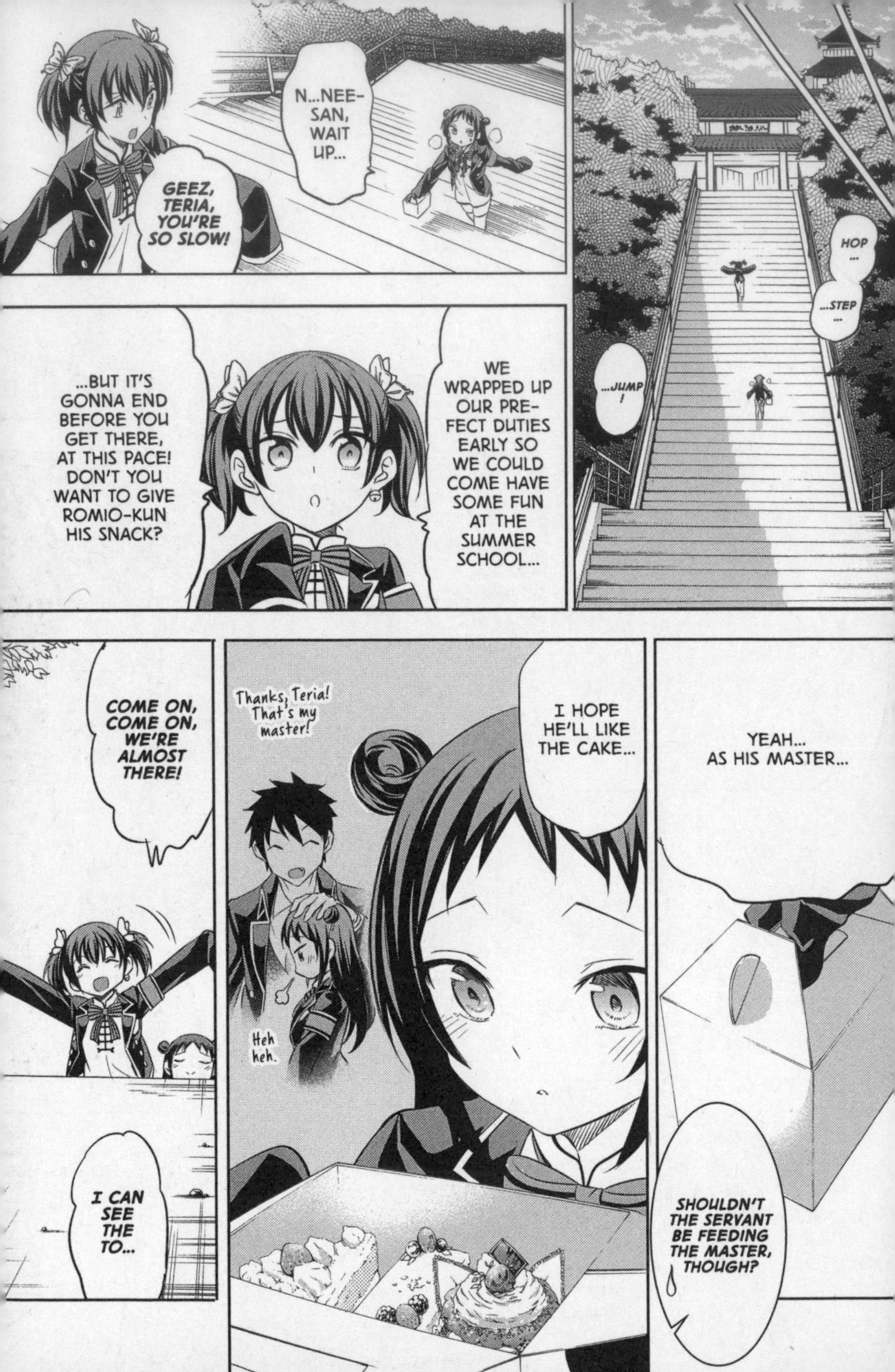
HOP ...
...STEP ...
...JUMP !
N...NEE-SAN, WAIT UP...
GEEZ, TERIA, YOU'RE SO SLOW!
WE WRAPPED UP OUR PRE-FECT DUTIES EARLY SO WE COULD COME HAVE SOME FUN AT THE SUMMER SCHOOL...
...BUT IT'S GONNA END BEFORE YOU GET THERE, AT THIS PACE! DON'T YOU WANT TO GIVE ROMIO-KUN HIS SNACK?
YEAH... AS HIS MASTER...
SHOULDN'T THE SERVANT BE FEEDING THE MASTER, THOUGH?
I HOPE HE'LL LIKE THE CAKE...
Thanks, Teria! That's my master!
Heh heh.
COME ON, COME ON, WE'RE ALMOST THERE!
I CAN SEE THE TO...

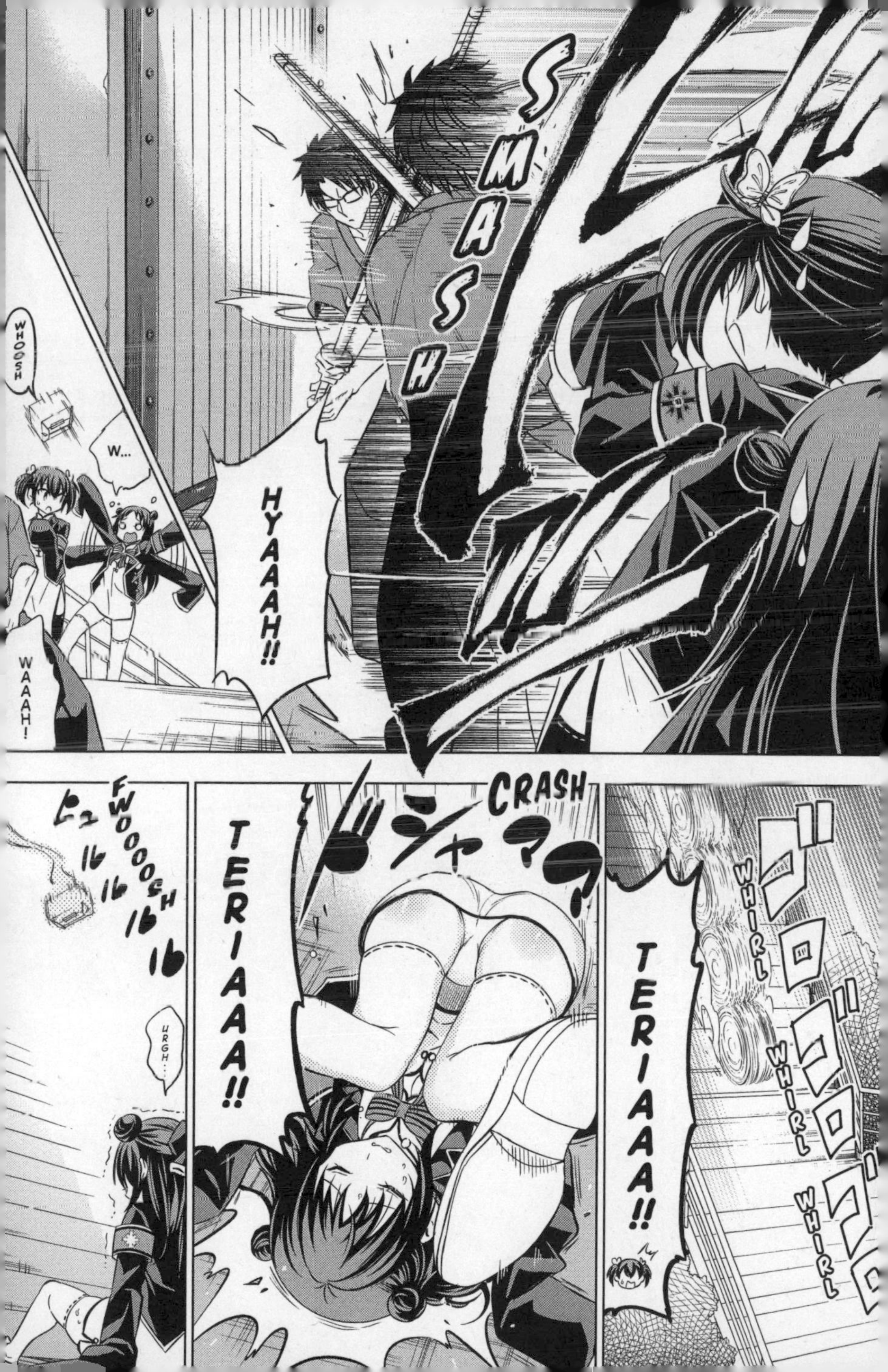
SMASH
HYAAAAH!!
WHOOSH
W...
WAAAAH!
WHIRL
WHIRL
WHIRL
TERIAAAA!!
CRASH
TERIAAAA!!
ヒュルルルル
FWOOOOSH
URGH...

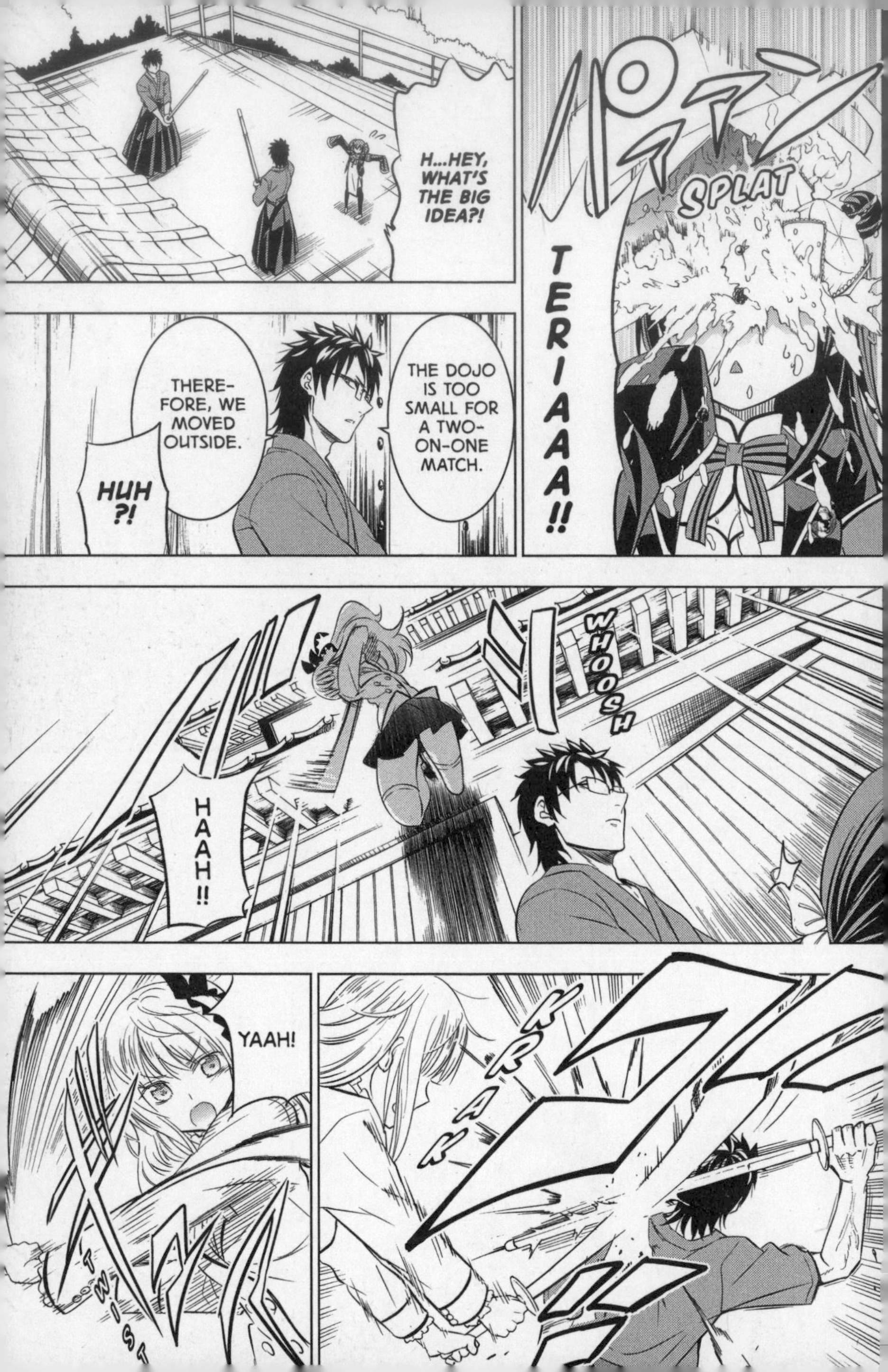
SPLAT
TERIAAAA!!
H...HEY, WHAT'S THE BIG IDEA?!
THE DOJO IS TOO SMALL FOR A TWO-ON-ONE MATCH.
THEREFORE, WE MOVED OUTSIDE.
HUH?!
WHOOSH
HAAAH!!
KRAAK
YAAH!
TWIST

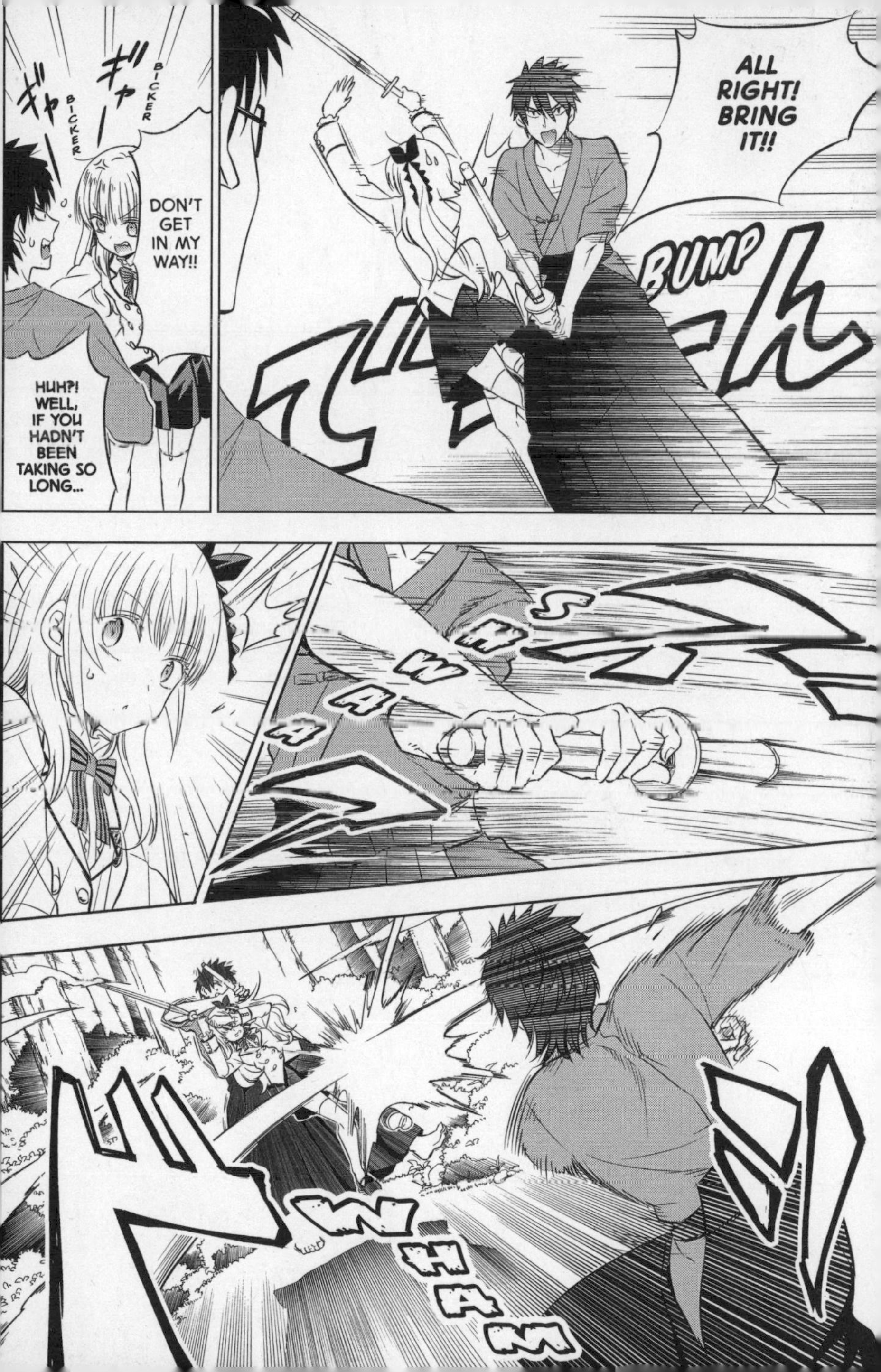ALL RIGHT! BRING IT!!
BUMP
ギャーギャー
BICKER BICKER
DON'T GET IN MY WAY!!
HUH?! WELL, IF YOU HADN'T BEEN TAKING SO LONG...
SHWAA
WHAM

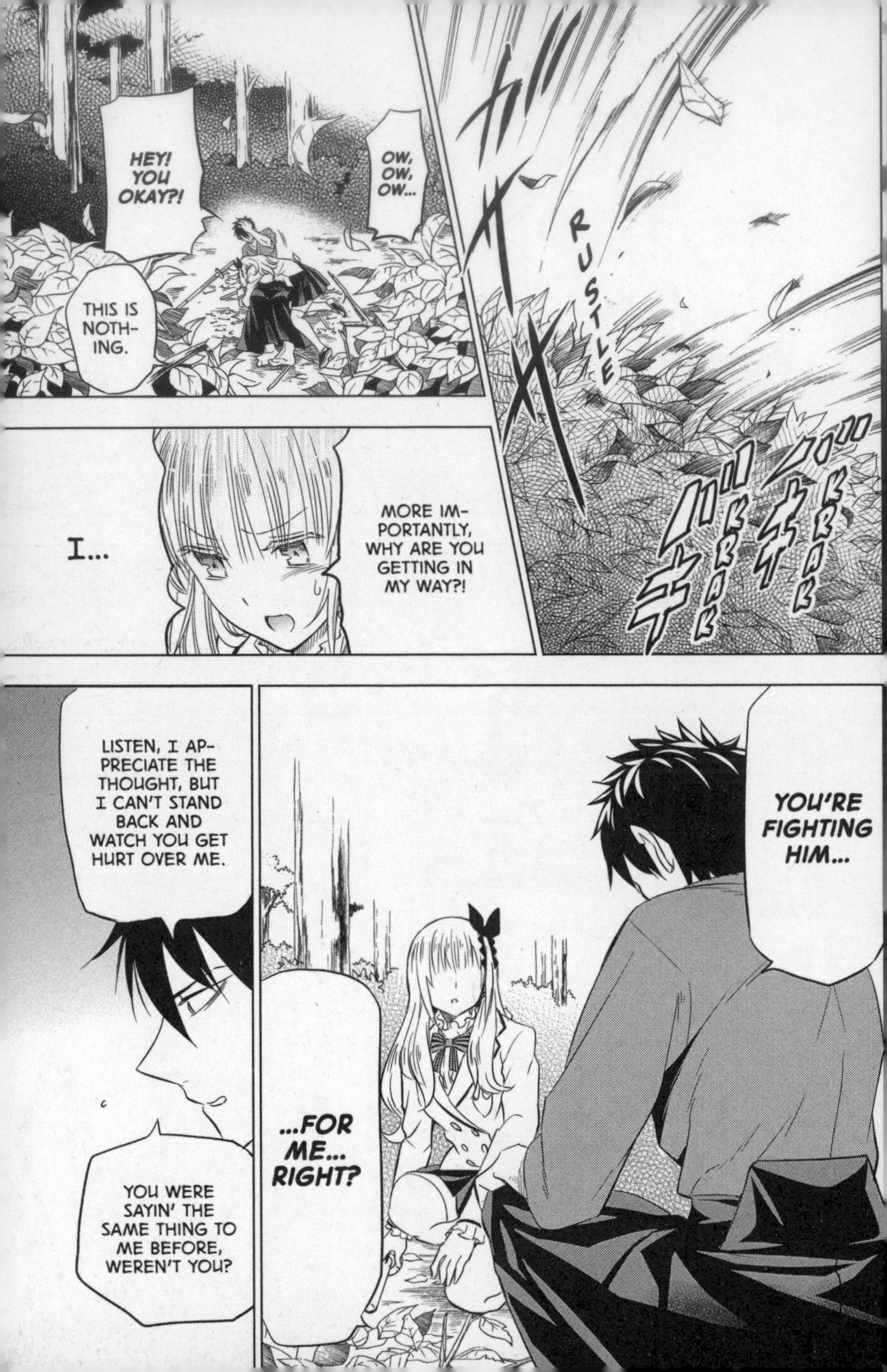
RUSTLE
KRAK
KRAK
OW, OW, OW...
HEY! YOU OKAY?!
THIS IS NOTH-ING.
MORE IM-PORTANTLY, WHY ARE YOU GETTING IN MY WAY?!
I...
YOU'RE FIGHTING HIM...
...FOR ME... RIGHT?
LISTEN, I AP-PRECIATE THE THOUGHT, BUT I CAN'T STAND BACK AND WATCH YOU GET HURT OVER ME.
YOU WERE SAYIN' THE SAME THING TO ME BEFORE, WEREN'T YOU?

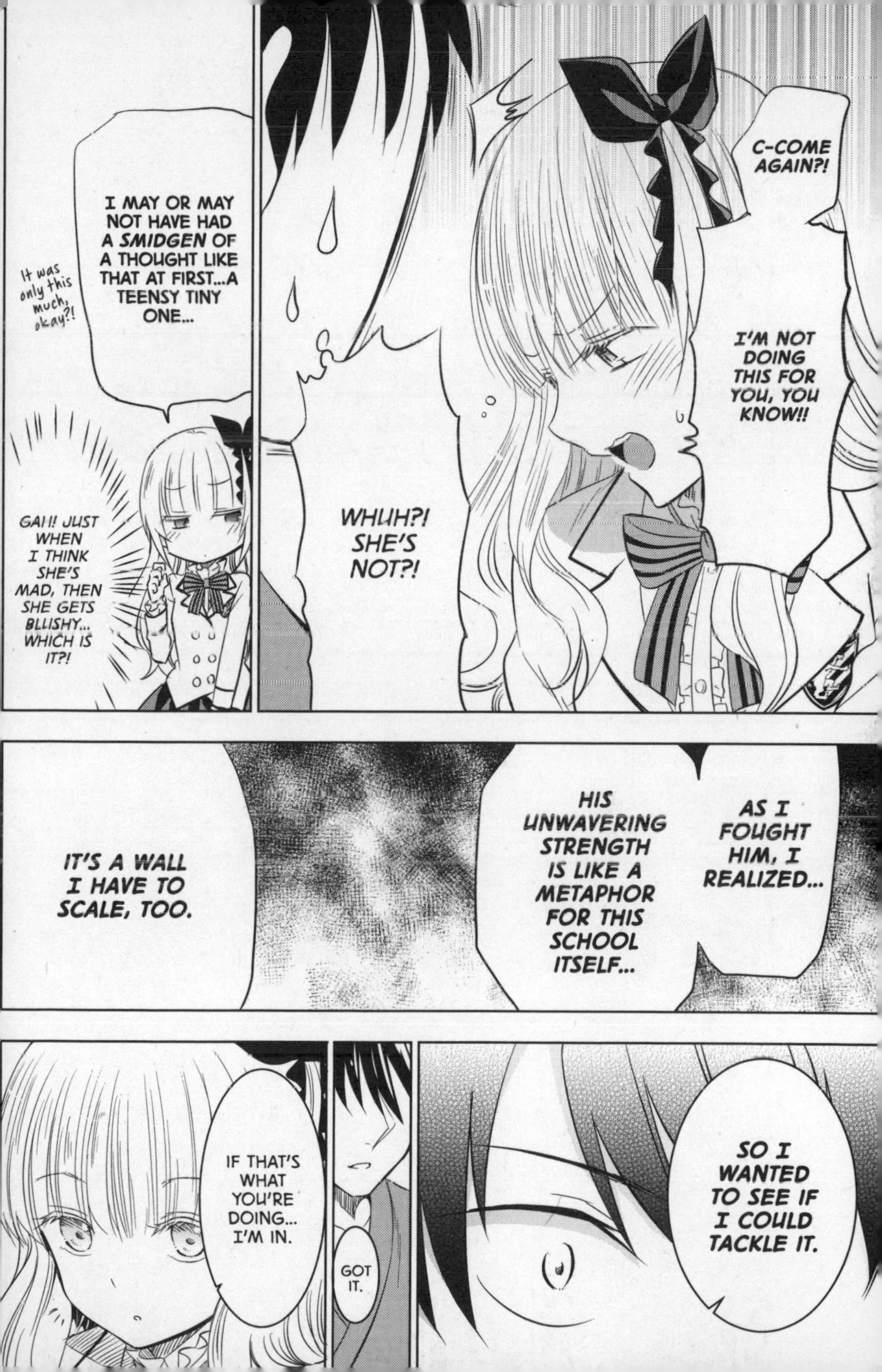
C-COME AGAIN?!
I'M NOT DOING THIS FOR YOU, YOU KNOW!!
WHUH?! SHE'S NOT?!
I MAY OR MAY NOT HAVE HAD A SMIDGEN OF A THOUGHT LIKE THAT AT FIRST...A TEENSY TINY ONE...
It was only this much, okay?!
GAH! JUST WHEN I THINK SHE'S MAD, THEN SHE GETS BLUSHY... WHICH IS IT?!
AS I FOUGHT HIM, I REALIZED...
HIS UNWAVERING STRENGTH IS LIKE A METAPHOR FOR THIS SCHOOL ITSELF...
IT'S A WALL I HAVE TO SCALE, TOO.
SO I WANTED TO SEE IF I COULD TACKLE IT.
IF THAT'S WHAT YOU'RE DOING... I'M IN.
GOT IT.

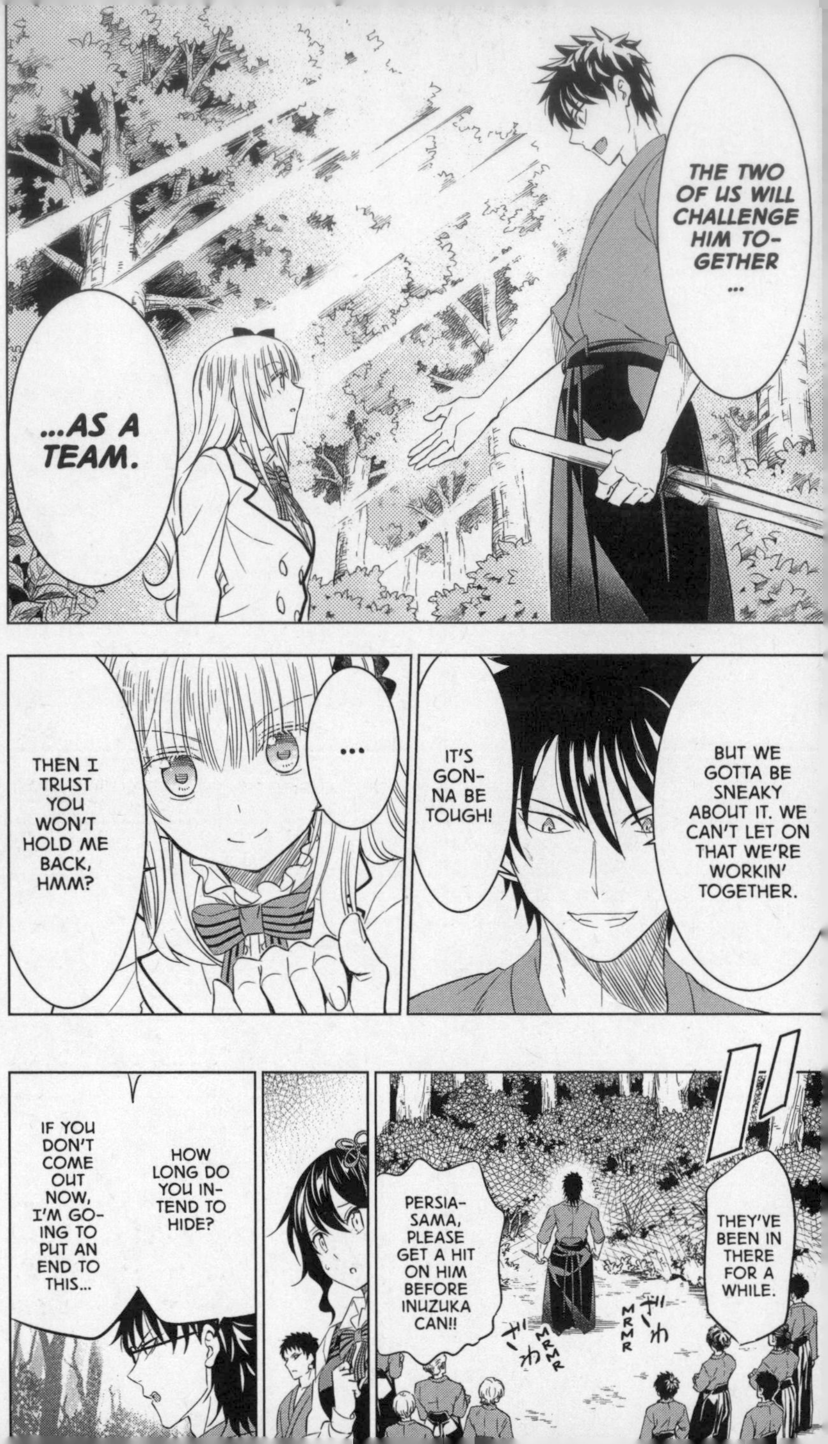
THE TWO OF US WILL CHALLENGE HIM TO-GETHER ...
...AS A TEAM.
BUT WE GOTTA BE SNEAKY ABOUT IT. WE CAN'T LET ON THAT WE'RE WORKIN' TOGETHER.
IT'S GON-NA BE TOUGH!
...
THEN I TRUST YOU WON'T HOLD ME BACK, HMM?
THEY'VE BEEN IN THERE FOR A WHILE.
MRMR
MRMR
PERSIA-SAMA, PLEASE GET A HIT ON HIM BEFORE INUZUKA CAN!!
HOW LONG DO YOU IN-TEND TO HIDE?
IF YOU DON'T COME OUT NOW, I'M GO-ING TO PUT AN END TO THIS...

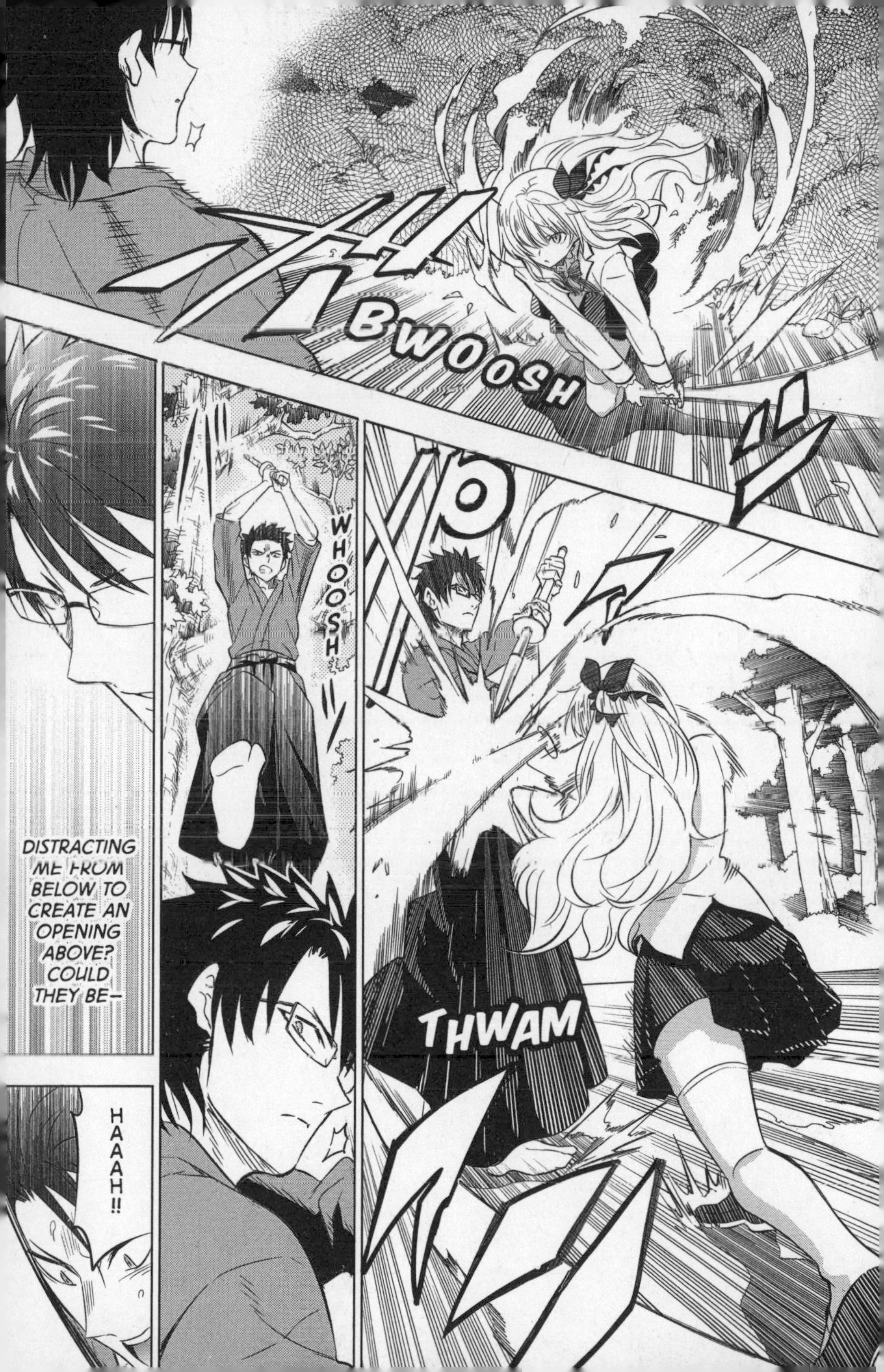
BWOOSH
THWAM
WHOOSH!!
DISTRACTING ME FROM BELOW TO CREATE AN OPENING ABOVE? COULD THEY BE—
HAAAH!!

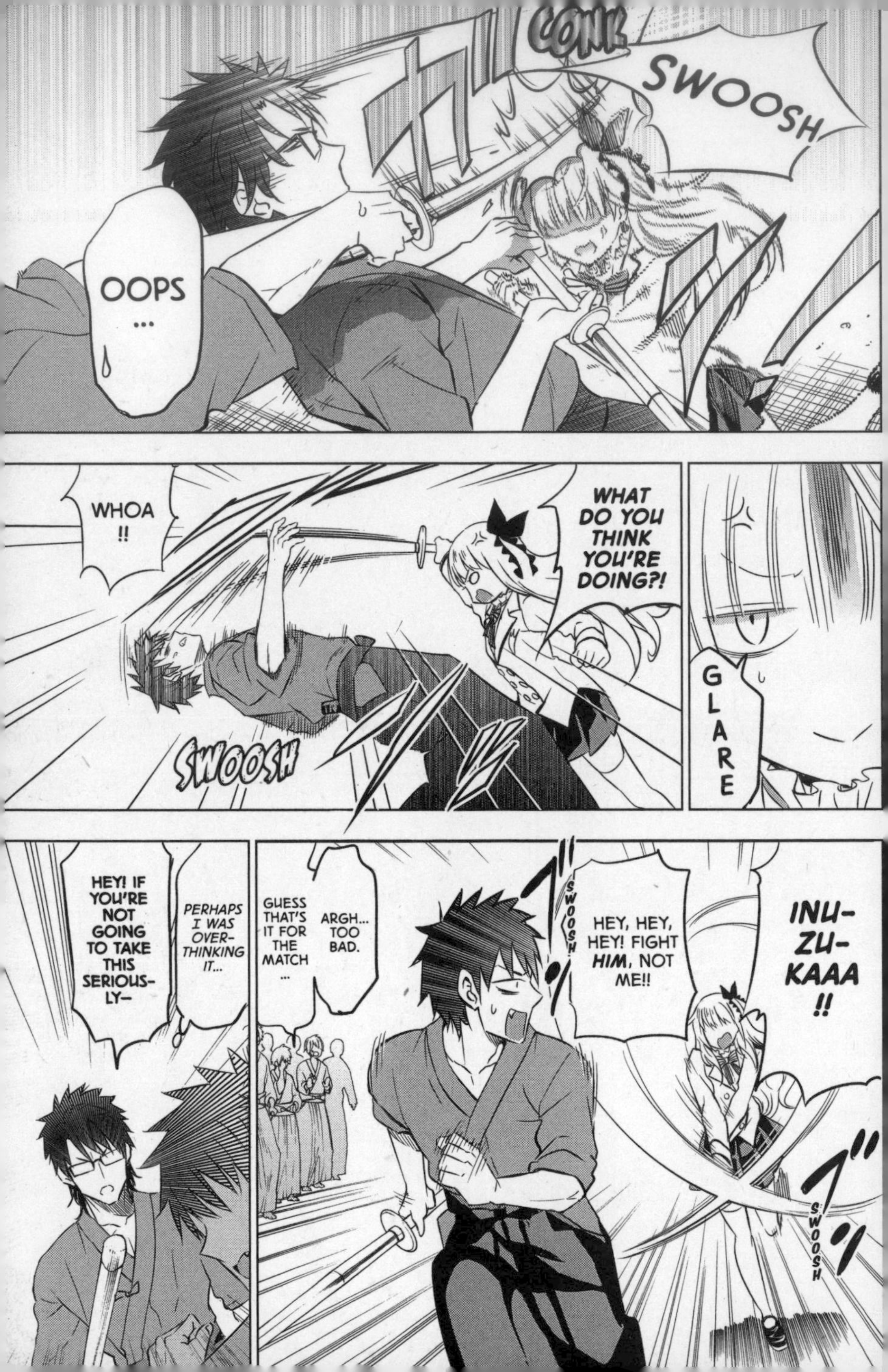
CONK
SWOOSH
OOPS ...
GLARE
WHAT DO YOU THINK YOU'RE DOING?!
WHOA !!
SWOOSH
INU-ZU-KAAA !!
SWOOSH
HEY, HEY, HEY! FIGHT HIM, NOT ME!!
SWOOSH
ARGH... TOO BAD.
GUESS THAT'S IT FOR THE MATCH ...
PERHAPS I WAS OVER-THINKING IT...
HEY! IF YOU'RE NOT GOING TO TAKE THIS SERIOUS-LY-

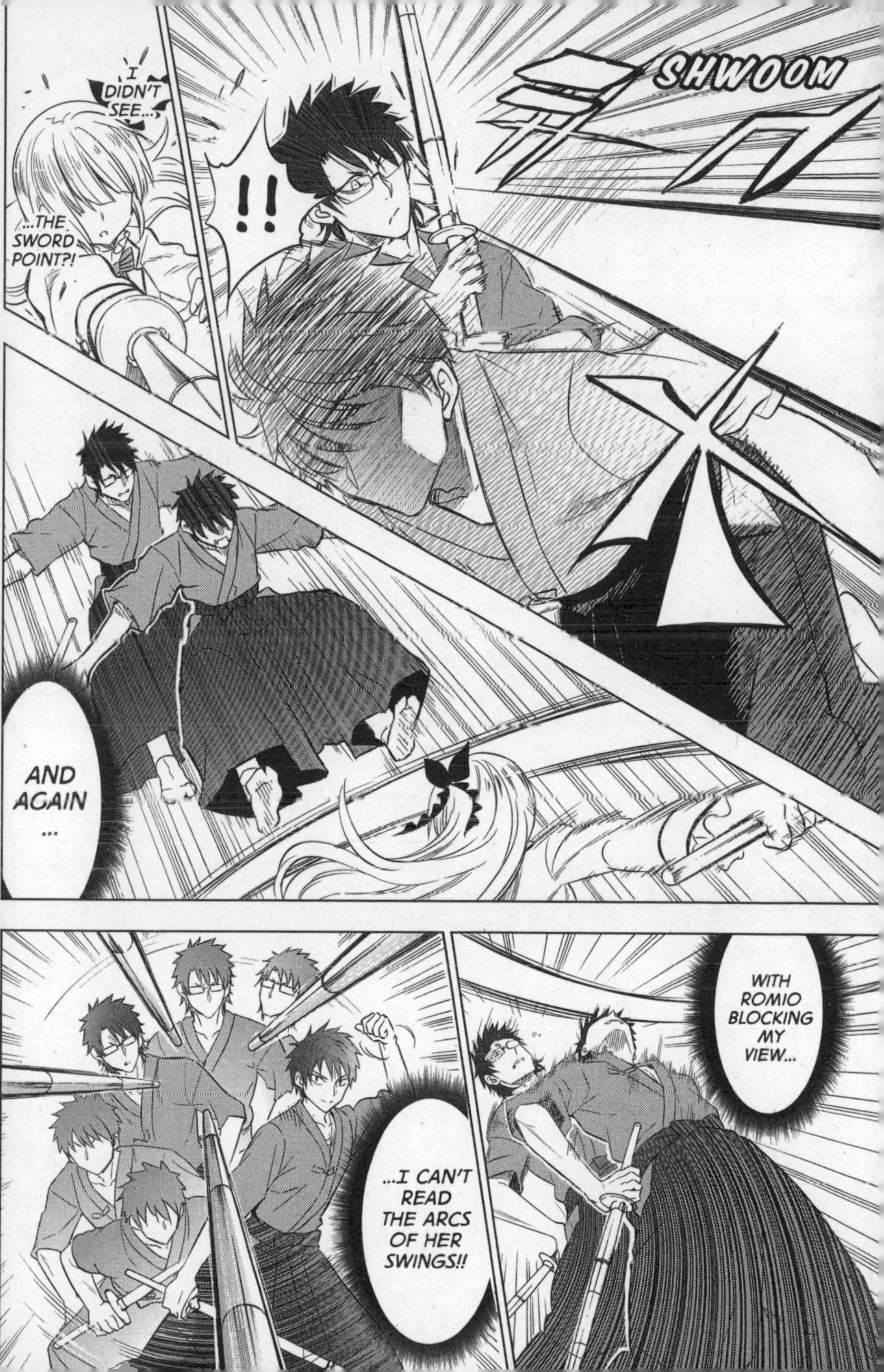
SHWOOM
!!
I DIDN'T SEE...
...THE SWORD POINT?!
AND AGAIN ...
WITH ROMIO BLOCKING MY VIEW...
...I CAN'T READ THE ARCS OF HER SWINGS!!

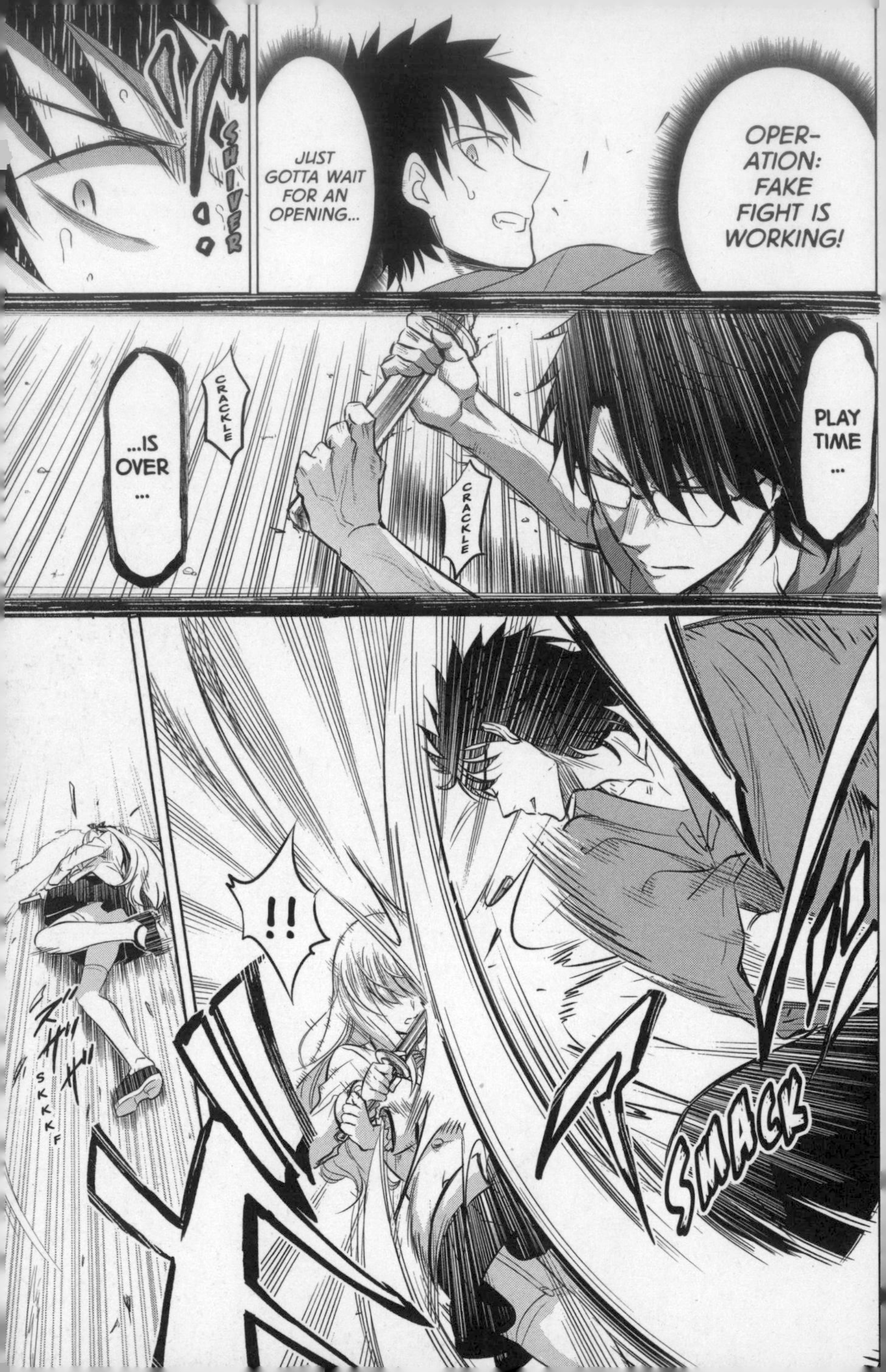
OPER-ATION: FAKE FIGHT IS WORKING!
JUST GOTTA WAIT FOR AN OPENING...
SHIVER
PLAY TIME ...
CRACKLE
CRACKLE
...IS OVER ...
SMACK
!!
SKKKF

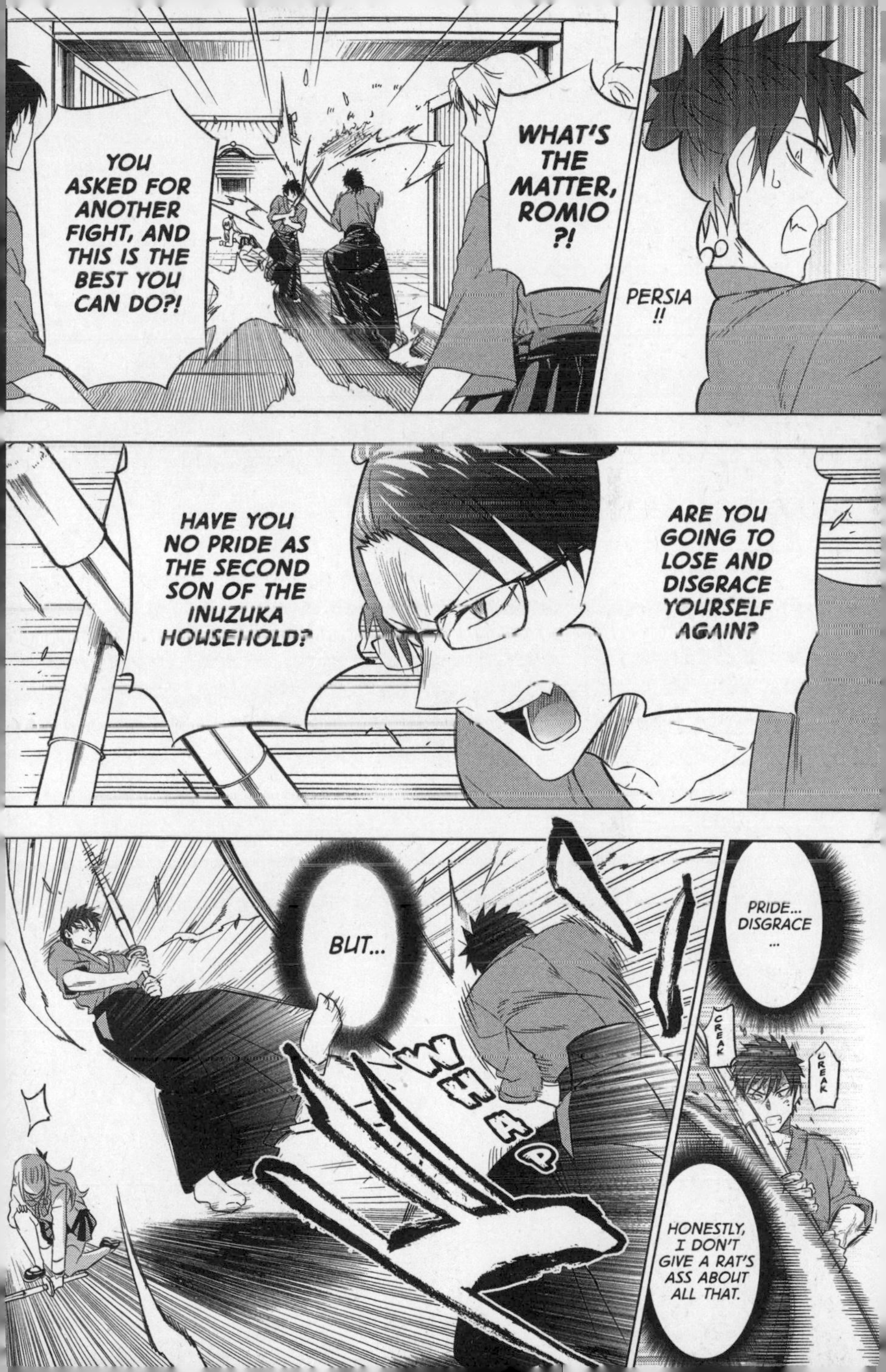
PERSIA !!
WHAT'S THE MATTER, ROMIO ?!
YOU ASKED FOR ANOTHER FIGHT, AND THIS IS THE BEST YOU CAN DO?!
ARE YOU GOING TO LOSE AND DISGRACE YOURSELF AGAIN?
HAVE YOU NO PRIDE AS THE SECOND SON OF THE INUZUKA HOUSEHOLD?
PRIDE... DISGRACE ...
CREAK
CREAK
HONESTLY, I DON'T GIVE A RAT'S ASS ABOUT ALL THAT.
BUT...
WHAP

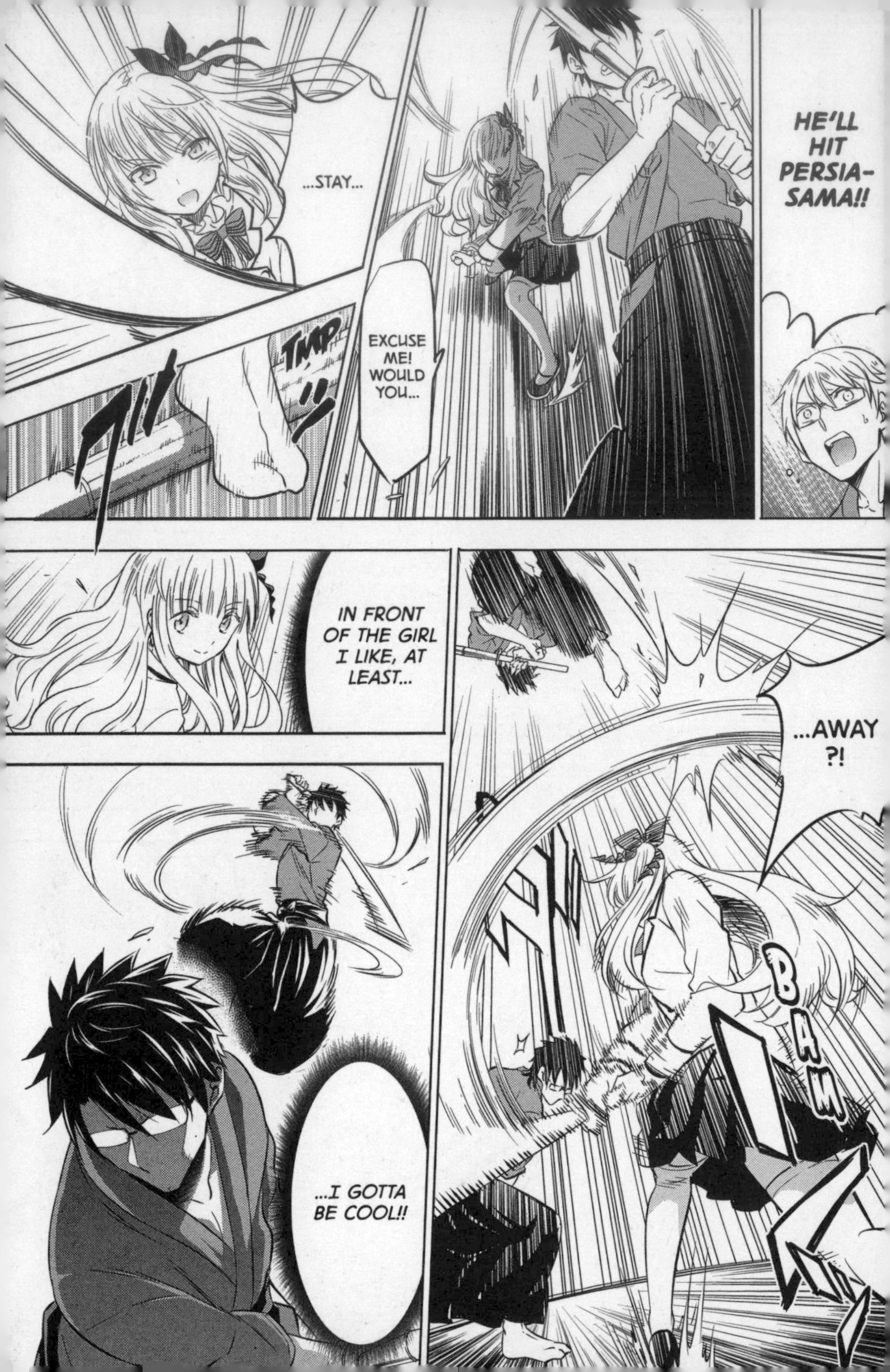
HE'LL HIT PERSIA-SAMA!!
EXCUSE ME! WOULD YOU...
...STAY...
TMP
...AWAY ?!
BAM
IN FRONT OF THE GIRL I LIKE, AT LEAST...
...I GOTTA BE COOL!!

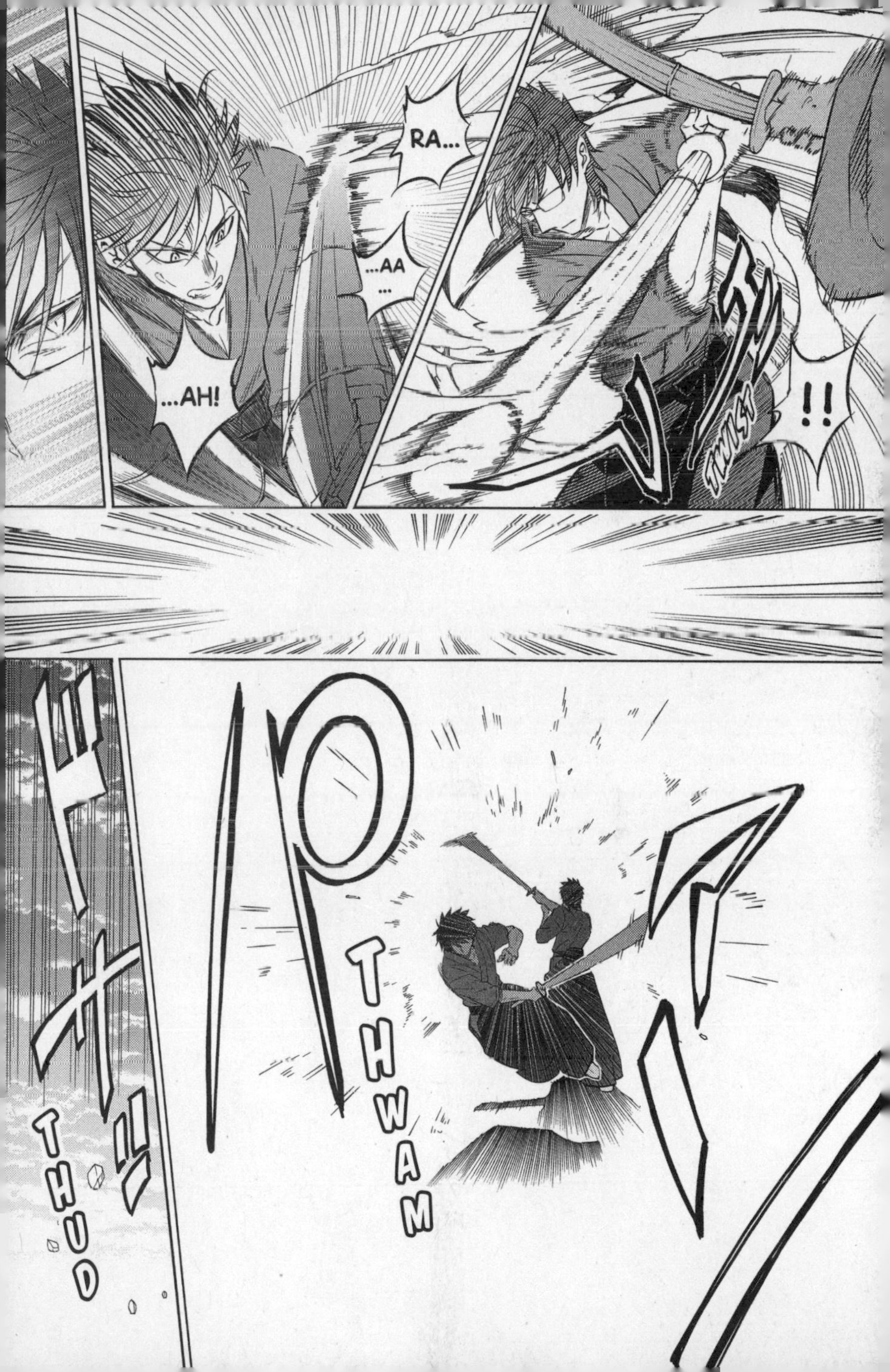

!!
TWIST
RA...
...AA ...
...AH!
THWAM
!!
THUD

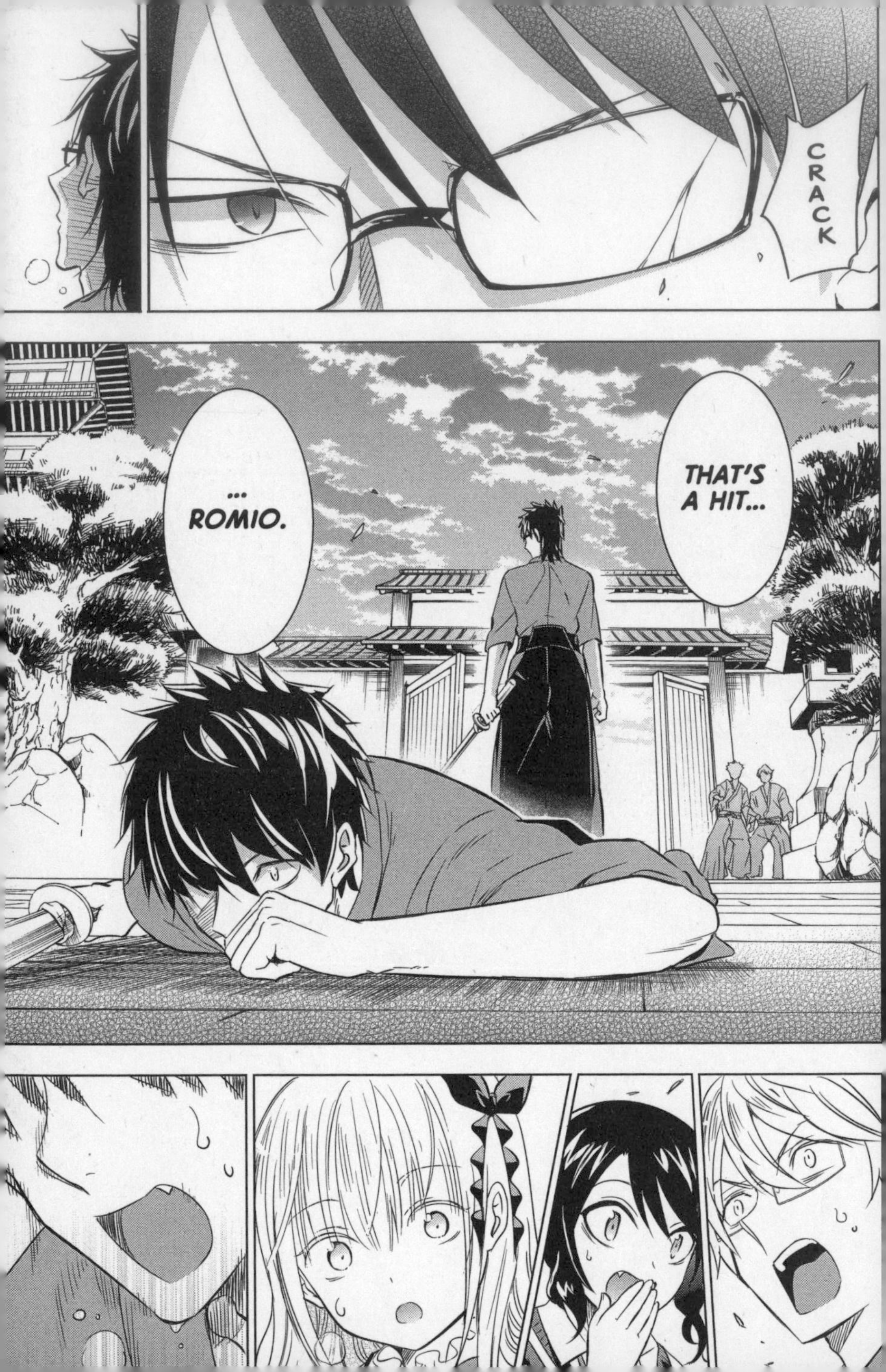
CRACK
THAT'S A HIT...
...ROMIO.

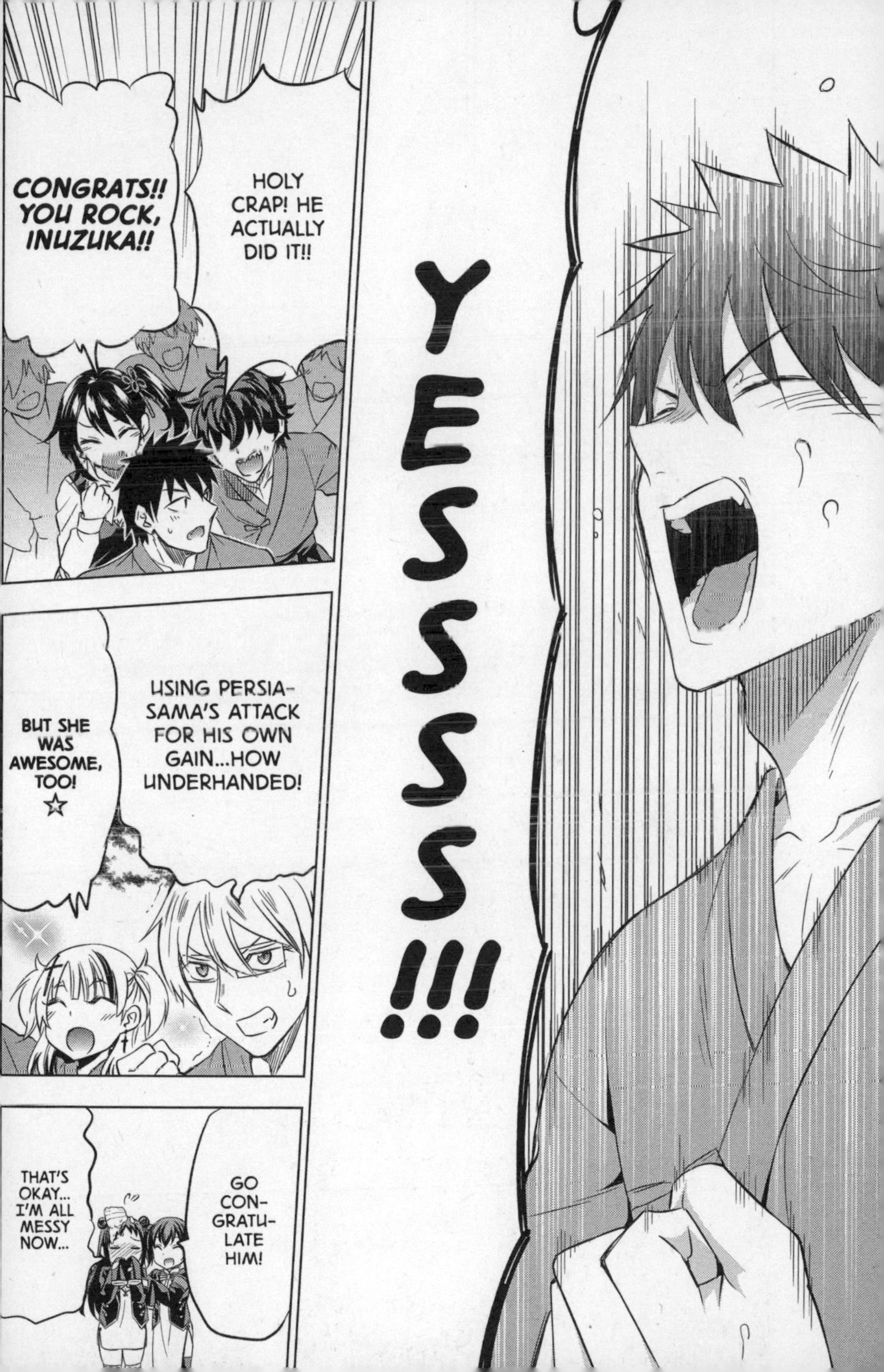
YESSS!!!
HOLY CRAP! HE ACTUALLY DID IT!!
CONGRATS!! YOU ROCK, INUZUKA!!
USING PERSIA-SAMA'S ATTACK FOR HIS OWN GAIN...HOW UNDERHANDED!
BUT SHE WAS AWESOME, TOO! ☆
GO CON-GRATU-LATE HIM!
THAT'S OKAY... I'M ALL MESSY NOW...

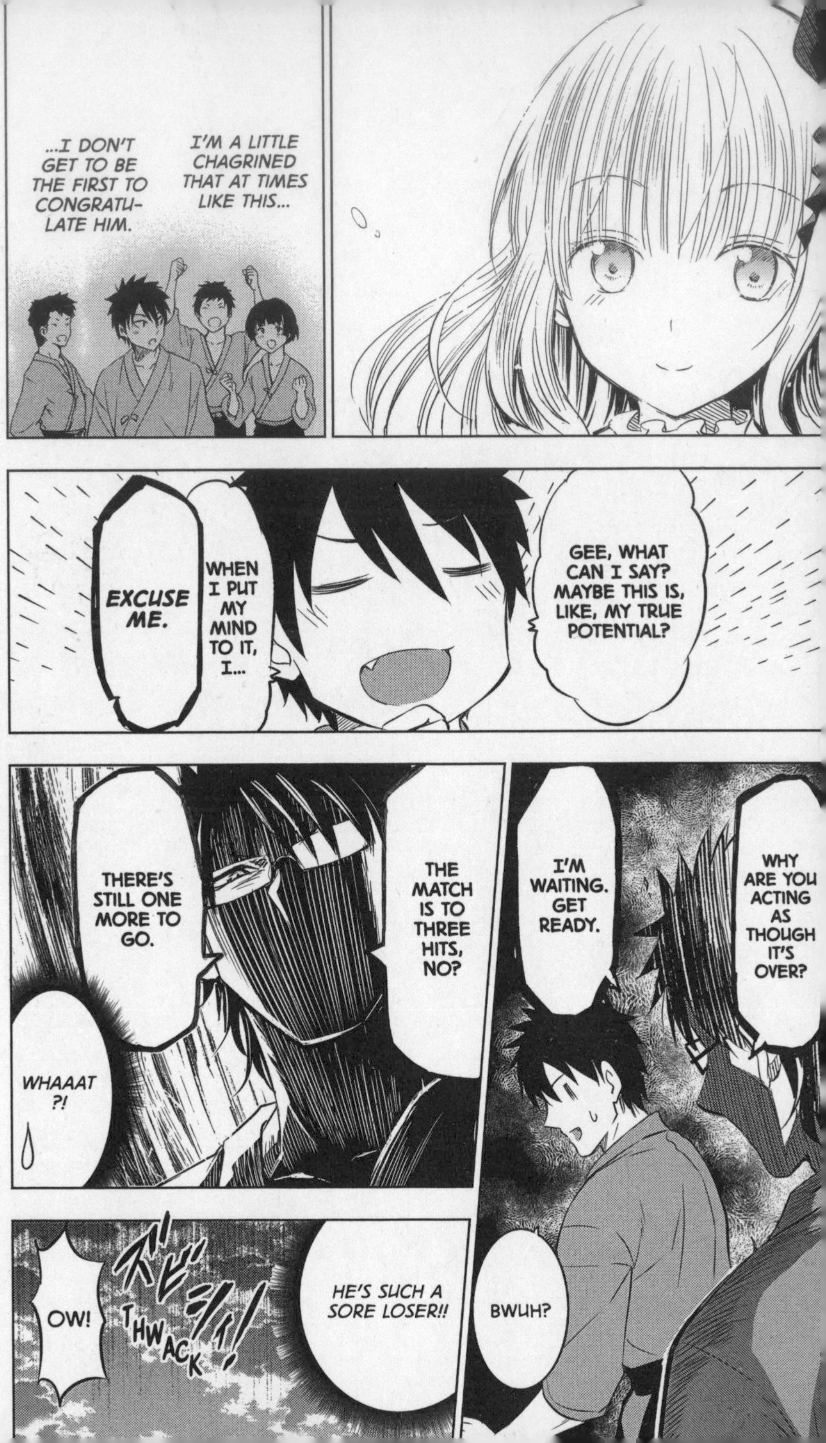
I'M A LITTLE CHAGRINED THAT AT TIMES LIKE THIS...
...I DON'T GET TO BE THE FIRST TO CONGRATU-LATE HIM.
GEE, WHAT CAN I SAY? MAYBE THIS IS, LIKE, MY TRUE POTENTIAL?
WHEN I PUT MY MIND TO IT, I...
EXCUSE ME.
WHY ARE YOU ACTING AS THOUGH IT'S OVER?
I'M WAITING. GET READY.
BWUH?
THE MATCH IS TO THREE HITS, NO?
THERE'S STILL ONE MORE TO GO.
WHAAAT?!
HE'S SUCH A SORE LOSER!!
THWACK
OW!

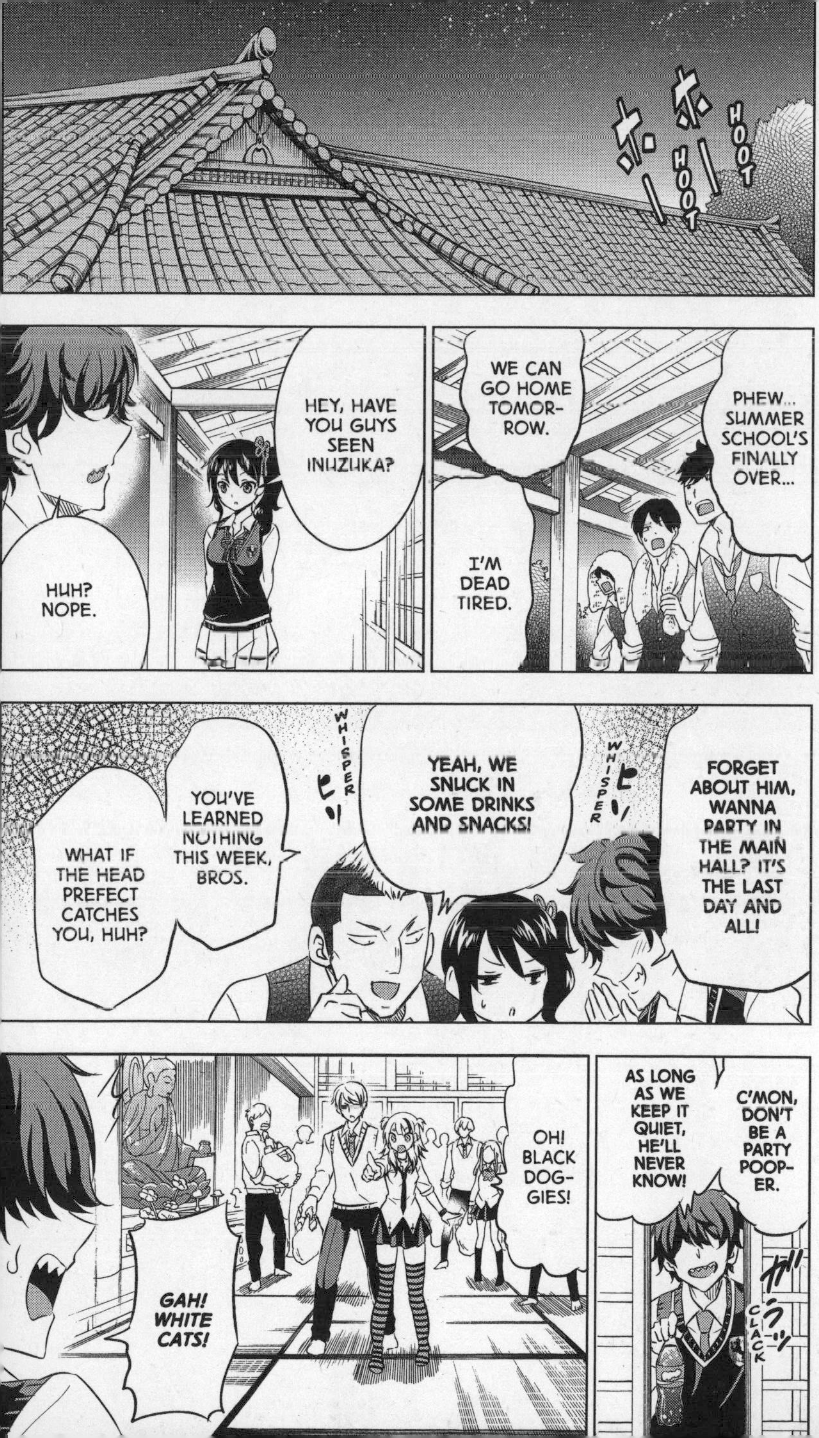
HOOT
HOOT
PHEW... SUMMER SCHOOL'S FINALLY OVER...
WE CAN GO HOME TOMORROW.
I'M DEAD TIRED.
HEY, HAVE YOU GUYS SEEN INUZUKA?
HUH? NOPE.
FORGET ABOUT HIM, WANNA PARTY IN THE MAIN HALL? IT'S THE LAST DAY AND ALL!
WHISPER
YEAH, WE SNUCK IN SOME DRINKS AND SNACKS!
WHISPER
YOU'VE LEARNED NOTHING THIS WEEK, BROS.
WHAT IF THE HEAD PREFECT CATCHES YOU, HUH?
C'MON, DON'T BE A PARTY POOPER.
AS LONG AS WE KEEP IT QUIET, HE'LL NEVER KNOW!
CLACK
OH! BLACK DOGGIES!
GAH! WHITE CATS!

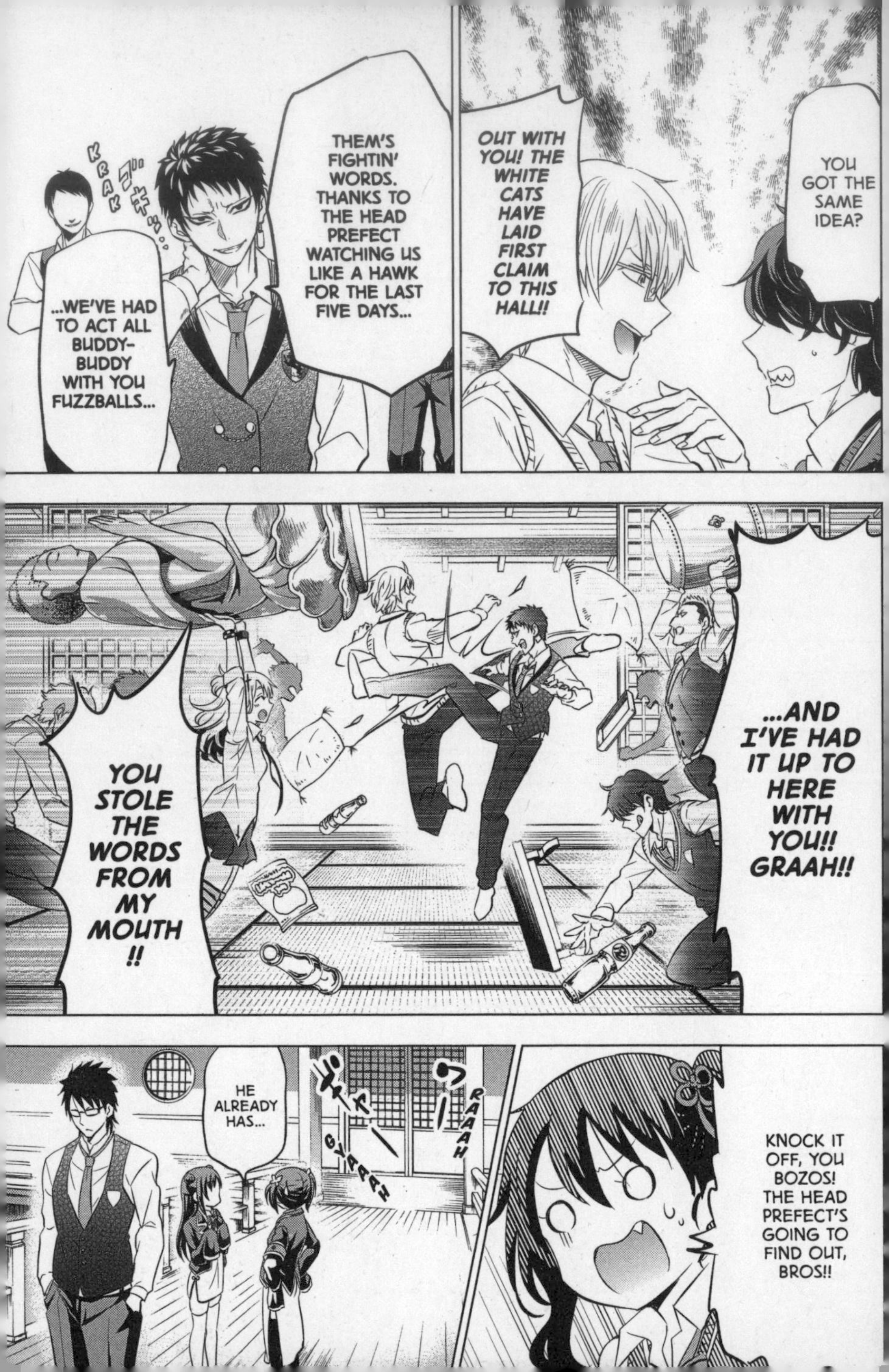
YOU GOT THE SAME IDEA?
OUT WITH YOU! THE WHITE CATS HAVE LAID FIRST CLAIM TO THIS HALL!!
THEM'S FIGHTIN' WORDS. THANKS TO THE HEAD PREFECT WATCHING US LIKE A HAWK FOR THE LAST FIVE DAYS...
KRAK
...WE'VE HAD TO ACT ALL BUDDY-BUDDY WITH YOU FUZZBALLS...
...AND I'VE HAD IT UP TO HERE WITH YOU!! GRAAH!!
YOU STOLE THE WORDS FROM MY MOUTH!!
KNOCK IT OFF, YOU BOZOS! THE HEAD PREFECT'S GOING TO FIND OUT, BROS!!
RAAAAH
GYAAAAH
HE ALREADY HAS...

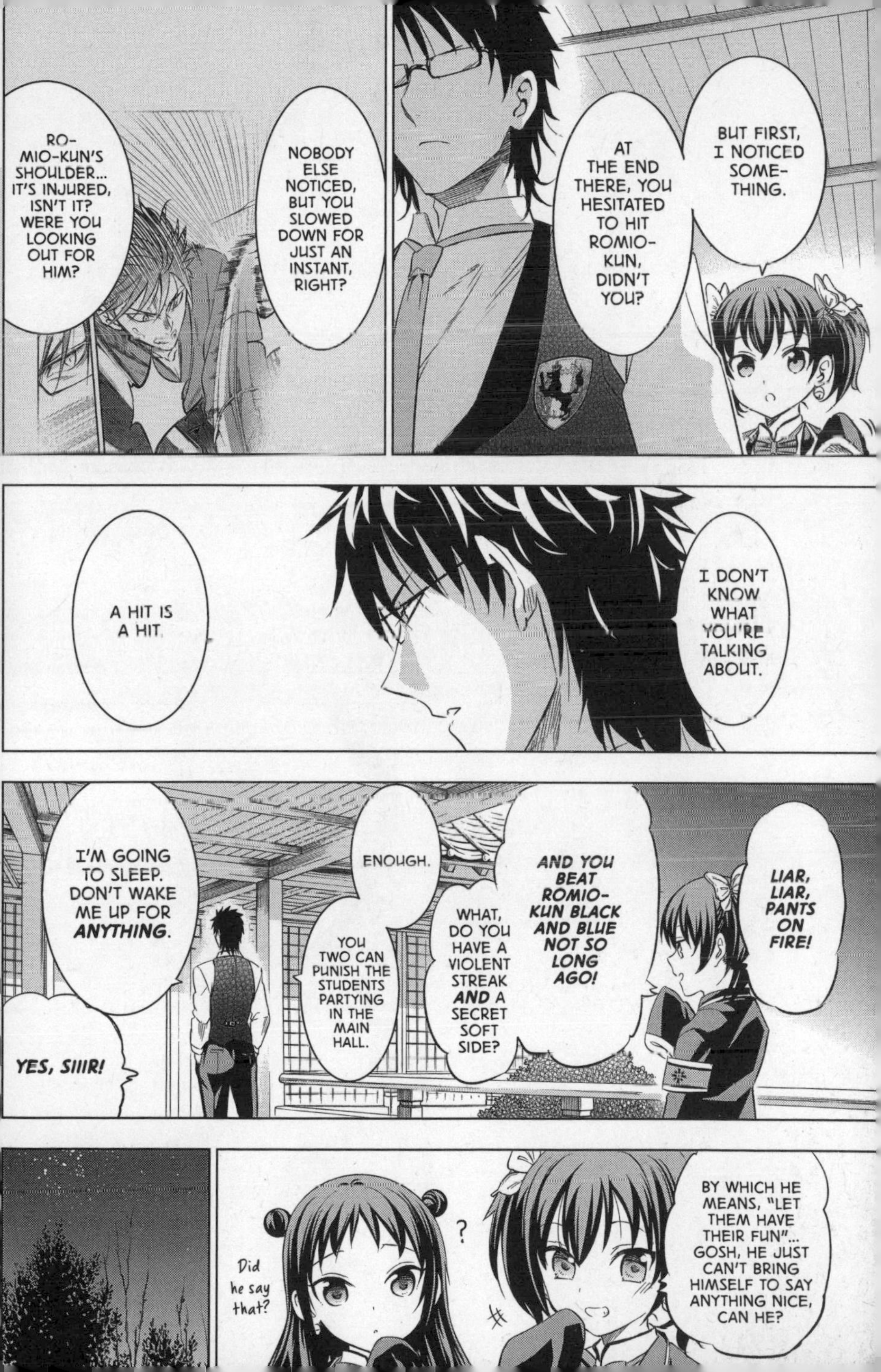
BUT FIRST, I NOTICED SOME-THING.
AT THE END THERE, YOU HESITATED TO HIT ROMIO-KUN, DIDN'T YOU?
NOBODY ELSE NOTICED, BUT YOU SLOWED DOWN FOR JUST AN INSTANT, RIGHT?
RO-MIO-KUN'S SHOULDER... IT'S INJURED, ISN'T IT? WERE YOU LOOKING OUT FOR HIM?
I DON'T KNOW WHAT YOU'RE TALKING ABOUT.
A HIT IS A HIT.
LIAR, LIAR, PANTS ON FIRE!
AND YOU BEAT ROMIO-KUN BLACK AND BLUE NOT SO LONG AGO!
WHAT, DO YOU HAVE A VIOLENT STREAK AND A SECRET SOFT SIDE?
ENOUGH.
YOU TWO CAN PUNISH THE STUDENTS PARTYING IN THE MAIN HALL.
I'M GOING TO SLEEP. DON'T WAKE ME UP FOR ANYTHING.
YES, SIIIR!
BY WHICH HE MEANS, "LET THEM HAVE THEIR FUN"... GOSH, HE JUST CAN'T BRING HIMSELF TO SAY ANYTHING NICE, CAN HE?
?
Did he say that?

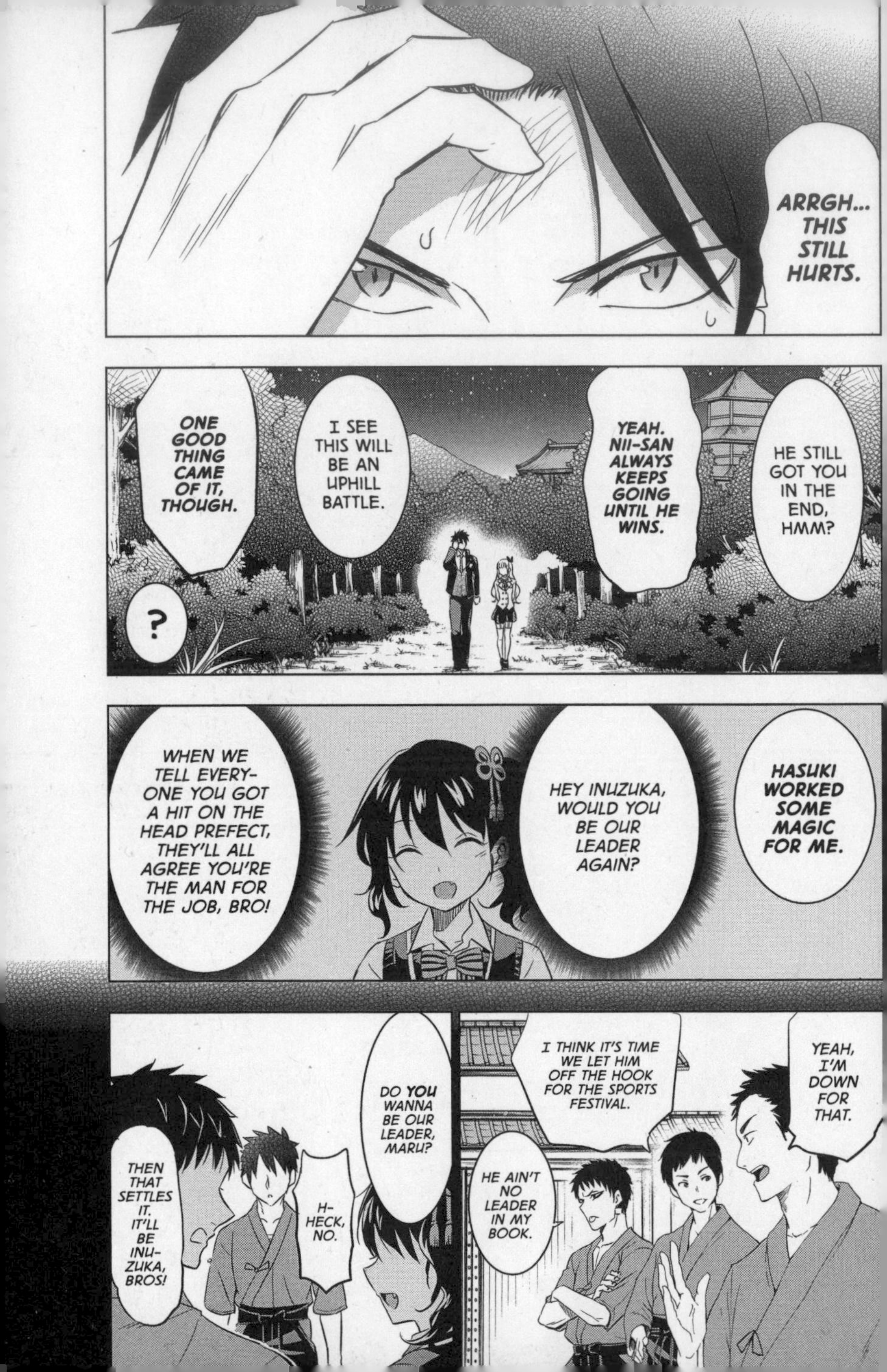
ARRGH... THIS STILL HURTS.
HE STILL GOT YOU IN THE END, HMM?
YEAH. NII-SAN ALWAYS KEEPS GOING UNTIL HE WINS.
I SEE THIS WILL BE AN UPHILL BATTLE.
ONE GOOD THING CAME OF IT, THOUGH.
?
HASUKI WORKED SOME MAGIC FOR ME.
HEY INUZUKA, WOULD YOU BE OUR LEADER AGAIN?
WHEN WE TELL EVERY-ONE YOU GOT A HIT ON THE HEAD PREFECT, THEY'LL ALL AGREE YOU'RE THE MAN FOR THE JOB, BRO!
YEAH, I'M DOWN FOR THAT.
I THINK IT'S TIME WE LET HIM OFF THE HOOK FOR THE SPORTS FESTIVAL.
HE AIN'T NO LEADER IN MY BOOK.
DO YOU WANNA BE OUR LEADER, MARU?
H-HECK, NO.
THEN THAT SETTLES IT. IT'LL BE INU-ZUKA, BROS!

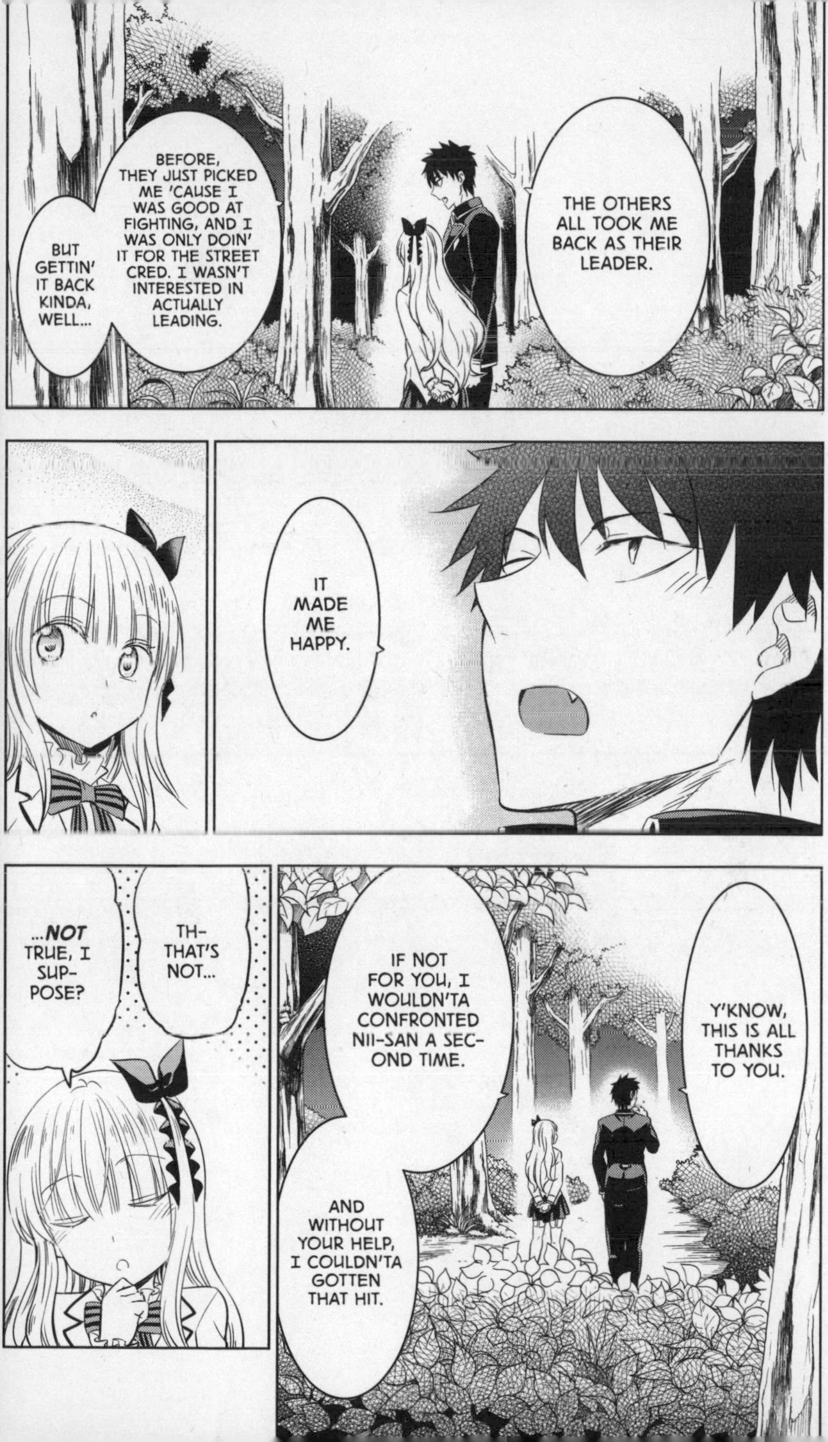
THE OTHERS ALL TOOK ME BACK AS THEIR LEADER.
BEFORE, THEY JUST PICKED ME 'CAUSE I WAS GOOD AT FIGHTING, AND I WAS ONLY DOIN' IT FOR THE STREET CRED. I WASN'T INTERESTED IN ACTUALLY LEADING.
BUT GETTIN' IT BACK KINDA, WELL...
IT MADE ME HAPPY.
Y'KNOW, THIS IS ALL THANKS TO YOU.
IF NOT FOR YOU, I WOULDN'TA CONFRONTED NII-SAN A SEC-OND TIME.
AND WITHOUT YOUR HELP, I COULDN'TA GOTTEN THAT HIT.
TH-THAT'S NOT...
...*NOT* TRUE, I SUP-POSE?

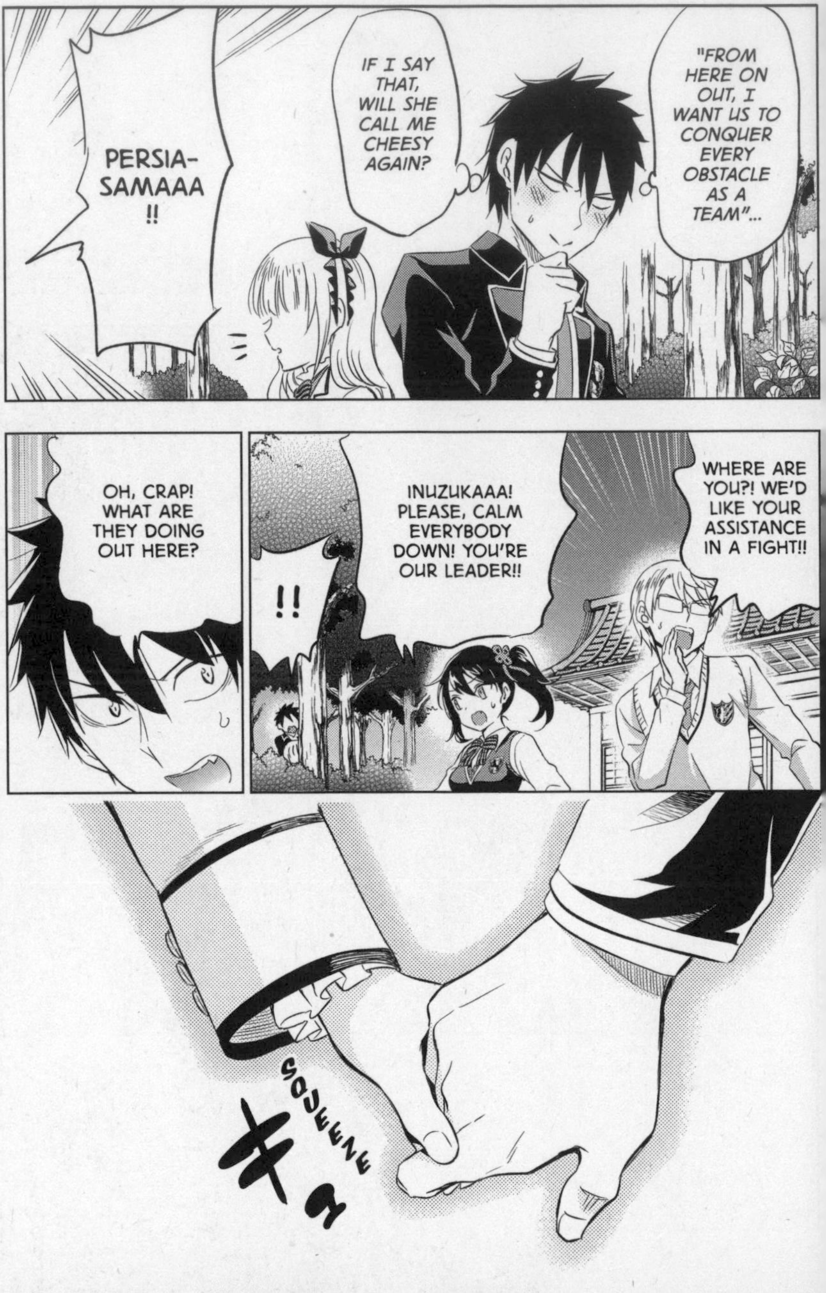
"FROM HERE ON OUT, I WANT US TO CONQUER EVERY OBSTACLE AS A TEAM"...
IF I SAY THAT, WILL SHE CALL ME CHEESY AGAIN?
PERSIA-SAMAAA!!
WHERE ARE YOU?! WE'D LIKE YOUR ASSISTANCE IN A FIGHT!!
INUZUKAAA! PLEASE, CALM EVERYBODY DOWN! YOU'RE OUR LEADER!!
!!
OH, CRAP! WHAT ARE THEY DOING OUT HERE?
SQUEEZE

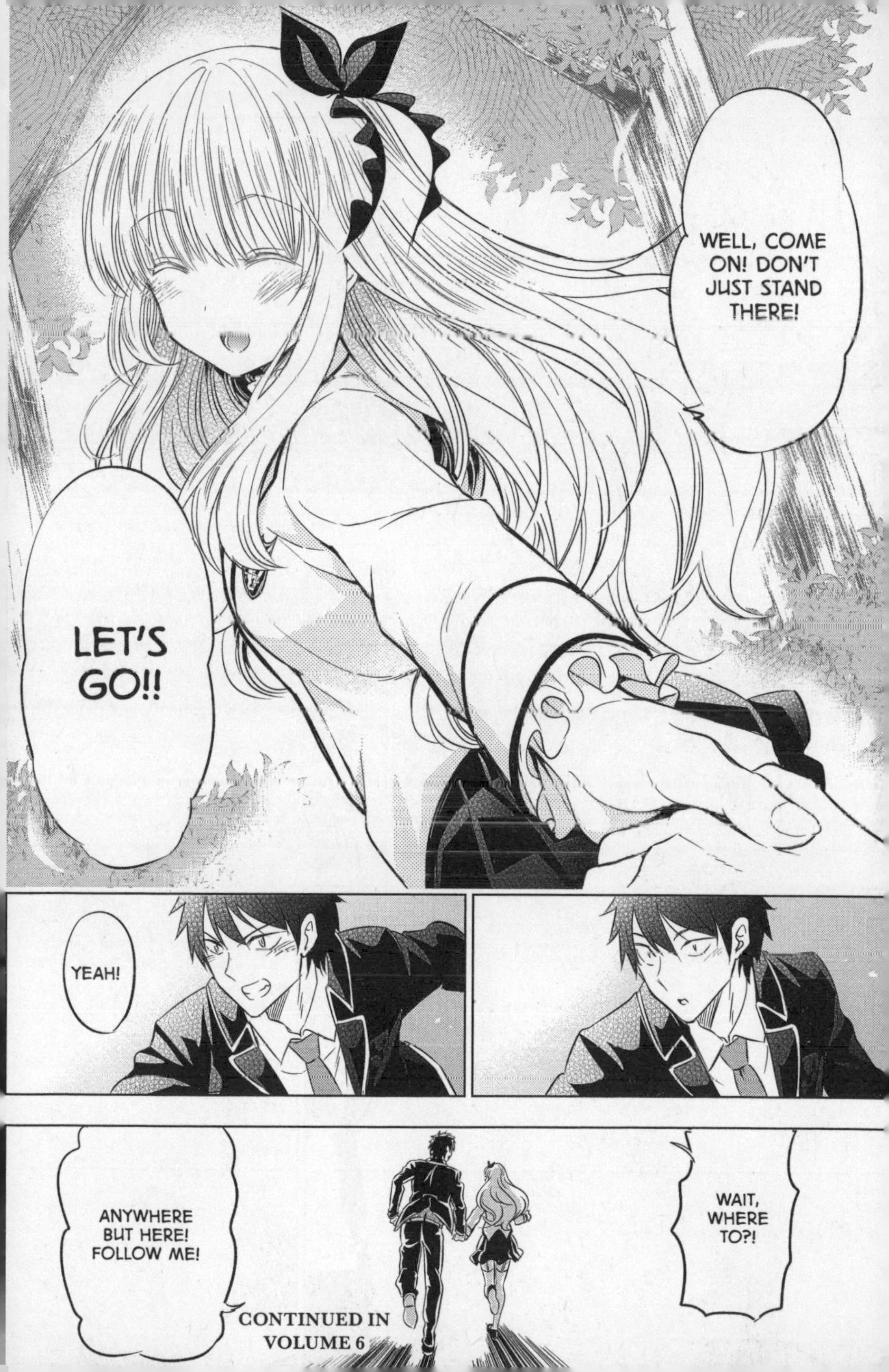
WELL, COME ON! DON'T JUST STAND THERE!
LET'S GO!!
YEAH!
WAIT, WHERE TO?!
ANYWHERE BUT HERE! FOLLOW ME!
CONTINUED IN VOLUME 6

BONUS PAGE: GO, REX, GO!

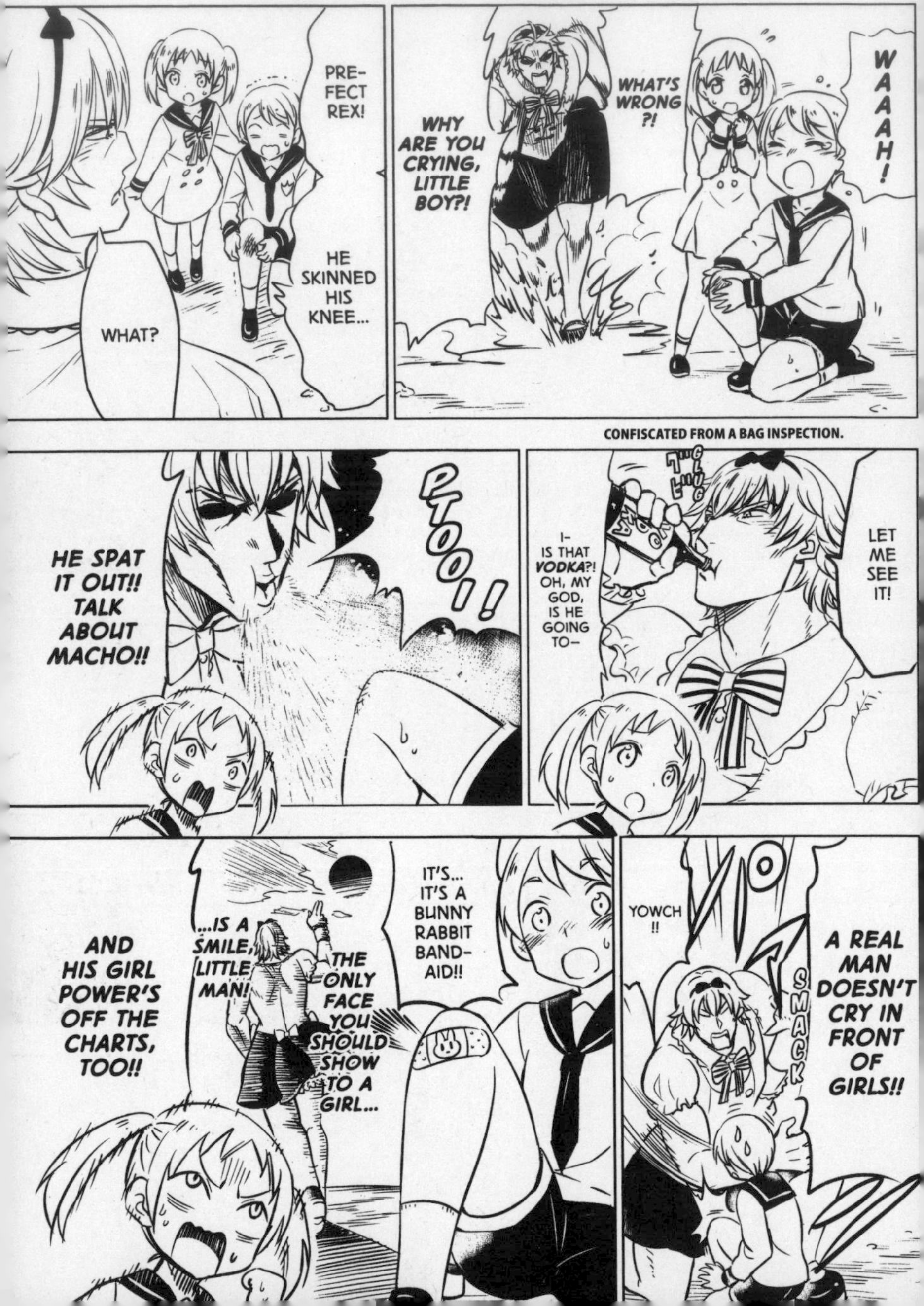
WAAAAH!
WHAT'S WRONG?!
WHY ARE YOU CRYING, LITTLE BOY?!
PRE-FECT REX!
HE SKINNED HIS KNEE...
WHAT?
CONFISCATED FROM A BAG INSPECTION.
LET ME SEE IT!
GLUG GLUG
I- IS THAT VODKA?! OH, MY GOD, IS HE GOING TO—
PTOOI!
HE SPAT IT OUT!! TALK ABOUT MACHO!!
A REAL MAN DOESN'T CRY IN FRONT OF GIRLS!!
SMACK
YOWCH!!
IT'S... IT'S A BUNNY RABBIT BAND-AID!!
THE ONLY FACE YOU SHOULD SHOW TO A GIRL...
...IS A SMILE, LITTLE MAN!
AND HIS GIRL POWER'S OFF THE CHARTS, TOO!!

AFTERWORD

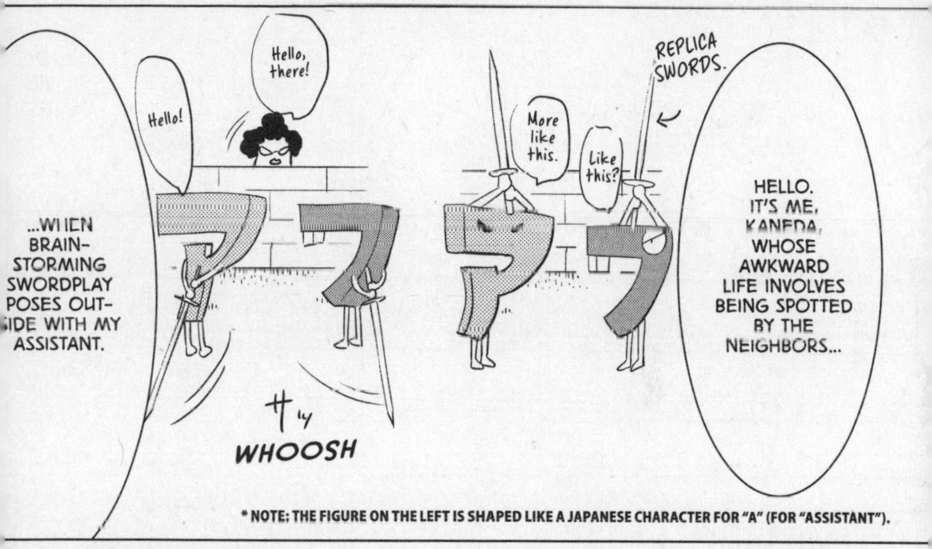
HELLO. IT'S ME, KANEDA, WHOSE AWKWARD LIFE INVOLVES BEING SPOTTED BY THE NEIGHBORS...
REPLICA SWORDS.
Like this?
More like this.
Hello, there!
Hello!
...WHEN BRAIN-STORMING SWORDPLAY POSES OUT-SIDE WITH MY ASSISTANT.
サッ
WHOOSH

* NOTE: THE FIGURE ON THE LEFT IS SHAPED LIKE A JAPANESE CHARACTER FOR "A" (FOR "ASSISTANT").

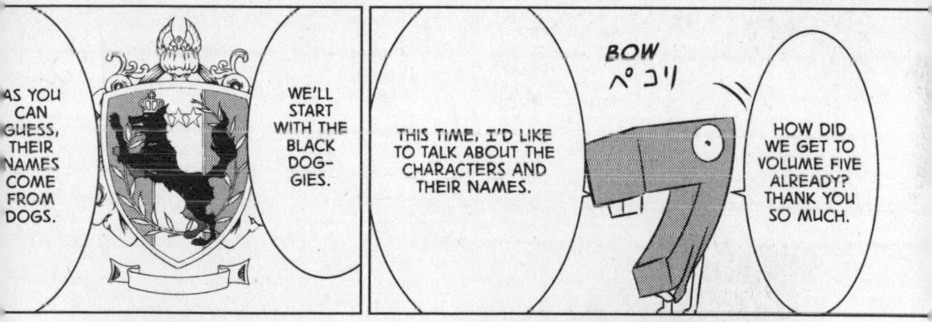
HOW DID WE GET TO VOLUME FIVE ALREADY? THANK YOU SO MUCH.
BOW
ペコリ
THIS TIME, I'D LIKE TO TALK ABOUT THE CHARACTERS AND THEIR NAMES.
WE'LL START WITH THE BLACK DOG-GIES.
AS YOU CAN GUESS, THEIR NAMES COME FROM DOGS.

ICONS I HAVE UP ON MY TWITTER ACCOUNT (@YOUSUKEKANEDA).

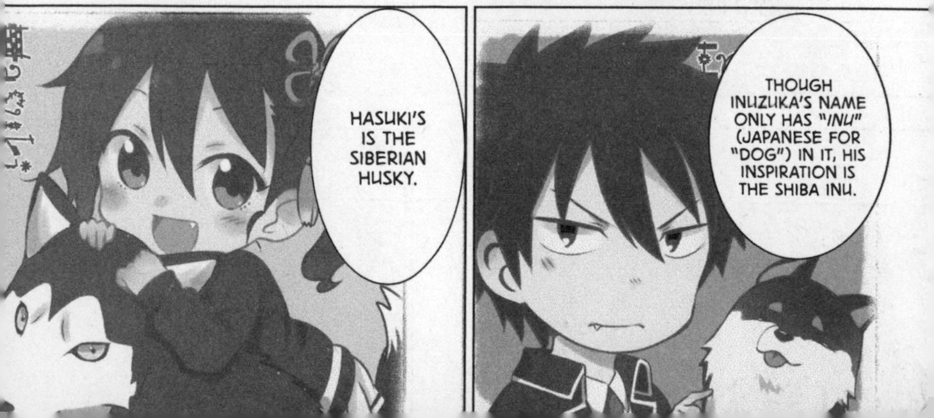
THOUGH INUZUKA'S NAME ONLY HAS "INU" (JAPANESE FOR "DOG") IN IT, HIS INSPIRATION IS THE SHIBA INU.
HASUKI'S IS THE SIBERIAN HUSKY.

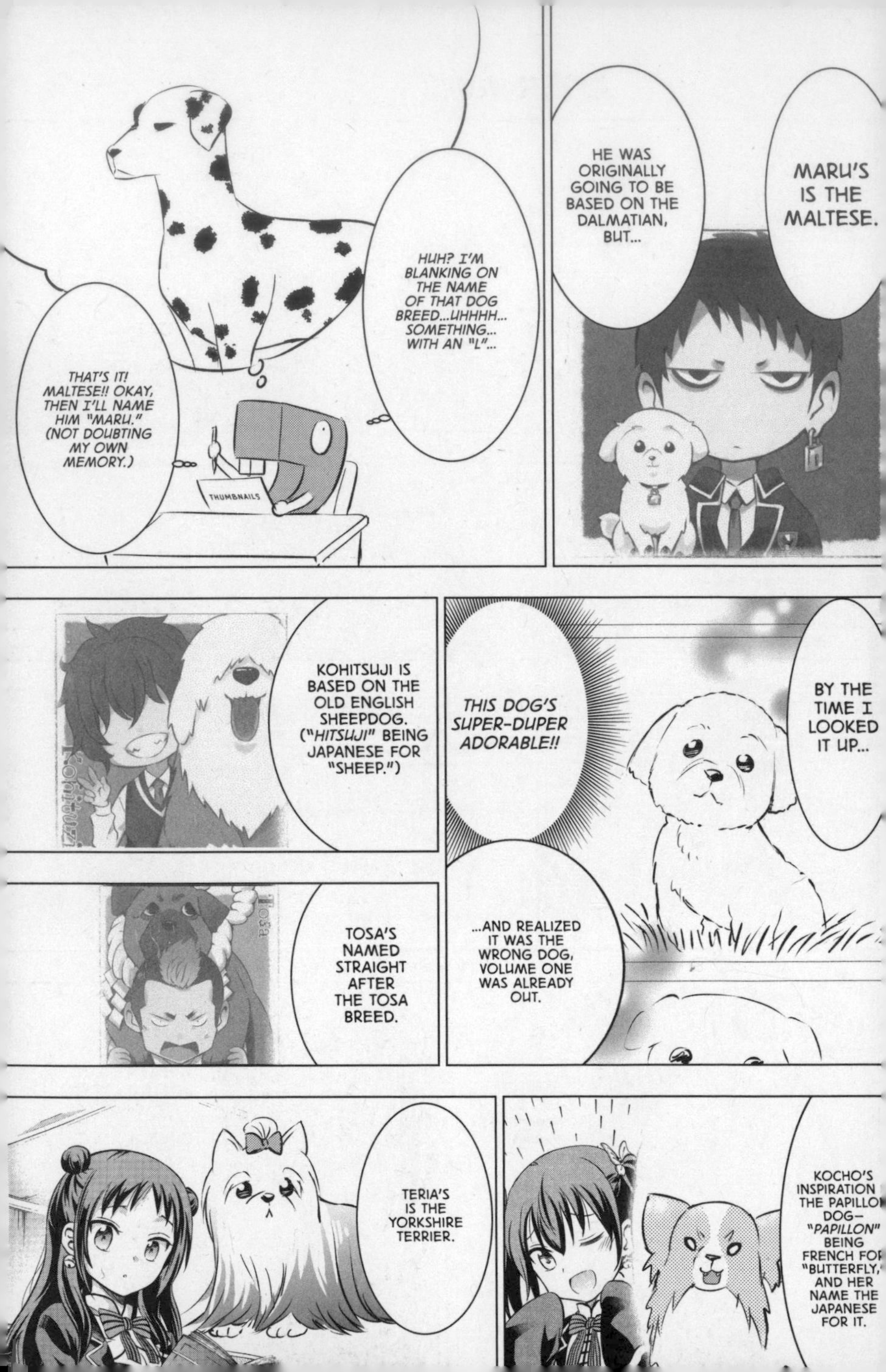
MARU'S IS THE MALTESE.
HE WAS ORIGINALLY GOING TO BE BASED ON THE DALMATIAN, BUT...
HUH? I'M BLANKING ON THE NAME OF THAT DOG BREED...UHHHH... SOMETHING... WITH AN "L"...
THAT'S IT! MALTESE!! OKAY, THEN I'LL NAME HIM "MARU." (NOT DOUBTING MY OWN MEMORY.)
THUMBNAILS
BY THE TIME I LOOKED IT UP...
THIS DOG'S SUPER-DUPER ADORABLE!!
...AND REALIZED IT WAS THE WRONG DOG, VOLUME ONE WAS ALREADY OUT.
KOHITSUJI IS BASED ON THE OLD ENGLISH SHEEPDOG. ("HITSUJI" BEING JAPANESE FOR "SHEEP.")
Tosa
TOSA'S NAMED STRAIGHT AFTER THE TOSA BREED.
KOCHO'S INSPIRATION THE PAPILLO DOG— "PAPILLON" BEING FRENCH FO "BUTTERFLY, AND HER NAME THE JAPANESE FOR IT.
TERIA'S IS THE YORKSHIRE TERRIER.

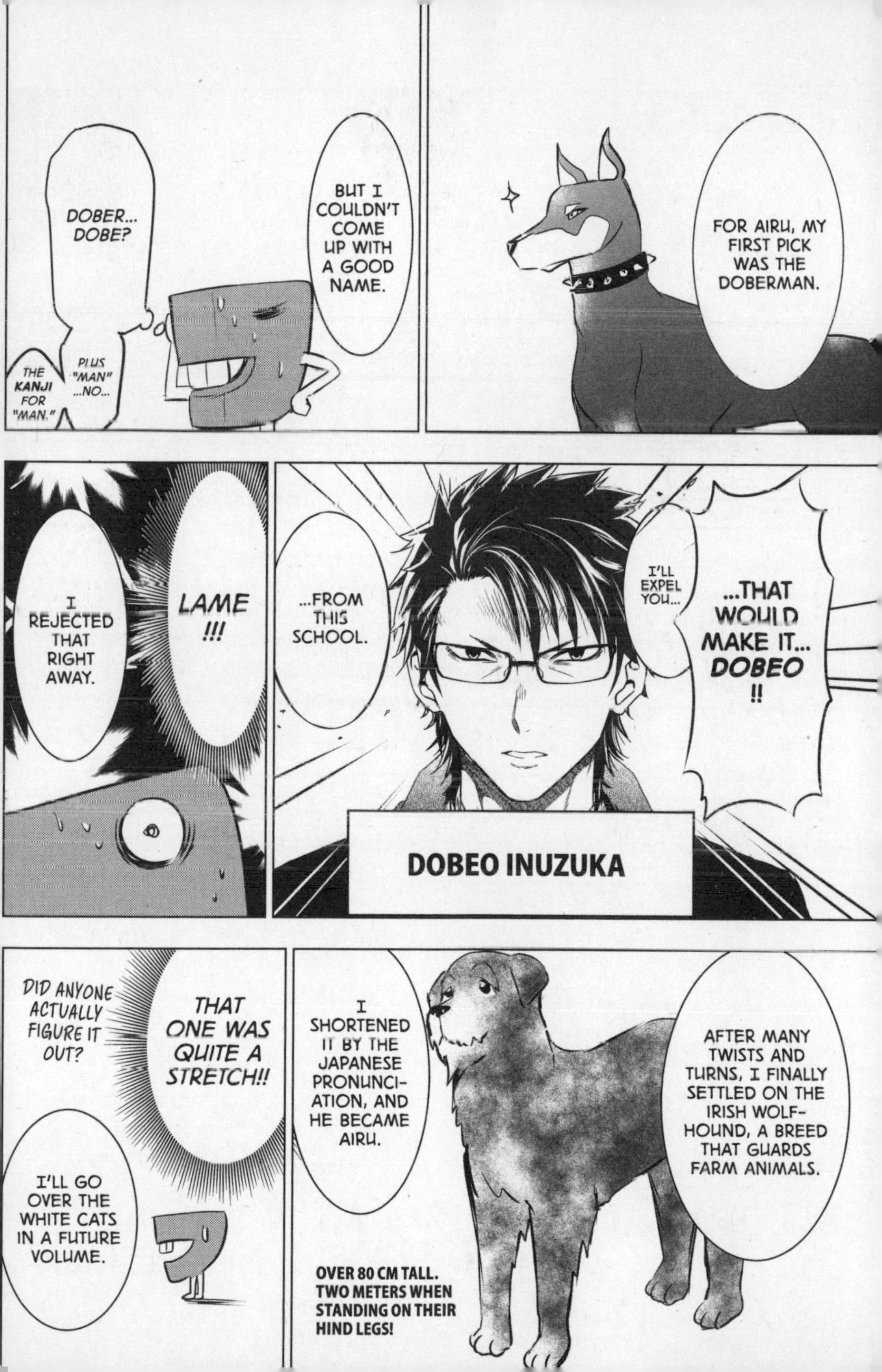
FOR AIRU, MY FIRST PICK WAS THE DOBERMAN.
BUT I COULDN'T COME UP WITH A GOOD NAME.
DOBER... DOBE?
PLUS "MAN" ...NO...
THE KANJI FOR "MAN."
...THAT WOULD MAKE IT... DOBEO !!
I'LL EXPEL YOU...
...FROM THIS SCHOOL.
DOBEO INUZUKA
LAME !!!
I REJECTED THAT RIGHT AWAY.
AFTER MANY TWISTS AND TURNS, I FINALLY SETTLED ON THE IRISH WOLF-HOUND, A BREED THAT GUARDS FARM ANIMALS.
I SHORTENED IT BY THE JAPANESE PRONUNCI-ATION, AND HE BECAME AIRU.
OVER 80 CM TALL. TWO METERS WHEN STANDING ON THEIR HIND LEGS!
THAT ONE WAS QUITE A STRETCH!!
DID ANYONE ACTUALLY FIGURE IT OUT?
I'LL GO OVER THE WHITE CATS IN A FUTURE VOLUME.

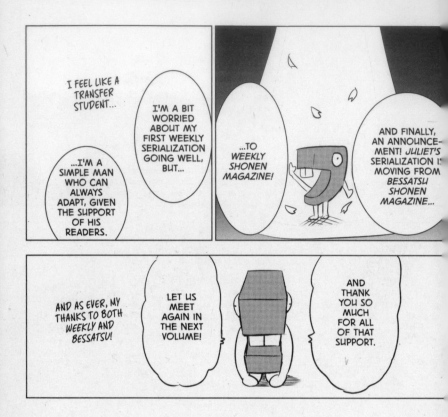

I FEEL LIKE A TRANSFER STUDENT...

...I'M A SIMPLE MAN WHO CAN ALWAYS ADAPT, GIVEN THE SUPPORT OF HIS READERS.

I'M A BIT WORRIED ABOUT MY FIRST WEEKLY SERIALIZATION GOING WELL, BUT...

...TO *WEEKLY SHONEN MAGAZINE!*

AND FINALLY, AN ANNOUNCEMENT! *JULIET'S* SERIALIZATION IS MOVING FROM *BESSATSU SHONEN MAGAZINE...*

AND AS EVER, MY THANKS TO BOTH *WEEKLY* AND *BESSATSU!*

LET US MEET AGAIN IN THE NEXT VOLUME!

AND THANK YOU SO MUCH FOR ALL OF THAT SUPPORT.

Boarding School *Juliet*

VOL. 6 ON SALE SOON!

Boarding School Juliet volume 5 is a work of fiction. Names, characters, places, and incidents are the products of the author's imagination or are used fictitiously. Any resemblance to actual events, locales, or persons, living or dead, is entirely coincidental.

A Kodansha Comics Trade Paperback Original.

Published in the United States by Kodansha Comics,
an imprint of Kodansha USA Publishing, LLC, New York.

Publication rights for this English edition arranged through
Kodansha Ltd., Tokyo.

First published in Japan in 2017 by Kodansha Ltd., Tokyo, as
Kishuku Gakkou no Jurietto volume 5.

ISBN 978-1-63236-755-6

Printed in the United States of America.

www.kodanshacomics.com

9 8 7 6 5 4 3 2 1

Translation: Amanda Haley
Lettering: James Dashiell
Editing: Erin Subramanian and Paul Starr
Kodansha Comics edition cover design: Phil Balsman